ISSUE
AND CRISIS
MANAGEMENT

ISSUE
AND CRISIS
MANAGEMENT

EXPLORING ISSUES, CRISES, RISK AND REPUTATION

TONY JAQUES

OXFORD
UNIVERSITY PRESS
AUSTRALIA & NEW ZEALAND

OXFORD
UNIVERSITY PRESS

Oxford University Press is a department of the University of Oxford.

It furthers the University's objective of excellence in research, scholarship, and education by publishing worldwide. Oxford is a registered trademark of Oxford University Press in the UK and in certain other countries.

Published in Australia by
Oxford University Press
253 Normanby Road, South Melbourne, Victoria 3205, Australia

National Library of Australia Cataloguing-in-Publication data

Jaques, Tony, author.
Issues and crisis management: exploring issues, crises, risk and reputation/Tony Jaques.

9780195529081 (paperback)

Issues management.
Crisis management.
Management.

658.401

Edited by Pete Cruttenden
Cover design by Kim Ferguson
Cover image: Getty Images/Michael Hitoshi
Typeset by diacriTech
Proofread by Carol Goudie
Indexed by Russell Brooks
Printed by Sheck Wah Tong Printing Press Ltd

Dedicated to the memory of my father, Pat Jaques, 1903–1980.

CONTENTS

LIST OF TABLES AND FIGURES

Tables

Figures

THE AUTHOR

Dr Tony Jaques is a consultant specialising in issue and crisis management and lectures in postgraduate programs at universities in Melbourne. Since working as Asia-Pacific Issue Manager for a US multinational, he has established an international reputation in the field, with speaking engagements and through publications in leading academic journals including *Public Relations Review, Journal of Communication Management, Journal of Public Affairs, Corporate Communication, International Journal of Strategic Communication* and *Asia Pacific Public Relations Journal*. In addition, he has written book chapters in Australia, Britain and the USA, most recently *The Sage handbook of public relations* (Sage, 2010), *Pre-crisis planning communication and management* (Peter Lang, 2012), *The handbook of research on crisis leadership in organisations* (Edward Elgar, 2013), *Workplace communication for the 21st century* (Praeger, 2013) and *Exploring public relations* (Prentice-Hall, 2014). He is a former Director of the Issue Management Council in Leesburg, Virginia, and writes Australia's only specialist online issue and crisis management publication, *Managing Outcomes* (www.issueoutcomes.com.au).

CONTRIBUTORS

Brendan Elliott

Brendan Elliott is the Community Relations Manager on a major Australian rail infrastructure project being delivered by John Holland in New South Wales. He has previously held Senior Media Advisor roles at NBN Co and Australia's largest urban water utility—Sydney Water. Brendan handled public affairs for the Australian Radiation Protection and Nuclear Safety Agency during consultation periods for the replacement research reactor at Lucas Heights and the Commonwealth Government application to site a national radioactive waste repository near Woomera in South Australia. He received a Masters in Communication Management from the University of Technology, Sydney in 2000.

Chris Galloway

Dr Chris Galloway is a senior lecturer in public relations at Massey University, Auckland, New Zealand. His research interests focus on reputation risk management; issue, crisis and risk communication; and the role of communication in emergency management. He is co-editor of *Public Relations Issues and Crisis Management* (Thomson, 2005) and his work has been published in journals including *Public Relations Review, Journal of Communication Management* and *Asia Pacific Public Relations Journal.*

Gwyneth Howell

Dr Gwyneth Howell has been teaching and researching the crisis and disaster communication for 15 years. She has published extensively in this area and today is one of Australia's leading researchers in social media response during and post disasters. She also consults to a range of NGOs and government agencies in the design and development of communication strategies for disaster response. In 2012 Dr Howell was awarded a national OLT Teaching Citation for her integrated and innovative delivery of crisis and issue management at the University of Western Sydney.

Tina Hunter

Dr Tina Hunter teaches and researches in the areas of national and international petroleum law, mining law, property law, administrative law and legal philosophy. After completing her PhD in comparative petroleum law at the University of Bergen, Norway, Dr Hunter has taught in Australia, the UK, Russia and Norway, and has provided consulting services to governments both overseas and in Australia. She drafted the resource management and administration regulations in Western Australia, and analysed petroleum laws in Western Australia and the Northern Territory. Prior to joining the TC Beirne School of Law, University of Queensland, Dr Hunter held positions at Bond University and the University of Bergen.

Joanne Chen Lyu

Joanne Chen Lyu is a PhD Candidate in the School of Journalism and Communication at the Chinese University of Hong Kong. Her research interests include public relations, crisis communication and management, relationship/*guanxi* studies and Chinese communication. Her research work has been published by *Public Relations Review* and Chinese scholarly journals. Previously, she worked in the public relations department of a transnational media corporation. The case study included in this textbook is adapted from her publication in *Public Relations Review*, which was awarded Top Student Paper in the Public Relations Division of the International Communication Association (ICA).

James Mahoney

James Mahoney is Head of the Discipline of Communication at the University of Canberra and convenes the Master of Strategic Communication and the Bachelor of Communication in Public Relations degrees. He is the author of *Public Relations Writing* (Oxford University Press, 2013) and *Strategic Communication Principles and Practice* (Oxford University Press, 2013) He has written on program evaluation and strategic communication for international academic journals and is a former Honorary National Secretary of the Public Relations Institute of Australia, of which he is a Life Fellow.

Lynette McDonald

Dr Lynette McDonald is a Lecturer in Public Relations at the University of Queensland in the School of Journalism and Communication. Lynette completed her PhD on the topic of consumer reactions to company crisis communication and management. She has multiple publications, including on different aspects of company crises, and has worked for a number of years as a public relations practitioner.

Gary Mersham

Gary Mersham is Professor of Communication at the Open Polytechnic in New Zealand and his research interests include e-learning and crisis communication. He has been a disaster management and crisis communication consultant to several large multinationals and to the South African and New Zealand governments. He has published widely in communication, authoring eight books and numerous peer reviewed research articles, including co-authoring the book *Disaster management: A guide to issues management and crisis communication* (Oxford University Press, South Africa, 2002) He has been a visiting professor at institutions in Australia, the USA and throughout Africa, and continues to consult to community, government and corporate clients.

Augustine Pang

Dr Augustine Pang is an Assistant Professor at the Wee Kim Wee School of Communication and Information at Nanyang Technological University, Singapore. Dr Pang's research interests include crisis management and communication, image management and repair, media management and public relations. Beside contributing chapters to leading textbooks such as the *Handbook of crisis communication* (Wiley-Blackwell, 2010) and *The Sage handbook of public relations* (2010), he has published widely in peer-reviewed journals. He is the regional editor for *Corporate Communications: An International Journal* and has co-guest-edited special issues in the *International Journal of Strategic Communication* and *Media Asia*.

Timothy Sellnow

Dr Timothy L. Sellnow is Professor of Communication at the University of Kentucky. He currently serves as theme leader for risk communication research at the National Center for Food Protection and Defense. His research focuses on risk and crisis communication in organisations and government agencies. He has worked globally on risk communication projects with such organisations as the World Health Organization and the International Food Information Council. He has co-authored five books on risk and crisis communication. His latest book, co-authored with Matthew Seeger, is *Theorizing crisis communication* (Wiley, 2103).

Mark Sheehan

Mark Sheehan combines almost 25 years of management marketing and public relations experience in the private sector with more recent academic experience as Senior Lecturer in Public Relations in the School of Communication & Creative Arts at Deakin University. He was the founding Postgraduate Course Director of the Master of Arts (Professional Communication) program from 2001 to 2006. From February 2007 to June 2009 he was SCCA Associate Head of School—Regional and Development. He has published widely and presented at Australian and international conferences in the areas of crisis management, public relations history and market research.

Manoj Thomas

Dr Manoj T. Thomas is an Associate Professor of Strategic Management at XLRI-Xavier School of Management, Jamshedpur, India. He has a doctorate in management from IRMA, Anand, and an MPhil in Economics from the Centre for Economic and Social Studies, Hyderabad. He has also trained as a civil engineer and has several years of working in consulting organisations on issues related to strategy and the environment.

Deborah Wise

Deborah Wise is a PhD candidate at the University of Newcastle, Australia. Her research interests are varied but they primarily concern the role of public relations in constructing and shaping socio-cultural discourses. Currently Deborah is examining the role of public relations in the positioning of the Australian carbon tax.

Katharina Wolf

Katharina Wolf is an academic at Curtin University in Perth, Australia, and course coordinator of the public relations program. She is passionate about student-centred, work-integrated learning; a commitment that has been recognised with a number of local and national awards. Katharina's industry experience encompasses communications and research roles in Germany, Spain, the United Kingdom and Australia. She is a former West Australian President of the Public Relations Institute of Australia and a director on the institute's national board. Her research interests include activism, the integrated use of new technologies, public relations education and career advancement in public relations.

Aimei Yang

Dr Aimei Yang is an Assistant Professor of Public Relations at the University of Southern California's Annenberg School for Communication and Journalism. Her work focuses on international public relations, activism studies, crisis communication and social network research. She has received research awards from both the International Communication Association and the National Communication Association. She has published numerous journal articles and book chapters in leading refereed journals in her field, including *Public Relations Review*, *Journal of International & Intercultural Communication*, and *Mass Communication and Society*.

ACKNOWLEDGMENTS

Thanks to the academics from around the world who adapted their published work to be included in the case studies; their names and achievements are listed in the earlier Contributors section of this book.

Thanks also to the many individuals whose support and encouragement made this book possible, in particular Dr Chris Galloway at Massey University, Auckland; Dr Robert Heath at University of Houston, Texas; Dr Peter Sandman; Dr Tim Coombs at University of Central Florida, Orlando; Dr Vince Covello of the Center for Risk Communication in New York; and Karen Hildebrandt at Oxford University Press, Melbourne.

Some parts of this book draw on previous publications by the author, which have been adapted for the present use and are identified at the end of the relevant chapters. Specific citations from the author's other publications are referenced in the normal way.

Thanks to Wayne Burns, CEO of Australasian Centre for Corporate Public Affairs, for permission to adapt material for figures in Chapter 3 and Chapter 12; Teresa Crane, CEO of the Issue Management Council in Leesburg, Virginia, for permission to use the Issue Management Best Practice Principles in Chapter 4; Dr Vince Covello for permission to use the message maps in Chapter 10; Harvard Business Review for permission to reprint the table in Chapter 11. The SCCT crisis response strategy guidelines in Chapter 11 are reprinted with permission from Macmillan Publishers Ltd: Corporate Reputation Review, 'Protecting Organization Reputations During a Crisis: The Development and Application of Situational Crisis Communication Theory' by Timothy Coombs, Copyright © 2007, Macmillan Publishers Ltd, published by Palgrave Macmillan. Also Dominic Cockram, Managing Director of Steelhenge Consulting, UK, for permission to use the leadership principles in Chapter 12.

INTRODUCTION

Where issue and crisis management intersect and converge with risk and reputation is one of the most dynamic and challenging areas of management and professional communication. Moreover, the new process approach to issue and crisis management reveals that these disciplines are not separate activities but form part of a continuum of management responsibilities that comprise a comprehensive response to events or developments which threaten organisational reputation or success.

This book introduces and explores each element, while at the same time emphasising the intimate relationship between them all.

The first chapter sets the framework, introducing the main elements of the book and placing them within an integrated, relational model.

Chapters 2–5 develop in detail the important concept of issue management, and Chapters 6–9 introduce and analyse the critical aspects of crisis management and the related concept of disaster management.

Chapter 10 introduces the basic elements of risk, risk management and risk communication, while Chapter 11 brings much of the previous discussion together in describing how the different elements combine to impact organisational reputation.

Chapter 12 summarises some of the main concepts; introduces corporate social responsibility as an integrated model; develops the role of leadership across the continuum of activity; and identifies some trends for likely future development.

While all the chapters contain frequent examples and references to illustrate key ideas, Chapters 2–11 also include two case studies relevant to the chapter theme. These case studies all focus on examples from the Asia-Pacific region, and are based on research or published journal articles by experts in their fields. Each contribution has been adapted by the original author especially for this book.

In addition to the main chapters, there are two additional features in this book. While each chapter lists the sources formally cited, there are many other useful sources that are referred to or that support each chapter. These additional references focus mainly on those published since 2000, although there are some exceptions for earlier publications that are of particular importance, or that reflect significant historical perspectives. They are listed in Further reading sections, also at the end of each chapter. Following the main chapters there is an Appendix with a fully worked example of a detailed issue management plan developed from the model introduced in Chapter 4.

Finally, in addition to the specific online resources referenced in the text, there is also a list of more general useful websites, which can be accessed by students or practitioners. This list appears at the end of the book before the index.

1

SETTING
THE FRAMEWORK

CHAPTER OBJECTIVES

This chapter will help you to:

+ understand the basic outline of issue management and crisis management

+ recognise the link to risk and reputation

+ assess the impact of the internet and social media

+ distinguish different approaches to defining an issue

+ learn how issue process models evolve

+ evaluate tactical crisis response versus strategic crisis management

+ differentiate between the categories of crises

+ appreciate how issue and crisis management align with other management disciplines.

Issue management and crisis management are core management disciplines, and they are also two of the most important elements of communications practice. Together they provide organisations with tools and processes to identify risks and issues early; take planned action to influence the course of those issues; respond effectively if issues develop into crises; and protect organisational reputation during and after a crisis.

Yet despite the acknowledged importance of issue management and crisis management to organisational success and the achievement of strategic goals, both disciplines suffer from a perceived lack of clarity about what they contribute and about the parameters that define them. In addition, the emergence of the internet and social media has added to this lack of clarity by further blurring the interrelationship between activities.

Not only has social media blurred distinctions, but it has also had a profound impact on each of the concepts addressed in this book—issue and crisis management, risk and reputation. While each of these concepts has its own established history, processes, tools and theoretical basis, the internet and social media now add a new dimension to the framework and operation of these activities.

For example, in issue management, social media has largely democratised the discipline by creating the capacity for individuals and community organisations to compete on a level playing field with big business and big government in identifying and engaging on issues.

In crisis management, social media now demands higher standards of transparency and consistency, and has introduced new methods of very rapid communication with stakeholders, both locally and around the world. In fact, the changes social media has made to crisis management have been branded 'the new normal' (Ziemnowicz, Harrison & Crandall, 2011).

In risk communication, the internet and social media have revolutionised the way in which people perceive risks, and brought with them new opportunities for improved understanding of risks, as well as new threats of increased misunderstanding and deliberate misrepresentation.

The cumulative effect of social media can be seen at perhaps its most striking when it comes to the crucial area of reputation, where threats to reputation—both for individuals and organisations—can emerge and escalate more quickly and dangerously than ever before. As the US reputation expert Leslie Gaines-Ross (2008, p. 18) commented:

> The Internet has spawned a new breed of critics and reputation assassins. Armed with little more than a computer and an opinion, these chat-room transmitters and bloggers can undo a company's reputation by disseminating misinformation and innuendo.

These and many other aspects of the importance of social media are explored and developed in the chapters that follow.

WHAT IS AN ISSUE?

In order to understand a concept well it is often most helpful to both define it and describe it. In other words, to present a concise definition—a carefully determined formula of words—and then characterise and describe it by discussing what it is and what it isn't, its shape and size, and how it relates to other things around it. This book follows that approach.

One reason why the term 'issue' is hard to define is because the concept is just not that simple. In the mid-1960s, in a US Supreme Court case about whether a particular film should be classified as obscene, Justice Potter Stewart famously wrote: 'I shall not today attempt to further define the kinds of material I understand to be embraced [as 'hard core pornography'] ... But I know it when I see it.' Issues are a bit like that. It is not easy to agree on defining exactly what an issue is. But for organisations that find themselves facing an issue, they 'know it when they see it'.

There is not much to be gained from getting caught up in duelling definitions. How to define an issue has been an acknowledged challenge since the discipline was first developed in the late 1970s and remains a subject of contention today.

The detailed nature of issues, and how they differ from simple problems, is addressed in Chapter 3. But for the present it is important to recognise that there are three main approaches to defining an issue—categorised as disputation, expectation gap and impact—and each has its advocates.[1]

DISPUTATION THEME

In the early days of issue management an issue was sometimes defined as 'a contested matter that is ready for decision'. This approach developed into what is now known as the 'disputation theme', which argues that an issue arises when there is a social and/or political dispute.

Heath and Coombs (2006) typified this approach when they characterised an issue as 'a contestable matter of opinion, a matter of fact, evaluation or policy that is important to the parties concerned' (p. 262). While the disputation theme is still used—sometimes called the controversy theme—some critics claim this approach is too broad. They argue that there are many disputes or contested matters that don't necessarily qualify as issues in the context of public relations. In other words, although every legitimate issue involves matters of dispute, not every dispute constitutes an issue.

EXPECTATION GAP THEME

Another common approach is the 'expectation gap theme', which says an issue exists when there is a gap—real or perceived—between an organisation's performance or the way it behaves, and the legitimate expectations of key stakeholders about how they think that organisation *should* behave.

The expectation gap—sometimes referred to as the legitimacy gap—remains a popular approach, first because it is simple to understand and communicate, and second because it aligns closely with the thinking of many activist and community groups who often have

---

1 For more discussion on the three approaches to issue definition, see Jaques (2010) in this chapter's Further reading section.

very firm opinions about what they regard as poor performance by target organisations, especially big business and big government.

Here, too, some critics think this approach is limited because it tends to focus on past events and behaviour, it can promote discord, and it can focus on a desire to punish perceived transgressions. As a result, the expectation gap approach can occasionally be confrontational rather than cooperative. This runs contrary to the view of some modern experts who believe issue management should, in fact, be used to promote social harmony. Robert Heath, for example, has defined issue management as 'a strategic set of functions used to reduce friction and increase harmony between organisations and their publics in the public policy arena' (2005, p. 460).

It can also be argued that the gap itself does not constitute an issue. However, a gap in stakeholder expectation can certainly *lead* to an issue, and analysis of the gap can help to *characterise* that issue. In addition, the expectation gap theme in particular has been boosted by the rise of social media, as is described in Chapter 2.

IMPACT THEME

The third approach is known as the 'impact theme', which characterises issues by their capacity to seriously impact the organisation concerned. Put simply, the impact theme defines an issue as any development that could have a serious adverse impact on the organisation and its interests.

Some critics suggest the impact theme minimises the fact that some issues contain opportunities as well as threats, and that this approach may divert attention from what might prove to be a positive opportunity. Some also argue that the impact theme is less appropriate for activist and community groups who often become involved in an issue, not necessarily because it impacts them directly but because they believe they are acting in the interests of a wider group or society as a whole.

Despite these shortcomings, the impact theme has been widely adopted, not least because it aligns closely with the processes and objectives of similar management disciplines, including crisis management, strategic planning and risk management.

Given that strategic alignment is an important theme of this book, the following modern version has been adopted as a working definition of 'issue' (adapted and updated from a version originally developed by the Conference Board[2] back in 1979):

> An issue is any trend or development—real or perceived—usually at least partly in the public arena which, if it continues, could have a significant impact on the organisation's financial position, operations, reputation or future interests, and requires a structured approach to achieve positive, planned outcomes.

---

2   The Conference Board is a New York–based organisation committed to the prosperity and security of business and improved business leadership (see www.conference-board.org). It published one of the first 'how to' manuals for issue management—see Brown (1979) in this chapter's Further reading section.

Within this definition are four important aspects that need close attention to fully understand the nature of issues.

The first is that an issue may not necessarily be 'real'. There is an old saying in public relations that 'perception *is* reality' and this applies nowhere more so than in issue management. Belief in an issue—even if it is false or doubtful—can create just as much public concern and consequent demands for action as one founded on solid fact.

An example might be the case for inoculation of young babies against common childhood illnesses, which is almost universally supported by medical experts around the world. Yet an international campaign by determined activists has made this a high-profile *perceived* issue of concern, especially among young mothers, whose decisions not to inoculate can have very real adverse health consequences for their own children and the wider community.[3] Dismissing an issue on the grounds that it is 'perceived and not real' can equally have serious consequences for the organisation concerned.

As Holladay and Coombs (2013, p. 452) concluded: 'A tenet shared by both risk communication and crisis management is that stakeholder perceptions matter. If stakeholders *think* there is a risk or crisis, there *is* one'.

The second important aspect of our working definition is that issues occur—at least in part—in the public arena. This doesn't necessarily mean the issue is on the front page of the newspaper or on the evening television news, or even trending on social media. But it is at least partly external to the organisation, which means it is not just an internal problem and, as a result, the organisation is usually not in control of all the contributing factors.

Also significant is the word 'significant' itself. Issues are not simply the passing 'problem of the day'. They genuinely threaten the well-being of the organisation and typically extend over weeks, months or even years. Although organisations face problems every day, of varying nature and importance, issue management is not a general-purpose problem-solving tool, but is most appropriately used when the impact is, or is likely to be, significant. The important difference between a day-to-day problem and a legitimate issue is explained in Chapter 3.

The final important element of our definition is that, regardless of which of the three approaches to defining an issue is used, one concept common to them all is that an issue 'requires a structured approach'. That means the need for an agreed, formal process, not just an ad hoc response. This importance of a planned issue strategy is a central principle of issue management.

Table 1.1 provides definitions of four important concepts discussed in this book and how they interrelate: issue, emergency, crisis and disaster. The further term 'catastrophe' is not included here, but is discussed in detail in Chapter 9.

---

3   For an overview of the anti-vaccination movement and its use of social media, see Kata (2012) and Shetty (2010) in this chapter's Further reading section.

Table 1.1 Definitional guide to key activities and their interrelation

Challenge	Management activity	Key focus
ISSUE Any trend or development— real or perceived—usually at least partly in the public arena, which, if it continues, could have a significant impact on the organisation's financial position, operations, reputation or future interests and requires a structured response.	**Issue management** A coordinated cross-functional effort to identify, prioritise and actively manage towards resolution those developments that most impact the organisation and where there is a capacity to make a difference.	To utilise resources across the organisation to make a difference and work towards planned, positive outcomes.
	Issue communication An element of the broader issue management process that contributes to and supports development and implementation of the strategic plan, including message development and effective delivery.	To ensure all communication meets stakeholder needs and supports and is consistent with the strategic plan.
EMERGENCY An unplanned or unwanted event that impacts the organisation locally and calls for immediate action. Low potential for adverse impact beyond the initial event. If badly managed can become a crisis.	**Emergency response** An immediate action plan to identify and manage the emergency. Local management is in charge and risk to reputation and media interest beyond the nearby area are low.	To bring the emergency under control and to prevent it from escalating.
CRISIS An event or development that can focus unwanted visibility on the organisation and is likely to endanger health or the environment, or seriously impact reputation or ability to do business. High potential for adverse impact beyond the initial event.	**Crisis management** A coordinated action that mobilises many functions to respond to the crisis, to assess potential impact, to provide resources, to minimise physical and reputational damage, to manage all stakeholders, to protect the organisation, and to capture post-event learnings.	To use resources from throughout the organisation to bring the crisis under control as quickly and effectively as possible and to minimise damage.
	Crisis communication What gets said by the organisation during and after the crisis. It also provides insight into societal concerns to help develop and communicate strategy.	To prioritise concerns among key stakeholders to ensure consistent accurate messages, and help protect organisational reputation.

Challenge	Management activity	Key focus
DISASTER A major adverse event that affects the broader society, such as natural disasters (floods, earthquakes, storms), social unrest (riots, political upheaval) or infrastructure breakdown (power outages). May trigger a specific crisis for individual organisations.	**Disaster management** A coordinated response, often managed by statutory or territorial authorities, that mobilises diverse forces. While the event may affect individual organisations, they face less risk to reputation and there is less focus on direct blame or accountability.	For government authorities, to protect people and property. For individual organisations, to protect people and business, with a focus on restoring normal operations and how to play a role in assisting the community.
	Business continuity Coordinated action to ensure an organisation's ability to do business during and after a crisis or disaster. Includes effective back-up and redundancy systems and key stakeholder communication.	To restore physical operations or to sustain supply to customers.

WHAT IS ISSUE MANAGEMENT?

It must be stated at the outset that issue management[4] is not about spin. It's not about image creation. And it's not about using communication to put a gloss on poor performance or to hide mistakes. It is a proven executive discipline that aligns with strategic planning and contributes directly to the business bottom line.

> Issue management is about steering the ship out of troubled water, while crisis management is about saving the ship after it has struck an iceberg.
>
> Tony Jaques (2000, p. 93)

It is an effective way for organisations to proactively engage in social, regulatory and political debates that have the potential to inhibit business and damage both individual and corporate reputation.

Most importantly, issue management is not just an activity for public relations and communications professionals. Communicators often have 'ownership' of the process and

---

4 The terms 'issue management' and 'issues management' are both commonly used. Howard Chase, the acknowledged 'father' of the discipline, once quipped that it should always be issue management in the same way that it is 'brain surgery', not 'brains surgery'. This book uses the form 'issue management' throughout.

can play a significant role in strategy development and implementation. But best practice around the world demonstrates that effective issue management requires the involvement and support of leaders and top executives across many functions departments and businesses in order to deliver the organisation's strategy and to develop and safeguard its good name. (The role of leadership is explored in Chapter 12.)

Building on the impact theme discussed above:

> Issue management is a coordinated, cross-functional effort to identify, prioritise and actively manage towards resolution those developments that most impact the organisation and where there is a capacity to make a difference.

It is also widely regarded as providing a structured framework and tools for identifying problems early to avoid issues becoming crises. This description is particularly helpful as it emphasises that, while issue management is a genuine management discipline and mindset, it is also a process and a set of tools.

At its core is a deceptively simple process, which, from the beginning of the discipline, has been built around five basic steps:

1. identification
2. analysis and prioritisation
3. strategy options
4. action plans
5. evaluation.

These steps—sometimes with different labels—are common across almost every issue management process today, irrespective of the industry sector, organisation size or organisation location. Many models add decision boxes at each stage, and some grow so complex and over-engineered that they become unwieldy and not particularly useful. But the basic idea of a formal process flow remains consistent. In addition, a variety of tools have been developed to support implementation of these process stages. Some typical tools are described in the next three chapters.

Yet the fundamental elements remain fairly simple and are based on the very first formal issue management process model, developed in 1977 by the pioneers Howard Chase and Barry Jones (see Figure 1.1).

This model shows the five basic steps in a continuous work flow, with key tasks at each step. Ray Ewing (1997), a colleague of Chase, asserted that all subsequent published models were based on this original construction, and, 30 years later, Coombs and Holladay (2007, p. 81) said it was still regarded as 'the most influential issue management model'.

The next chapter discusses the development of issue management, how it is applied and how it grew from a largely corporate discipline to be adopted by governments, activist organisations and community groups around the world. But first it is necessary to introduce crisis and crisis management.

Figure 1.1 Common steps in the issue management process

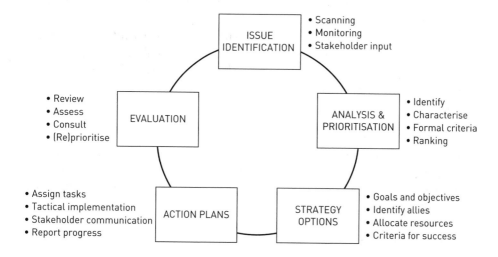

Source: adapted from Chase and Jones (1977).

WHAT IS A CRISIS?

Unlike the challenges around how to define an issue, there is much less disagreement about what is a crisis. The two are clearly linked, and issue management and crisis management have even been called the 'Siamese twins' of public relations (Jaques, 2002). In fact, there is a maxim that 'a crisis is an issue that wasn't managed' and many crises do arise from a mismanaged issue or a badly handled emergency.

Regardless of how crises originate, there is not much doubt about what a crisis is. Jaques (2009) cites well over a dozen definitions that reflect different approaches. A typical basic definition would be:

> A crisis is an event or development that can focus unwanted visibility on the organisation and is likely to endanger health or the environment, or seriously impact reputation or ability to do business.

However, many scholars believe this is too general, and one definition that is widely used was developed by Pearson and Clair (1998, p. 60):

> An organisational crisis is a low probability, high impact event that threatens the viability of the organisation, and is characterised by ambiguity of cause, effects and means of resolution, as well as by a belief that decisions must be made swiftly.

Following the principle of describing rather than defining something, Gregory (2005) undertook an extensive review of the literature and concluded that crises are characterised as 'high consequence, low probability, overlaid with risk and uncertainty, conducted under time pressure, disruptive of normal business and potentially lethal to organisational reputation' (p. 313).

An important aspect of all three approaches is the consistent reference to the importance of a high level of significance. Pearson and Clair, for example, described a crisis as threatening the viability of the organisation, and Gregory referred to it as being disruptive of normal business and potentially lethal to organisational reputation.

> At a time when almost anything and everything is called a crisis, recognition and diagnosis of a crisis has become a problem in itself. Although crisis is not a precise concept (quite the contrary, as a concept it is vague) it is important to understand its specificity to distinguish between a crisis and other situations that might be close but whose management would be significantly different.
>
> Michel Ogrizek and Jean-Michel Guillery (1999, p. xii)

This degree of impact is an essential element of a real crisis. Yet within business and society the word 'crisis' has been seriously devalued by overuse, until it is now sometimes applied to describe just about any embarrassment or minor problem.

When the keynote speaker fails to turn up at your conference it is embarrassing and awkward, but it is not a crisis. When a CEO inadvertently utters a profanity during a national television interview he or she might be revealing something about themselves, but it isn't a crisis. And, contrary to one IT reporter, when someone misplaces the piece of paper with the computer admin access passwords, it isn't a crisis (unless perhaps the passwords fall into the hands of a competitor, or a hacker determined to destroy the organisation's entire database).

The multiple impacts of a crisis were well captured by Weiner (2006, p. 1):

> Few circumstances test a company's reputation or competency as severely as a crisis. Whether the impact is immediate or sustained over months and years, a crisis affects stakeholders within and outside of the company. Customers cancel orders. Employees raise questions. Directors are questioned. Shareholders get antsy. Competitors sense opportunity. Governments and regulators come knocking. Interest groups smell blood. Lawyers are not far behind.

While it is true that crises come in all shapes and sizes, throughout this book the term 'crisis' will be used in the conventional sense of a serious development or event that can genuinely threaten the organisation's long-term reputation or ability to do business.

Experts have identified a variety of different types of crisis,[5] but broadly they fall into some fairly well-recognised categories:

---

5   For some analyses of crisis types, see Fearn-Banks (2011), Lerbinger (1997), Pearson and Mitroff (1993) and Rosenthal and Kouzmin (1993) in this chapter's Further reading section. See also discussion in Chapter 11.

1. *Operational crises.* Generally these originate in plant or operational facilities, and typically arise from physical incidents such as spills, leaks, fire or explosions, but might also result from sabotage, a workplace shooting, social unrest, riots or even terrorism.

2. *Environmental crises.* These often emerge in the aftermath of an operational incident and may include community exposure to pollution, or release of toxic substances into the environment, such as chemical emissions into the air, poisons discharging into lakes or rivers, or contamination of underground sources of drinking water.

3. *Management or employee misconduct crises.* These typically arise from moral or ethical lapses, such as misuse of company money, corruption, bribery, scandalous misbehaviour, nepotism, industrial espionage, theft or other criminal activity. These can occur at all levels of the organisation.

4. *Management/legal crises.* Negative structural decisions, such as layoffs or shut-downs or offshoring, can be a cause of potential crises, along with allegations of managerial wrongdoing, such as price-fixing, tax evasion, trademark, patent or copyright infringement, or claims of unfair or improper competition.

5. *Technological crises.* These usually result from a technology failure or breakdown, including collapse of computer systems, hacking, breaches of privacy, loss of data, or infrastructure breakdown such as a prolonged loss of power.

6. *Product crises.* Crises directly affecting products can be deliberate (such as product tampering or extortion) or accidental (such as contamination or manufacturing error, or a design fault which causes illness, injury or even death). Product crises can lead to recalls, boycotts or product liability litigation.

7. *Labour relations crises.* These may arise from specific industrial disputes, such as a strike or lockout, or from allegations of wrongful behaviour towards employees, such as racial or sexual discrimination, bullying, wrongful dismissal, or unfair or dangerous working conditions.

8. *Social concerns.* Organisations sometimes find themselves facing an operational or reputational crisis because they are caught up in a social concern, such as animal testing, use of genetically modified organisms or packaging derived from endangered rainforest, or suppliers who use exploited labour or underage workers.

9. *Natural disasters.* Crises may strike in the form of natural disasters such as floods, earthquakes, hurricanes and bush fires, but (as defined earlier in Table 1.1) disaster management is a standalone discipline usually implemented at a societal level. This means it is different from the response to organisational crises, even though a natural disaster can trigger an operational crisis for an individual organisation. Disasters are discussed as a separate topic in Chapter 9.

Although these categories capture the broad range of potential crises, it is essential to recognise that, depending on severity, some of the examples given would not necessarily develop into a full-scale crisis. They may have been successfully dealt with earlier as an incident, an emergency or even an issue. One of the key factors that can determine how far they develop is the effectiveness of crisis management.

WHAT IS CRISIS MANAGEMENT?

At one level it is not difficult to describe crisis management:

> Crisis management is often presented as a coordinated action that mobilises functions and resources from throughout the organisation to bring the crisis under control as quickly and effectively as possible and to minimise damage.

Over recent years that simple approach has been overtaken by a more sophisticated way of thinking about crisis management as a more strategic and proactive discipline.

The traditional view of what an organisation does to get ready *in case* a crisis strikes and how it acts *after* the crisis strikes (including communication) is now increasingly understood as being crisis *response*. By contrast, the wider concept of crisis *management* is now understood to include the steps an organisation takes to prevent a crisis happening in the first place, as well as its actions during the potentially dangerous phase after the triggering event itself has been resolved.

Referring to this important difference between largely tactical crisis response and more strategic crisis management, the pioneering scholars Pauchant and Mitroff (1992, p. 11) coined a vivid distinction:

> *Crisis management* is not the same as *crash management*—what to do when everything falls apart. Obviously this is important, but it is only one part of total crisis management effort. Here we focus not only on crash management—what to do in the heat of a crisis—but also on why crises happen in the first place and what can be done to prevent them.

Another easy way to remember this difference is to think about home security. A responsible homeowner will take out insurance to provide financial assistance in the event that the home suffers fire, flood or burglary. But the insurance policy itself does nothing to prevent the fire or flood or to deter the burglar. It comes into play only after the event, and can be seen as the equivalent of reactive crisis response—only useful when the event has already occurred. However, the responsible homeowner doesn't just take out insurance. They also install burglar alarms, smoke detectors and security locks on doors and windows. That is taking protective action before the event, and might be called the equivalent of crisis prevention.

Most importantly, the responsible homeowner would never do just one task and think the job was done. Effective home security requires both proactive actions to keep the home safe, and well as some advanced planning to provide protection if it all goes wrong. Or, in Pauchant and Mitroff's phrase, 'when everything falls apart'.

> Crisis management must not be viewed as another stand-alone program. Unless it is integrated with other programs, it will not succeed, and neither will the other programs.
>
> Ian Mitroff (2001, p. 30)

The need for an integrated approach lies at the heart of modern crisis management. Its development has seen a progression from largely tactical crisis response, closely linked to emergency incident management, towards a more sophisticated broad approach, more closely aligned with strategic planning.

This emergence of crisis management as a comprehensive, formal business discipline—and the role of public relations in all its phases—is expanded on in Chapter 6. But for now it highlights not just how crisis management developed but also how crisis management, issue management and the related management disciplines are increasingly seen to fit together into the broader spectrum of organisational activities.

One popular way to illustrate this relationship is the graphic representation known as the 'issue life cycle', discussed in the next chapter. The life cycle illustrates that a public concern can develop into a problem, then into an issue, and can even develop into a full-blown crisis, which in turn reaches some form of resolution. This approach is useful in emphasising the basic importance of early intervention—taking steps to prevent the situation getting worse. But the reality is that issue management is seldom a linear process. Moreover, many crises don't move neatly forward to resolution, but circle back to a renewed phase of the original issue or even to a fresh or transformed issue.

As Bigelow, Fahey and Mahon (1993, p. 29) concluded:

> Issues do not necessarily follow a linear, sequential path, but instead follow paths that reflect the intensity and diversity of the values and interests stakeholders bring to an issue and the complexity of the interaction among the ... factors.

Advancing this idea, the relational model illustrated in Figure 1.2 attempts to show that the relationship between different activities is not a stepwise, linear process (Jaques,

Figure 1.2 Issue and crisis management relational model[6]

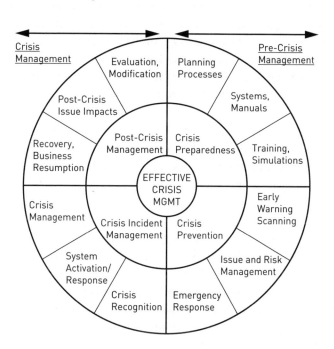

Source: Jaques (2007).

---

6   This relational model was first published in Jaques (2007) and has subsequently appeared in other publications.

2007). It comprises clusters of related and integrated disciplines that may be undertaken in sequential fashion, but equally may operate simultaneously. In fact, two of the major segments—crisis prevention and crisis preparedness—most often *should* happen at the same time. It also shows that the flow of activities circles back to deliver learning and continuous improvement.

The model is divided into halves (crisis management and pre-crisis management) and comprises four major segments (crisis preparedness, crisis prevention, crisis incident management and post-crisis management), each built around clusters of activities and processes.

One important purpose of this construction is to illustrate how the various separate management disciplines fit together and how they comprise an integrated whole. The four major segments from the model are now discussed in turn.

CRISIS PREPAREDNESS

Crisis preparedness is the group of activities previously compared to taking out home insurance. These activities don't prevent a crisis striking, but they do help prepare the organisation to respond well and to minimise any damage.

The bottom-line importance of being properly crisis prepared was demonstrated by seminal research at Oxford University (Knight & Pretty, 1999). This respected study showed that companies with effective crisis plans in place suffered on average a 5 per cent fall in share value, and after 12 months their share value on average had recovered to 7 per cent above the pre-crisis level. By contrast, companies with no effective crisis plan in place saw their shares fall by an average of 10 per cent, and after 12 months their shares were 15 per cent below the pre-crisis level. In other words, for companies without effective planning in place, the share price initially fell twice as far, and a year later there was a difference of 22 per cent of the organisation's market value compared with the well-prepared companies.

Many subsequent studies around the world have reinforced the dire financial and reputational cost of *not* being prepared with effective crisis planning in place. For example, Coleman (2004) analysed Australian crises over an entire decade and found that more than a quarter cost the organisations concerned in excess of $100 million.

The first important aspect of crisis preparedness focuses on systems, manuals and other crisis management infrastructure, such as equipment in place, 'war room' established, resources allocated and documentation prepared. Key items typically include selection and induction of the crisis management team; agreement on reporting and authority lines in the event of a crisis; functional checklists; pre-prepared materials such as approved media statement templates, organisational information, product data sheets and executive profiles; stakeholder contact lists; and logistical resources for the centralised crisis management centre, such as phones, radio, television, computer access and back-up files of all material. (Details of elements of a crisis plan are discussed in Chapter 7.)

However, none of this preparation is of real value without familiarisation programs such as table-top exercises, live simulations and communication system testing. While most organisations regularly practise emergency response, such as fire drills and office evacuation,

isis management manual is often left unrehearsed in a dusty
…en a crisis strikes the team is unprepared and the manual itself is
…rly prepared, crisis management response should be exercised at
… a year. And the manual should be a 'living' electronic document,
…otely accessed.

…ften reluctant to talk about crisis preparedness (or lack of it), but an
…isis planning can be seen in the case of financial services giant Morgan
…e single largest tenant in New York's World Trade Center. Following
…ttack on the building, the company upgraded its crisis plan and
…es, including establishment of a back-up site twenty-two blocks away.
When the first plane hit the World Trade Center more than eight years later on 11
September 2001, Morgan Stanley immediately started evacuating almost 3000 employees,
even though the public address system was telling occupants to remain in place. Within
20 minutes the back-up site had been activated and senior management had established a
command centre at a second back-up site. Thousands died when the twin towers collapsed
and over 500 businesses in the buildings were destroyed. But only thirteen Morgan Stanley
employees lost their lives and 2687 were safely evacuated. When the New York Stock
Exchange resumed on 17 September the company was fully functioning.[7]

CRISIS PREVENTION

It is a truism that the best method of crisis management is to take steps to prevent the crisis
happening in the first place. Unlike the previous segment of the model—which focuses
on getting ready to respond when the triggering event has occurred—the activities and
processes under the crisis prevention segment are designed to help reduce the likelihood of
the crisis occurring at all. This second section also highlights the link to the preventive role
of other management disciplines.

The first step is early warning and scanning, which includes processes such as audits,
preventive maintenance, issue and environmental scanning, social forecasting, anticipatory
management and future studies. However, receiving a warning of advance information and
doing something about it are obviously not the same thing. Case studies of real-life crises
repeatedly reveal that there were ample early warnings or 'red flags' that were either ignored,
or that were reported but no action was taken.

For example, in the aftermath of the $65 billion Madoff investment fraud scandal in the
USA, SEC Inspector General David Kotz admitted that his agency missed 'numerous red
flags' from 1992 until the fraudster was arrested in December 2008. Kotz conceded that
five separate failed investigations into Madoff's operation had been bungled (Jaques, 2013).

Similarly, following Victoria's Black Saturday bushfires in February 2009, which resulted
in 173 deaths, it was revealed that there had been clear warnings about allegedly inadequate
maintenance of power lines, which caused at least some of the fires (see the case study on
the Victorian bushfire disaster at the end of Chapter 9).

---

7   For a fuller description of Morgan Stanley's experience after 11 September, see Couta (2002) in this chapter's
    Further reading section.

Taking action on early warnings is where issue management and risk management link directly to other management tools and processes. Both of these disciplines are strategic activities with significance far beyond just early warning for crisis prevention. But they provide a vital framework to help identify problems early, and to effectively manage those problems to reduce the chance of them becoming a crisis.

The third area of crisis prevention is less obvious, but no less important, and that is emergency response. Not every crisis is triggered by an emergency, but any emergency that is badly handled can lead directly to a crisis, especially when the impact of the emergency starts to spread because of mismanagement.

For example, a small fire in an electricity substation could cause a brief power blackout, and that would be classified as an emergency. But if the recovery system failed because of management mistakes, or the blackout spread to other areas and lasted hours or even days, then the power company could be facing a real crisis. Similarly, if a chemical company had a moderate-sized spill it would probably constitute an emergency. But a series of repeated spills over a short period could well trigger regulatory intervention, a crisis of confidence and damaged reputation.

Organisations need effective emergency response, and public relations can be an important part of that response.[8] Moreover, they also need training that would enable emergency responders and local communicators to identify the possibility that it *could* become a crisis, plus processes which allow the organisation to escalate in a planned way from emergency response to crisis incident management.

> Sooner or later every business will be confronted by a crisis of some type. Its ability to manage the crisis successfully can mean the difference between survival and disaster.
>
> John E. Spillan (2003, p. 61)

CRISIS INCIDENT MANAGEMENT

Much of the crisis management literature is very tactical in nature, and often focuses primarily on the segment called crisis preparedness—planning, manuals and training—and then on management of the crisis itself. Crisis incident management is certainly a critical and high-profile phase, and it is also a period when public relations professionals are likely to play a key role as crisis communicators.

When a crisis arises from an emergency or major physical incident, it is usually easy to identify. It is much harder to identify when an ongoing problem has the potential to become a crisis. In fact, crisis recognition is a definite skill. It requires judgment, leadership and honesty, and sometimes senior managers will try to deny that a crisis is threatening or has already happened. Indeed, one of the important roles of a crisis leader is to recognise that a crisis exists.

---

8   For discussion of the role of communication in emergency response, see Hyer and Covello (2005) and Jabro (2013) in this chapter's Further reading section.

Steven Fink (1986) wrote one of the most important early books on crisis management, which firmly positioned it as a formal executive responsibility. He warned: 'You should accept almost as a universal truth that when a crisis strikes it will be accompanied by a host of diversionary problems. As a manager your task is to identify the real crisis' (p. 73).

Of course, crisis recognition alone is not enough. Response systems must be activated immediately and rapidly. When Hurricane Katrina struck Louisiana in 2005, system activation and response at many levels was slow and inadequate. The report of the Congressional Committee set up to investigate the preparation and response was tellingly titled *A Failure of Initiative*. It concluded that while there was no failure to predict the inevitability and consequences of a monster hurricane, there was a failure of initiative to take action and improve the level of protection in place (Select Bipartisan Committee, 2006, p. 97).

Managing any crisis incident has two distinct streams of activity. One is responding to the triggering event and mitigating subsequent damage. The other critical stream is stakeholder management and media response, and this is where the public relations professional can be so important. Experience shows that although the incident itself is well handled, mismanagement of communication—or even *perceived* mismanagement of communication—can prolong the crisis and contribute to lasting financial or reputational damage.

POST-CRISIS MANAGEMENT

The fourth segment of the relational model addresses this risk of lasting financial or reputational damage that is sometimes the main concern after the crisis incident itself has been resolved.

The obvious first step is recovery and the resumption of operations—sometimes known as 'business continuity'. This generally sees a focus on operational resumption, financial costs, market retention, business momentum and share price protection. Many business continuity programs concentrate primarily on protecting the organisation against infrastructure problems such as power outages, computer failure and breakdown of logistics and distributions systems.

But it is a major mistake to think that post-crisis management is limited to business recovery and continuity. The reality is that the risks to an organisation post-crisis can be even greater than during the crisis itself (sometimes described as the 'crisis after the crisis').

Long after the organisation has returned to 'business as usual' there remains the very real threat of post-crisis issue impacts, such as coronial inquests, judicial inquiries, prosecution, litigation, prolonged reputational damage and seemingly endless media scrutiny.

These need to be effectively managed and this is where issue management is the preferred discipline to support the broader strategy. Lawyers and public relations professionals have to be ready to work together to face months or even years of effort to address these longer-term issues. A study in Australia (Coleman, 2004) showed that about one in four organisations struck by a crisis do not survive in the long run. Organisational survival has also been studied in many other countries. Importantly, the capacity to survive is often directly related to how well the organisation tried to prevent the crisis and how well its plans and processes operated in response, including how well it managed communication to the public and key stakeholders.

The final stage of post-crisis management is evaluation and modification—to undertake a root cause analysis; to honestly assess the performance of management and the organisation; to review the existing process; and, possibly, to implement change and improvement.

This phase can be difficult, because there is a very human desire to move on rather than to dwell on what went wrong. But the post-crisis phase provides a genuine opportunity to change whatever helped create the potential for a crisis in the first place, which in turn leads us right back to crisis preparedness and crisis prevention.

This chapter has introduced issue and crisis management and outlined how these disciplines fit together with other management activities. The remaining chapters address in detail the essential elements of issue management, crisis management and risk communication and their impact on reputation.

Note: parts of this chapter draw on Jaques (2007).

KEY POINTS

+ There are three approaches to issue management: the disputation theme, the expectation gap theme and the impact theme.

+ Issue, emergency, crisis and disaster are distinctly different concepts and must be separately defined.

+ Issue management is a stepwise process to identify potential threats or opportunities early in order to deliver planned, positive outcomes.

+ Crisis management is not just about incident response, but also about preparing for a crisis before it happens and taking proactive steps to prevent it from taking place.

+ Issue and crisis management are closely linked and need to be well integrated into a comprehensive continuum of management activities.

≡ ACTIVITIES AND DISCUSSION

1. What are the strengths and weaknesses of the disputation theme, the expectation gap theme and the impact theme when it comes to defining an issue? Which approach do you think is best suited to a social-media driven issue. Why?

2. Review the nine categories of crises and identify some high-profile cases within each category. Are some categories of crises typically more difficult to manage than others? Why?

3. Lawyers and professional communicators often need to work very closely in responding to an issue or a crisis. Discuss why you think this relationship is sometimes so difficult and challenging.

4. Identify possible reasons why some senior managers are reluctant to properly examine what went wrong during a crisis. How does this inhibit organisations in learning from what happened?

REFERENCES

Bigelow, B., Fahey, L. & Mahon, J. F. (1993). A typology of issue evolution. *Business and Society, 33*(1), 18–29.

Chase, H. W. & Jones, B. L. (1977). CPI presents. *Corporate public issues and their management, 2*(14), 1–4.

Coleman, L. (2004). The frequency and cost of corporate crises. *Journal of Contingencies and Crisis Management, 12*(1), 2–13.

Coombs, W. T. & Holladay, S. J. (2007). *It's not just PR: Public relations in society.* Malden, MA: Blackwell.

Ewing, R. P. (1997). Issue management: Managing trends through the issue lifecycle. In C. L. Caywood (Ed.), *The handbook of strategic public relations and integrated communications* (pp. 173–187). New York: McGraw-Hill.

Fink, S. (1986). *Crisis management: Planning for the inevitable.* New York: American Management Association.

Gaines-Ross, L. (2008). *Corporate reputation: 12 steps to safeguarding and recovering reputation.* Hoboken, NJ: John Wiley.

Gregory, A. (2005). Communication dimensions of the UK foot and mouth disease crisis, 2001. *Journal of Public Affairs, 5*(3/4), 312–328.

Heath, R. L. (2005). Issues management. In R. L. Heath (Ed.), *The encyclopedia of public relations* (vol. 1, pp. 460–463). Thousand Oaks, CA: Sage.

Heath, R. L. & Coombs, W. T. (2006). *Today's public relations: An introduction.* Thousand Oaks, CA: Sage.

Holladay, S. J. & Coombs, W. T. (2013). Successful prevention may not be enough: A case study of how managing a threat triggers a threat. *Public Relations Review, 39*(5), 451–458.

Jaques, T. (2013). The leadership role in crisis prevention. In A. DuBrin (Ed.), *The handbook of research on crisis leadership in organisations* (pp. 270–289). New York: Edward Elgar.

Jaques, T. (2009). Issue and crisis management: Quicksand in the definitional landscape. *Public Relations Review, 35*(3), 280–286.

Jaques, T. (2007). Issue management and crisis management: An integrated, non-linear, relational construct. *Public Relations Review, 33*(2), 147–157.

Jaques, T. (2002). Towards a new terminology: Optimising the value of issue management. *Journal of Communication Management, 7*(2), 140–147.

Jaques, T. (2000). *Don't just stand there: The Do-it Plan for effective issue management.* Melbourne: Issue Outcomes.

Knight, R. F. & Pretty, D. J. (1999). Corporate catastrophes, stock returns and trading volume. *Corporate Reputation Review, 2*(4), 363–378.

Mitroff, I. I. (2001). *Managing crises before they happen.* New York: American Management Association.

Ogrizek, M. & Guillery, J-M. (1999). *Communicating in crisis.* New York: Aldine de Gruyter.

Pauchant, T. C. & Mitroff, I. I. (1992). *Transforming the crisis-prone organisation: Preventing individual, organisational and environmental tragedies.* San Francisco: Jossey-Bass.

Pearson, C. M. & Clair, J. A. (1998). Reframing crisis management. *The Academy of Management Review, 23*(1), 59–76.

Select Bipartisan Committee. (2006). *A failure of initiative: Final report of the select bipartisan committee to investigate the preparation for and response to Hurricane Katrina.* Washington, DC: US Government Printing Office.

Spillan, J. E. (2003). An explanatory model for evaluating crisis events and managers' concerns in non-profit organisations. *Journal of Contingencies and Crisis Management, 11*(4), 160–167.

Weiner, D. (2006). Crisis communications: Managing corporation reputation in the court of public opinion. *Ivey Business Journal, 70*(4), 1–6.

Ziemnowicz, C. H., Harrison, G. & Crandall, W. (2011). The new normal: How social media is changing the way organisations manage a crisis. *Central Business Review, 30*(1), 17–24.

FURTHER READING

Arnold, J. E. & Ewing, R. P. (2012). Issues management methods for reputational management. In C. L. Caywood (Ed.), *The handbook of strategic public relations and integrated marketing communication* (pp. 335–352). New York: McGraw Hill.

Brown, J. K. (1979). *This business of issues: Coping with the company's environments.* New York: The Conference Board.

Coombs, W. T. & Holladay, S. J. (2014). *It's not just PR: Public relations in society* (2nd ed.). Malden, MA: Wiley-Blackwell.

Coombs, W. T. & Holladay, S. J. (2010). *PR Strategy and application: managing influence.* Malden, MA: Wiley-Blackwell.

Couta, D. L. (2002). How resilience works. *Harvard Business Review*, pp. 2–8.

Dalton, J. (2011). Reputation and strategic issue management. In A. Hiles (Ed.), *Reputation management: Building and protecting your company's profile in a digital world* (pp. 203–216). London: Bloomsbury.

Dougall, L. (2008). *Issues management.* Institute for Public Relations, Miami. Retrieved from www.instituteforpr.org/topics/issues-management.

Fearn-Banks, K. (2011). *Crisis communications: A casebook approach* (4th ed.). New York: Routledge.

Heath, R. L. (Ed.). (2010). *The Sage handbook of public relations* (2nd ed.). Newbury Park, CA: Sage.

Hyer, R. N. & Covello, V. T. (2005). *Effective media communication during public health emergencies: A WHO handbook.* Geneva: World Health Organization. Retrieved from www.who.int/csr/resources/publications/WHO_CDS_2005_31/en/.

Jabro, A. D. (2013, 6–10 March). *New media, emergency planning and scaled-up drills: Risky business.* Paper presented at the 16th International Public Relations Research Conference, Coral Gables, Miami.

Jaques, T. (2010). Embedding issue management: From process to policy. In R. L. Heath (Ed.), *The Sage handbook of public relations* (2nd ed., pp. 435–446). Newbury Park, CA: Sage.

Kata, A. (2012, 28 May). Anti-vaccine activists, Web 2.0, and the postmodern paradigm: An overview of tactics and tropes used online by the anti-vaccination movement. *Vaccine, 30*(15), 3778–3789.

Lerbinger, O. (1997). *The crisis manager: Facing risk and responsibility.* Mahwah, NJ: Lawrence Erlbaum.

Overbay, Z. (2004). Exploring reputational risk. *Risk Management, 51*(10), 50.

Pearson, C. M. & Mitroff, I. I. (1993). From crisis prone to crisis prepared: A framework for crisis management. *Academy of Management Executive, 7*(1), 48–59.

Rosenthal, U. & Kouzmin, A. (1993). Globalising an agenda for contingencies and crisis management: An editorial statement. *Journal of Contingencies and Crisis Management, 1*(1), 1–12.

Seymour, M. & Moore, S. (2000). Issues management and risk communication: Two linked disciplines. In *Effective Crisis management: Worldwide Principles and Practice* (pp. 159–189). London: Cassell.

Shetty, P. (2010, 20 March). Experts concerned about vaccination backlash. *The Lancet, 375*(9719), 970–971. Retrieved from www.thelancet.com/journals/lancet/article/PIIS0140-6736(10)60421-7/fulltext.

Tench, R. & Yeomans, L. (Eds.). (2014). *Exploring public relations* (3rd ed.). Harlow: Pearson Education.

2

ISSUE MANAGEMENT— DEVELOPMENT AND TOOLS

CHAPTER OBJECTIVES

This chapter will help you to:

+ learn how issue management came about

+ discover some of the pioneers who championed its development

+ gain an overview of the theoretical framework

+ recognise how issue management developed beyond its corporate origins

+ understand the emergence and importance of discipline tools and processes

+ evaluate the impact of the rise of social media.

Issue management is an ambiguous, even contradictory, activity. On one hand it is a formal executive-level discipline with an explicit strategic intent, built on sophisticated academic theory. On the other hand it is a tactical set of practical tools and processes, often implemented well beyond the confines of the executive suite, and sometimes far beyond the corporate world.

While some authors try to focus just on the management theory or just on the practical tactics, it is not possible to properly understand issue management without looking at the development and evolution of the discipline alongside the parallel development of the hands-on tools and processes.

There are very few management disciplines where the time and place of formal birth can be pinpointed as precisely as for issue management. The occasion was 15 April 1976, when Howard Chase (1910–2003) produced the first issue of his new publication *Corporate Public Issues and their Management* (CPI), which saw the first recorded use of the term 'issue management'.

Chase's colleague Ray Ewing later commented that the actual practices of issue management existed 'in protean form' before 1976, but that giving it a name was the decisive step permitting corporate communicators, who were effectively already doing issue management, to share approaches and to evolve the process itself.

Chase, then already 66 years old, devoted himself to promoting what he called the 'new science' of issue management (Chase, 1977, p. 1). In fact, he not only launched the good ship Issue Management, but also spent the rest of his long life keeping the ship on course, modernising and refurbishing the vessel to meet new trends, mentoring and coaching new crew members as they come on board, and actively playing every role from captain on the bridge to stoker in the engine room (Jaques, 2008). At the age of 90, Chase was continuing to dispense advice on the future of the discipline and was described as still being 'congenitally upbeat' (Chase, 1999, p. 13).

For Chase and his fellow issue pioneers, the challenge from the beginning was very clear. Looking from a corporate perspective, they recognised a change in the way public policy was being developed—and they didn't like what they saw. Archie Boe, an insurance industry CEO and one of the early adopters of issue management, described it as a response to 'an unprecedented battering of business'. Boe (1979, p. 4) said that, prior to this time, crisis and post-crisis management had been the only responses open to chief executive officers:

> During the past few years, however, intensive study of the processes and forces which have brought about these changes has resulted in the belief that business can move to a pre-crisis management posture and participate in the public policy process that resolves these larger demands on business. The pre-crisis management approach is called issues management and is an important management tool available to today's business leaders.

Community activists and other non-governmental organisations (NGOs) were seen to be increasingly influencing the direction of public policy, which often impacted directly upon the way the way corporations were able to operate. As the corporate advocates assessed it, traditional lobbying—talking directly to elected politicians and regulators—was no longer sufficient to counter the much broader groundswell of community and activist concerns. What they needed, they believed, was a mechanism to restore corporations to a more equal footing to participate in, and not simply respond to, policy issues that might affect them. That mechanism was issue management, and Chase himself described it as 'a methodology by which the private sector can get out of the unenviable position of being at the end of the crack-the-whip political line' (1980, p. 5).

On another occasion, in his ground-breaking book *Issue management: Origins of the future* (1984a), Chase wrote that issue management would enable the private sector to be 'co-equal with the government and citizens in the formation of public policy, rather than being the tail of a policy kite flown by others' (p. 10). In a less flamboyant tone, Chase (1982, p. 1) described issue management specifically as

> ... the capacity to understand, mobilise, coordinate and direct all strategic and policy planning functions, and all public affairs/public relations skills, toward achievement of one objective: meaningful participation in creation of public policy that affects personal and organisational destiny.

Regardless of how it was expressed, it is important to note that the early advocates of issue management did not see issue management as a way to overpower opponents or to exert undue influence. Their stated objective was to have a fair share of the debate and to be 'co-equal' in the formation of public policy.

> No issue can be negotiated unless you first have the clout to compel negotiation.
>
> Saul Alinsky (1972, p. 119)

In his characteristically bold language, Chase introduced issue management as 'a breakthrough in corporate management design' (1976, p. 1); 'a vital new form of management science' (1977, p. 26); and 'a vital tool in the total executive management decision making process' (1980, p. 6). Not surprisingly, Chase's unbounded enthusiasm—and maybe deliberate over-statement—led to a healthy dose of scepticism, particularly among established academics and practitioners, including within the prestigious Public Relations Society of America (PRSA), of which Chase was one of the six founders in 1947 and president in 1956.

In a much-cited paper, the public relations scholars William Ehling and Michael Hesse (1983) used a survey of PRSA members to question whether issue management was, in fact, a new concept or simply a 'pretentious' new term for everyday activities with 'nothing that is scientific either in the conceptualisation or in analytical techniques' (p. 23). They were also critical of Chase, Jones and Ewing, who they characterised as 'promulgators and propagators' of issue management.

Predictably, Chase wasn't going to take that lying down. Shortly afterwards he wrote an opinion piece for the *Wall Street Journal* (Chase 1984b, p. 28), which he impishly titled *No matter how well packaged, corporate fads fail fast*. In it he declared:

> Issue-oriented management process, systematically integrated into line-management decision-making, is the enemy of corporate faddism. Once the high-priority issue is identified, filtered through issue task forces drawn from both line and staff, the designated issue action program produces more lasting results than any quick-fix dreamed up by the most inventive faddists. When all is said and done, the issue management process offers the opportunity for alleged rugged individualists to act less like sheep.

A more objective assessment at that time was a still-respected paper by Steven Wartick and Robert Rude (1986), which bore the arresting title *Issues management: Corporate fad or corporate function?* They warned: 'If issue management is to be anything more than a passing corporate fad, both practitioners and academicians must work towards resolving the identity problem related to issue management' (p. 139). They concluded that if those involved in issue management could work towards establishing the filling of a void and professionalisation as complements instead of substitutes, then the future of issue management was bright.

In 1986, Wartick and Rude—and Chase himself for that matter—could not have predicted the changes that issue management was to undergo, with its adoption by non-corporate organisations and the impact of digital communication. Yet Chase and his colleagues certainly had the last laugh over their critics, with issue management not only filling a void and building professionalisation, but also growing and evolving into a universally accepted discipline.

While the first decade of issue management was largely devoted to establishing definitions and promoting the 'new science', some of the longer-term themes for scholarship and development for the subsequent decades were already in place, and an overview of theory will help to explain how issue management developed and expanded.

THE EMERGING THEORETICAL FRAMEWORK

One of the most thorough conceptual analyses of the overall field of issue management is that by Janet Bridges (2004) who addressed six theoretical frameworks—'loosely referred to as theories'—and provided detailed references and sources for each. Summarised in Table 2.1, they are systems theory, powerful stakeholder theory, legitimacy gap theory, issue life cycle theory, rhetorical analysis and social exchange theory. (Note that the expectation or legitimacy gap was examined in Chapter 1 and the concept of the issue life cycle is discussed more fully later in this chapter.)

Bridges noted that 'although initially these theoretical approaches may seem discrete, closer analysis indicates that they are important parts of a single perspective' (2004, p. 69). She proposed that the different theories for issue management are, in fact, interdependent and she concluded that, from an applied perspective, none of them provides definitive empirical evidence about corporate issues campaigns. However, she concluded that 'each provides a partial foundation for corporate campaign decision making, and most can provide some application to social-issue campaigns' (Bridges, 2004, p. 73).

Bridges had also argued that many theoretical approaches fail to recognise that issue management operates both to avoid or mitigate threats and also to promote opportunities, and she suggested that a relational approach is the preferred option to address this threat–opportunity duality. (An example of a modern relational model is depicted in Figure 1.2 in Chapter 1.)

Beyond these theoretical frameworks, Bridges and other scholars have identified two mass communication theories that have very real relevance to issue management: agenda-setting and framing. These two theories are closely linked, with many areas of overlap, and are often discussed together.

Table 2.1 Six theoretical frameworks for issue management

Systems theory	Each organisation is a system of integrated interdependent parts. In issue management those system units are possible stakeholders, each with the potential to affect the organisation in some way.
Powerful stakeholder theory	Issue campaign behaviour is prioritised because of the influence a particular group or finite public has on the organisation. The theory attempts to describe those stakeholder roles in the organisational system that are most important at the time.
Legitimacy gap theory	Issues arise from discrepancies between the organisation's behaviour and society's expectations of that organisation, which threaten its status as a legitimate member of the business community.
Issue life cycle theory	This theory discusses issues from the perspective of the process of development, suggesting that issues begin from societal concern and evolve through increasing stakeholder involvement to eventual resolution.
Rhetorical analysis	This approach acknowledges that words and events have different meanings to various groups in a dialogue, and that dialogue creates understanding, leading eventually to proposed solutions to a contested issue.
Social exchange theory	This theory advocates a win-win approach arising from negotiation of mutual benefits, which ties issue campaigns to an exchange in which each party expects a gain. It can be applied to organisational-stakeholder relations.

Source: adapted from Bridges (2004).

AGENDA-SETTING

Agenda-setting is a concept that began by arguing that news media editors, reporters and broadcasters filter news events, and that their reporting sets an agenda by how much attention is given to a particular story, and its positioning within a physical or online newspaper, or the prominence it receives in a radio or television news bulletin. The early media expert Bernard Cohen (1963) famously said: 'The press may not be successful much of the time in telling people what to think, but it is stunningly successful in telling its readers what to think *about*' (p. 130).

The theory gained impetus from a well-known study of the 1968 US presidential election[1] that compared the nature and amount of news coverage given to particular issues (known as salience) and the public perception of the most important election issues. While the concept quickly attracted attention for analysing elections around the world, it soon became clear that the longer term result of media involvement in issues has two effects that are very important to issue management. First is the creation of a public agenda, built on what the public believes to be the most important issues or concerns (sometimes measured by opinion surveys). Second is the formation of policy agenda-setting, where politicians

---

1   The US political study that boosted agenda-setting theory is McCoombs and Shaw (1972) in this chapter's Further reading section.

and regulators respond to real or perceived public concerns or trends and move to develop and introduce new laws or regulations.[2]

> He who defines the issues and determines their priority is well on the way to winning.
>
> Australian journalist and commentator Owen Harries (1991)

Although the idea of agenda-setting originated with the 'gatekeeper' role of newspapers and other traditional outlets, the rise of the internet and social media has rapidly broadened the capacity of non-media organisations and individuals to set the agenda. Internet-mediated agenda-setting has dramatically increased the number of 'gatekeepers', so that bloggers and other online activists now have powerful new tools to push their own priorities onto the public agenda. As the Arthur W. Page Society (2007, p. 21) commented: 'With the development of "Web 2.0" capabilities such as blogs, wikis, podcasts, content syndication and immersive virtual worlds, it is literally the case that any literate person today can become a global publisher for free in five minutes, drawing on a richer array of communications capabilities than [the great newspaper barons] ever dared imagine.' This in turn influences the media agenda, as journalists increasingly monitor and transfer online events across to the so-called mainstream media. In this way online agendas not only spill over into the mainstream but also help to shape the public policy agenda.

FRAMING

Very closely linked to agenda-setting is framing, which some scholars argue is, in fact, a subset of agenda-setting (sometimes called second-level agenda-setting). Framing is a process by which an event or message is placed within a frame—very much like a photograph or a painting—in order to focus attention on certain elements and to exclude competing, distracting or contradictory elements.

Whereas agenda-setting is about how often and how recently the public is exposed to an event or message, framing is about contextualisation, attempting to get the public to 'see' the event or message in a particular way and, most importantly, to focus on that viewpoint when forming opinions.

Contextualisation relies to a large extent on what is called the individual or group 'construct of reality', and these varying interpretations can have a direct effect on behaviour and on the public policy debate. To take an example, the problem of drink-driving and the resultant road toll can be interpreted in different ways. At one level it can be seen simply as a problem of irresponsible drunk drivers. But it can also be interpreted as a problem of inadequate crash-protection and safety devices in motor vehicles; poor road design and construction; legal speed limits set too high; a transport system too dependent on cars; social acceptance of excessive drinking; or failure of friends to prevent drunks getting behind the wheel. Each of these could be a valid perspective, and the media, interest groups and politicians can strongly influence which interpretation is high on the public agenda at any time, and how it then shapes the issue and public policy.

---

2   For a recent overview of agenda-setting, see Ragas (2013) in this chapter's Further reading section.

Another common example is seen in the controversy over abortion, which can be framed as a health issue focusing on abortion as a medical procedure; as a defining religious stance; as a societal moral concern; or as an issue of freedom of choice. The abortion controversy also highlights another important aspect of framing, which is the naming or labelling of an issue.

What an issue is called—and who gets to name it first—can substantially change the way the issue is perceived and debated. For example, the terms 'pro-abortion' and 'anti-abortion' are now rarely used, having been replaced by 'pro-choice' and 'pro-life' as a better way to frame each side of the issue. This is by no means just a matter of slippery semantics. And it is certainly not an argument in support of euphemisms (such as describing innocent civilian casualties on a battlefield as 'collateral damage', or using terms such as 'downsizing', 'right-sizing' or 'restructuring' to sugar-coat lay-offs or redundancies).

Euphemisms such as these are designed primarily to distort or mask the truth. By contrast, choosing specific language to describe an issue is more likely intended to provide an alternative frame. In issue management this naming or labelling can be a critical factor in determining success or failure. The company wanting to install a 'secure landfill' can easily have its plans overturned if opponents label it as a 'toxic waste dump' and if that terminology secures media currency and shapes the debate. Similarly, a company's plan for a new high-temperature incinerator might have a greater chance of success if the proponent and other stakeholders refer to it as a 'thermal oxidation unit'.[3]

A famous critique of the selective use of language by the public relations industry was the US book *Toxic sludge is good for you: Lies, damn lies and the public relations industry* (Stauber & Rampton, 1995), which included a description of the failed campaign to rename sewage sludge as 'biosolids'. An Australian case study (Mackey, 2001) considered the same definitional failure and described how community outrage derailed a proposed biosolids project in Victoria.

Rather more successful was the effort by the Government of Singapore to introduce water for household use recycled from sewage under the name 'new water'. By contrast, an analysis of the general failure of the same issue in Australia[4] reinforces the importance of framing and labelling when it comes to persuading the public to accept recycled water.

Another significant success was the campaign to relabel 'global warming' as the less alarming sounding 'climate change'. This initiative was reportedly supported by the Bush White House, and climate change has now been widely adopted throughout the English-speaking world as preferred terminology.

To name an idea or object is to influence attitudes towards it, and these examples are all about the planned way in which the choice of words can be a decisive factor in an issue management strategy. The importance of framing and reframing for issue management success was examined by Mahon and Wartick (2003) who detailed how framing was used to position the pharmaceutical manufacturer Johnson & Johnson as 'victims' in the notorious

---

3   For discussion on how high-profile issues can be framed by documentary film-makers, see Martz-Mayfield and Hallahan (2009) in this chapter's Further reading section.

4   For details on the failure of a water-recycling project in Australia, see Kemp et al. (2012) in this chapter's Further reading section.

CHANGE A WORD TO CHANGE AN IMAGE

One of the best examples of an industry reframing its greatest image weakness by turning it into its most beneficial strength is the 'gaming' industry, formerly known as the 'gambling' industry. By changing just that one word, Las Vegas transformed the old, unsavoury associations—such as organised crime, pawnshops, prostitution, addiction and foolishly losing one's fortune—to a 'lighter, brighter image of good clean fun'.

Gambling is seen as a vice, while gaming is positioned as a choice. Same poker machines, same deck of cards, same dice, same casino advantage. But the switch from gambling to gaming contributed to a fundamental change in how Americans see the gambling industry. And it's a change that rapidly spread, with gaming now the preferred term by both industry and governments around the world.

Source: Frank Luntz (2007, pp. 129–131).

1982 Tylenol poisoning case, when unknown persons fatally laced the company's headache capsules with cyanide. (For details of the case see Chapter 7.) Mahon and Wartick explored the practical application of framing in issue management and went so far as to conclude that framing should, in fact, be the first step for every organisation in its preliminary analysis.

A further factor in the context of issue management is that the unexpected intervention of headline events can sometimes dramatically change the overall frame of a major issue. A vivid example is the Three Mile Island nuclear accident in Pennsylvania in 1979, which changed the frame of nuclear power from a largely favourable progressive innovation to alarming runaway technology.[5] Although the incident resulted in little or no health or environmental damage, it effectively put a halt to any new nuclear power projects in the USA, just as the Chernobyl nuclear disaster in the Ukraine in 1986 triggered new concerns about the safety of nuclear power in Europe.

Later the rise of the climate change debate and concern about carbon emissions from traditional electricity generation triggered the rehabilitation of nuclear power and put it firmly back onto the political and social agenda as a viable option. Politicians and others who previously would not have even countenanced nuclear power began to talk about it openly as a technology that had to be at least considered. Mahon and Wartick (2009) described this as 'one of the clearest examples of framing that can be offered' (p. 30).

However, that new increasingly positive frame was shaken to its core by the Fukushima nuclear disaster in March 2011, which not only renewed questions about the technology, but also led directly to policy decisions to shut down or phase out nuclear power stations in a number of countries.[6] Such dramatic and high-profile interventions may be exceptions, but they highlight that framing is a very important element of issue management.

---

5   For analysis of the Three Mile Island incident, see Dionisopoulos and Crable (1988) in this chapter's Further reading section.

6   The Fukushima disaster and its aftermath have been extensively analysed. See, for example, Goodman (2014) in this chapter's Further reading section.

THE EVOLVING DISCIPLINE

Before considering the tools available to issue managers, it is important to explore the evolution of issue management and how it developed from a narrowly focused corporate effort to the broad and comprehensive discipline it has become today. This is most easily done by reviewing three different areas of development that are separate, though closely linked:

1. the expanding focus of issue management

2. the increasing emphasis on strategic alignment

3. migration beyond the corporation.

1 THE EXPANDING FOCUS OF ISSUE MANAGEMENT

As previously described, issue management was unambiguously born within a corporate environment and much of the early literature focused on issue management as a vehicle for the contest between corporations and other parties—both government and non-government—attempting to establish control through public policy.

But as it developed beyond a focus primarily on public policy, a substantial definitional gap opened up. William Miller (1987, p. 125) captured the problem succinctly:

> Issue management isn't quite public relations. Neither is it government relations, nor public affairs, nor lobbying, nor crisis management, nor futurism nor strategic planning. It embraces all of these disciplines, and maybe a few more.

Out of this definitional confusion, two principal approaches to issue management emerged:

1. The public policy process approach—which builds upon where issue management began, as a mechanism by which organisations can participate in the formation of public policy to advance the interests of the organisation.

2. The internal process approach—which focuses more on the internal mechanisms by which organisations mobilise resources to achieve a better balance between an organisation and its stakeholders in pursuit of what has been called 'social harmony'.

Table 2.2 examines comparative definitions and demonstrates the way in which the broad thinking about issue management tends to align with one of these two approaches. It also demonstrates that there is a good deal of overlap and that the two approaches are in many ways complementary rather than competitive. Most importantly these approaches can both be applied in many organisations—both corporate and non-corporate—and neither is inherently better or more advanced than the other.

In addition to these generic categories, a number of novel constructs have been formulated that attempt to conceptualise particular aspects of the discipline. These have gained varying degrees of support, and include the following:

+ *Anticipatory management* focuses on uncovering emerging issues to enable leaders to anticipate and shape the organisation's future.

+ *Risk issues management* focuses on real or perceived risks to public health, safety or the environment where stakeholder interest groups compete to steer outcomes towards a preferred policy option.
+ *Reputation risk management* focuses on current and emerging risks that pose both threats and opportunities for reputation, and attempts to optimise outcomes.
+ *Environmental issues management* focuses on events in the environmental domain, or involving environmental stakeholders, that could impact on the ability of the enterprise to reach its objectives.
+ *Strategic issue management* can be seen either as strategically managing issues or managing strategic issues (see the following section).

Table 2.2 Issue management comparative definitions

Public policy process approach	Internal process approach
'Issue management is the management of organisational and community resources through the public policy process to advance organisational interests and rights by striking a mutual balance with those of stakeholders and stakeseekers' (Heath & Coombs, 2006)	'Issue management is the management process whose goal is to help preserve markets, reduce risk, create opportunities and manage image as an organisational asset for the benefit of both an organisation and its shareholders' (Tucker, Broom & Caywood, 1993)
'Issue management is systematic identification and action regarding public policy matters of concern to an organisation' (Public Relations Society of America, 1987)	'Issue management is the process by which the corporation can identify, evaluate and respond to those social and political issues which might significantly impact on it' (Johnson, 1983)
'Issues management is a process to organise a company's expertise to enable it to participate effectively in the shaping and resolution of public issues that critically impinge upon its operations' (Arrington & Sawaya, 1984)	'The overriding goal of an issues management function is to enhance the current and long-term performance and standing of the corporation by anticipating change, promoting opportunities and avoiding or mitigating threat' (Renfro, 1993).
'Issues management is not the management of issues through public policy forums or management of the public policy process itself. It is the management of an institution's resources and efforts to participate in the successful resolution of issues in our public policy process' (Ewing, 1987)	'Issue management is the orchestrating of a positive plan for dealing with issues rather than merely reacting to them. It is a tool used in corporations and trade associations to come to an earlier and more constructive understanding of the issues an organisation or industry will face in the next few years' (Coates et al., 1986)
'Issues management is a program which a company uses to increase its knowledge of the public policy process and enhance the sophistication and effectiveness of its involvement in that process' (Public Affairs Council, 1978)	'Issues management is the strategic use of issues analysis and strategic responses to help organisations make adaptations needed to achieve harmony and foster mutual interests with the communities in which they operate' (Heath, 1997)

(continued)

Table 2.2 Issue management comparative definitions (*continued*)

Public policy process approach	Internal process approach
'Issue management is the capacity to understand, mobilise, coordinate and direct all strategic and policy planning functions, and all public affairs/public relations skills, towards achievement of one objective: meaningful participation in creation of public policy that affects personal and institutional destiny' (Chase, 1982)	'Issue management attempts to minimise surprises which accompany social and political change by serving as an early warning system for potential environmental threats and attempts to promote more systematic and effective responses to particular issues by serving as a coordinating and integrating force within the corporation' (Wartick & Rude, 1986)

Sources: Arrington, C. B. & Sawaya, R. N. (1984). Issues management in an uncertain environment. *Long Range Planning, 17*(6), 17–24.

Chase, W. H. (1982). The corporate imperative: Management of profit and policy. *Public Relations Quarterly, 27*(1), 25–29.

Coates, J. F., Coates, V. T., Jarratt, J. & Heins, L. (1986). *Issues management—How you can plan, organise and manage for the future.* Mt Airy, MD: Lomond Publications.

Ewing, R. P. (1987). *Managing the new bottom line: Issues management for senior executives.* Homewood, IL: Dow Jones Irwin.

Heath, R. L. & Coombs, W. T. (2006). *Today's public relations: An introduction.* Thousand Oaks, CA: Sage.

Heath, R. L. (1997). *Strategic issues management: Organisations and public policy challenges.* Thousand Oaks, CA: Sage.

Johnson, J. (1983). Issues management—What are the Issues? *Business Quarterly, 48*(3), 22–31.

Public Affairs Council (1978). *The fundamentals of issue management.*

Public Relations Society of America. (1987). Report of Special Committee on Terminology. *International Public Relations Review, 11*(2), 6–11.

Renfro, W. (1993). *Issues management in strategic planning.* Westport, CT: Quorum Books.

Tucker, K., Broom, G. & Caywood, C. (1993). Managing issues acts as bridge to strategic planning. *Public Relations Journal, 49*(11), 38–40.

Wartick, S. L. & Rude, R. E. (1986). Issues management: Corporate fad or corporate function? *California Management Review, 29*(1), 124–140.

2 THE INCREASING EMPHASIS ON STRATEGIC ALIGNMENT

The second area of development parallels the last of these constructs and builds on the central idea of strategic alignment. It has been suggested (John Mahon, cited in Greening, 1992, p. 3) that a key difference between strategic planning and issue management is that strategic planning focuses on identifying opportunities and threats to products and markets, while the emphasis of issue management is on identifying and addressing social and political issues not usually addressed in the market place.

While this understates the fact that some issues arise directly from product problems in the market, the importance of aligning the two disciplines has never been in doubt. In fact, Heath (1997) said issue management simply cannot have its full impact if it is not part of the strategic planning process. (See Chapter 4 for a full comparative analysis of issue management and strategic planning.)

From early in the life of issue management there was an effort to align the new discipline more explicitly with business strategy development, and one outcome was the new term 'strategic issue management' (SIM) to convey this alignment. (It is sometimes presented as SIMS—strategic issue management systems).

One of the earliest scholars to champion this new language was Igor Ansoff, who used the term 'strategic issue management' as the title of a seminal paper (1980) that crystallised his thinking. Ansoff argued that the concept of 'strategic issues' first appeared during the evolution of strategic planning, and that strategic issue management was a process not just for *planning* the response but also for *resolving* the issue.

However, this distinction was soon lost and in many places the term 'strategic issue management' has become virtually synonymous with 'issue management'. This can lead to the mistaken belief that issue management methods should be applied only (or preferentially) to priority or strategic issues. And this, in turn, can lead to the belief that issue management has no appropriate application to less important issues. But as Dutton and Ashford (1993) concluded: 'No issue is inherently strategic. Rather, an issue becomes strategic when top management believes it has relevance for organisational performance' (p. 397).

In addition, using the terms 'issue management' and 'strategic issue management' interchangeably encourages the idea that the only issues that merit management attention are strategic ones. In reality, issues can be tactical, operational or strategic, and issue management as a discipline can be equally relevant in addressing each category. In fact, responsible managers *should* consider all possible issues and contingencies, not just those in high-priority areas.

Rather than trying to suggest that strategic issue management means the management only of strategic issues, a common view is emerging that the most important point is that issue management should be seen as a strategic management activity. In other words, there is increasing acceptance that it is the process itself, not the specific issue, that is strategic. This is certainly the meaning adopted throughout this book—that issue management is one of the important, effective processes available to organisations to assist in pursuit of their strategic goals.

3 MIGRATION BEYOND THE CORPORATION

Corporations are not the only organisations that have strategic goals, and this brings us to the third important area of the development of issue management: migration of the discipline beyond its corporate origins.

This development follows two distinct streams, although they occurred pretty much simultaneously. The first was the adoption of issue management by governments and government agencies, and the other was its adoption by activists and community groups. Overall this was a healthy development that has helped invigorate issue management and reflects to a large degree both the changing nature of the discipline and society's maturing expectations in terms of both transparency and participation.

Initially, issue management began as a corporate response to adverse public policy and the desire to move from reaction to participation. This eventually led to both business and government using issue management processes to promote their positions. It also led to consumer and activists groups utilising issue management processes not only to resist big business and big government, but also to demand greater public participation.

This in turn led to an increased expectation that big government and big business *should* properly provide for greater public participation, and issue management processes began to be used by big government and big business to facilitate that participation. This is often seen when a controversial government or corporate policy fails, and the blame is assigned to 'failing to manage the issue'.

Nowhere is this changing expectation of participation more evident than in the area of environmental issues, where the key reasons were succinctly itemised by Yosie and Herbst (1998). They said forces driving the evolution of environmental stakeholder processes include:

+ a lack of public confidence and trust in the environmental decision-making of many government agencies and corporations
+ increasing transparency of institutions whose decisions affect environmental quality
+ greater societal expectations for improved environmental quality
+ enhanced ability of citizens to participate in stakeholder processes
+ growing diffusion of information technology and an associated decentralisation of decision-making in large institutions
+ policy commitments made by industry and government agencies to expand stakeholder participation in their decision-making processes.

While these scholars developed this overview specifically to support an exploration of stakeholder processes in environmental decision-making, it provides a sound template to help explain the broader maturing of issue management and participation, both inside and beyond the corporate environment. And as these shifts have taken place, so too has issue management migrated to become a process and tool for all the different sectors concerned, from business to government to NGOs and activists.

ADOPTION BY GOVERNMENT

After corporations, the second area that has seen migration of issue management techniques is among government legislatures and government agencies, where the tools and processes are used not to resist or modify public policy as originally conceived by the corporate founders of the discipline, but to promote and implement such policies. For example, Galloway (2005) examined its application by Australian local governments in community engagement, and Weaver and Motion (2002) explored how a New Zealand government agency tried to create favourable public opinion in support of genetic engineering research.

Governments and government agencies have not only recognised the value of issue management for promoting their own programs and policies, but in their role as regulators they have also accelerated the adoption of issue management by NGOs through new requirements for proponents to demonstrate community participation. In fact, such participation is increasingly presented not as a voluntary commitment on the part of proponents but as a mandated obligation. For example, the planning approval process in many state and national jurisdictions now requires evidence of public participation and/or consultation as a precondition for submitting a planning application. And many government contracts for big projects now require commitment to such consultation as part of the tender process.

This is usually not specifically referred to as issue management—it is most often defined by terms such as 'stakeholder engagement' or 'community consultation'—but it is in reality an application by all parties of the tools and processes of issue management to help bridge corporations, governments and the community.

ADOPTION BY COMMUNITY GROUPS AND ACTIVISTS

It is somewhat ironic that issue management, which began as a mechanism to allow corporations to regain a level playing field to influence public policy, was then adopted by governments to promote their own programs. Now those same tools and processes have been adopted by community groups and activists to counter what they see as an unfair advantage of both big business and big government in forming policy.

Chapter 5 explores in detail the rise of modern activism and its use of issue management as a key tool for success. However, the adoption of issue management by community groups and activists is a very important element in understanding the migration of issue management beyond its original corporate origins.

The term 'activism' can embrace an enormous range of activities and programs. At one end are neighbourhood initiatives such as angry residents banding together to oppose an ugly high-rise development that will overshadow historic homes; concerned parents protesting against a fast-food restaurant opening up next to their local primary school; or a small country town pressing for a motorway bypass to protect their local residential streets from the noise and danger of heavy, long-distance trucks.

At the other end of the scale are massive international activist campaigns to protect threatened rainforest, to ban landmines or to save endangered whales. And some of these initiatives are so large that they can become virtually indistinguishable from government interests, especially through alignment with quasi-government agencies such as branches of the United Nations like the United Nations International Children's Emergency Fund (UNICEF) or the United Nations Environment Programme (UNEP).

At the same time, some non-government activist organisations have become so big that they are themselves multinational entities, with multimillion dollar budgets and huge professional infrastructure, including Greenpeace, Amnesty International and the World

Wildlife Fund for Nature (websites for these organisations appear in the Useful Websites section at the end of this book).

Regardless of whether it is a local group of socially motivated mothers or a multinational NGO, the tools and processes of issue management have been widely adopted and have proved remarkably durable.

TOOLS AND PROCESSES

The terminology used in issue management varies widely, and outside the corporate environment there is sometimes a deliberate effort *not* to adopt the same language used by those who may be regarded as 'corporate opponents'. But the benefits afforded by issue management as a discipline far outweigh such concerns, which is why it has proved so resilient. Two principal tools are the process flow model and the issue life cycle, and these are now examined in turn.

PROCESS FLOW MODEL

One of the important requirements for effective issue management at any level is to establish an agreed process. In the same way that issue management is a framework for strategy development and implementation, the flow diagram is a tool that provides a framework for the issue management process itself.

The Best Practice Indicators developed by the US-based Issue Management Council begin by specifying two important tools (note that the best practice concept is addressed in detail in Chapter 4). The first best practice tool is that there should be an 'established mechanism to identify current and future issues through environmental scanning/issue analysis' (Issue Management Council, 2005). (Identification and prioritisation are discussed in detail in Chapter 3.) The second critical tool is that the organisation has adopted a formal process to assign and manage issues.

> While emerging issues may be complicated and difficult to understand, the process by which issues are dealt with should not be.
>
> William Ashley (1996, p. 245)

The process flow model can be as basic as the pioneering Chase-Jones model (Figure 1.1) in Chapter 1, or it can be a complex flow process with dozens of distinct steps and decision boxes. Moreover, it doesn't much matter whether the flow diagram represents the method used by a local nature group trying to protect a rare frog threatened by a damaging land development, or the planning approach for an international NGO working to eliminate child labour. Whatever format is adopted, the value of the process flow is that it provides a readily understood graphic representation that is easy to communicate to others, and that simplifies the task of measuring progress. Most importantly it is an *agreed* process, which enables the organisation to focus on developing and implementing strategy and avoid backsliding into unhelpful debate about how the process should be working.

A common weakness of some process flow models is that they become too complicated or include a confusing mix of both strategic and tactical steps and options. This is sometimes called the 'Christmas tree effect', which happens with the attempt to load the tree with every possible decoration. The lights and decorations look good, but their weight may overwhelm the basic structure of the tree itself.

The same applies to the issue management flow model. It is best to build a simple sturdy framework and leave the specific action options to the next step: strategy development. The model depicted in Figure 2.1 is an example of how to keep the process flow diagram simple and unambiguous, yet sufficiently self-explanatory to keep the organisation united in a step-wise program.

Figure 2.1 Issue management model process flow

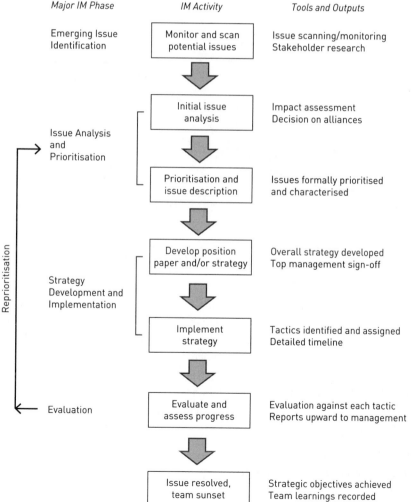

ISSUE MANAGEMENT PROCESS FLOW

Major IM Phase	IM Activity	Tools and Outputs
Emerging Issue Identification	Monitor and scan potential issues	Issue scanning/monitoring Stakeholder research
Issue Analysis and Prioritisation	Initial issue analysis	Impact assessment Decision on alliances
	Prioritisation and issue description	Issues formally prioritised and characterised
Strategy Development and Implementation	Develop position paper and/or strategy	Overall strategy developed Top management sign-off
	Implement strategy	Tactics identified and assigned Detailed timeline
Evaluation	Evaluate and assess progress	Evaluation against each tactic Reports upward to management
	Issue resolved, team sunset	Strategic objectives achieved Team learnings recorded

Reprioritisation

ISSUE LIFE CYCLE

The other core tool is the issue life cycle, which was also a very early innovation. Despite the scores of different versions developed over the years, issue life cycles typically illustrate three fundamental concepts (see Figure 2.2):

1. Issues progress along a fairly predictable continuum (though not always at the same pace).

2. Issues left unaddressed tend to become more difficult to manage.

3. As issues escalate, the available options decrease and the cost of intervention increases.

Figure 2.2 Life cycle of a strategic issue

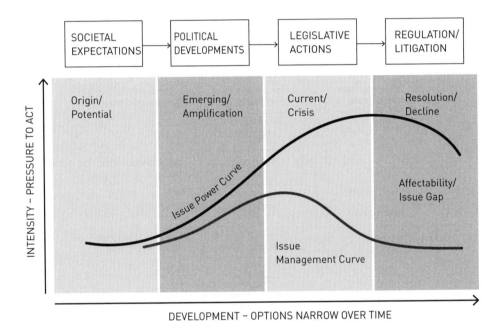

As with the process flow models, the life cycle graphic can vary from basic to very advanced, and the labels and terminology vary widely between the many different approaches available. While alternative models may label the axes or the phases differently, the purpose of every life cycle remains unchanged: to illustrate in graphic form the importance of early intervention; of starting to participate in the issue near the beginning of the cycle; and that non-intervention can be a very costly decision.

Some organisations threatened by an issue will try to find ways to avoid getting involved, using phrases like:

+   'It's not *our* issue.'

+   'It will die down if we don't interfere.'

+   'Let's not *make* it an issue.'

+ 'It's not worth exposing our brand.'
+ 'Let's wait until it gets worse and we'll throw resources at it.'
+ 'Someone else will intervene.'

These and other similar phrases are frequently just excuses for not committing resources to deal with a potential issue. The issue life cycle is a powerful tool to counteract this attitude and to demonstrate that the earlier an organisation gets involved and implements an effective issue management strategy, the greater its chance of achieving a planned, positive outcome.[7]

These two established tools have become generic to the issue management process itself. Other processes specific to particular issues—including the issue profile, the alliance decision, the prioritisation process and the strategy development tool—are discussed in detail in Chapters 3 and 4.

IMPACT OF INTERNET AND SOCIAL MEDIA

The final area to be considered in the development of issue management, and the tools available, is the impact of the rise of social media.

One of the most obvious impacts of the internet and social media on issue management has been the so-called democratisation of the discipline, which has seen a major realignment of power away from big business and big government towards typically resource-poor NGOs, activists and community groups.[8] As a result, these hitherto disadvantaged players can now readily elevate issues onto the public and media agenda in a way previously undreamed of, and can mobilise resources quickly and cheaply as never before. Significantly, some public issues are now able to be played out largely or entirely in the digital media.

> Resources that were once the preserve of governments and large corporations, such as access to intelligence and an ability to communicate and mobilise (both globally and instantaneously), are now available to anyone for the price of a cup of coffee in a cybercafé.
>
> Simon Titley (2003, p. 86)

This 'levelling of the playing field' and its impact on activism is discussed more fully in Chapter 5. But beyond this broad process of democratisation, the internet has also had other important effects on issue management itself.

The first area where digital media has made a big difference is on the process aspects of issue management—particularly scanning, monitoring and tracking of issues. The internet and social media mean organisations now have new avenues to scan for potential issues

---

7   For discussion on the impact of social media on the traditional life cycle model, see Pop (2013) in this chapter's Further reading section.

8   NGOs' use of the internet is explored in Boyer and McCallum (2012), Brainard and Siplon (2002), Naude, Froneman and Atwood (2004), Reber and Kim (2006), Seo, Kim and Yang (2009) and Waters et al. (2009) in this chapter's Further reading section.

and new e-tools to do it quickly and cheaply. The same applies to monitoring existing issues, where inputs and perspectives from many different actors can be accessed almost instantaneously. It also applies to tracking the pace and flow of an issue, and can facilitate very accurate tracking, such as monitoring key words and key messages across multiple platforms.

The two-way communication capacity provided by the internet and social media has dramatically increased and accelerated an organisation's ability to manage a wide variety of issue stakeholders rapidly and efficiently. However, at the same time it has exposed them to a broader range of stakeholders with increasing expectations of how the organisation should perform. In fact, the 'expectation gap' approach discussed in Chapter 1 has been substantially revitalised as a result of this increased stakeholder mobilisation.

Another impact of social media on large organisations—especially multinational businesses—has been the globalisation of issues, which can now spread across borders at digital speed. It has also become much harder for companies to confine an issue to a particular country or region, and a multinational organisation can no longer contemplate handling a single issue in different ways in different parts of the world. Stakeholders now expect and demand global consistency and transparency.[9]

Globalisation of issues has also produced a less obvious and less expected impact: the broadening assault on global brands.[10] As part of this development, some activist organisations are moving their focus from engagement at a local or national level on narrow concerns to targeting large organisations across a range of different issues and geographies.

HOW A SOCIAL MEDIA CAMPAIGN DEFEATED A GLOBAL GIANT

The power of social media across borders was demonstrated after the massive expansion of Starbucks into China. One of their coffee outlets was near Beijing's Forbidden City, also known as the Palace Museum. It operated successfully for seven years until a social media campaign was started by Chenggeng Rui, a celebrity blogger and news anchor for English-language programs on China Central Television. Rui argued that the fast-food outlet within the museum precinct was an 'offence to national dignity'. His blog campaign attracted hundreds of thousands of supporters, and soon spread to mainstream media in China and the USA. In July 2007, Seattle-based Starbucks closed the store, ending months of controversy and negative publicity.

Source: Gang Han & Ai Zhang (2009).

For such organisations the resulting impact on their whole approach to issue management has been significant. Not only do they face multiple issues on multiple fronts,

---

9   On the use of social media by both activists and corporations, see Price (2011) and Temin (2012) in this chapter's Further reading section.

10   A classic critique of the power of brands is Klein (2000) in this chapter's Further reading section.

but there is also a growing recognition that for some activist organisations the fundamental purpose of raising and prosecuting issues is evolving in parallel with the rise of social media.

For some large-scale campaigns, the target is evidently not so much the issue as the organisation itself. Indeed, in some campaigns issue management has become part of the extensive anti-corporate/anti-globalisation social justice movement and is used as a tool to attack the very structure of the organisation, or to achieve change at a societal level.[11]

For example, a study of the anti-genetically modified (GM) food issue in Canada (West & Larue, 2005) concluded that much anti-GM activism is more likely motivated by anti-corporate or anti-globalisation attitudes and a desire for social reform than food safety. Similarly, it would appear that some campaigns against big-brand fast-food producers may be motivated less by stated concern about obesity and more by concern about the global commoditisation of food and by 'corporate colonialism'.

The purpose here is not to suggest a value judgment about these developments, but rather to highlight how such internet-mediated campaigns have forced big organisations to rethink their approach to issue management as a whole, particularly the way they may identify and characterise issues in a broader context rather than as a stand-alone problem.

Taking into consideration this whole combination of effects led to what has been described as the e-issue life cycle,[12] or the viral life cycle,[13] which is effectively the post–social media version of the classic issue life cycle (described earlier in this chapter). Importantly, the life cycle principles remain largely unchanged—that issues progress along a continuum and become increasingly difficult to manage. However, the 'new economy' model has a number of key differences—some positive and some negative:

+ Issues can escalate much faster and may be over more quickly.

+ Multiple platforms increase media momentum and potential impact on the organisation.

+ There is a higher risk of synergy with, or contagion to, other issues.

+ Damaging material can remain 'live' on the internet long after the issue's apparent resolution.

+ There are better opportunities for more and earlier participation.

+ More stakeholders can be reached quickly and easily.

The internet and social media has unquestionably impacted issue management and the way it is implemented. But the continuing relevance of the basic ideas and tools developed from the earliest days reinforces the resilience of issue management as a fundamental management discipline.

Note: parts of this chapter draw on Jaques (2008) and Jaques (2009).

---

11 There is a strong, established literature on anti-corporate campaigning. See, for example, Beder (2006), Dinan and Miller (2007), Lubbers (2002) and Starr (2000) in this chapter's Further reading section.

12 For a description of the e-issue life cycle, see Wernli and Frank (2000) in this chapter's Further reading section.

13 The concept of the viral life cycle is developed in Rogers, Chapman and Giotsas (2012) in this chapter's Further reading section.

KEY POINTS

+ Issue management began in 1976 as a defensive corporate discipline, but was soon successfully adopted by governments, NGOs and community groups.

+ Framing and agenda-setting have emerged as the two key theoretical frameworks that support the practice of issue management.

+ The two principal strands of development are the public policy process approach and the internal process approach.

+ Two key tools are the process flow model and the issue life cycle. Process flow models are basic tools used to develop responses, while the issue life cycle shows that issues ignored progress along a continuum and become harder and more costly to manage.

+ Although big business and big government were early adopters of formal issue management, the internet has levelled the playing field and given activists unprecedented ability to raise and influence issues.

≣ ACTIVITIES AND DISCUSSION

1. Why would governments, community groups and activists be so enthusiastic to adopt the tools and processes of issue management, yet be seemingly so reluctant to adopt its original corporate language?

2. Think of some recent government communications campaigns. Which are purely informational and which are attempting to change behaviour through issue management?

3. Why do you think 'pro-choice' and 'pro-life' have largely replaced 'anti-abortion' and 'pro-abortion'? Is it just language or is it something more fundamental?

4. What are some other examples of how language has been used to frame high-profile issues? Is framing sometimes used improperly to hide the truth?

5. Why do many organisations resist intervening early enough in issues that may affect them? What can a communication practitioner do to help overcome this reluctance?

ISSUES THAT PREVENT ANTI-SMOKING CAMPAIGNS FROM WORKING

James Mahoney

University of Canberra

Anti-cigarette-smoking messages, often fear-based, have been directed at young people for most of their lives. They have seen anti-smoking advertisements, undergone school-based health programs that warn them of smoking dangers and, more recently, found scary messages on cigarette packets.

Despite this concentration of anti-smoking messages, many young people still smoke. In Australia, where anti-smoking school education and mass media campaigns about the health dangers of smoking have been pursued for almost the entire lifespan of the oldest members of Gen Y, a significant number of young people report that they have at some time smoked, or still do.

Research has found that anti-smoking campaigns, especially those using fear-based social marketing, and education, have no significant effect on smoking behaviour. On the other hand, workplace smoking bans and health warnings on cigarette packs do decrease consumption, and there is evidence that taxation of tobacco products is the most effective way of reducing aggregate tobacco consumption.

This suggests that health communication strategists may not have effectively engaged in issues identification and analysis prior to implementing anti-smoking campaigns. Had they undertaken carefully planned research to identify and analyse issues that concern the target publics for these campaigns, they may have been more successful. A key question would be: 'Why do many people, especially young people, not heed anti-smoking health messages?' That would have produced data showing:

+ Most adolescent smokers are addicted to nicotine and report they want to quit but are unable to do so. Many smoke because they enjoy it, or because smoking relaxes them, or because their friends smoke.

+ Adolescents with lower levels of school achievement, with fewer skills to resist pervasive influences to use tobacco, with friends who smoke, and with lower self-images are more likely than their peers to smoke.

+ Adolescent smokers feel less in control of their lives than do non-users and, as one consequence of this, may be unable to adapt to anti-smoking communication to achieve positive health outcomes.

+ Smoking could be integrated and embedded behaviour.

+ Warning messages on cigarette packages can lead to anti-smoking behaviour.

+ Death-related warnings are not effective.

These are all issues that need to be analysed in the context of improving campaigns.

In addition, health promotion strategists should consider the practical campaign design issues that content and process communication theories raise. For example, McClelland's acquired needs theory suggests that individuals are motivated by three underlying needs: achievement, affiliation and power. The theory could help identify how such 'needs' can be applied in the design and delivery of anti-smoking campaigns; for example, in designing messages to reach young people who smoke because their peer group smokes. Vroom's expectancy theory posits that individuals calculate the benefits of behaving in certain ways, or do what they can when they want to. That is, people place a value (or 'valence') on, for example, work outcomes after they assess the effort (or 'expectancy') involved in performing a task and the probability that performing the task (or 'instrumentality') will lead to a rewarding outcome. Anti-smoking messages appear to apply elements of this theory. However, identifying ways in which young people who say they smoke because it 'relaxes them' can be convinced to more effectively calculate the 'zero valence' of smoking may be an area for further investigation by strategic health communicators.

Effective issue analysis would have informed the selection of message delivery strategies because it would have found, for example, that women are more likely to listen to anti-smoking messages from doctors, and that males may react more effectively to advertising using credible role models than they appear to react to fear-based messages that do not employ such role models.

The issue health communication strategists face is not that young people reject health-based anti-smoking messages; rather, it is that young people smoke for more entrenched, perhaps irrational, reasons. Addressing this involves resolving complex and interrelated issues. These issues cannot be resolved overnight: they are about embedded behaviours and the solutions to them require long-term approaches.

Strategic communication principles suggest that anti-smoking campaigns for young people should reflect the different ways in which males and females prefer to receive messages. One campaign planning issue that needs to be addressed is how information can be presented in ways that address the needs of young people, and the reasons they smoke, rather than to scare them into changing behaviour.

While anti-smoking campaigns designed in this way may be more costly than the current approach, and take longer to implement, they will have a better chance of delivering more positive results. They certainly would not deliver instant impressions that something is being done about an urgent health issue. But they would improve strategists' chances of overcoming an equally important issue: research consistently suggests that fear-based campaigns don't work.

Source: This case study is based on James Mahoney's research.

PLANNED AND REACTIVE RESPONSES TO CONFECTED OUTRAGE

Brendan Elliott

Sydney

In this age of climate change, many Australian capital cities have at least one desalination plant to back up the drinking water supply for their growing populations, with the exception of Canberra (landlocked), and Darwin and Hobart (no water shortage). However, widespread use of this water technology did not reduce published and broadcast expressions of outrage about the planning and construction of the reverse osmosis desalination plant at Kurnell, in Sydney's south, which began pumping water to the city in January 2010.

The New South Wales Government's 2006 *Metropolitan Water Plan* said construction contracts for such a plant would be awarded if Sydney's dam storages reached 'around 30 per cent'. When then Premier Morris Iemma announced on 6 February 2007 that a request for tender documents would be issued to two shortlisted consortia, Sydney's dams were at 33.9 per cent and falling fast. The government and Sydney Water were not prepared to wait any longer and risk future supply.

As Senior Media Adviser to Sydney Water at that time I backgrounded as many domestic and overseas journalists as possible over the tendering, design and construction phase of the project. Planned issue management activities included escorting journalists from the USA, Britain, New Zealand and other countries around the plant. International media were interested to learn about Australia's response to increasingly unpredictable rainfall.

By contrast, many Sydney journalists were mainly interested in reporting controversy. Their focus was fuelled by government and opposition members who engaged in vigorous, critical debate about water policy in the lead-up to the March 2007 NSW election. Briefing notes, so-called 'Dorothy Dixers' (friendly questions in Parliament) and budget estimates hearings played a leading role in addressing these parliamentary issues. Outside parliament, talkback radio and some television networks were occasionally shrill about project need, cost, water quality and alleged business losses (the latter relating to construction impacts).

Sydney Water's response was a combination of targeted backgrounding and suggesting story leads that journalists may not have thought about—or 'shifting focus' as it is sometimes described in issue management. Several in-depth interviews were arranged with Sydney Water's then Managing Director, Dr Kerry Schott. One controversial talkback host, who prefers not to talk to people he doesn't regard as his equal, was sent written responses to some of his more colourful on-air claims. I spoke to the *Daily Telegraph* newspaper and Channel 9 about a couple who erroneously claimed their investments had been devalued.

One valuable lesson for anyone trying to mitigate confected outrage is not to rely solely on official channels to understand a latent or emerging issue. It pays to occasionally walk in the shoes of residents, business owners, councils and journalists, too. For example, when dealing with community complaints and media reports about noise from the plant, I made a point of driving past homes said to be affected at different times, including after hours. This enabled me to triangulate all information at my disposal, and challenge my own assumptions.

The other type of vigilance required is to constantly monitor news coverage. This takes time and resources, but the public narrative around issues can rapidly turn against you if you are slow to respond. In order to be better prepared, we developed draft talking points on emerging aspects of the issue for approval before they were needed.

Sydney Water's broader, proactive communications strategy for the desalination project could best be described as 'no surprises'. A mix of communication tools and tactics was used to keep all key stakeholders well informed of progress. These methods included regular briefings of internal stakeholders, preparation of questions and answers on issues, regular site visits for external stakeholders, and planning and promotion of major milestones. The project was normalised, which made it harder for misconceptions to spread.

When the NSW Government directed Sydney Water to undertake the desalination project, it became a political story in the hands of most media and other commentators. This story prism meant that the project drivers and context were often ignored, and there were instances of misinformation. A classic illustration of this was a radio caller identified as 'Jack from Cronulla'. On 8 February 2010 'Jack' alleged on commercial radio 2UE that his water smelled of formaldehyde, and he repeated this claim a fortnight later on radio 2GB. By a curious coincidence this was the same day Parliament resumed sitting.

At that time, Sydney Water wasn't supplying any water derived from the desalination plant to the southern end of its network where Jack claimed to be calling from. Radio host Ray Hadley at 2GB gave the caller short shrift. But to tackle the issue directly, I made an on-air offer for Sydney Water quality technicians to pay Jack a visit and test the water in his taps, in case there was a problem we should know about. Significantly, no address was ever forthcoming.

For more detailed discussion of this case see:

Elliott, B. (2011). 'There's formaldehyde in my water': Absurd discourse about the Sydney desalination project—a case study. *Asia Pacific Public Relations Journal, 11,* 75–82.

REFERENCES

Alinsky, S. D. (1972, March). A candid conversation with the feisty radical organiser. *Playboy Magazine*. Reprinted and retrieved from *The Progress Report* at www.progress.org/2003/alinsky2.htm.

Ansoff, H. I. (1980). Strategic issue management. *Strategic Management Journal, 1*(2), 131–148.

Arthur W. Page Society. (2007). The authentic enterprise. Retrieved from www.awpagesociety.com/images/uploads/2007Authentic-Enterprise.pdf

Ashley, W. C. (1996). Anticipatory management: Linking public affairs and strategic planning. In L. B. Dennis (Ed.), *Practical public relations in an era of change* (pp. 239–250). Lanham, MD: Public Relations Society of America.

Boe, A. R. (1979). Fitting the corporation to the future. *Public Relations Quarterly, 24*(4), 4–6.

Bridges, J. (2004). Corporate issues campaigns: Six theoretical approaches. *Communication Theory, 14*(1), 51–77.

Chase, W. H. (1999). Chase foresees dismal future for public relations—It's been captured by marketing. *Public Relations Quarterly, 44*(4), 13–18.

Chase, W. H. (1984a). *Issue management: Origins of the future.* Stamford, CT: Issue Action.

Chase, W. H. (1984b, 12 November). No matter how well packaged, corporate fads fail fast. *The Wall Street Journal,* p. 28.

Chase, W. H. (1982). Issue management conference: A special report. *Corporate Public Issues and Their Management, 7*(3), 1–2.

Chase, W. H. (1980). Issues and policy. *Public Relations Quarterly, 25*(1), 5–6.

Chase, W. H. (1977). Public issue management: The new science. *Public Relations Journal, 33*(10), 25–26.

Chase, W. H. (1976). Objectives of CPI. *Corporate Public Issues and their Management 1*(1), 1.

Cohen, B. C. (1963). *The press and foreign policy.* Princeton: Princeton University Press.

Dutton, J. E. & Ashford, S. J. (1993). Selling issues to top management. *Academy of Management Review, 18*(3), 397–428.

Ehling, W. P. & Hesse, M. B. (1983). Use of 'issue management' in public relations. *Public Relations Review, 9*(2), 8–35.

Galloway, C. (2005). *Engaging activist communities.* Paper presented at the International Conference on Engaging Communities, Brisbane 14–17 August.

Greening, D. W. (1992). *Integrating issue management activities into strategic planning: An empirical analysis of inter-industry differences.* Leesburg, VA: The Issue Exchange.

Han, G. & Zhang, A. (2009). Starbucks is forbidden in the Forbidden City: Blog, circuit of culture and informal public relations campaign in China. *Public Relations Review, 35*(3), 395–401.

Harries, O. (1991). A primer for polemicists. *Tactical Notes #10.* Retrieved from www. libertarian.co.uk/lapubs/tactn/tactn010.htm.

Heath, R. L. (1997). *Strategic issues management: Organisations and public policy challenges.* Thousand Oaks, CA: Sage.

Heath, R. L. & Coombs, W. T. (2006). *Today's public relations: An introduction.* Thousand Oaks, CA: Sage.

Issue Management Council. (2005). *Best practice indicators.* Retrieved from http:// issuemanagement.org/learnmore/best-practice-indicators.

Jaques, T. (2008). Howard Chase: The man who invented issue management. *Journal of Communication Management, 12*(4), 336–343.

Jaques, T. (2009). Integrating Issue Management and Strategic Planning: Unfulfilled promise or future opportunity? *International Journal of Strategic Communication, 3*(1), 19–33.

Luntz, F. (2007). *Words that work.* New York: Hyperion.

Mackey, S. (2001). How world's best public relations practice was not, but might have been achieved, in respect of a biosolids project. *Asia Pacific Public Relations Journal 3*(2), 59–72.

Mahon, J. F. & Wartick, S. L. (2003). Dealing with stakeholders: How reputation, credibility and framing influence the game. *Corporate Reputation Review, 6*(1), 19–35.

Miller, W. H. (1987, 2 November). Issue management: No longer a sideshow. *Industry Week, 3,* 125–128.

Public Affairs Council (1978, December). *The fundamentals of issue management.* Pamphlet published by Public Affairs Council, Washington DC.

Stauber, J. & Rampton, S. (1995). *Toxic sludge is good for you: Lies, damn lies and the public relations industry.* Monroe, ME: Common Courage Press.

Titley, S. (2003). How political and social change will transform the EU public affairs industry. *Journal of Public Affairs 3*(1), 83–89.

Wartick, S. L. & Rude, R. E. (1986). Issues management: Corporate fad or corporate function? *California Management Review, 29*(1), 124–140.

Weaver, C. K. & Motion, J. (2002). Sabotage and subterfuge: Public relations, democracy and genetic engineering in New Zealand. *Media, Culture & Society, 24*(3), 325–343.

West, G. E. & Larue, B. (2005). Determinants of anti-GM food activism. *Journal of Public Affairs, 5*(3/4), 236–250.

Yosie, T. F. & Herbst T. D. (1998). *Using stakeholder processes in environmental decision making: An evaluation of lessons learned, key issues and future challenges.* Ruder Finn Washington, DC. Retrieved from www.riskworld.com/Nreports/1998/stakehold/html/nr98aa03.htm.

FURTHER READING

Beder, S. (2006). *Suiting themselves: How corporations drive the global agenda.* London: Earthscan.

Bowen, S. A. (2005). A practical model for ethical decision making in issues management and public relations. *Journal of Public Relations Research, 17*(3), 191–216.

Boyer, R. & McCallum, S. (2012). Nongovernmental organisations: Solving society's problems. In C. L. Caywood (Ed.), *The handbook of strategic public relations and integrated marketing communication* (2nd ed., pp. 289–310). New York: McGraw Hill.

Brainard, L. A. & Siplon, P. D. (2002). The internet and NGO–government relations: Injecting chaos into order. *Public Administration and Development, 22*(1), 63–72.

Cooper, A. (2009). *Two-way communication: A win-win model for facing activist pressure: A case study on McDonalds and Unilever's responses to Greenpeace.* Institute for Public Relations. 12th Annual International Public Relations Research Conference, Coral Gables, Florida. Retrieved from www.instituteforpr.org/ipr_info/two_way_communication_facing_activist_pressure.

Dinan, W. & Miller, D. (Eds.). (2007). *Thinker, faker, spinner, spy: Corporate PR and the assault on democracy.* Pluto Press: London.

Dionisopoulos, G. N. & Crable, R E. (1988). Definitional hegemony as a public relations strategy: the rhetoric of the nuclear power industry after Three Mile Island. *Central States Speech Journal, 393*(2), 134–145.

Goodman, A. (2014, 17 January). Fukushima is an ongoing warning to the world on nuclear energy. *The Guardian.* Retrieved from www.theguardian.com/commentisfree/2014/jan/16/fukushima-is-a-warning.

Heath, R. L. (2010). *Evolution of issues management: John Hill, tobacco controversy and the battle of scientists.* First International History of Public Relations Conference (pp. 138–154). Bournemouth University. Retrieved from http://blogs.bournemouth.ac.uk/historyofpr/proceedings.

Heath, R. L. (2002). Issues management: Its past, present and future. *Journal of Public Affairs, 2*(4), 209–214.

Heath, R. L. & Palenchar, M. J. (2009). *Strategic issues management—Organisations and public policy challenges* (2nd ed.). Thousand Oaks, CA: Sage.

Heath, R. L. (Ed.). (1998). *Strategic issues management: How organisations influence and respond to public interest and policies.* San Francisco: Jossey-Bass.

Heugens, P. P. M. A. R. (2006). Environmental issue management: Towards multi-level theory of environmental management competence. *Business Strategy and the Environment, 15*(6), 363–376.

Jaques, T. (2014). Issue management. In R. Tench & L. Yeomans (Eds.), *Exploring Public Relations* (3rd ed., pp. 300–312). Harlow: Pearson Education.

Jaques, T. (2012). Is issue management evolving or progressing towards extinction? *Public Communication Review, 2* (1).

Kemp, B., Randle, M., Hurlimann, A. & Dolnicar, S. (2012). Community acceptance of recycled water: Can we inoculate the public against scare campaigns? *Journal of Public Affairs, 12*(4), 337–346.

Kent, M. L., Taylor, M. & Veil, S. R. (2011). Issue management makeover: A facelift for an aging theory. *Business Research Yearbook, Balancing Profitability and Sustainability: Shaping the Future of Business, 18,* 534–541.

Klein, N. (2000). *No logo: Taking aim at the brand bullies.* New York: Picador.

Laufer, D. G. (2005). *A practical process guide to issue management.* Washington, DC: Public Affairs Council.

Lubbers, E. (Ed.). (2002*). Battling big business: Countering greenwash, infiltration and other forms of corporate bullying.* Melbourne: Scribe.

Martz-Mayfield, M. & Hallahan, K. (2009). Filmmakers as social advocates—A new challenge for issues management: Claims-making and framing in four social issue documentaries. *Public Relations Journal, 3*(4).

McCoombs, M. E. & Shaw, D. L. (1972). The agenda-setting function of mass media. *Public Opinion Quarterly, 36*(2), 171–187.

McGrath, C. (2007). Framing lobbying messages: Defining and communicating political issues persuasively. *Journal of Public Affairs, 7*(3), 269–280.

Naude, A. M. E., Froneman, J. D. & Atwood, R. A. (2004). The use of the internet by ten South African NGOs—a public relations perspective. *Public Relations Review, 30*(1), 87–94.

Pop, R. (2013). *Issue management within the U.S. Navy: Toward a revised issue lifecycle model.* Paper presented at the 16th International Public Relations Research Conference, 6–10 March, Coral Gables, Miami.

Price, T. (2011). *Beyond control: How social media and mobile communication are changing public affairs.* Washington DC: Foundation for Public Affairs.

Ragas, M. W. (2013). Agenda-building and agenda-setting: Which companies we think about and how we think about them. In C. E. Carroll (Ed.), *Handbook of communication and corporate reputation* (pp. 153–165). New York: Wiley.

Reber, B. H. & Kim, J. K. (2006). How activist groups use websites in media relations: Evaluating online press rooms. *Journal of Public Relations Research, 18*(4), 313–333.

Rogers, M., Chapman, C. & Giotsas, V. (2012). Measuring the diffusion of marketing messages across a social network. *Journal of Direct, Data and Digital Marketing Practice, 14*(2), 97–130.

Seo, H., Kim, J. Y. & Yang, S. (2009). Global activism and new media: A study of transnational NGOs' online public relations. *Public Relations Review, 35*(2), 123–126.

Starr, A. (2000). *Naming the enemy: Anti-corporate movements confront globalisation.* Armadale, NSW: Pluto Press.

Temin, D. (2012). What boards must know about social media. *The Corporate Board, 33*(194), 11–15.

Waters, R. D., Burnett, E. B., Lamm, A. & Lucas, J. (2009). Engaging stakeholders through social networking: How nonprofit organisations are using Facebook. *Public Relations Review, 35*(2), 102–106.

Wernli, J. & Frank, U (2000). Global issues management in the new economy. *PR World Congress*, Chicago, 23 October. Retrieved from www.ipra.org/members/archive/conference_papers/chicago/chicago/page21a.htm.

Zyglidopoulos, S. C. (2003). The issue life cycle: Implications for reputation for social performance and organisational legitimacy. *Corporate Reputation Review, 6*(1), 70–81.

3

ISSUE MANAGEMENT – IDENTIFICATION AND PRIORITISATION

CHAPTER OBJECTIVES

This chapter will help you to:

+ learn to identify the difference between an issue and a problem

+ understand the basics of environmental scanning

+ recognise how issues are identified and flagged

+ assess some methodologies for prioritisation

+ appreciate more fully how issues can evolve into crises.

Two of the most frequently asked questions in issue management are: Where do issues come from and how do you identify them? And how do we know which ones to work on? While this chapter will focus on those two crucial questions, the first part of the challenge with identifying issues is to understand exactly what an issue is.

In Chapter 1 we defined an issue in a broad sense:

> An issue is any trend or development—real or perceived—usually at least partly in the public arena which, if it continues, could have a significant impact on the organisation's financial position, operations, reputation or future interests, and requires a structured approach to achieve positive, planned outcomes.

Furthermore, Table 1.1 in Chapter 1 positioned an issue to distinguish it from an emergency, a crisis and a disaster.

To more specifically identify particular issues—those requiring the structured response of formal issue management—a further distinction is required; namely, to clarify the difference between an issue and a problem. One of the commonest mistakes in this respect is to treat every problem as an issue, and to regard issue management as an all-purpose problem-solving tool.

Issue management is undoubtedly useful for addressing some problems. But not all problems are issues in the context of requiring the mobilisation of resources and a full issue management strategy. And not all issues are problems. Some represent genuine opportunities. Understanding the difference can have a real bottom-line impact on the way organisational resources are deployed. (For fuller discussion about 'problem versus issue' see Jaques, 2007.)

Managers generally are expected to handle a wide variety of problems, and their key to success is to use the correct problem-solving tool for each challenge. For instance, to understand the financial implications of a proposed project, the correct tool might be *cost-benefit analysis*; to examine in detail why an incident happened, the correct tool might be *root-cause analysis*; and to analyse and assess an organisation's communication capability, the correct tool might be a formal *communications audit*.

In these and similar areas, a specific management tool is often available to address a particular type of problem. Issue management as a tool is no different, but it's frequently misapplied through careless use of the word 'issue'.

Some managers tend to describe any challenge they face as an 'issue', be it market share, staff retention, interest rates, competitive pricing, timing a product launch, cash flow or getting a new advertising campaign completed on schedule. This misuse of the terminology sometimes results from carelessness and sometimes from a belief that using the label 'issue' may secure additional attention or resources.

There is no question that the examples given may be important challenges, but one of the key skills and responsibilities that typically separate managers from other employees is the capacity to identify and solve problems, using the correct tool.

Those situations properly defined as issues—which warrant the application of a formal issue management process—are not day-to-day problems that functional or departmental managers need to just get on and deal with. Typically issues are situations that:

+ involve external parties (and are thus at least partly beyond the organisation's direct control)

+ have no black and white or 'right' answer

+ may involve public policy or regulation
+ are driven by emotions rather than hard data
+ happen in public or in the news media (conventional or online)
+ may be controversial, with strongly held contending opinions
+ are likely to attract interest beyond the immediate stakeholders
+ often have a moral or ethical component
+ have the greatest potential risk in the event of failure
+ and, most crucially, if left unmanaged, have the capacity to become a crisis and threaten the entire organisation.

The cumulative effect of these explicit characteristics can be expressed in the following phrase:

PROBLEMS ARE SOLVED, ISSUES NEED TO BE RESOLVED.

This is much more than simply semantics or a clever maxim. To take a dictionary definition approach, to _solve_ is to explain, to find the answer or solution—for example, when solving a mathematical equation, solving a crossword puzzle or solving a detective mystery. You know there is a right answer, and you just need to find and present the solution.

By contrast, the Oxford English Dictionary says to _resolve_ is to separate a thing into its component parts or elements; to reduce by mental analysis into more elementary forms, principles or relations; to change from discord to harmony; or to determine on a course of action. Such a pursuit of resolution is very much the hallmark of issues. There is seldom any ready-made solution or 'right answer'. In this way, unlike a problem, which can be solved, an issue has to be resolved.

This means seeking out and developing a balanced way forward from a range of possible actions, all of which may have conflicting risks and rewards. Furthermore, the absence of a single 'right answer' reinforces the need for a process that helps to define and clarify the issue; to set a clear, agreed objective; and to develop and implement effective strategies and tactics.

This is where issue management delivers its essential value—providing a framework within which to apply the standard tools of communications and a management discipline to establish a process that orders the optimal sequence of activities.

> Managing an issue management system is not the same as managing an issue.
>
> Andrew Griffin (2008, p. 117)

Furthermore, in accordance with the dictionary definition, issue management is increasingly seen as a formal process that helps bring about 'change from discord to harmony'. As referenced in Chapter 1, the issue scholar Robert Heath specifically defines issue management as a strategic set of functions used to 'reduce friction and increase harmony' between organisations and their publics in the public policy arena.

A need to address discord and promote harmony can be readily seen in some common examples of issues that an organisation could face. Unlike the case studies and brief examples included in this book, which focus on real-life issues or crises, the following situations are generic—yet they illustrate typical issues that could lend themselves to active issue management (although some very much have the potential to escalate into a crisis):

+ meeting community opposition to controversial zoning proposals
+ addressing regulatory concern over use of an environmentally sensitive chemical
+ recognising public awareness about identify theft to position new security technology
+ anticipatory planning for adverse public reaction to scheduled plant closures or job layoffs
+ ongoing accusations of racial or sexual harassment or discrimination
+ responding to online rumours of faulty products or rude service
+ addressing hostile response to foreign buyout of an iconic local brand
+ promoting public acceptance of nuclear power generation
+ combating parental resistance to vaccinating babies against childhood diseases
+ reacting to charges of worker exploitation by contractors in the developing world
+ managing hostility to introducing recycled water into a town drinking supply
+ replying to an internet campaign alleging that charity donations have been misspent
+ facing anger over demolition of historic buildings to make way for a new highway
+ preparing for reputational damage from upcoming high-profile litigation
+ countering claims that product packaging comes from endangered rainforest
+ encouraging legislative support for wind farms.

The list goes on and the variety of potential issues is seemingly inexhaustible. However, not all issues are so obvious, and obvious issues are sometimes deliberately ignored.

There is effectively a three-step process:

1. scanning for and identifying potential issues
2. prioritising which issues to work on
3. then, and only then, assigning resources and putting plans in place.

This chapter focuses on the first two steps. The next chapter explores in detail the development and implementation of issue management plans.

SCANNING AND IDENTIFICATION

The process of scanning for potential issues—sometimes called environmental scanning or horizon scanning or scouting the terrain—can vary enormously, from the least formal individual professional judgment through to dedicated review teams linked directly to corporate strategic planning (see Figure 3.1).

Figure 3.1 Levels of formality in identifying emerging issues ✖

MORE FORMAL	APPROACHES TO IDENTIFYING EMERGING ISSUES	
	Dedicated resources	Online systems or a formal monitoring group
	Cross-business cross-function teams	Meet regularly to identify issues. IM staff in support to provide structure and tools
	Regular inter-functional review; including Issue Management, Government Affairs, Public Affairs, Communications	Brainstorming, issue reviews, joint assessment. Mainly by communication professionals
	External audits, community and corporate advisory panels	Multi-faced commitment to an 'outside in' perspective
	Government relations scanning capability	Mainly through legislative and regulatory review and public opinion polling
	Employee scanning capability and a formal process for raising issues	Particularly through public/stakeholder interface and participation in trade associations
	Electronic services	Internal or commercial monitoring of mainstream and social media
LESS FORMAL	No formal process, but an integral part of public affairs/issue management	Largely based on professional experience and goal-setting

Source: Issue Outcomes.

Recognising these different levels of formality, the best practice indicators developed by the US-based Issue Management Council (discussed in Chapter 2) do not attempt to specify a universally preferred model. Instead, the Issue Management Council indicators propose only that there is 'an established mechanism to identify current and future issues through environmental scanning/issue analysis'. They also propose that 'formal channels exist for managers at all levels to identify and elevate potential issues for possible integration into broader strategic planning, including external stakeholder management' (Issue Management Council, 2005). Here, again, they describe what is needed without specifying a preferred method. The indicators are presented in full in Chapter 4.

The key here is not to be prescriptive about the nature of the process and the level of formality, but rather to emphasise the importance of an agreed methodology that is appropriate for the organisation, considering its size, exposure, history, geographic spread and other factors.

In some multinational companies in the issue-rich energy and chemical sector, for example, the process is taken to very advanced levels of sophistication. Dupont (2007) pioneered the use of a Strategic Issue Council to identify emerging issues that might otherwise fall between the organisational boxes. It has a cross-business/cross-functional membership, supported by a team of government affairs and issue management professionals. For its part, the energy company Shell has added another level of input, undertaking regular large-scale scenario reviews that draw on people from across its worldwide structure, not just to identify probable issues but also to 'consider a range of plausible futures and how these could emerge from the realities of today', which then feed directly into strategic planning.[1]

Whatever system is chosen, a team approach has been shown to be very effective, especially where the team has cross-business/cross-functional membership and support. This cross-functional method has some particular benefits as it:

+ reduces silo thinking
+ prevents issues falling between groups
+ addresses issues that cover multiple businesses, functions or geographies
+ includes issues that exist primarily as a corporate function
+ ensures consistency of approach and governance across the organisation.

Some organisations extend this approach by broadening the review process to involve external opinion. For example, the multinational chemical company BASF gives priority to an outside view, with a Global Stakeholder Survey scanned into what is called a materiality matrix. Another example is the Sustainability External Advisory Council (SEAC) created by Dow Chemical, which was set up with external experts—including environmentalists and people from 'the other side'—specifically to help the company gain a diverse and sometimes critical 'outside-in perspective' on environment, health and safety, and sustainability issues for the company.

For individual organisations the scanning and identification process can be reasonably formal, yet may not require this level of complexity and cost. Regardless of how sophisticated or basic the issue scanning process is, an important reality is that the sources of live and emerging issues are, in fact, often quite simple and easily overlooked, and do not need to rely on excessively complicated tools.[2]

ISSUE SOURCES

The first and most obvious source of potential issues is effectively monitoring the mainstream news media and the social media. This can range from reading the local newspaper, watching the television news and using a daily online word search, right through to professional monitoring, which can be very comprehensive and costly. Often it is a combination of both.

---

1   Examples of the Shell issue scenarios can be seen at www.shell.com/global/future-energy/scenarios.html.
2   For more discussion of the role of scanning, see Davidson (1991) in this chapter's Further reading section.

> For most organisations, key issues will be found from reading headlines rather than tea leaves.
>
> George McGrath (1988, p. 77)

Although daily news monitoring is an obvious requirement, case studies reveal that organisations are constantly caught unaware by issues that emerge in the media and develop rapidly. Regardless of discussion about the changing importance of traditional and digital media, and the roles of professional reporters and 'citizen journalists', news scanning will likely remain a crucial element in issue identification. Of course, none of this is of substantive value if the scanning does not link to an effective action process.

Beyond basic mainstream and social media scanning, there is a range of very important and low-cost sources of issue information that are frequently under-utilised. These include:

+ industry and political conferences
+ scientific and trade publications
+ regulatory and legislative updates
+ trade association meetings and newsletters
+ CEO forums
+ the organisation's own business/operating units
+ websites and information from critics and opponents
+ industry and business allies, and joint venture partners
+ surveys of clients, customers, employees and other stakeholders
+ analysis by experts
+ feedback from staff who deal with external people and organisations.

Most of these are inexpensive yet can yield priceless information.

One specific internal source is the organisational risk register. Many organisations have a formal risk register, sometimes associated with financial risk assessment or insured risk. While the risk register will typically contain many elements that relate to matters well outside the scope of potential public issues as defined in this chapter, it can be a useful pointer to areas of vulnerability which might otherwise be overlooked.

In fact, internal sources are often under-appreciated, even though an organisation's employees may be close to potential issues. For instance, a pattern of customer complaints can signal a potential issue in product quality or customer relations, but that potential risk can be recognised only if the information is collected and acted upon.[3]

As previously mentioned, the IMC best practice indicators propose that formal channels exist for managers at all levels to identify and elevate potential issues, and the same applies to employees at other levels. Case analysis around the world shows that after almost every crisis or major issue, someone inside the organisation will come forward and say: 'Oh yes, I knew about that.' Sometimes they will add: 'I tried to raise it, but no one took any notice.'

---

3   For discussion of the importance of signal detection, see Coombs (1999) in this chapter's Further reading section.

An important element of effective issue scanning is to provide a simple process by which people throughout the organisation know how to raise a potential issue, and be confident they will be listened to. Moreover, best practice issue management requires a mechanism to receive and evaluate that information, and to feed back to the person who raised the concern.

RISK VERSUS RESOURCES

Before companies progress as far as starting to prioritise the identified issues, it is a very common mistake to assess issues in terms of resources available rather than the potential risk to the organisation. In other words, prioritising on the basis of 'Have we got the people to deal with it?' rather than 'How important is it and how could it affect us?' In this way, important issues may be discounted at the first pass on the grounds that they are too big, too controversial, too sensitive or demand too many resources.

A vital step here is to recognise that an organisation is rarely alone when it comes to facing an issue. There are often allies or those with a common interest who are willing and able to play a part. Moreover, these potential allies may not be the obvious ones, as is demonstrated by the alliance between food giant Cargill and NGOs to develop the Brazilian Forest Code on deforestation for soy production; the German refrigerator manufacturer Foron merging resources with Greenpeace to promote the famous CFC-free 'green fridge'; World Wildlife Fund working with the Australian Minerals Council to improve environmental reporting practices; or the alliance between Dupont and the NGO Environmental Defence to develop a nano-risk framework.

The factors that shape activist–corporate partnerships, from both the corporate and the activist perspective, are complex and involve balancing a number of important competing interests. This balancing act is explored, for example, in Coombs and Holladay (2009), and the subject is also discussed in more detail in Chapter 5.

A BENEFICIAL ALLIANCE

A good example of an organisation joining in an alliance to deal with a genuine issue occurred when a major public health problem arose from the increasing use of petrol as an inhalant in remote Indigenous communities in Australia. But for BP Australia it was recognised as both a potential new business and a high-profile, reputation-building opportunity. In 2005, in partnership with the Federal and Northern Territory governments, Indigenous communities and educational bodies, BP developed Opal fuel, a variety of fuel that contains only 5 per cent aromatics compared with 25 per cent in typical unleaded petrol.

This means it has less of the toluene and other solvents that produce the 'high' that inhalant users are seeking. It is more expensive to produce, but BP receives a substantial government subsidy, which offsets the high social and health costs of petrol sniffing. A government report five years later (Marshall, 2010) showed that the introduction of Opal in 106 communities across remote and regional Australia had led to a 70 per cent drop in petrol sniffing in those communities. For more detail on this issue see www.opalfuel.com.au.

When undertaking the preliminary assessment of issue resources, and deciding whether an organisation will take the lead or simply contribute to an issue, the thinking behind the question 'Do we have to do this alone?' needs some process, such as the alliance decision flow chart (see Figure 3.2).

Figure 3.2 Alliance decision flow chart

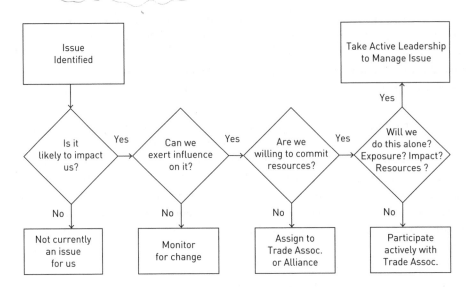

Source: Issue Outcomes.

The strategic use of allies is critical here. In one case, the issue may be assigned entirely to a trade association or formal alliance, with the company doing no more than monitoring and assessing progress. This could apply when the organisation regards the issue as important, but does not want to have its name or brand directly associated with the issue.

This same outcome might also be achieved by a more active participation; for example, being part of the industry association committee or alliance overseeing the issue (sweat equity) or by providing expertise or even a 'loan executive' to work directly to the issue but still under the trade association's identity.

Importantly, this decision process does not apply only to commercial organisations. Not-for-profits (NFPs) and community organisations equally can benefit from alternative participation models, which may preserve resources in order to optimise joint objectives. In fact, ad hoc alliances are sometimes more common in the NFP and activist communities than in the corporate world. Broadly, however, these are all very real ways in which the organisation can influence or even drive the issue without necessarily being seen as the active issue leader or depleting limited resources.

In addition to utilising existing structures, such as a trade association or a community coalition, the organisation can also 'share responsibility' by helping to establish a purpose-built alliance to address a specific issue of common concern. A good example is the 'measured dose inhaler' alliance established in the 1990s. The world applauded when the Montreal Protocol was implemented to phase out ozone-depleting chlorofluorocarbons (CFCs), but the ban would have affected millions of asthmas sufferers whose 'puffers' used these chemicals as a propellant. Even though NGOs and governments around the world said there should be 'no exemptions', developing an alternative could take up to 10 years. Industry leaders formed the International Pharmaceutical Aerosols Consortium (IPAC) and a successful international issue management strategy gave manufacturers time to develop non-CFC alternatives.[4]

An example in the NFP sector was the ad hoc coalition organised in Australia to oppose government legislation to limit private gun ownership after the Port Arthur Massacre in 1996 when thirty-five people died at the hands of a lone gunman. The rapid creation of this diverse and influential coalition took some politicians and commentators by surprise, although gun control was eventually implemented.[5]

It is important to recognise that such alliances need to be open and transparent.[6] There is no legitimate place for phoney front alliances to disguise a company's involvement in an issue. Just before the 2010 Australian federal election, a television campaign was launched by the newly created Alliance of Australian Retailers to oppose a plan to introduce plain packaging for cigarettes. The organisation described itself as 'Owners of Australian corner stores, milk bars, newsagents and service stations who are fed up with excessive regulation that is making it harder for us to run our businesses' and the advertisements featured small business owners speaking out against the proposed legislation. But it was soon revealed that the alliance was, in fact, almost entirely funded by three of the world's largest tobacco companies.[7] Standardised plain packaging for cigarettes became law in Australia in December 2012.

PRIORITISATION

Only after consideration of possible alliance options can the real work of prioritisation proceed. At the start of the scanning process just about everything looks like an issue and a common mistake is to think that the longer the list of issues identified, the better prepared the company is to achieve its corporate goals and protect its reputation.

However, no organisation can actively manage every issue in their environment and some issues can appropriately be assigned to an allied organisation (as described above) or can safely be placed into a passive management or monitoring phase.

This might involve, for example, an individual employee or small internal group being given responsibility to track the issue and identify any change in status; a decision to monitor the issue and to revisit on an agreed schedule; or an informed, conscious decision

---

4   For discussion of the asthma puffer case see Regester and Larkin (2005) in this chapter's Further reading section.
5   For an overview of issue management and the Australian gun debate, see Reynolds (1997) in this chapter's Further reading section.
6   For an example of an alliance between a fast food company and an environmental activist group, see Livesey (1999) in this chapter's Further reading section.
7   For a review of the case for plain packaging, and tobacco industry support of the campaign opposing it, see Quit Victoria (2011) in this chapter's Further reading section.

to categorise as 'not an issue *for us*' or 'not an issue for us *at present*'. It is important to stress, however, that this should be a planned, *agreed* decision, not just consigning the issue to the 'too hard basket' as an excuse to do nothing.

It is also important to stress that categorisation is not the same as prioritisation. Dividing potential issues into categories can make them easier to understand and help to identify common characteristics, but it doesn't help to decide on prioritisation; namely what we need to work on and where we need to commit resources.

When it comes to full-scale proactive issue management—which involves a formal issue management team, goals and strategies, a communication plan, implementation schedules and commitment of substantial resources—even the largest organisations recognise that the number of priority strategic issues under proactive management must be limited. Many experts believe six to twelve top-level issues is an optimum number, even though many others may be in passive or inactive mode.

> Having no problems is the biggest problem of all.
>
> Pioneer leader of the Toyota Production System,
> Taiichi Ohno[8]

Prioritisation is the essential process to progress from a comprehensive list of all potential issues to a workable list of the proactive few—and do it in a way that is fully aligned with the company's capabilities, culture and strategic objectives.[9] Principles that apply to successful prioritisation include the following:

+ Leading organisations have a clearly defined process for identifying emerging issues, not just the issues that are addressed day to day.

+ Emerging issues are seen as those that are still developing and may or may not require a planned management response.

+ The process can range from informal, through structured, to highly sophisticated, but needs a good variety of inputs.

+ The need for more advanced processes increases as organisations:
    – increase in size
    – have exposure to issues across borders
    – operate in potentially controversial markets
    – develop a high-profile brand
    – have brands that are vulnerable to actions of subsidiaries, joint ventures or associated entities.

One common issue prioritisation model is to simply look at two criteria: probability and impact (see Figure 3.3). In other words, how likely or how soon could it happen, and how badly would it impact us if it did?

---

8   For more on the work of Taiichi Ohno, see Ohno (2006) in this chapter's Further reading section.

9   For discussion of prioritising, see Ferguson (1994) and Rawlins (2006) in this chapter's Further reading section.

Figure 3.3 Probability–impact matrix

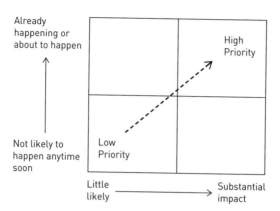

The probability–impact method is rather crude and not very helpful. If it was entirely effective, how could the same issue be a high priority for one organisation and a lower priority for another?

The difference is logically within the organisation itself. Because of this, an effective prioritisation process needs to consider not just the issue on its own, but also the organisation; its capacity to influence the issue; whether it is willing or resourced to exercise that influence; and whether the issue is actually susceptible to influence. In other words, can the organisation actually make a difference and is it prepared to commit both resources and reputation to deliver that outcome? From this comes the significance–influence approach (see Figure 3.4), where priority is a function of the likely significance of the issue and capacity to influence.

Figure 3.4 Significance–influence matrix

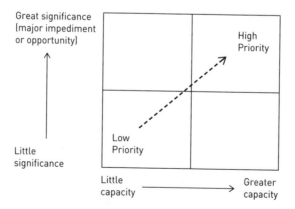

The significance–influence model is a more useful approach, in that it considers the capacity of the organisation to influence the issue. But it fails to address how susceptible the issue is to influence, and whether the organisation has the resources and/or the willingness to exercise that capacity to influence. In reality, both models over-simplify prioritisation, which requires more than just a two-dimensional matrix. Moreover, an effective prioritisation process doesn't just assess each issue itself but also evaluates relative priority between different issues, and prioritises issue management effort and the allocation of resources.

One approach is to assign numerical values against key criteria, which creates a quantified, numerical assessment rather than relying on intuition or 'gut feel'. Furthermore, such systems typically provide a weighting against the selected criteria to meet the needs of the particular organisation. Table 3.1 is an example of six different criteria that can be used as the basis for the prioritisation assessment (with nominal maximum values to illustrate the process). The agreed numerical value totalled out of 100 provides a firm and informed foundation on which to prioritise.

Table 3.1 Prioritisation assessment

Category	Description	Discussion	Maximum value*
Impact	Potential magnitude for the organisation if the issue is left unmanaged	Impacts may include reputation (particularly with key stakeholders); financial (both profitability and share value); regulatory (including licence to operate, fines and penalties); and legal (current and potential litigation)	20
Salience/ legitimacy (sometimes called social consensus)	How widely in society the issue is regarded as a concern	Assesses not just the present situation, but also whether attention to the issue is likely to change substantially soon; it reflects what influential stakeholders and society regard as important, not the opinion of the organisation concerned	20
Visibility	Extent of coverage in the news media and social media	Considers both the nature and quantity of media attention: is the coverage confined to news reports, or does it include opinion pieces/columns/blog? Which media are active?	20
Affectability/ leverage	The organisation's capacity to influence the issue	How much influence could be achieved, setting aside for the moment questions about resources available—if it is important enough, resources can usually be found	20
Proximity/ timing	When the issue is likely to reach its maximum impact	Although issue management is about early intervention, potential timing of competing issues helps to decide the order in which they are addressed; the question of likely peak timing assumes no prior intervention	10
Profile	Willingness of the organisation to expose its brand or reputation	A core product or activity may warrant greater commitment than for a minor or peripheral activity; however, minor products can generate disproportionate reputational and financial damage	10

*The higher the score, the greater the priority.

From an issue management perspective, the strategic benefit of this process comes not simply from deriving a numerical value for each issue, but also from the *process* of thinking through the key elements of prioritisation and the development of a formal framework to agree on *why* some issues are more important than others. As Prussian Field Marshal Helmuth von Moltke reportedly said 'Plans are nothing. Planning is everything.'

This planning discussion also helps to focus attention beyond the inherent nature of the issue itself and drives consideration of the organisation's specific position in relation to the issue.

Using this approach, and the numerical values assigned to each of the criteria, an organisation can better understand the importance of each issue relative to other issues. It can then determine the priority for the organisation in terms of the appropriateness and level of issue management effort and what resources may be required to work towards a positive, planned outcome. Of course, the numerical value is not absolute. Prioritisation is essentially a formal, structured way to compare between issues in order to determine where the company should invest its effort.

A common question which arises is how an organisation incorporates the fact that issues can be highly volatile and priorities may change quickly. This is a serious consideration, but experience shows it is a mistake to keep revisiting the priority list. However, a formal process does allow for a comparative assessment against changing criteria. For example:

+ Issues evolve over time, especially in terms of public and media interest.

+ Organisational exposure can change, such as entering a new market or new geography.

+ New facts or data may emerge that substantially alter a particular issue, either increasing or decreasing its priority.

+ Available resources can change. New expert staff may be employed. A new interest group may be established.

+ Relative importance of issues can change. As old issues get resolved, other issues rise towards the top.

+ Organisational change can alter priorities, such as acquiring a business with legacy issues.

The final important aspect of prioritisation is: who decides? Issue prioritisation is not an abstract or theoretical exercise. It can lead to important decisions on investment and resource allocation. It can also have direct impact such as reputation, capacity to do business, investor confidence, expansion and acquisition plans, recruitment and retention, compliance cost and risk exposure. For that reason a strategic team approach to prioritisation is essential and senior management must be involved.

FORMAL ISSUE PRIORITISATION

There are ten good reasons to adopt formal issue prioritisation:

+ *Commitment*—involves key players, ensures their buy-in and reduces backsliding and dissent.

+ *Objectivity*—demonstrates to top management that a proper process was followed and didn't rely on 'gut feel'.

+ *Confidence*—provides confidence that the organisation is not only doing things right but is doing the right things.

+ *Rigour*—helps resist pressure from individuals, sometimes very senior, who demand resources for their 'pet issue'.

+ *Speed*—can be achieved quickly without having to reinvent the process.

+ *Efficiency*—optimises use of resources and minimises duplication and waste.

+ *Neutrality*—reduces the risk of distortion by turf rivalries or dominant personalities.

+ *Simplicity*—can be implemented by line managers and senior executives with minimal facilitation once the format is embedded.

+ *Flexibility*—criteria can be easily adapted to fit the needs of different parts of the organisations, different markets or joint ventures.

+ *Repeatability*—provides a consistent objective basis for future updates to assess whether priorities or conditions have changed.

Brian's word too?

Note: Parts of this chapter draw on Jaques (2007).

KEY POINTS

+ Not all problems are issues, and not all issues are problems.

+ Problems are solved, but issues need to be resolved.

+ Issues can be more effectively defined by their characteristics rather than a formula of words.

+ Many sources of potential issues are simple and low cost, but are often under-utilised.

+ Cross-functional issue identification improves depth and helps avoid gaps.

+ Alliances or coalitions are a powerful tool to optimise issue management resources and impact.

+ Prioritisation needs to assess much more than just 'how soon' and 'how bad'.

≡ ACTIVITIES AND DISCUSSION

1. Identify other potential issues to add to the list of generic examples provided in this chapter. How many of them reflect two or more of the criteria listed?

2. Review the catalogue of potential issue sources listed here. Discuss reasons why some obvious sources are often overlooked or under-used.

3. Research examples of issue alliances between big business and NGOs. What are the characteristics that contribute to successful outcomes?

4. What are some of the attitudes that inhibit objective issue prioritisation? How can these barriers be overcome?

SUPER SIZE ME—A TALE OF TWO NATIONS

Mark Sheehan

Deakin University, Melbourne

The issues that affect organisations are sometimes not particularly dramatic in nature, but all too often are of the organisation's own making. The release of the documentary film *Super Size Me*—described in publicity blurbs as a film of 'epic portions'—was clearly an issue identified when McDonald's Corporation in the USA was scouting the terrain. But their strategic reaction to what was in many ways this largely foreseeable event was quite unlike the response from McDonald's in Australia.

The corporation in each nation chose to respond to the challenge of the film and its maker very differently, which meant some actions had a far greater effect on organisational reputation with consumers, franchisees and government.

The documentary revolved around film-maker Morgan Spurlock making himself a human guinea pig, by conducting an experiment to eat only McDonald's for 30 days. And, as the title suggests, when asked if he wanted to super-size his serve—increase the size of the portion—he would agree every time. With three doctors monitoring his health, he documented the effects of a McDonald's diet on his body.

McDonald's recognition of nutrition and diet as key factors in organisational success was acknowledged in the US corporate head office with a specific role of Director of Worldwide Nutrition. So the issue of diet and their products was clearly identified.

As part of standard issue identification, it is recognised that an issue can change due to change in evaluative criteria; for example, a new sense of social responsibility. For McDonald's, *Super Size Me* brought about this change. The connection between 'fast food' and obesity had been unambiguously made.

Scanning of the issues horizon would have given McDonald's US four months' lead time to develop a response to the film between its debut in January 2004 and commercial launch in May. This would have been adequate time to craft a strategy to address the documentary's claims about the supposed adverse health effects of eating McDonald's meals. The company could not claim to have been surprised or to have had insufficient information. A critical element of issue identification is knowing which issues will benefit from communication and which will benefit from re-evaluating policy or procedural, or from altered stakeholder engagement. The company had clear time in which to consider and deliver these thoughtful responses.

Prior to the documentary's May 2004 US release, McDonald's spokespersons were attempting to discredit Spurlock, saying he was 'a comedian that made a gross-out movie' and accusing him of gluttony and sloth. However, it was clear that in the eyes of consumer stakeholders, *Super Size Me* placed responsibility for the national obesity issue squarely

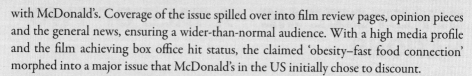

with McDonald's. Coverage of the issue spilled over into film review pages, opinion pieces and the general news, ensuring a wider-than-normal audience. With a high media profile and the film achieving box office hit status, the claimed 'obesity–fast food connection' morphed into a major issue that McDonald's in the US initially chose to discount.

In June 2004 *Super Size Me* was released in Australia. Existing controversy surrounding the film ensured it was a box office success, presenting the local McDonald's organisation with a crisis-level dilemma: ignore the moviemaker's claims or convince consumers that the film's premise—that McDonald's food is unhealthy—was false. McDonald's Australia chose the latter course and developed a responsive plan that included positive communication and stakeholder engagement.

Research told McDonald's Australia that customers were 'disappointed' at the company's previous lack of response. So Australian CEO Guy Russo sought the views of the many hundreds of McDonald's franchisees and thousands of employees and suppliers around the country.

Procedurally McDonald's Australia was well placed due to the strategic relationship it had with stakeholder group The Food Group Australia (a group of accredited practising dieticians), which it had worked closely with to improve menus and develop new menu items. Russo stated he 'thought long and hard' about whether to comment and concluded that 'at the end of the day we believe we owe it to you, our valued customers' to come out with a position.

The company's proactive strategy, in television and print advertising and other in-store communication tools (brochures and posters), rebutted the movie's claims. The in-store material made a point of not mentioning the name of the movie—a policy Russo followed in his extensive media interviews and in the company's advertising. Russo undertook a forthright media strategy. As Spurlock toured Australia promoting his documentary in media interviews, Russo sought right of reply within 24 hours, with himself as spokesperson.

McDonald's Australia issue response program showcased the company's ability to build on existing community goodwill, allowing McDonald's a fair hearing in the court of public opinion. Moreover, responding to Spurlock's publicity tour through the same media channels he was using gave the company an opportunity tell its positive story.

A real winner in the issue was McDonald's UK. When *Super Size Me* was due for release there a few months later, the UK organisation had watched and analysed the US and Australian responses to the issue—and chose the Australian way.[10]

For more detailed discussion of this case see:

Sheehan, M. (2005). *Super Size Me*: A comparative analysis of responses to a crisis by McDonald's America and McDonald's Australia. In C. Galloway & K. Kwansah-Aidoo (Eds.), *Public Relations Issues and Crisis Management* (pp. 67–79). Melbourne: Thomson.

---

10 For analysis of how the American retailer Walmart responded to a highly critical Hollywood documentary film, see Barbaro (2005) in this chapter's Further reading section. Walmart launched a large-scale counter-offensive that included establishment of a 'war room'.

EARLY ISSUE IDENTIFICATION FOR CRISIS PREVENTION

Tony Jaques

RMIT University, Melbourne

When two 14-year-old New Zealand schoolgirls challenged the advertising claims of Ribena blackcurrant drink—then owned by global giant GlaxoSmithKline (GSK)—they triggered a sequence of events that led to prosecution and public embarrassment. But the resulting international damage to an iconic brand could have been largely avoided if the company had recognised the issue early and responded without delay.

Ribena has been marketed since the 1930s as a source of healthy vitamin C, and in 2004 the two Auckland teenagers tested Ribena, along with other drinks, as a high school experiment to assess vitamin C. They tested the pre-diluted ready to drink (RTD) variety of Ribena, which is conveniently packaged for school lunchboxes, but found it did not contain 'four times the vitamin C of oranges' as advertised.

They wrote to GSK in New Zealand to complain about what they said was misleading advertising. But instead of recognising a potential issue, the company dismissed the complaint. The two teenagers then went to the top-rating consumer program, *Fair Go*, which broadcast the story on national television. GSK declined to appear on the program, but provided a written statement that apologised to the girls for the way their complaint had been dealt with, but defended the advertising as being correct.

Most importantly, despite all the warning signs of a growing problem, the company continued using a television commercial with the 'four times' claim for another 18 months. Meanwhile, the two girls took their complaint to the government consumer watchdog, the New Zealand Commerce Commission.

As the issue emerged, the company attempted a number of strategies, which included suggesting the girls had tested the 'wrong product'; asserting that vitamin C levels fall when product is left on the shelf too long; and trying to argue that the advertising claim was true on a 'weight for weight' comparison between blackcurrants and oranges in their natural state. They also attempted to separate the problems with RTD Ribena from concentrated syrup. However, analysis showed commentators, consumers and the general public made little or no distinction between Ribena syrup and its pre-diluted RTD variety.

When government regulator tested the RTD formulation of Ribena and found it contained no vitamin C at all, the company admitted that their own testing method was unreliable, though they were unaware of that at the time.

With supermarket sales of all forms of Ribena falling, the company appeared in the Auckland District Court in March 2007 and pleaded guilty to fifteen charges relating to false advertising and incorrect labelling. Imposing a heavy fine, the judge described their

packaging statement as 'not just incorrect but wholly false'. He ordered GSK to place corrective advertising in New Zealand and Australian newspapers, as the company said this particular formula was marketed only in those two countries (the story received much less publicity in Australia).

While the judge stopped short of ordering a television campaign, because it had been years since the misleading advertisements had run, the company also voluntarily placed television advertising in both countries 'to show the mothers who trusted the brand over the years we are sorry and we wanted to fix it'.

Yet the story and resulting reputational damage spread far beyond the local media, driven in part by the extraordinary circumstances by which the case arose. As the *New Zealand Herald* commented: 'Seldom has a case of commercial chicanery been exposed so delightfully as that of the sugar drink Ribena.'

Notwithstanding GSK's efforts to geographically contain the issue, the story received disproportionate publicity around the world, undoubtedly amplified by the involvement of the two photogenic schoolgirls, now aged 17, who gave extensive interviews before and after the court hearing. A sampling of just a few international headlines captures the tone of the coverage—'Ribena shamed by New Zealand schoolgirls' (*Australian*); 'Schoolgirls rumble vitamin claims' (*Guardian*); 'Schoolgirls expose firms claim of vitamin C in drink' (*Times of India*); and 'Schoolgirls expose drink scandal' (*Bangkok Post*).

In the wake of the court case, the company tried reframe the issue by arguing that there was never an intention to mislead, and that Ribena syrup remained a rich source of vitamin C: 'It was never our intention to mislead consumers in Australia and New Zealand, so we moved quickly to amend our advertising, labelling and testing procedures when the issue came to light'. However, that statement was made three years after the two teenagers raised the issue ... and were ignored.

For more detailed discussion of this case see:

Jaques, T (2008). When an icon stumbles: The Ribena issue mismanaged. *Corporate Communications, 13*(4), pp. 394–406.

REFERENCES

Coombs, W. T. & Holladay, S.J. (2009). Cooperation, co-optation or capitulation: Factors affecting activist–corporate partnerships. *Ethical Space: The International Journal of Communication Ethics, 6*(2), 23–29.

Dupont. (2007). *DuPont and Environmental Defense launch comprehensive tool for evaluating and addressing potential risks of nanoscale materials.* Retrieved from http://investors.dupont.com/phoenix. zhtml?c=73320&p=irol-newsArticle&ID=1018133&highlight=.

Griffin, A. (2008). *New strategies for reputation management: Gaining control of issues, crises and corporate social responsibility.* London: Kogan Page.

Issue Management Council. (2005). *Best practice indicators.* Retrieved from http:// issuemanagement.org/learnmore/best-practice-indicators.

Jaques, T. (2007). Issue or problem? Managing the difference and averting crises. *Journal of Business Strategy, 28*(6), 25–28.

Marshall, A. (2010, 24 June). Opal fuel leads to 70pc drop in petrol sniffing. *ABC News.* Retrieved from www.abc.net.au/news/2010-06-24/ opal-fuel-leads-to-70pc-drop-in-petrol-sniffing/879990.

McGrath, G. B. (1998). *Issues management: Anticipation and influence.* San Francisco: IABC.

FURTHER READING

Barbaro, M. (2005, 1 November). A new weapon for Wal-Mart: A war room. *New York Times.* Retrieved from www.nytimes.com/2005/11/01/business/01walmart.ready. html?pagewanted=all/&_r=0

Coombs, W. T. (1999). Signal detection. In *Ongoing Crisis communication: Planning, Managing and Responding* (pp. 17–27). Thousand Oaks, CA: Sage.

Davidson, W. H. (1991). The role of global scanning in business planning. *Organisational Dynamics, 19*(3), 5–16.

Deegan, C. & Blomquist, C. (2006). Stakeholder influence on corporate reporting: An exploration of the interaction between WWF-Australia and the Australian minerals industry. *Accounting, Organisations and Society, 31*(4/5), 343–372.

Femers, S., Klewes, J. & Lintmeier, K. (2000). The 'life of an issue' and approaches to its control. *Journal of Communication Management, 4*(3), 253–265.

Ferguson, S. D. (1994). Prioritising and managing the organisation's issues: Deciding what's important and what to do about it. In *Mastering the Public Opinion Challenge* (pp. 51–79). New York: Irwin Publishing.

Gillions, P. (2009). Issues management. In R. Tench & L. Yeomans. (Eds.), *Exploring Public Relations.* (2nd ed., pp. 364–383). Harlow: Prentice Hall.

Hallahan, K. (2001). The dynamics of issues activation and response: An issues processes model. *Journal of Public Relations Research, 13*(1), 27–59.

Livesey, S. M. (1999). McDonald's and the Environmental Defense Fund: A case study of a green alliance. *Journal of Business Communication, 36*(1), 5–39.

Millett, I. (2005). Management by Issues: An organisational system for processing problems and opportunities. *Knowledge Management Research and Practice, 3*(3), 173–182.

Murphy, J. J. (1989). Identifying strategic issues. *Long Range Planning, 22*(2), 101–105.

Ohno, T. (2006). *Ask 'why' five times about every matter.* Retrieved from www.toyota-global.com/company/toyota_traditions/quality/mar_apr_2006.html.

Palese, M. & Crane, T. Y. (2002). Building an integrated issue management process as a source of sustainable competitive advantage. *Journal of Public Affairs, 2*(4), 284–292.

Pedregal, V. D. & Nguyen, N. L. (2009). Is fresh milk powdered milk? The controversy over packaged milk in Vietnam. In A. Lindgreen, M. K. Hingley & J. VanHamme (Eds.), *The crisis of food brands: Sustaining safe, innovative and competitive food supply* (pp. 65–85). Farnham, Surrey: Gower.

Quit Victoria. (2011). *Plain packaging of tobacco products: A review of the evidence.* Cancer Council Victoria. Retrieved from www.heartfoundation.org.au/SiteCollectionDocuments/Evidence-Paper-Plain-Packaging.pdf.

Rawlins, B. L. (2006). *Prioritising stakeholders for public relations.* White paper for Institute for Public Relations, Florida. Retrieved from www.instituteforpr.org/topics/prioritising-stakeholders.

Regester, M. & Larkin, J. (2005). CFCs—find an essential breathing space. In *Risk Issues and Crisis Management: A Casebook of Best Practice* (pp. 107–113). London Kogan Page.

Regester, M. & Larkin, J. (2005). Issues management defined. *In Risk Issues and Crisis Management: A Casebook of Best Practice* (pp. 38–47). London: Kogan Page.

Reynolds, C. (1997). Issue management and the Australian gun debate. *Public Relations Review, 23*(4), 343–360.

Taylor, S. (2003). The internal dimensions of issues management practice: Conflict, or collaboration and consensus? *PRism.* Retrieved from www.praxis.bond.edu.au/prism.

Watkins, M. D. & Bazerman, M H. (2003). Predictable surprises: The disasters you should have seen coming. *Harvard Business Review, 81*(3), 72–80.

4

ISSUE MANAGEMENT – PLANNING

CHAPTER OBJECTIVES

This chapter will help you to:

+ appreciate the importance of planning in issue management

+ explore the relationship between issue management and formal strategic planning

+ learn about the commonest barriers to effective issue management

+ introduce a proven effective issue planning model

+ identify issue management best practice for planning, implementation and evaluation.

Issue management is fundamentally an analysis and planning tool—albeit at a sophisticated level. It enables organisations to identify and respond to issues early and, most importantly, to work towards planned, positive outcomes.

It is obvious that planning is important in many areas of management, but none more so that in dealing with issues. Issue management and strategic planning are both formal planning disciplines, though they have important differences (see the 'Issue management and strategic planning' box). However, it is widely accepted by experts in both issue management and strategic planning that there are real benefits if the two are integrated as much as possible to operate in the overall best interests of the organisation. Certainly, issue management activity needs to be fully aligned with its strategic objectives (Jaques, 2009).

> Planning without action is futile. Action without planning is fatal.
>
> Anon.

As cited in Chapter 2, Robert Heath (1997) argued that issue management cannot have its full impact if it is not part of the strategic business planning process. Similarly, Australian academic Bruce Perrott (1995) warned: 'With a myopic focus on issues management alone, there is a risk of losing perspective of the strategic framework and direction of the organisation as a whole' (p. 61).

But experience suggests that this integrated approach to planning is talked about more than it is actually achieved. Research among major public corporations in Britain (Regester & Larkin, 2005, p. 41) indicated that while there was an acknowledgment by corporate communication and public affairs functions of the importance of managing issues, only 10 per cent of the sample considered that their senior management proactively dealt with issues as part of the strategic planning process. Furthermore, less than 5 per cent considered their organisation applied an integrated approach to linking planning, communication, regulatory affairs and other appropriate functions to assess, prioritise and plan for the impact of near and longer-term issues on corporate objectives.

ISSUE MANAGEMENT AND STRATEGIC PLANNING

Strategic planning as a formal business discipline was born in the 1960s and it has been claimed that few management techniques have swept through corporate and governmental enterprise more rapidly and more completely (Murphy, 1989).

After issue management took off in the early 1980s these two planning activities began to develop in parallel. At the basic level, 'Issue management links strategic planning with communication planning and improves the effectiveness of both disciplines' (McGrath, 1998, p. ii). But they are distinct disciplines, and the differences between the two need to be acknowledged.

Table 4.1 identifies some of the important distinctions.

Table 4.1 Issue management versus strategic planning ✕

Issue management	Strategic planning
Flexible timing for real time response	Locked in to periodic planning or budget cycle
Sometimes isolated from senior management	Directly linked to senior management
Perceived as a cost to business	Perceived as an investment for business
Emphasis on social and political issues not usually resolved in the market place	Emphasis on opportunities and threats to product/market issues
Regarded as a communication activity	Accepted as a core business discipline
Compromised by historic association with 'spin'	Regarded as an objective management 'science'
Corporations may be reluctant to admit they are 'managing issues'	No corporation would admit to having no strategic plan
Attempts to infuse current standards of corporate social responsibility	Attempts to balance social responsibility with corporate financial obligations
Outside-in focus (considers impacts on stakeholders)	Inside-out focus (search for opportunities and threats)
Focus on early identification of issues to manage their impact—either positive or negative	Focus on formulation of strategies to achieve positive organisational objectives
Produces an outcome	Produces a product; that is, a competitive strategic plan
Evaluation is usually 'soft,' sometimes measured in terms of crises avoided or reputation preserved	Evaluation is usually 'hard', measured in terms such as sales, production and market share
Able to respond to weak signals	Tends to respond to strong signals
Promotes non-traditional modes of thought and action	Emphasises analysis and outputs by existing structure and power relationships
Stakeholder focused	Organisation focused
Applies to business, not-for-profits, NGOs and community organisations	Primarily a corporate business discipline

Source: Jaques (2009).

It has been suggested that one of the reasons for this lack of integration is that 'corporate strategic planners focus their efforts on creating sustainable competitive advantages while public issue managers try to anticipate and respond to a growing number of social problems with little appreciation for the firm's competitive position or comprehension of its long term business plans' (Marx, 1986, p. 141).

While that may be a somewhat harsh judgment, another important reason can be found in the nature of issues themselves and the type of challenges they address. While formal strategic planning is readily accepted for many areas of management—especially those that rely on numbers, analysis and hard data—responding to issues is often seen quite differently. For example, communication professionals are often seen as having an advocacy role to bring issues into the organisation. Van Ruler and Vercic (2005) noted: 'What distinguishes communication managers from other managers when they sit down at the table is that they contribute special concern for broad societal issues and approaches to problems' (p. 264).

By contrast, senior executives whose professional training and reputation is built on solving problems and finding the 'right answer' sometimes feel uncomfortable dealing with issues that, by their nature, are difficult, awkward, emotive and occasionally downright embarrassing.

These are situations where there is no right answer, and when a lifetime of academic excellence and professional expertise may be publicly challenged by opponents whose knowledge of the subject is based mainly on research through the internet. It's also when the experts may be called on to negotiate with people who not only challenge their expertise but may even challenge their honesty, ethics or motivation: 'Why should the community believe you? You're just paid by the company to say what suits them.' Under these circumstances it is not surprising that even the most experienced of experts can feel angry or resentful, and may lead their organisation to do or say something they may later regret.

It is exactly these circumstances that make calm, objective planning even more important when it comes to issues. Because issues can often involve situations where emotions prevail over facts, planning becomes critical to success.[1]

Formal issue management planning not only helps provide an objective framework for strategy development, but also delivers some other important benefits. For example, it:

+ helps to demonstrate that issue management is a true business discipline
+ ensures strategic thinking and long-term planning
+ avoids reliance on 'gut feel'
+ simplifies evaluation
+ coordinates action for agreed objectives
+ reduces duplication and wasted effort
+ prioritises to focus on what is important
+ clarifies roles and responsibilities
+ helps to prevent issues becoming crises.

A formal planning process also helps to address four of the commonest barriers to effective issue management: remaining in reactive mode, legal response syndrome, ad hoc management and unclear goals. These are now examined in turn.

---

1   For a firsthand case study of how US footwear company Timberland planned and executed a campaign to counter environmental claims by Greenpeace, see Swartz (2010) in this chapter's Further reading section.

REMAINING IN REACTIVE MODE

This problem arises when organisations are unwilling, or feel themselves unable, to make decisions and take action. Issue management demands a proactive mindset rather than being in reactive mode. This barrier sometimes manifests itself as a focus on minutes, memos and meetings rather than actions and outcomes. Or it becomes reflected in a feeling that the issue is overwhelming and nothing can be done. Developing an issue management plan enables the organisation to realistically assess the options and opportunities, and to mobilise its resources to deliver planned positive outcomes.

LEGAL RESPONSE SYNDROME

The legal response syndrome is seen when an organisation treats each issue as if legal considerations override all others. Many issues have a legal perspective and it is important that all legal angles are appropriately addressed. However, it is rare that any issue is solely legal in nature and all aspects need adequate attention. It is a well-known maxim that an organisation can 'win in the court of law and lose in the court of public opinion'. In other words, the organisation may act in a way that is legally correct, yet results in damage to business or reputation. The planning process allows development of a proper balance between the legal considerations and the many other important considerations that may apply.

> Often companies allow legal considerations to trump all others, forgetting that the defensive posture necessary to avoid or gird for litigation also imposes reputational costs.
>
> Lance Morgan and Sally Squires (2012, p. 11)

AD HOC MANAGEMENT

Lack of a formal issue management structure with clear responsibility and accountability is another major barrier to success. This is typically seen when organisations are reluctant to establish a formal issue management team to take command. An ad hoc approach often results when the issue is assigned to an informal group that may lack the necessary skills or resources, or to an existing group that is already heavily committed to other tasks. Issues are best managed by a dedicated team set up with the right people and the right resources, and tasked specifically to develop and implement a strategically aligned plan.

UNCLEAR GOALS

Of all the barriers to effective issue management, one of the most prevalent is unclear goals and, with it, a lack of focus on action. This is where planning proves its value. There are many planning models available in different areas of business, and most start with a clear focus on establishing clear goals and objectives. This is regarded as the foundation of any effective plan, though the language and terminology may differ between disciplines. The same importance also applies in issue management, where a clear goal needs to be established in relation to the issue under consideration. Only then is it possible to ensure the organisation is working together towards a consistent, agreed outcome.

THE VALUE OF A PLANNING MODEL

The need to establish a planning process has led to the development of a very wide range of issue management models. As described in Chapter 1, the original recognised model was the basic five-step process devised by Jones and Chase (1979):

1. identification

2. analysis

3. strategy options

4. action plans

5. evaluation.

Chase (1984) later expanded this model into the detailed Programme Evaluation and Review Technique (PERT) chart, which included eighty-eight distinct 'steps' illustrated in a series of concentric circles. A researcher who worked with Chase later conceded that this chart was intentionally made complicated in an attempt to gain 'legitimacy' in the eyes of the CEO and board (Jaques, 2008).

Such thinking, and an excessive focus on process, has led to some extraordinarily complex planning models, where the process itself can threaten to overshadow the very purpose of issue management. One large multinational corporation developed an in-house issue management work process that was built on a flow chart with twenty-nine separate step-point symbols, supported by eighteen new 'system tools' and twelve defined roles, each with its own acronym. The company later replaced this process with a much simpler and more practical approach.

This situation very much parallels the fact that the original five-step Chase-Jones model has survived to this day while Chase's fold-out PERT chart is now little more than an historic artefact. As Bryan (1977) concluded: 'Issue management can easily become too process-oriented for effective response to nearer term threats or opportunities' (p. 13).

The lesson is very clear. A process is not a plan, and the planning process needs to lead to real outcomes. Tom Catania (2002, p. 3), Government Relations VP for a major US whitegoods manufacturer, neatly summed up the problem when speaking to an international conference of issue managers:

> It's so important not to let the process be seen as a surrogate for actual outcome. If the business people you deal with don't understand how you add value and how your activities are integrated with their activities, it doesn't matter how bullet-proof your process is. If the connection between the business activity and your activity is too attenuated or takes too convoluted an explanation, you're just not going to be successful.

The key to an effective issue planning process can be captured in six essential values:

1. *Utility*—it is useful and can be put into practical action.

2. *Simplicity*—it uses unambiguous language and a minimum number of steps.

3. *Clarity*—it is not only easy to follow, but also easy to explain to top management and others.

4. *Relevance*—it focuses only on what directly adds value to addressing the issue.

5. *Versatility*—it is meaningful for many types of issues, regardless of scope and scale.

6. *Assessability*—it allows assessment of ongoing progress as well as achievement of outcomes.

> The best laid plans are worthless if they cannot be communicated.
>
> Michael Regester and Judy Larkin (2005, p. 209)

INTRODUCING AN ISSUE MANAGEMENT MODEL

A major weakness in some process models is managing the crucial transition from problem identification to tactical implementation. This reflects a natural human response—see a problem and immediately focus on actions. It also reflects a very common error in issue management—to confuse 'what are we trying to achieve' with 'what do we need to do'; in other words, confusing strategic objectives with tactics.

The danger here is that an organisation's actions may lack a consistent purpose and may even fall into the trap of activity for its own sake: 'We must be seen to be taking action.' And if these actions are mainly 'gut response' and not part of a planned strategy, they can lead to duplication, waste and even outcomes that contradict the strategic purpose.

This danger brings us back to the essence of issue management: developing and implementing a planned response designed to deliver positive outcomes. While there are many different published process models, one simple proven model is the Do-it Plan© (Jaques, 2000a), which takes its name from four sequential steps—definition, objective, intended outcomes and tactics (see Figure 4.1).[2]

Figure 4.1 The Do-it Plan©

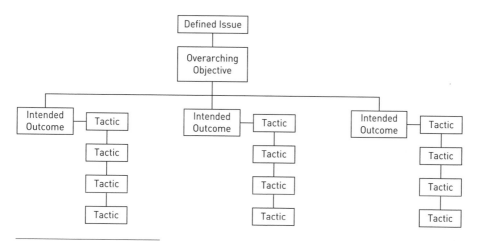

---

2   The Do-it Plan was first published in *Don't just stand there—The Do-it Plan for effective issue management* (Jaques, 2000a) and has subsequently appeared in other publications.

A strength of this model is that it has only four steps, and those four steps embrace the fundamentals of issue management. (A fully worked example of an issue strategy using this approach can be seen in the Appendix.)

STEP ONE: DEFINITION

Before an organisation can even consider the objective—'What are we trying to achieve'—it is essential to clearly define the issue—'What is the problem and how does it affect us?'

To busy managers trying to get on with the job, formally defining the issue might seem obvious and a waste of time. But experience shows that, while there may be broad agreement on the outline of the problem, different parts of the organisation can easily perceive it in different ways (Jaques, 2000b). It's only natural, for instance, that the lawyer will tend to see it in legal terms; an HR person will see it in personnel terms; an engineer will focus on technical aspects; a public relations person will look to a communication solution; and so on through the executive team.

If the organisation can't agree on the definition of the issue, it is virtually impossible to work towards a practical and realistic objective. An effective method to accurately define an issue is to agree on a single sentence based on the following formula (Jaques, 2000a):

PROBLEM + IMPACT = ISSUE

This approach has two distinct benefits. First, it forces the organisation to define the issue in a concise way that can be easily understood and communicated (problem) rather than relying on a complex situational analysis and pages of descriptive text. Second, it drives the focus beyond just the problem itself to why it is important to the organisation (impact).

This is most easily explained by a realistic example. If a senior manager said the issue that needed to be addressed was 'water', it could be interpreted in many different ways. How much better if the issue was defined as:

> There is a growing scarcity of water in the community where our factory is located (problem) and a water shortage would threaten our planned increase in production (impact).

Or:

> We use a large volume of water in a dry area (problem) and local farmers claim our wells are lowering the water table and their livestock are starving (impact).

Or:

> Our production process needs to discharge large quantities of contaminated water (problem) and government regulators are threatening to close us down if we continue to pollute the nearby river (impact).

In each case the problem and its impact are unambiguously stated, and the definition would lead directly to the subsequent objectives and tactics. However, it is important to recognise that the organisation is seldom alone in defining the issue. Government, the news media and various publics can have a significant, sometimes even decisive, influence on determining what is regarded as an issue.

A classic example occurred when it was announced that shark fin soup would be on the wedding menu at the soon-to-be-opened Disneyworld in Hong Kong. Global and local environmental activist groups used the announcement to highlight the cruelty of the 'finning' process and called for a boycott. In response, Disney protested that shark fin soup is a traditional Chinese delicacy, served in high-class restaurants throughout Hong Kong and around the world, and the issue had nothing to do with them. But after a month of adverse publicity and damage to its reputation, Disney agreed to remove shark fin soup from its wedding menu.[3]

The role of activist publics in defining and framing issues is discussed in detail in Chapter 5. For more on issue definition see Jaques (2004).

STEP TWO: OBJECTIVE

A well-chosen and carefully worded definition establishes the firm foundation for effective issue management. More specifically, it provides the basis upon which the organisation can reach consensus on an agreed objective.

For the purposes of planning it is preferable that there is a single overarching objective. Often there are various possible alternatives, and these must be properly weighed in terms of what is reasonably achievable and what resources are available. While there are sometimes several possible objectives, one usually stands out above the others.

Consider our previous hypothetical example: our production process needs to discharge large quantities of contaminated water, and government regulators are threatening to close us down if we continue to pollute the nearby river. In this case there would be a number of possible strategic approaches to determine what the focus should be:

1. Buy time to substantially reduce the volume of contaminated water generated (operational).

2. Call on independent experts to demonstrate there is no real adverse impact on the local river (technical).

3. Argue no change is needed because the discharge is within the operating licence (legal).

4. Raise concerns about the risk to local jobs and taxes if the plant closes (government and community affairs).

These and other possible strategies might all be appropriate, or perhaps a combination of more than one may ultimately be implemented. But for the purposes of planning, it would make an enormous difference whether the agreed objective was: (a) to recognise there is a problem and commit to make improvement; or (b) to deny there is a problem and gather evidence to support the need for no change. It is that decision that would determine the objective and set the framework for the entire strategic plan. For detailed discussion on objective setting see Jaques (2005a).

---

3   For discussion of the shark fin case, see Swann (2008, pp. 295–298) in this chapter's Further reading section.

> Objectives should not represent whatever levels of achievement management thinks would be 'nice'. Wishful thinking has no place in objective setting. For objectives to serve as a tool for stretching an organisation to reach its full potential, they must be challenging but achievable.
>
> Arthur Thompson and Lonnie Strickland (1995, p. 34)

Beyond this hypothetical example, in broad terms a strategic objective for managing any major issue should meet the following criteria:

+ There should be a single, overarching issue objective.
+ The issue objective must be fully aligned with relevant organisational strategies and objectives.
+ It should specifically address or respond to the issue.
+ It must be clear, unambiguous and measurable.
+ It must be easily stated and communicated.
+ It must have top management understanding, support and commitment.

STEP THREE: INTENDED OUTCOMES

While setting a clear objective is essential, some issues can appear to be almost overwhelmingly broad or complex. Therefore it is useful to divide the overall objective into discrete, comprehensible and manageable tasks, which can be called sub-objectives, or 'bite size pieces'. These manageable tasks simplify the transition from objectives to tactics, and in the Do-it Plan© they are called 'intended outcomes'.

The term 'desired outcomes' is commonly used in management systems, but 'intended outcomes' has a different and much more active meaning. Desired outcomes are what we would like to *see* happen. Intended outcomes, by contrast, are what we plan to *make* happen. The difference is significant as it moves the thinking from 'Wouldn't it be nice if ...' to 'What we plan to do is ...' In essence, it captures the difference between talking about it and doing it, and issue management is fundamentally a discipline about proactive, planned action.

Each intended outcome makes a positive contribution to achieving the overarching objective by identifying a specific outcome that will help deliver that objective. As a sub-objective, the intended outcome typically describes what needs to be done in a discrete area. Facing a hypothetical issue, the objective might be broken up into intended outcomes such as the following:

+ Government regulators understand and agree with our strategy.
+ Independent experts speak out in support of our approach.
+ Community leaders are engaged and their concerns have been addressed.
+ Detailed information has been assembled to counter claims by activist opponents.
+ A proactive media strategy ensures neutral-to-positive coverage.

While these are generic, they illustrate that agreeing on intended outcomes focuses effort on what must be achieved, and provides an easily understood framework for tactics.

STEP FOUR: TACTICS

As previously described, it is a very human response to want to leap from identifying the problem straight to proposing tactics. This is sometimes referred to as working on the answer before making sure the question is clear.

Using the Do-it Plan© ensures that the tactics are focused on delivering each of the agreed outcomes, which in turn support the overarching objective. Of the four steps in the plan, identifying tactics is by far the easiest and most intuitive. This is where the standard tools of public relations come into play.

Take just one of the hypothetical intended outcomes above: 'Community leaders are engaged and their concerns have been addressed.' The detailed tactics to achieve this outcome might include:

+ Identify the key community leaders.
+ Decide how they will be initially approached.
+ Develop briefing materials.
+ Organise an appropriate forum for ongoing engagement.
+ Nominate and train selected organisation participants.
+ Secure mutual agreement on the engagement process.
+ Listen to and record community concerns.
+ Agree on how any unsolved differences will be managed.
+ Develop feedback and reporting mechanisms.

This list is not in sequence and is not exhaustive, but it illustrates that the tactics fall very easily out of the intended outcomes. In addition, to be effective, each tactic must be accompanied by the name of the individual who will implement that tactic, and the timeframe by which progress and completion is required. That doesn't mean the person named will necessarily actually do the task, or will do it alone. But it does mean that the person named is accountable to make sure the task is completed, and on schedule.

When all the tactics are recorded for each intended outcome, the cumulative result is an issue management plan that is practical and workable; is easily communicated upwards in the organisation; and, most importantly, is focused on delivering an agreed objective in order to make a difference to the issue.

EVALUATION

Evaluation in public relations is the subject of an extensive literature, and generates heated debate among students, practitioners and academics. And if evaluation is an acknowledged challenge in public relations generally, it is regarded as even more difficult when it comes to issue management.

The challenge, of course, is that much of the effort in issue management is spent on anticipating problems before they get worse. In other words, evaluating the impact of what *could* have happened if the issue had not been managed; the cost of the crisis that *might* have happened, but was successfully avoided.

This conundrum was neatly captured by Australian practitioner David Goodwin (2000), who tells the anecdote of an External Affairs Manager who, under pressure to describe her role, says, 'I keep the elephants away.' 'But there are no elephants,' comes the reply from a sceptical CEO. To which she responds: 'See what a great job I'm doing!'

'Effective issues management is like that,' Goodwin concluded. 'Inconspicuous when it is successful, and valued most highly in its absence' (2000, p. 5). As a result, the most effective issue management is sometimes the issue management you don't see.

Another distinct challenge for evaluation in this field is that issue campaigns can last months or years and it is genuinely difficult to assess incremental changes. For instance, the campaign against Nestlé in relation to the marketing of baby formula has been running for more than 30 years (see www.info.babymilkaction.org and Cohn, 2000). Another high-profile example is the ongoing campaign by public health activists to limit the damage caused by cigarette smoking, and the dogged counter-campaign waged by the big tobacco companies. Derry and Waikar (2008) have analysed this prolonged effort over a period of more than 50 years.

Although it is rare for issues to continue at a high level of intensity over such a long period, the tobacco case in particular highlights an important lesson for evaluating the success of issue campaigns; namely that such campaigns are incremental and the evaluation needs to reflect the incremental nature of the plan. In other words, the campaign against cigarettes has seen progressive advances over decades, even though the overarching objective of eliminating cigarette smoking as a public health risk is still far from being achieved. However, no one would seriously claim on that basis that the campaign so far had not been successful. There have been major advances, such as eliminating tobacco sponsorship of sport, and banning smoking in cinemas and in many restaurants. Each of these achievements (and many others) is a victory (or an intended outcome) for the anti-smoking issue along the path towards it ultimate goal (the overarching objective).

Similarly, conventional, shorter-term issue strategies can also be effectively evaluated by assessing success against progressive elements. In the case of the Do-it Plan©, for example, evaluation should be against successful implementation of each of the intended outcomes, which it has been agreed will deliver the objective.

In this way, the key to evaluating an issue campaign is not necessarily to assess against immediate achievement of the overall objective but rather to measure the successful implementation of intermediate tactical steps towards the ultimate goal. Given the complexity and intractability of some issues, the most practical evaluation should therefore be against the plan, not necessarily against the issue.

A plan is a list of actions arranged in whatever sequence is thought likely to achieve an objective.

Author and cofounder of the Strategic Planning Society, John Argenti

ISSUE MANAGEMENT BEST PRACTICE

Planning for issue management extends beyond a process to develop and implement a successful plan to deal with a particular issue or cluster of issues. It also includes planning for how to introduce the actual process and structure of issue management into an organisation, and how to evaluate the effectiveness of the discipline itself.

Bridges and Nelson (2000) highlighted that issue management is a continuous process that emphasises monitoring the environment and making adjustments to feedback from both the external and internal environments. Although not identified specifically as best practice, they captured what they called 'ten functions of effective issue management' (p. 97):

1. integrating public policy issues analysis and audits into strategic planning

2. monitoring standards of organisational performance to discover key publics' perceptions of the organisation

3. developing and implementing ethical codes of organisational social accountability

4. assisting senior management make decisions on goals and policies in reaction to public opinion

5. identifying, defining, prioritising and analysing issues of greatest operational, financial and political significance

6. creating multidimensional proactive and reactive response plans from among issue-change strategy options

7. establishing relationships with like-minded individuals and groups, including the media

8. communicating on the most important issues for the organisation and publics to establish an agenda and build external support

9. influencing public opinion in order to stall or thwart undesirable legislation or regulation

10. evaluating issues management objectives to measure success, direct improvement and make recommendations to management.

These ten functions have been widely cited and used as a basis upon which emerging planning systems can be assessed.

Subsequently, the US-based Issue Management Council (IMC, 2005) developed nine best practice indicators that have become a de facto standard. The IMC recognised that it was not possible to propose a single 'best practice model' given the enormous variation between the demands of different issues and the needs and resources of different organisations. Therefore the nine indicators were developed to identify common criteria among successful issue managers, and at the same time to provide aspirational or stretch goals.

An organisation would not necessarily need to have all nine standards in place to be best in class and, as needs and emphases vary greatly between different fields of enterprise, they carry no weighting. However, they crystallise the wisdom and experience of practitioners and academics, and set out the goals for those who aspire to perform and contribute to issue management at the highest level.

Basically, they help organisations answer two questions:

1. How do we do it? That is, what steps do we need to take to implement best practice issue management?

2. How are we doing? That is, how does our process compare when benchmarked against leading organisations?

The indicators are divided into three categories: structure, implementation and integration.

STRUCTURE

1. There is an established mechanism to identify current and future issues through environmental scanning/issue analysis.

2. The organisation has adopted a formal process to assign and manage issues.

3. Responsibility for stewardship of the issue management process is clearly assigned and mechanisms are in place to build organisational expertise in the discipline.

IMPLEMENTATION

4. 'Ownership' of each major issue is clearly assigned at an operational level with accountability and results linked to performance reviews.

5. Progress against key issues is formally reviewed with organisational 'owners' on a regular basis and the status of each is monitored at the highest management level.

6. The Executive Committee or Board of Directors has fiduciary oversight of issue management; has mechanisms in place to report progress to directors and/or external stakeholders; and has authority to intervene in the event of non-compliance or misalignment.

INTEGRATION

7. Formal channels exist for managers at all levels to identify and elevate potential issues for possible integration into broader strategic planning, including external stakeholder management.

8. Management of current and future issues is well embedded within the strategic planning and implementation processes of organisational clients or owners.

9. Issue management is recognised and organisationally positioned as a core management function that is not confined to a single function or department.

Recognising that different organisations may interpret achievement of each best practice indicator in different ways, IMC later developed five specific reference points for each indicator. In the same way that the indicators are not standards but are intended as guidance to what can be achieved by organisations operating at best practice, so too the reference points are not intended as audit checks or compulsory requirements. (Use of the best practice indicators is discussed in further detail in Jaques, 2005b.) The reference points provide practical examples of what procedures or documentation an organisation might establish to demonstrate achievement of a particular best practice indicator.[4]

Note: parts of this chapter draw on Jaques (2000a) and (2005b).

KEY POINTS

+ Issue management and strategic planning should be closely aligned, but are distinctly different disciplines.

+ Formal planning not only provides a framework for strategy development but also delivers other important benefits.

+ There are recognised barriers to effective issue management and a lack of a clear goal is one of the most important.

+ Planning needs to follow simple, clear and assessable steps.

+ Objective setting highlights the difference between 'what we are trying to achieve' and 'what we need to do'.

+ Progress on issues can realistically be assessed against the plan, not necessarily against the issue.

+ Best practice indicators help understand how to implement issue management and also how to benchmark against successful organisations.

☰ ACTIVITIES AND DISCUSSION

1. Why do some planning processes become too complicated? What can be done to resist excessive complexity?

2. Discuss the risks that can occur if an issue is managed without following a plan. Will a plan address all these risks?

3. Identify a current issue and work through the Do-it Plan©, drafting a formal definition and objective, intended outcome and some tactics (using the worked example in the Appendix as a guide).

4. Research the best practice indicators and forty-five reference points developed by the Issue Management Council. Which do you think may be mainly for organisations starting out, as opposed to those that might be more for advanced systems?

---

4 The full IMC document with all reference points can be seen at www.issuemanagement.org/learnmore/best-practice-indicators.

NATIONALISM VERSUS ANIMAL RIGHTS—VALUE ADVOCACY IN CORPORATE ISSUE MANAGEMENT

Aimei Yang

University of Southern California

In 2012, the China Securities Regulatory Commission published a list of companies to be registered for public trade on the stock exchange market. The list triggered a national controversy because one of the companies was Guizhentang Pharmaceutical Company, a company that harvests Asian black bear bile. Asian black bear bile is valued in traditional Chinese medicine. However, the Asian black bear is also an endangered animal, and the process by which bile is extracted is considered cruel to the bears. The daily extraction process results in severe physical problems and a high mortality rate.

Soon after publication of the list, Animals Asian Foundation (AAF) teamed up with a group of Chinese NGOs and seventy-two celebrities to send petition letters to the China Securities Regulatory Commission. Guizhentang's application for being listed on the market was halted and the company was negatively covered in the media as being immoral and cruel to animals. During the peak of public outrage, thousands of Chinese submitted online complaints and petition letters to stop Guizhentang's plan to expand its bear farm once publicly traded. The company's website was hacked several times.

The public outcry against Guizhentang reflected a changing public opinion about animal rights in China. In recent decades, NGOs and environmental activists had made great efforts to educate the Chinese public and raise societal awareness of animal rights. Many Chinese perceive the movement towards ethical treatment of animals to also be a sign of societal progress and modernisation, particularly in medicine.

Traditional Chinese medicine treats patients with natural plant, animal and mineral remedies, including the use of animal parts from endangered wild animals. These practices violate international conservation agreements and further threaten already endangered species. Activists sought to highlight the Guizhentang case as part of a broader initiative to promote ethical treatment of animals and a more modern approach to Chinese medicine.

Organisations that fail to live up to social expectations and values may incur serious social disapproval that can substantially jeopardise the development of those organisations. One source of organisational issues is when a gap opens up between the way an organisation behaves and the way key stakeholders believe it should behave. In this case, the discrepancy between the changing public opinion about animal rights in China and the way Guizhentang treated Asian black bears undermined the legitimacy of the company and created a potential reputational crisis.

In response to the public outcry, Guizhentang and the Chinese Medicine Association held a press conference and launched a series of press releases arguing that some of the NGOs, specifically AAF, had financial connections with international pharmaceutical companies, and that AAF was using this opportunity to sabotage the development of traditional Chinese medicine.

Framing is a key element in planning an issue management strategy, and Guizhentang's response framed itself as a company that cares about animal rights and contributes to sustainable development and Chinese medicine. The response also framed the NGOs as front groups for foreign businesses striving to hurt the future of Chinese medicine. Although Guizhentang's response did not completely change the tone of media coverage, it successfully influenced the topics of the discussion and introduced the concern for nationalism into the public discourse of what started as an animal rights issue. After the distraction of public attention, despite the previous criticism and nationwide negative news, Guizhentang managed to survive this potential crisis.

Guizhentang's response fits well within framing theory and the concept of advocacy speech. Advocacy speech is used to create a relationship between the public and the organisation based on their mutual support of a specific social value. The value Guizhentang sought to promote was nationalism. In the era of global economic and technological interdependence, nationalism has remained an influential force for economic behaviours and consumer preference in China. Guizhentang and the Chinese Medicine Association were able to promote nationalism and take pride in traditional Chinese medicine, while accusing the activists of supporting Western medicine and values.

When the news media published excerpts from the press releases and statements, the frame of the news coverage changed. While Guizhentang's treatment of animals continued to be an underlying storyline, analysis showed the importance of supporting nationalism and traditional Chinese medicine became the most prominent frame in both the online and print news coverage.

This case demonstrates that value advocacy speech as a strategy can indeed influence media coverage. Advocating for nationalism to a certain extent restored Guizhentang's legitimacy while threatening the legitimacy of AAF by criticising the activists' stance on such an important societal value. Practitioners need to consider carefully the ethical implications of prioritising one value over another. Further, globalisation increases the chance for corporations to be affected by political and economic conditions in multiple countries. In the globalisation era, nationalism may have a profound influence over international public relations practice.

For more detailed discussion of this case see:

Yang, A. & Veil, S. (2013, May). *Animal rights versus nationalism: A semantic network analysis of values advocacy in corporate crisis*. Paper presented at the annual conference of International Communication Association (Public Relations Division), London.

LOST IN TRANSLATION—TOURISM AUSTRALIA'S 'WHERE THE BLOODY HELL ARE YOU?' CAMPAIGN

Mark Sheehan

Deakin University, Melbourne

Images of nations are the major marketing tools in global tourism. Successive Australian tourism campaigns for international travellers have selectively used recognisable identities, stereotypes and locales for appropriate markets; for example, well-known cricketers and cricket grounds for the UK and India.

But such recognisable images can become clichéd and tourist authorities sometimes turn to an evocative slogan or catchphrase; for example, something that reflects a nation's wonders ('Incredible India') or diversity ('Malaysia—truly Asia').

In 2006 Tourism Australia chose to spice up the country's images with a very Australian invitation—but failed to identify a potential issue and failed to plan for how to deal with the issue. 'So where the bloody hell are you?' was a $180 million advertising campaign that featured Australians getting ready to receive visitors to their country. The 'Australian invitation' campaign was intended to reach 'a more sophisticated global traveller' with income and education, who is open-minded and well travelled. Tourism Australia designed the campaign for a large market that they labelled 'experience seekers' who 'seek out and enjoy authentic personal experiences they can talk about, involve themselves in holiday activities ... are active in their pursuits and come away having learnt something, are somewhat adventurous and ... place high value on contrasting experiences'.

Prior to its release, aspects of the campaign were tested in fifty-four focus groups involving participants from Australia's top seven tourism markets, presumably reflecting the 'experience seeker'. But market research is no substitute for stakeholder analysis. Messages in the mass media reach not only the intended market, but also other stakeholders including the wider public and the bodies who regulate communication. This lack of planning methodology was the making of a crisis for Tourism Australia.

The 'Australian invitation' featured a range of print and audio-visual materials featuring iconic Australian landscapes including the outback, the beach and rainforests, as well as urban areas. Ordinary Australian characters introduced each of the scenes with comments like: 'We've poured you a beer; we've had the camels shampooed; we've saved you a spot on the beach; we've got the sharks out of the pool and we've got the 'roos off the green.' The last scene of the television advertisement featured bikini-clad Sydney model Lara Bingle asking: 'So where the bloody hell are you?'

The target market appeared to embrace such a bold catchphrase and the campaign itself received extensive media coverage, but for all the wrong reasons. In March 2007 it was banned by the UK's Broadcast Advertising Clearance Centre, which would not allow the word 'bloody' in television versions of the commercial. Following lobbying by Tourism Australia, including a visit to the UK by Australia's tourism minister Fran Bailey and model Lara Bingle, the ban was lifted, although a 9 p.m. 'curfew' was imposed on television commercials.

In the meantime, the UK's Advertising Standards Authority (ASA) ordered the removal of roadside billboards bearing the slogan. The ASA said it had received thirty-two complaints and warned Tourism Australia to refrain from using profanity in future billboards. The advertisement was also banned by regulators in Canada, owing to the implication of 'unbranded alcohol consumption' by the opening line: 'We've poured you a beer.' There was also concern in Canada at the word 'hell' being used as an expletive. In Singapore, the advertisement campaign was presented as, 'So where are you?'—with the offending words removed.

The campaign was intended to attract visitors to Australia from Japan, Germany and the UK, but tourist figures show that during October 2006 the number of Japanese tourists visiting Australia fell by 5.7 per cent compared with the same period in 2005. German tourists were down 4.7 per cent and UK visitors dropped 2.3 per cent, although there was a slight increase in tourists from the USA and also China (where the advertisement was not screened).

In Japan it was culture and not prudishness that brought about the slogan's demise because it proved impossible to translate, leaving Tourism Australia to ask: 'So? Why don't you come?' superimposed over the original invitation.

Incoming Labor Prime Minister Kevin Rudd described it as 'rolled gold disaster'. It wasn't just the language that caused problems. The catchphrase question gave rise to humorous alternative answers and even more questions. Parodies appeared on comedy shows in Australia and New Zealand and went viral on YouTube. The British press taunted Australia with the question after the UK surpassed Australia's medal tally at the Beijing Olympics and England scored a cricket test victory in Australia, asking: 'Where the bloody hell were you?'

The choice to use only 'experience seeker' focus groups was a serious error in issue planning and analysis. In countries where the message was changed it caused confusion and image uncertainty in the target audience. For others it may have simply reinforced an Australian reputation of boorishness that continued long after the question was answered.

For more detailed discussion of this case see:

Sheehan, M. (2012). *The language of tourism: Perfecting soft skills in a flat world*. Paper presented at the 34th All India Public Relations Conference—Communication strategies for travel and tourism, 29 September–1 October 2012, Shimla HP, India.[5]

---

5   See also Winter and Gallon (2008) in this chapter's Further reading section.

REFERENCES

Bridges, J. & Nelson, R. A. (2000). Issues management: A relational approach. In J. A. Ledingham & S. D. Bruning (Eds.), *Public relations as relationship management: A relational approach to the study and practice of public relations* (pp. 95–115). Mahwah, NJ: Lawrence Erlbaum.

Bryan, J. L. (1977). The coming revolution in issues management: Elevate and simplify. *Communication World, 14*(7), 12–14.

Catania, T. F. (2002). Whirlpool integrates issue management for strategic gain. *Corporate Public Issues and their Management, 24*(1), 1–7.

Chase, W. H. (1984). *Issue management: Origins of the future.* Stamford, CT: Issue Action Publications.

Cohn, R. (2000). When Nestlé crackled. In *The PR crisis bible: How to take charge of the media when all hell breaks loose* (pp. 84–90). New York: Truman Talley.

Derry, R. & Waikar, S. V. (2008). Frames and filters: Strategic distrust as a legitimation tool in the 50-year battle between public health activists and Big Tobacco. *Business & Society, 47*(1), 102–139.

Goodwin, D. (2000). Issues management: The art of keeping the elephants away. *Corporate Public Affairs, 10*(1), 5–8.

Heath, R. L. (1997). *Strategic issues management: Organisations and public policy challenges.* Thousand Oaks, CA: Sage.

Issue Management Council. (2005). *Best practice indicators.* Retrieved from http:// issuemanagement.org/learnmore/best-practice-indicators/.

Jaques, T. (2009). Integrating issue management and strategic planning: Unfulfilled promise or future opportunity? *International Journal of Strategic Communication, 3*(1), 19–33.

Jaques, T. (2008). *Refocusing issue management: Bridging academic and practitioner perspectives.* PhD Dissertation, RMIT University, Melbourne, Australia.

Jaques, T. (2005a). Systematic objective setting for effective issue management. *Journal of Public Affairs, 5*(1), 33–42.

Jaques, T. (2005b). Using best practice indicators to benchmark issue management. *Public Relations Quarterly, 50*(2), 8–11.

Jaques, T. (2004). Issue definition: The neglected foundation of effective issue management. *Journal of Public Affairs, 4*(2), 191–200.

Jaques, T (2000a). *Don't just stand there—The Do-it Plan for effective issue management.* Melbourne: Issue Outcomes.

Jaques, T. (2000b). Developments in the use of process models for effective issue management. *Asia Pacific Public Relations Journal, 2*(2), 125–132.

Jones, B. L. & Chase, W. H. (1979). Managing public policy issues. *Public Relations Review, 5*(2), 3–23.

Marx, T. G. (1986). Integrating public affairs and strategic planning. *California Management Review, 29*(1), 141–147.

McGrath, G. B. (1998). *Issues management: Anticipation and influence.* San Francisco: IABC.

Morgan, L. & Squires, S. (2012, Spring). Before crisis hits. *Food and Drink,* 10–11.

Murphy, J. J. (1989). Identifying strategic issues. *Long Range Planning, 22*(2), 101–105.

Perrott, B. E. (1995). Strategic issue management: An integrated framework. *Journal of General Management, 21*(2), 52–64.

Regester, M. & Larkin, J. (2005). *Risk issues and crisis management: A case book of best practice* (3rd ed.). London: Kogan Page.

Thompson, A. A. & Strickland, A. J. (1995). *Strategic management: Concepts and cases.* Chicago: Irwin.

Van Ruler, B. & Vercic, D. (2005). Reflective communication management: Future ways for public relations research. In P. Kalbfleisch (Ed.), *Communication Yearbook, 29* (pp. 239–273). Mahwah, NJ: Lawrence Erlbaum.

FURTHER READING

Cothran, H. & Clouser, R. (2009). *Strategic planning for communities, non-profit organizations and public agencies.* Institute of Food and Agricultural Science, University of Florida. Retrieved from www.csus.edu/indiv/s/shulockn/Executive%20Fellows%20PDF%20readings/U%20FL%20Strategic%20Planning.pdf.

Holzer, B. (2008). Turning stakeseekers into stakeholders: A political coalition perspective on the politics of stakeholder influence. *Business and Society, 47*(1), 1–18.

Matera, F. R. & Artigue R. J. (2000). The issues campaign: Managing molehills before they become mountains. In *Public relations campaigns and techniques: Building bridges into the 21st century* (pp. 164–171). Needham Heights, MN: Allyn & Brown.

McDaniel, P. A., Intinarelli, G. & Malone, R. E. (2008). Tobacco industry issues management organisations: Creating a global corporate network to undermine public health. *Globalisation and Health, 4*(2).

Rose, C. (2009). The Gurkhas campaign: Lessons from Lumley. *Campaign Strategy Newsletter, 52.* Retrieved from www.campaignstrategy.com.

Swann, P. (2008). *Cases in Public Relations.* New York: McGraw-Hill.

Swartz, J. (2010, September). How I did it: Timberland's CEO on standing up to 65,000 angry activists. *Harvard Business Review*, 39–43.

Veil, S. R. & Kent, M. L. (2008). Issues management and inoculation: Tylenol's responsible dosing advertising. *Public Relations Review, 34*(3), 399–402.

Winter, C. & Gallon, S. (2008). Exploring attitudes toward Tourism Australia's 'Where the bloody hell are you?' campaign. *Current Issues in Tourism, 11*(4), 301–314.

5

ISSUE MANAGEMENT— ACTIVISM

CHAPTER OBJECTIVES

This chapter will help you to:

+ understand the impact of activism in the evolution of issue management

+ introduce some of the 'rules' for effective activist campaigning

+ differentiate between criteria that separate corporate and activist strategies

+ learn how digital media has increased activist capability

+ assess the arguments for negotiation versus confrontation

+ identify issue redefinition as an effective activist strategy

+ recognise the different corporate responses to activist attacks.

Activism and the organisational response to activist campaigns are major factors in the creation of the modern face of issue management. But while the tools available to activists have progressed substantially in recent years, the basic concept of activism remains largely unchanged.

More than 20 years ago the influential US academic Larissa Grunig (1992, p. 504) developed a definition that is still valid and widely used today:

> An activist public is a group of two or more individuals who organise in order to influence another public or publics through action that may include education, compromise, persuasion tactics or force.

Various different terms are now used to describe what Grunig called 'an activist public', including community groups, citizen campaigns, single-issue lobby groups, pressure groups, grass-roots campaigns, advocacy groups, special interest groups and non-government organisations. One reason for these alternative terms is that, to some people, the word 'activist' has a narrow and even disparaging meaning, suggesting people confronting police in violent demonstrations or lying in front of bulldozers rather than sitting in the boardroom negotiating change. These associations may be regarded as negative, and something to be avoided.

In this chapter the term 'activist' is used in the neutral way defined by Grunig. However, it is true that various activist groups choose very different issue strategies to promote their objectives, and these are discussed shortly.

> The focus on corporations is relatively new. Activists traditionally focused on governments as the targets for achieving change. While governments continue to be targeted, corporations are increasingly seen as valid targets due to the growing economic and political power they wield.
>
> Duane Raymond (2003, p. 214)

Although modern tools and media operations have greatly increased the capability and profile of activist groups, activism is nothing new. Social and community activism blossomed in the mid nineteenth century with the great campaigns against slavery and child labour. It continued into the early twentieth century with women's suffrage and prohibition, then on through feminism, the anti-war movement, land rights and racial equality, up to campaigns concerning AIDS, globalisation and the environment (Jaques, 2006). In fact, Ingrid Newkirk, founder of the modern animal rights group PETA, has said she sees herself as part of a long history in liberating the weak and the unprotected—slaves, blacks, children and women. Animals, she says, are just one more link in the chain of freeing a species of the universe (cited in Burke, 2005, p. 42).

Much of the early activism proceeded largely within a framework of national politics rather than the more recent context of organised community action. While national political activism remains strong, activism overall has become a much more widely applied concept, both within and between countries. Indeed, Doh and Guay (2006) described the rising influence of NGOs as 'one of the most significant developments in international affairs over the past 20 years' (p. 51).

One of the first people to develop written guidelines for community action, which provided form and focus, was the Chicago community organiser Saul Alinsky (1909–1972), who wrote the seminal book *Rules for radicals: A practical primer for realistic radicals* (1971), which remains a classic source. It is significant that issue management as a corporate discipline was born just a few years later, when business leaders began to understand that the rules of the game in terms of influencing public policy had changed.

Even though Alinksy himself was sometimes anarchic in his programs of direct action,[1] one of his major contributions was to recognise the importance of planning and structure to achieve strategic outcomes—very much in line with the principles of issue management. As elaborated and explained in his book, the rules for activism set out by Alinsky were:

- Power is not only what you have but what the enemy thinks you have.
- Never go outside the experience of your people.
- Wherever possible go outside the experience of the enemy.
- Make the enemy live up to their own book of rules.
- Ridicule is man's most potent weapon.
- A good tactic is one that your people enjoy.
- A tactic that drags on too long becomes a drag.
- Keep the pressure on.
- The threat is usually more terrifying than the thing itself.
- The major premise for tactics is the development of operations that will maintain a constant pressure on the opposition.
- If you push a negative hard and deep enough it will break through into its counterside.[2]
- The price of a successful attack is a constructive alternative.
- Pick the target, freeze it, personalise it and polarise it (Alinsky, 1971, pp. 127–130).

Over the subsequent years, an enormous body of material has emerged on the how-to of activism, which often reflects a contemporary application of Alinsky's original 'rules' (see Jaques, 2006). More broadly it deals with the hands-on implementation of activism, such as planning and strategy; dealing with the media; creating an organisation; raising funds, organising a demonstration or event; and building coalitions and alliances (see the box, 'How to be an activist issue manager' for online and printed resources).

---

1 Alinsky described some of his more outrageous direct actions in a 1972 interview with *Playboy* magazine shortly before his death, reprinted and online in *The Progress Report* at www.progress.org/2003/alinsky2.htm.

2 Alinsky explained that if a corporate target comes under severe enough pressure, it may do something unwise or even illegal that may damage it, such as sending someone to break into the activists' office or illegally hacking in to their computers.

HOW TO BE AN ACTIVIST ISSUE MANAGER

There is a veritable treasure trove of how-to sources in relation to activism. In fact, the production and distribution of such guidelines and manuals has in itself become an activist strategy to motivate and mobilise community action.

One rich resource of material is the European-based organisation Community Builders, which has an online library of more than forty activist manuals in downloadable format from around the world (www.communitybuilders.ro/library/manuals), on subjects including coalition-building, how to organise boycotts, strategic planning, engaging stakeholders, and motivating and involving youth.

Another valuable source is the UK-based National Council for Voluntary Organisations (www.ncvo-vol.org.uk/campaigning-resources), which has a fifty-two-page handbook on campaigning, plus fact sheets and focus guides on subjects such as how to analyse issues, building a strategy, using social media, and identifying routes of influence (all free and downloadable).

Similarly, the California-based organisation Net Action focuses on online activism and promoting citizen action campaigns, and has extensive materials including a free downloadable virtual activist training course (www.netaction.org).

Then there are websites with links to dozens of online manuals and other resources, such as the Emory University School of Law (www.law.emory.edu/ihr/advlinks.html) or the UK e-campaigning forum (http://southwarkorganising.wordpress.com/reading-about-activism-campaigning), which catalogue scores of books and manuals, many with free downloads and others linking to paid sites.

Another online resource is manuals produced by activist organisations themselves. A good example is the 320-page downloadable *Campaigning Manual* produced by Amnesty International (www.amnesty.org/en/library/info/ACT10/002/1997). Briefer, more issue-specific manuals include the PETA guide, *Effective Advocacy: Planning for Success* (www.mediapeta.com/peta/PDF/EffectiveAdvocacyGuide_FINAL300.pdf) or the series of How to Win campaign guides, published by Friends of the Earth, UK (www.foe.co.uk/community/resource/how_to_win_guides.html).

In addition to this brief sampling of online resources, there is also a substantial library of conventional books on activism. More recent how-to titles include the following:

+ *The activists' handbook: A step-by-step guide to participatory democracy* (Aidan Ricketts, Zed Books, London, 2012)

+ *Going public: An organiser's guide to citizen action* (Michael Gecan, Anchor/Doubleday, New York, 2004)

+ *Getting started in communication: A practical guide for activists and organisations* (Michael Norton and Purba Dutta, Sage, New Delhi, 2003)

+ *The global activist's manual: Acting locally to change the world* (Mike Prokosch and Laura Raymond (Eds.), Nation Books, New York, 2002)

+ *The Protesters' Handbook* (Bibi van Derzee, Guardian Books, London, 2010)

+ *How to win campaigns: Communicating for Change* (2nd ed.) (Chris Rose, Earthscan, London, 2010)

+ *Counterpower: Making things happen* (Tim McGee, New Internationalist, Oxford, UK, 2011)

+ *The everyday activist: Everything you need to know to get off your backside and start to make a difference* (Michael Norton, Boxtree (Macmillan), Basingstoke, 2007).

The term 'issue management' is seldom if ever used in this activist material, most likely because of its perceived negative association with big business and big government. But any sampling of the how-to literature reveals that the tools and processes of issue management have been widely and enthusiastically adopted and embraced by activist organisations.

ACTIVISM AND THE IMPACT OF TECHNOLOGY

Without doubt the greatest advance in issue management in the last 20 years has been the rise of the internet and social media (as introduced in Chapter 2). For activists, the digital revolution has brought particularly profound change, giving them a new weapon that can alter the organisation–stakeholder dynamic, potentially increase the power of activist groups, and make their concerns more salient to organisations and society.[3] According to Coombs (1998, p. 300), 'The reason for the power increase is the Internet's potential to alter organisational stakeholder networks so that an activist group's power to influence is increased while an organisation's ability to resist is reduced.'

In summary, the internet and digital communication provide activists with a low-cost tool to secure information from companies and governments; to share information and disseminate ideas more widely; to recruit members, raise funds and build relationships with stakeholders; to generate letters and petitions; to drive issues onto the public agenda; to organise actions such as meetings, protests and marches; and to generate web attacks such as hacking or coordinated social media campaigns (Jaques, 2006). Moreover, social media has provided an increasingly powerful political activist tool, as shown during the so-called Arab Spring, which began in late 2010 and saw the overthrow of governments in the Middle East.[4]

Smith and Ferguson (2010) counsel moderation in the emphasis on the technological aspects and reminded us that, while there is no mistaking the impact of the internet and other inexpensive forms of communication on activism, it should remembered that activists continue to use a variety of tactics, not just the internet, to achieve their goals. However, the opportunities provided by electronic communications are very real. Using these new tools in early 2013, a young Australian anti-coal activist with a laptop distributed a fake news release with false bad news that triggered a $300 million crash in the share value

---

3 For discussion of activist use of social media, see Illia (2003), Joyce (2010), Kahn and Kellner (2004) and Tesh (2002) in this chapter's Further reading section.

4 The role of social media in the 'Arab Spring' protests in the Middle East has been widely discussed in the literature. See, for example, Newsom and Lengel (2012) in this chapter's Further reading section.

HOW ACTIVISTS WON THE TOY WAR

When the Santa Monica-based online toy retailer eToys.com won a US court ruling to strip a similar domain name from a European art collective, an online campaign was launched to damage the retailer in the busy pre-Christmas shopping period. Activists encouraged email complaints to the retailer's management; hacked into the company's e-commerce process to disrupt purchase transactions; and posed as investors on internet forums to talk down the company's value. In the space of two months the shares fell from $67 to $15 and the company surrendered, conceding the original domain name.

Source: Chris Thomas (2003, p. 120)

---

of coalminer Whitehaven ('Whitehaven coal share plunge', 2013). When the hoax was exposed, the share price quickly recovered and the hoaxer found himself under arrest. Similarly, Greenpeace used social media to mount an attack on Mattel in order to highlight their environmental campaign against rainforest logging (Stine, 2011). Such cases and many other examples are a reminder that the capability of activists has changed forever.

ACTIVIST STRATEGIES—PRIORITISING EFFORT

In Chapter 3 we covered the formal way in which issues are identified and prioritised. We also covered the fact that organisations themselves don't necessarily decide what is an issue for them. Other stakeholders, particularly activist organisations, play a major role in deciding what is an issue, and also deciding what target organisation, or group of organisations, will be presented as the 'poster child'[5] for the issue, or the public face of the perceived problem.

The discussion of identification and prioritisation in Chapter 3 was largely from the perspective of business or government, most often in response to external events or developments which force the issue on them. But the way in which activist organisations select issues, and their motivation for getting involved in issue management, is typically very different.

Like corporations, activists sometimes feel themselves driven to get involved in issues that arise from external developments and directly affect them or their community, such as a planned new highway that will reduce the value of their homes; a proposed new regulation that will limit the choice of school for their children; or new restrictions that may reduce access to certain medication.

But unlike most business organisations, activists may also *choose* to get involved with issues that do not directly impact them but present a moral or ethical imperative, such as the slaughter of whales; the plight of child-soldiers in Africa; threats to freedom of the press in far distant countries; or human trafficking around the globe.

---

5   A poster child was originally a child afflicted by starvation or a disease used in posters to raise funds for a cause. It now also means a person or organisation that represents or embodies a cause, an issue or a problem.

> Activist groups vary in size, range of issue involvement, tactics and effectiveness—but all (especially the smallest, most active ones) are potentially damaging to the target organisation.
>
> Larissa Grunig (1992, p. 513)

While activist organisations have embraced many of the tools and processes of issue management as developed in the world of business, the question of issue identification and selection is one area where activists and business leaders have very different objectives and motivation. Whereas corporate issue managers tend to set measurable, specific goals aligned to defined strategic objectives in order to 'resolve' the issue, for some activist organisations the process of agitation and activism can be a legitimate goal in itself: 'By acting against the enemy, activist organisations declare themselves winners even when no territory is gained because of member fulfillment' (Derville, 2005, p. 530).[6]

This is a common theme in the activist literature, which frequently emphasises that a key purpose is to give members a sense of meaning and self-worth, and belief that they are improving society, plus, of course, the need to recruit new supporters and raise funds.[7] Clearly this doesn't generally apply to corporate issue managers. In line with this very different interpretation of 'success', activist organisations have quite distinct criteria when selecting issues.

Writing about this distinction, the German academics Matthias Winter and Ulrich Steger (1998) produced comparative checklists to illustrate their findings. The first was a conventional checklist for corporations to consider in defending their position on issues, which included plausibility, emotion, the strength of the company and its opponents, connection to other company or industry issues, the availability of allies, media impact, and the ease of achieving a solution. By contrast, they developed a very different issue checklist to inform the selection of issues by activist organisations.[8] According to Winter and Steger (1998, p. 83), for an activist issue to be successfully campaigned:

1. The campaign should have a clear aim or goal.

2. The issue is easily understood by the general public.

3. The issue has high symbolic value.

4. The issue has the potential to damage the image of the target company.

5. The opponent is strong enough (to avoid an 'underdog' effect that evokes sympathy).

6. The issue can be 'packaged' in a campaign in which the public can get involved.

---

6 The paper by Derville provides a thorough analysis of activist motivation and tactics, and the differences between radical and moderate activist organisations.

7 For interviews with consumer activists about individual motivation, see Kozenits and Handelman (2004) in this chapter's Further reading section.

8 Winter and Steger (1998) not only defined the business and activist processes for issue section and described them in detail, but also devoted almost half of their book to real-life case studies analysed against the two sets of criteria.

7. There are solutions that are confrontations, not gradual.

8. There could be a dramatic element to the campaign to engage the media.

THE POWER OF GLOBAL COALITIONS

The Bakun hydro-electric power scheme in Sarawak was planned to produce up to 15 per cent of the electricity requirements of Malaysia. The project was led by Swedish-Swiss ABB, one of the world's largest engineering companies, and attracted large-scale opposition. While local activists in Malaysia faced major hurdles to have real impact on environmental issues domestically, an international alliance of over 200 NGOs focused on ABB across environmentally conscious Europe and at their Swiss headquarters near Zurich. Even though construction had already begun, the controversial dam was halted and ABB was able to withdraw. A few years later the project resumed, this time led by a well-connected local company.[9]

For a non-academic approach to how activists should select issues, we can turn to three US social issues campaigners, Kim Bobo, Jackie Kendall and Steve Max. Their activist manual (1991) is a little dated, but is a remarkably thorough and practical publication, which sets out sixteen criteria for activists to choose an issue. The issue should:

1. result in a real improvement in people's lives (it will make a tangible difference)

2. give people a sense of their own power (the victory is for them, not for lawyers or experts)

3. alter the relations of power (it changes the way the other side makes decisions)

4. be worthwhile (members feel good about the cause)

5. be winnable (there is a good chance of success)

6. be widely felt (many people believe it's a real problem)

7. be deeply felt (people feel strongly enough to do something)

8. be easy to understand (the problem shouldn't require a long or difficult explanation)

9. have a clear target (that is, the person or people who can give you what you want)

10. have a clear timeframe (it needs a beginning, a middle and an end)

11. be non-divisive (it avoids issues that divide your constituency)

12. build leadership (the campaign needs leadership and also builds leaders)

13. set up the next campaign (it should lead to new campaigns on related issues)

14. have a pocketbook angle (that is, issues that earn or save people money)

15. raise money (it should provide opportunities to secure funding for the campaign)

16. be consistent with your values and vision (it should reflect your values and vision for an improved society) (Bobo, Kendall & Max, 1991, pp. 16–17).

---

9   For details on the Bakun campaign, see Winter and Steger (1998).

Unlike corporations, which typically believe the most successful issue management is issue management that is effective but out of sight, the activist criteria specifically prioritise issues that focus on conflict, will be fought out in public and have the greatest potential to attract media attention.[10] Activist tactics to support such issues are discussed later in this chapter.

> If protest tactics are not considered significant by the media, protest organisations will not succeed. Like a tree falling unheard in the forest there is no protest unless protest is perceived and projected.
>
> Michael Lipsky (1968, p. 1151)

ACTIVIST STRATEGIES—DEFINING THE ISSUE

Having selected a target issue, the activist organisation can choose from a range of strategic issue management approaches. The first and most direct is where activists are part of what is called a 'single issue group', where the basic principle of issue definition as previously described often applies—to be clear, precise and focused.

One example of this approach is where the issues revolve around a very specific proposition to be the subject of a vote of a regulatory bureaucratic decision. In these cases the issue needs to be formulated in a very clear and unambiguous way. It might be a local council decision whether to change Sunday shopping hours; or a referendum question put to public vote, such as whether the country should become a republic, or whether the law should be changed to recognise same-sex marriage. Or it might be a resolution to be voted on at a corporation annual general meeting, such as a proposal to withdraw investment in a country controlled by a brutal dictatorship, or a proposal to ban animal testing for the company's products.

Such issues—which typically revolve around a yes or no response—need to be extraordinarily focused if they are to be successful. The US activist Randy Shaw (2001) has examined the strategies behind ballot initiatives—which are common in the USA—and concluded that 'lack of simplicity' is all too often the fatal flaw leading to failure.[11]

ISSUE REDEFINITION

Clarity when defining the issue may be appropriate for ballot proposals or a one-off decision and is recommended for corporate issue managers trying to keep the debate focused. However, there is a counter-intuitive mechanism that lies behind many activists' strategies;

---

10 For discussion of activist strategies against corporate reputation, see Manheim and Holt (2013) in this chapter's Further reading section.

11 Ballot initiatives often take place at the same time as a government or local body election and ask electors to vote on specific issues affecting the community, such as a proposal to change a contentious regulation or whether to spend public money on a controversial local project.

namely to constantly redefine the issue in order to gain and retain the initiative. As Robert Heath (1997, p. 168) concluded:

> Activists use redefinition to place a new interpretation on a situation, a product (such as cigarettes) or a service, a corporation or industry, or a governmental agency. If the reinterpretation catches on, especially with reporters and followers, the company, industry or agency has become vulnerable to change.

From analysis of activist campaigns we can identify three distinct approaches to issue redefinition: moving target, transitional target and multiple target. The three approaches are summarised in Table 5.1 and then described in more detail.

Table 5.1 Activist issue redefinition grid

	Moving target approach	Transitional target approach	Multiple target approach
Field of debate	Remains generally within a given objective discipline	Deliberately moves from objective fact to subjective responses	Covers as many different fields as possible, both subjective and objective
Timing	Issue progressively redefined as each concern is addressed	Moves ground before objective concerns can be addressed	Multiple concerns and allegations are raised simultaneously
Broad purpose	Maintains appearance of objective debate but keeps responder off balance with fresh plausible allegations	Maximises emotive content of issue by focus on areas of opinion such as ethics, values or standards	Confuses responder, exhausts his resources and maximises the number and variety of different stakeholders

Source: Jaques (2004).

THE MOVING TARGET APPROACH

This applies where the issue is progressively redefined but remains within a given discipline, constantly moving the grounds of debate to keep the responder off balance, often over a prolonged time frame.

For example, activists who want to force withdrawal of a controversial medication might initially argue that the product has a range of potential adverse side effects that have not been adequately researched. As the manufacturer initiates new research and supportive information starts to emerge, activists move the target, alleging that the real problem is unknown risk to vulnerable patients such as children. Later the issue may move again, to allegations that there are synergistic risks when the product is used in conjunction with certain other medications, which have not been properly examined, or claims that long-term use of the product causes subtle and hard-to-disprove effects such as learning deficits or inhibition of development.

The US academics Celeste and Diedre Condit coined the expression 'incremental erosion' to describe this process and concluded that activists create points of view to which the targeted companies must continually respond and where issues are slowly and incrementally redefined to the advantage of the attacker (cited in Heath, 1997, p. 180).

Using this approach, activists are not required to prove their claims. They need only raise 'plausible allegations' to force the target company to commit resources in response, and for their allegations to raise doubts in the minds of the public and regulators. This moving target approach depends on the old adage of 'where there is smoke there must be fire'. This is not to suggest that activist claims of this type are necessarily untrue, but they create continuous fresh doubt, in the hope the target company will eventually conclude that the cost of defending the product is just not worth it in terms of financial cost, reputational damage or the flow-on risk to other products.

> Most activists are not kooks, antibusiness zealots, or publicity-hungry egotists. Except for a small few, they are sincerely and genuinely interested in the cause they are espousing. Some may be more passionate and strident in their behavior than others in advancing their cause, but that does not mean that they are any less genuine or sincere.
>
> Edmund Burke (2005, p. 42)

THE TRANSITIONAL TARGET APPROACH

This technique focuses on moving the issue away from an area that can be addressed in terms of measurable facts or science or statistics, to an area where opinion and emotion prevail. As described in Chapter 3, issues by definition often involve emotions, feelings, ethics, values and matters of opinion, and the transitional target approach deliberately moves issues into this area.

A hypothetical example could be public funding for a 'morning after' abortion pill. Initially, the activist opposition campaign might follow the moving target approach—raising conventional concerns such as whether the pill is effective; what the physical side effects are; and whether it's safe to use in the long term. But the issue could then quickly move into the transitional target mode, where the questions are not about science and health but about moral, ethical and religious implications: Is it ethically right to use a morning after pill? Will it encourage immoral behaviour? Will it undermine the sanctity of marriage? Will it increase the spread of sexually transmitted diseases? Will it threaten accepted community standards?

Not only are such questions challenging to answer in any objective way, but, more importantly, the new issue focus is also much more likely to generate headlines, to encourage protest and to mobilise a broader spectrum of opinion.

MULTIPLE TARGET APPROACH

Unlike the first two categories—where the issue is progressively redefined to continually change the grounds of debate—the multiple target approach attacks on many issue fronts simultaneously, making it much harder for the organisation to respond in a meaningful way, and opening up the inevitable accusation that they 'deliberately ignored' one or other aspect.

When a high-profile fast-food chain proposed to open an outlet in a largely residential suburb of Melbourne, which is home to a substantial Turkish community, the range of arguments in the ensuing activist campaign exemplified the multiple target approach. They included the following:

+ The restaurant will create noise and traffic problems.

+ It is unhealthy to have a fast-food outlet near a school.

+ Property values will be adversely impacted.

+ Fast food undermines local Turkish cuisine.

+ The development will involve demolition of a historically valuable building.

+ Fast food is bad food.

+ The proposed restaurant is architecturally incompatible with local homes.

+ Multinational corporations are just not welcome in our community.

The US public relations commentator Ross Irvine (1999) illustrated this same approach with a hypothetical example of the pressure on an organisation facing a broad ranging activist campaign. He said a company that is talking with a local environmental group about forestry practices on a parcel of land may find itself:

+ facing a consumer boycott of its products on the other side of the world

+ entering costly legal battles over property rights

+ meeting with indigenous groups concerned about the historical importance of the land

+ researching the population and habitat of a bird that may have been seen in the trees

+ calculating the impact of the tree harvest on global warming

+ determining the impact of the harvest on a watershed or ecosystem hundreds of times the size of the proposed harvest area

+ battling the media coverage generated by rock musicians and movie stars who have come to rescue the trees

+ responding to politicians who have little knowledge of the situation.

Similarly, the coal seam gas case study at the end of Chapter 10 illustrates an activist issue campaign that ranges across a huge spectrum of concerns, including economic, scientific, environmental, social, political and cultural. From the activist perspective, this 'scatter gun' style has many attractions, not the least of which is that multiple targeting can fortuitously hit unexpectedly vulnerable points.

In terms of the organisational issue management response, it also has another very important effect. Not only do these multiple attacks come from different areas, but they may also come from different, often unrelated, activist groups. As a result, the target organisation finds itself forced to deal with a wide range of diverse stakeholders, each with their own strategy, and each competing to elevate their particular concern onto the media and political agenda. It is a popular activist issue strategy because it can be exciting, motivating and, above all, very effective. (For further detail on these three activist approaches to issue redefinition, summarised at Table 5.1, see Jaques, 2004).

ACTIVIST STRATEGIES—CONFRONTATION VERSUS ENGAGEMENT

Many large-scale activist groups and NGOs have begun to adopt business principles as they themselves become national or multinational organisations with multimillion-dollar budgets and teams of full-time employees (Jaques, 2006). One result of this growing professionalisation is that many activist organisations are increasingly inclined to accept that, strategically, more can be achieved by sitting at the board table negotiating than standing outside the board room with protest placards. This trend to negotiation is regularly encouraged by both business organisations and government agencies, which promote the management of issues through a 'mutual gains' approach.[12]

For businesses, this often leads to a choice between dealing with 'solutions focused' activist organisations, rather than those that remain committed to direct actions or publicity events, often staged for television. In terms of corporate issue management, this approach may make sense and may seem to be the most likely to help progress towards planned, positive outcomes.

But the strategy that corporates might describe as 'constructive engagement' is sometimes regarded by parts of the activist community as 'sleeping with the enemy'.[13] Some activist organisations—such as those motivated by a strong anti-corporate or anti-capitalist ideology—reject engagement and continue to favour confrontation as the preferred way to dramatically highlight perceived misdeeds on the part of big business and big government, and as the most direct way to force change. As one writer put it: 'Activist organisations that use militant tactics believe they are more effective by influencing their targets through outside means than they would be through strategies such as *bargains with offenders*' (Derville, 2005, p. 529; emphasis added).

The Australian activist academic Sharon Beder is one issue expert who has written extensively and very critically on what she calls 'misguided and ineffective' cooperation between activists and industry.[14] She believes that 'solution oriented' engagement on

---

12 For discussion on working with activists, see Cooper (2009), Price (2006), Susskind and Field (1996), Watson, Osborne-Brown and Longhurst (2002) and Zietsma and Winn (2008) in this chapter's Further reading section. See also Burke (2005).

13 For a business perspective on 'living with the enemy', see 'Non-governmental organizations and business' (2003) in this chapter's Further reading section.

14 See Beder (1997, 2002, 2006) in this chapter's Further reading section.

selected aspects of a corporation's activities compromises the activist organisation and may force it to turn a blind eye to misdeeds elsewhere in the company it works with.

This strategic debate within activist organisations has occasionally become very public, most famously when Patrick Moore, the co-founder and former CEO of Greenpeace, left the organisation, arguing that it had been 'hijacked' by extremists. Moore later argued that the environment movement more broadly had abandoned science and logic in favour of emotion and sensationalism, whereas the emerging concept of sustainable development, he said, was propounding balancing environmental, social and economic priorities to find win-win solutions by bringing all interested parties together (Moore, 2005). It's little wonder some of his former colleagues branded him the first 'eco-Judas'.

More recently, the campaign against genetically modified food in the UK was similarly shaken when one of its high-profile warriors, Mark Lynas, publicly recanted, apologising for destroying GM crops and saying anti-GM activists had demonised an important technology and 'could not have chosen a more counter-productive path' (Storr, 2013).[15]

The purpose here is not to offer judgment on these competing approaches, but rather to highlight that the strategic choice between engagement and confrontation is critical for the way issue management is implemented by both 'sides' of any issue. In the same way that business and government agencies facing activist issues need to make smart choices about how they will engage and with whom, so too activist organisations need to decide and agree on what strategy will best suit their objectives.

ACTIVIST TACTICS

The tactics commonly used by activists in support of their cause are usually pretty public and can be seen in the news media every week. Most of the manuals and how-to guides listed earlier in this chapter provide clear instructions on how to increase awareness of issues, build support, manage campaigns and influence people with capability to make a difference.

> There are occasions when activists can either inadvertently or deliberately mislead. By the time the truth emerges, if in fact it does, it is often too late to save the pressured organisation's reputation.
>
> Denise Deegan (2001, p. 12)

Another way to observe activist tactics is through published issue management case studies. One such is a recent analysis of the activist organisation PETA, which has used largely media tactics to become one of the world's best-known and best-funded animal

---

15 For a detailed case study of GE activism in New Zealand, see Henderson (2005) in this chapter's Further reading section.

rights activist organisations.[16] The authors (Brummette, Miller & Zoch, 2013) identified eight PETA publicity tactics:

+ shocking advertisements (depicting brutal treatment of animals)

+ protesting opponents' events (disrupting public events to embarrass opponents)

+ celebrity activists (using film stars and celebrities to increase media attention)

+ naked people, mainly women (for example, naked models used in anti-fur protests)

+ throwing substances (for example, throwing flour bombs at fur-clad models at fashion shows)

+ unreasonable public demands (for example, asking an opponent to abandon their main business activity)

+ dysphemism (using graphic language to label opponents; for example, fishermen are 'lip-rippers')

+ threatening senseless legal action (that is, threats over actions that are not actually illegal).

WARRIOR PRINCESS VERSUS OIL GIANT

A protest demonstration in the New Zealand port of New Plymouth in January 2012 was a high-profile example of using activist celebrity power to capture the media. New Zealand actress Lucy Lawless—better known as television's Xena Warrior Princess—joined six other Greenpeace protesters to climb the drilling rig of the oil exploration ship *Noble Discoverer*, due to depart to search for oil in the Arctic on behalf of Shell Oil. Their made-for-television occupation continued for more than 70 hours, attracting massive international media attention and publicising the previously little-known Greenpeace campaign against exploitation of Arctic mineral resources. The protesters pleaded guilty to trespass and faced up to three years in prison. Shell also sought over $500,000 in reparations. In court 12 months later, Lawless and her co-accused were each sentenced to 120 hours of community service and ordered to pay $651.44 in damages to the port authority.[17]

One of the most controversial activist tactics is to deliberately break the law in support of a cause. This can range from civil disobedience, such as blocking the road to a nuclear power plant; through trespassing to stage a sit-in or to hang a banner on the side of a building; on to physical damage such as destroying genetically modified crops or releasing laboratory test animals; and as far as violent criminal activity such as firebombing petrol stations or even murdering doctors who provide abortions.

---

16 For a detailed case study of a PETA campaign affecting sheep-farm practice in Australia, see Jopson (2012) in this chapter's Further reading section. The PETA online how-to manual is referenced in the 'How to be an Activist Issue Manager' box earlier in this chapter.

17 For details on the case, see Lucy Lawless fined (2013).

At the civil disobedience end of the spectrum, many activists are willing to break the law knowing that the public will support them and the courts will probably be lenient. A typical example occurred when housewives in Sydney and Melbourne staged a brief sit-in at big supermarkets to support a Greenpeace protest against what they claimed were genetically modified ingredients in baby formula. When they appeared in court and pleaded guilty to trespass, the magistrate placed them all on a good-behaviour bond, saying she recognised their 'high moral standing' and their right to peaceful protest. But she warned them that protest had to be carried out within the confines of the law. 'You will confine yourself to legal behaviour,' she said, 'or it will come to nothing' (Jaques, 2011).

When it comes to more serious illegal activities, the activist community itself can be deeply divided about whether a just cause can make law-breaking a legitimate tactic. While Derville (2005) distinguished between what she called radical or extreme activists and more moderate groups, there is no doubt that, from an activist's perspective, when peaceful issue management methods fail, other tactics may sometimes become accepted as the only remaining option.

CORPORATE RESPONSE TO ACTIVIST CAMPAIGNS

An issue by definition has 'contending parties' who hold opposing views, and the relationship between those parties can be critical to how issue management plays out. Where one of those parties is an activist organisation, a significant factor in response strategies can be a disparity in public trust.

Studies around the world consistently show that business is at a substantial disadvantage when it comes to trust and reputation.[18] By contrast, activist organisations such as NGOs have a strong and increasing reputation in terms of trust and believability.[19] For example, the well-respected Edelman Global Survey shows that NGOs remain the most trusted institutions in four out of five markets, with the overall highest trust levels in Asia-Pacific (Edelman, 2013). In 2013, trust in NGOs in China was the second highest in the world at 81 per cent (up from 48 per cent in 2008), closely followed by Malaysia (76 per cent), Hong Kong (76 per cent), Singapore (75 per cent) and India (69 per cent), ahead of Australia at 64 per cent.

Given such challenges, there is no 'best way' for an organisation to respond to activist pressure. For example, the gay health case study at the end of this chapter illustrates how two companies responded in very different ways to competing activist campaigns.[20] Not surprisingly, it depends on variables such as the qualities of the target organisation, the subject matter of the issue, and the nature of the activist group.

---

18 See the 2013 Roy Morgan Survey of trust that shows directors of public companies and business executives in the bottom half of the list, along with journalists, politicians, real estate agents and advertising people (www.roymorgan.com/findings/image-of-professions-2013-201305020534).

19 It has been suggested even the acronym NGO itself has become an international 'brand'. See Beaudoin (2009) in this chapter's Further reading section.

20 See also Walton (2007) in this chapter's Further reading section for a case study of how competing activist groups argued for and against a coal mine in New Zealand.

From the business perspective it is important to remember that corporations are made up of people, and the response to an activist attack can be seen very much in human terms. The eminent psychiatrist Elizabeth Kübler-Ross (1926–2004) is best known for her model known as the 'five stages of grief'—denial, anger, bargaining, depression and acceptance— and the first three of these stages can be seen in the possible corporate responses to an activist attack.

STAGE ONE: DENIAL—DO NOTHING

For organisations facing pressure by activists it is very easy to come up with reasons why ignoring the attack and doing nothing seems like a good idea:

- It's not really 'our issue'.
- Our lawyers' advice is not to do or say anything.
- Whatever we do or say can be turned against us.
- If we respond it will only 'give them oxygen'.
- We don't want to look like bullies.
- The group is so small they don't really represent any threat.
- We should leave it to our trade association.
- If we wait long enough they will give up and pick another target.
- They are so extreme they will never listen to reason.
- We are too busy trying to run our business.
- The news media will soon lose interest in the story.
- Our stakeholders don't really care about their allegations.

Although these and similar management responses are very familiar to public relations practitioners, there are many case studies that demonstrate the principle illustrated by the issue life cycle set out in Chapter 2—issues ignored usually don't go away, but instead get worse and harder to deal with. As the British writer Denise Deegan (2001, p. 23) concluded:

> Ignoring activists tends to be a knee-jerk response by those feeling the heat rather than a positive and pre-planned strategy. In fact, if one is honest, many of the 'reasons' given by organisations for not responding to activists are in reality excuses for inaction.

STAGE TWO: ANGER—FIGHT BACK

Following the 'five stages of grief' model, after denial comes anger, and anger in a corporate context is sometime seen as a decision to fight back. For an organisation under attack it can be very tempting to launch a counter-campaign to discredit the activist organisation, or perhaps even to discredit its leaders personally. Other reactions might be to initiate costly and time-consuming legal action against the activist organisation or its leaders;[21] or to strike

---

21 Legal actions intended to inhibit activist or community opposition are sometimes called SLAPP suits—Strategic Legal Action Against Public Participation.

back by using corporate power to cut off the organisation's funding; or to influence others to withhold financial support.

Another trigger for corporate anger can occur when the activist strategy draws directly from the Saul Alinksy playbook and personalises the attack. A few protesters with placards picketing the corporate headquarters may be a minor embarrassment. But when those same few activists picket the CEO's home and name him or her as personally responsible for the cause of their protest, the idea of fighting back quickly becomes even more attractive.

Of course, this is exactly what the activists want, because they know that when a company fights back it may initially seem to be a success, but the company itself can suffer badly in terms of reputation and public opinion. In any conflict between David and Goliath, the public and news media will nearly always be on the side of David, even if Goliath is actually in the right.[22]

There is one other way of fighting back that is even more risky, and that is when the organisation under pressure resorts to 'dirty tricks'. Such strategies are probably less common than some activists would suggest, but when they are publicly revealed—as often eventually happens—the negative reaction can cause serious damage.[23]

One 'dirty trick' is so popular it even has its own name: astroturfing, or creating fake 'community groups' to appear to represent genuine grass-roots opinion. In Chapter 3 we met the seemingly independent 'Alliance of Australian Retailers', which was actually funded by big tobacco to oppose plain packaging for cigarettes. In another notorious case, Australian and New Zealand companies trying to trying to introduce plastic milk containers found themselves facing a well-organised campaign by 'Mothers against Pollution', which described itself as 'Australia's largest environmental group'. The campaign spokeswoman 'Alana Maloney' was eventually exposed as a Brisbane-based public relations consultant with a different name whose work was funded by the manufacturers of cardboard milk cartons.

An even more serious example of astroturfing involved a proposed shopping development in the Sydney suburb of Homebush, which faced opposition from an apparently local activist group called 'North Strathfield Resident Action Group'. After legal action was launched in the Australian Federal Court, shopping mall giant Westfield admitted it had been behind the supposed activist group, and went even further, confessing it had been involved in eleven other 'grass-roots' campaigns against rival retail developments.[24]

However, one of the most infamous cases of a secret fight-back strategy against activists is undoubtedly that by the New Zealand Government-owned timber company Timberlands, which masterminded an eight-year campaign against activists opposed to logging in native forests (see the box, 'Fighting back against environmentalists').

---

22 One of the most famous examples of misjudged legal action against activists was when McDonald's sued two unemployed British critics. The so-called McLibel case turned into the longest-running case in British history and badly embarrassed the fast-food maker around the world. See www.mcspotlight.org/index.shtml.

23 For a highly critical activist view of corporate 'dirty tricks', see Lubbers (2002) in this chapter's Further reading section.

24 For detail of the milk packaging case and manufactured opposition to shopping centre development, see Burton (2007, pp. 44–51) in this chapter's Further reading section. For a US legal view on the use of front organizations see Fitzpatrick and Palenchar (2006) in this chapter's Further reading section.

FIGHTING BACK AGAINST ENVIRONMENTALISTS

For eight years between 1991 and 1999 the New Zealand government-owned company Timberlands ran a multimillion-dollar campaign against activists trying to halt logging in rainforest on the west coast of New Zealand's South Island. The strategy included spying on activist groups, trying to undermine their funding, threatening legal action, pressuring critical journalists, destroying a tree-top protest camp, and setting up a local campaign to support logging. The strategy came crashing down when internal company documents were leaked and appeared in a controversial book. The resulting political scandal contributed to the downfall of the government at the next election and the company was forced to curtail its logging of native timber.

Source: Nicky Hager and Bob Burton (1999).

STAGE THREE: BARGAINING—DIALOGUE AND NEGOTIATION

On the face of it, negotiation with activists who oppose you is a logical and positive corporate response. It demonstrates willingness to compromise and commitment to a win-win or mutual-gains outcome. It is also consistent with the 'two-way symmetrical' model of communication championed by James and Larissa Grunig, which became a cornerstone of public relations orthodoxy. The two-way symmetrical model uses balanced communication to negotiate with publics, resolve conflicts and promote mutual understanding and respect between the organisation and its publics. It was first published by Grunig and Hunt (1984) and remains a popular and desirable approach (see also Grunig, 1992).

However, there is a growing view that such dealing with activists tests the practicality of this theory. In fact, Coombs and Holladay (2012) argue that some activist strategies are deliberately asymmetrical—in other words, it suits the activists to be seen as 'powerless underdogs' who have to use publicity stunts to break through the news clutter to promote their cause.

In her book on managing activism, Deegan (2001) strongly supported the idea of the two-way symmetrical model and spelled out in extensive detail how and when to work with activist groups and how to know which ones offered the best chance of success.[25] However, she also recognised that there are a number of good reasons why some activist groups may decline to negotiate, and this is a critical concern.

Negotiation requires that both parties believe there is value in dialogue, and for activist organisations that rely on unpaid volunteers, even more important is a return on that commitment of time and resources. This brings us back to the challenge of negotiation versus confrontation, discussed earlier in this chapter. While there are many excellent examples of activists and target organisations working together on areas of common interest to deliver positive outcomes that benefit society (see Chapter 3), there are also many situations where the opposing 'sides' cannot or will not work together.

---

25 For detailed discussion on the process of negotiation with activists, see Hon (2006) in this chapter's Further Reading section.

Discussing what she calls 'radical extremists', Derville (2005) says such groups can be characterised by aggressive tactics such as 'vitriolic rhetoric, disruptive image events, actions that provoke violent backlashes, unreasonable demands, pressure against targets' accomplices, harassment and sabotage' (p. 529). As she concluded, the use of such tactics may give activist groups a sense of fulfilment that would never be obtained through collaboration and negotiation.

In this way, sometimes the objectives and methods of activists and their targets are so far apart that meaningful dialogue to achieve persuasion is not only impossible but may actually have the opposite effect. When an activist group is focused primarily on disruptive media stunts and making wildly outrageous demands that they know will never be accepted, but will generate good headlines, the target organisation can legitimately ask whether negotiation really is a viable option.

Note: parts of this chapter draw on Jaques (2004) and Jaques (2006).

KEY POINTS

+ Activism is not new, but modern tools and technology have greatly increased the capability and profile of activist groups and their ability to put issues on the public agenda.

+ The 'rules' devised by Saul Alinsky in 1971 remain as core guidelines for many of today's activists.

+ Activist issue selection criteria differ greatly from the way corporates decide how to prioritise issues.

+ Issue redefinition is a proven effective activist tactic used against target companies.

+ Corporates facing activist pressure can choose to deny, to fight back or to negotiate.

+ Whether to engage or confront is a critical question both for activists and for business.

≡ ACTIVITIES AND DISCUSSION

1. Access one or more of the online activist how-to manuals listed earlier in this chapter. Identify common themes and discuss activities that align with conventional issue management.

2. From the perspective of an activist organisation, evaluate the advantages and disadvantages of engaging with business versus confrontation.

3. Why is the expectation gap theme of issue management a focal point for activists?

4. The chapter mentioned community groups, citizen campaigns, single-issue lobby groups, pressure groups, grass-roots campaigns, advocacy groups, special interest groups and non-government organisations. Are these terms defined differently? If so, what are the main differences?

5. If you were a business receiving unwanted activist attention, would you rather suffer a high-profile demonstration that attracted extensive adverse media headlines but was over in a few days, or commit time and resources to lengthy negotiation with an activist group who you suspect may never really change their mind about you?

6. Research the McLibel legal case between McDonald's and two British critics. What lessons can be learned from this famous example for activists and for their targets?

7. Identify a current activist campaign and assess how it compares with the checklist of criteria developed by Winter and Steger.

8. Some activists believe breaking the law is a legitimate tactic in support of a just cause. Discuss whether different rules should apply when activists go beyond the normal legal limits.

RECOGNISING ACTIVISTS AS EXPERT ISSUE COMMUNICATORS

Katharina Wolf

Curtin University, Perth

The Western Australian anti-nuclear movement (WA ANM) has been a prominent voice in Australian politics and social commentary for over four decades. Emerging out of the global mass demonstration movement in the 1960s, the WA ANM became particularly prominent in the late 1970s, when the state was positioned as the future nuclear powerhouse of Australia. When in September 2008 the newly elected Liberal government overturned a ban on uranium mining in Western Australia (WA), the movement reformed with new energy and focus.

WA is the largest of Australia's states and territories, covering around one-third of the country. WA's economy is largely driven by the extraction and processing of mineral and petroleum commodities, and West Australians proudly refer to their state as the 'powerhouse' of Australia and as a major contributor to ensuring the county remained largely unaffected by the 2007–10 global recession. But due to a downturn in global prices for WA's 'traditional' resources, such as aluminium and iron ore, attention shifted to the potential role of uranium ore to secure a continuation of resources growth.

Anti-nuclear activists have publicly challenged this focus on economic benefits, instead positioning uranium as the 'asbestos of the 21st century' by highlighting claimed long-term health, environmental and cultural consequences. Activists have also questioned the industry's positioning of nuclear power as a low-carbon solution in the fight against global warming.

However, the activist–corporate relationship is characterised by vast differences in access to (economic) resources and hence power. This has resulted in the resources and energy sector dismissing activists as 'disorganised troublemakers' who do not pose a realistic threat to corporate objectives. The so-called 'relationship' is therefore not only characterised by irreconcilable differences, but also by lack of engagement or even acknowledgment. Essentially, the WA ANM does not feature on mining corporations' stakeholder maps.

A contributor to anti-nuclear activists being easily dismissed as ineffective, chaotic and unprofessional is difference in communication styles. By definition, community movements are typically dynamic collectives of volunteers, often characterised by a lack of a clear reporting structure. In this way, the WA ANM has struggled to put any long-term strategic plans into place. Their use of street theatre, song, dance and humour (such as the enlisting of a Clown Army) contrasts with the polished corporate approach to communication. However, this does not mean they are necessarily less effective. In reality, anti-nuclear activists have had no desire to engage with corporate representatives. Instead, they have been more effective in challenging the viability of uranium mining by targeting corporations' key stakeholders, as illustrated by two examples:

By 'planting seeds of doubt' anti-nuclear activists have challenged shareholders' investment decisions. Since the reversal of the uranium ban, anti-nuclear activists and their supporters have ensured their continuous presence at the annual general meetings of resources corporations with an interest in uranium mining. Here the focus has not been on challenging the management team, but on questioning the long-term viability and return on investment of uranium ore projects. Furthermore, by highlighting potential environmental, cultural and health implications of uranium operations in the Australian outback, activists have forced shareholders to consider ethical implications of their investment decisions.

Simultaneously, anti-nuclear activists have set out to 'undermine the government agenda' by mobilising public opposition to the mining and export of uranium. This has been done via a range of tactics: the collection of signatures and online petitions; the distribution of campaign postcards; information sessions and public debates; regular vigils for the victims of the nuclear industry; and public events around anniversaries of major nuclear incidences, as well as continuous calls for individuals to write to the state newspaper or ring their local member of parliament. The WA ANM also initiated a '100 Weeks of Public Breakfasts' campaign outside the WA Premier's electoral office, to provide 'like-minded groups' with a public platform to challenge the neoliberal government agenda.

Mining corporations and anti-nuclear activists use dissimilar communication styles and operate in different public spheres. In the context of this case study, there has been very limited meaningful engagement between corporate representatives and activists, due to a lack of interest from either side. However, the difference in resources, tactics and ultimately power does not imply that corporations can afford to underestimate or even dismiss grass-roots activists like the WA ANM. The ultimate goal of anti-nuclear activists is the withdrawal of shareholder and government support for the mining and export of uranium ore, thereby eventually making uranium operations nonviable.

This ideological battle between the nuclear industry and anti-nuclear activists is still taking place, with no clear 'winner' in sight. However, as the WA ANM continues to demonstrate, activists can be effective, experienced and knowledgable issue communicators. In challenging the status quo, they perform a prominent role in modern Western societies.

For detailed discussion of this case see:

Wolf, K. (2011). *Anti nuclear activism & social change in Western Australia.* Paper presented at the International PR conference, Barcelona, 28–29 June.

ACTIVIST CAMPAIGNING AND THE IMPORTANCE OF ISSUE FRAMING

Tony Jaques

RMIT University, Melbourne

When the Brisbane-based Queensland Association of Healthy Communities (QAHC) launched a $64,000 local advertising campaign in 2011 promoting safe gay sex, the outcome was a Christian lobbying campaign that back-fired badly but made the poster one of Australia's most complained-about outdoor advertisements.

The poster was a black-and-white photograph showing a fully clad gay couple, both men facing the camera in a chaste embrace, with one holding an unopened condom packet. Text promoted the condom brand, Rip & Roll, with the advertiser's strapline—'A safe sex message from Healthy Communities'—and a phone number.

To the local branch of the Australian Christian Lobby (ACL), the poster—that appeared on outdoor hoardings and bus-shelters—was an affront to decency and family values, which inappropriately exposed children to condoms. And they claimed that the fact one of the men was wearing a crucifix was 'offensive to Christianity'.

Local ACL director and campaign spokesperson Wendy Francis emphasised that her objection to the advertisement was the sexualisation of children through exposure to condom use and that her opposition had 'absolutely nothing to do with gay couples'. However, many complaints lodged by her supporters with the Advertising Standards Board (ASB), the outdoor advertising companies and the Brisbane City Council revealed an unmistakable anti-gay or homophobic tone.

As complaints built up, the two outdoor advertising companies involved in the program began to feel the heat. Goa Billboards, the local company which carried the poster on city hoardings, announced it saw no reason to make any change. By contrast, the Sydney-based national company Adshel, whose Brisbane bus-shelter advertising panels were the subject of particular criticism, caved in under the pressure, and removed the posters. However, their decision to yield to activist pressure triggered an extraordinary social media backlash far beyond a few advertising sites in just one city.

In the wake of Adshel withdrawing the poster, Michael O'Brien, one of the men in the advertisement, personally spearheaded a campaign to force Adshel to reinstate the advertisement. He appeared as a spokesperson in the news media across the country, and started a Facebook page that attracted more than 30,000 followers in just two days, calling on them to complain to Adshel.

The story gained national and international exposure, and a massive internet presence. The campaign against Adshel briefly occupied six of the top ten trending topics in Australia

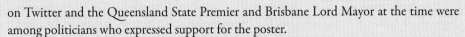

on Twitter and the Queensland State Premier and Brisbane Lord Mayor at the time were among politicians who expressed support for the poster.

In the face of public pressure, and a protest outside its Brisbane office, Adshel back-flipped next day and agreed to reinstate the advertisements, claiming it did so only after they realised the complaints were not individual concerns but part of a coordinated campaign.

Wendy Francis of ACL denied she had orchestrated the campaign, but the ASB eventually received 222 formal complaints, many using near-identical wording. This made Rip & Roll the most complained-about billboard advertisement for many years. (Complaints to ASB typically attract fewer than fifty separate objections.)

Dismissing the complaint on all grounds, the ASB ruled that the depiction of a same-sex couple in an advertisement should be treated no differently from an image of a heterosexual couple, and it also found that younger children would not understand what a condom is.

The case provides a contrasting study in how the two activist campaigns utilised (or failed to utilise) the concept of issue framing to communicate their viewpoint. Framing of the ACL campaign was ambiguous and inconsistent. Although campaign spokesperson Wendy Francis argued that the main focus was against condom advertising in places where children would be exposed, and that the effort was not anti-gay, media coverage reinforced the perception that the central issue was homophobia. Indeed, the ASB itself, in rejecting the complaints, specifically referred to 'people's attitudes in relation to homosexuality' as one of the main reasons for the record high number of objections received.

This ambiguity of framing played into the hands of their critics and detracted from the purported objective of the campaign. By contrast, the response by QAHC and their volunteer spokesperson was unwavering from the beginning. They framed the issue as free speech in advertising in the face of homophobia, and this construction was widely adopted.

Of the two advertising companies that found themselves caught in the crossfire of a high-profile and contentious moral issue, local operator Goa maintained a high level of direct management involvement and took a principled position on the issue.

The national company, Adshel, may have considered itself in a no-win position, but its response to issue activism appeared to misread the local situation. The company specifically declined to take a position on the controversial advertisement itself, and its stated reasons for withdrawing and then promptly reinstating the poster were poorly thought through and poorly communicated. Adshel may have believed this was a minor issue, involving a relatively small amount of advertising revenue in a single local market. But they clearly underestimated the national and international potential of the issue, which undoubtedly damaged their reputation.

For more detailed discussion of this case see:

Jaques, T. (2013). Ensnared in a gay health controversy:
A comparative study in responding to issue activism.
Journal of Public Affairs, 13(1), 53–60.

REFERENCES

Alinsky, S. D. (1971). *Rules for radicals: A pragmatic primer for realistic radicals.* New York: Random House.

Bobo, K., Kendall, J. & Max, S. (1991). *Organising for social change: A manual for activists in the 1990s.* Washington, DC: Seven Locks Press.

Brummette, J., Miller, L. & Zoch, L. (2013, 7–8 March). PETA: media reputation and press agentry in the context of animal rights activism. Paper presented at the *16th International Public Relations Research Conference*, Miami. pp. 124–137.

Burke, E. M. (2005). *Managing a company in an activist world.* Westport, CT: Praeger.

Coombs, W. T. (1998). The internet as a potential equaliser: New leverage for confronting social irresponsibility. *Public Relations Review, 24*(3), 289–303.

Coombs, W. T. & Holladay, S. J. (2012). Fringe public relations: How activism moves critical PR toward the mainstream. *Public Relations Review, 38*(5), 880–887.

Deegan, D. (2001). *Managing activism: A guide to dealing with activists and pressure groups.* London: Kogan Page.

Derville, T. (2005). Radical activist tactics: Overturning public relations conceptualisations. *Public Relations Review, 31*(4), 527–533.

Doh, J. P. & Guay, T. R. (2006). Corporate social responsibility, public policy and NGO activism in Europe and the United States: An institutional-stakeholder perspective. *Journal of Management Studies, 43*(1), 47–73.

Edelman. (2013). *Edelman trust barometer, 2013 annual global survey.* Retrieved from www.edelman.com/insights/intellectual-property/trust-2013.

Grunig, J. E. & Hunt, T. (1984). *Managing public relations.* New York: Holt, Rinehart & Winston.

Grunig, L. A. (1992). Activism: How it limits the effectiveness of organisations and how excellent public relations departments respond. In J. E. Grunig (Ed.), *Excellence in Public Relations and Communications Management* (pp. 503–530). Hillsdale, NJ: Lawrence Erlbaum.

Hager, N. & Burton, B. (1999). *Secrets and lies: The anatomy of an anti-environmental PR campaign.* Nelson, NZ: Craig Potton Publishing.

Heath, R. L. (1997). *Strategic issues management: Organisations and public policy challenges.* Thousand Oaks CA: Sage.

Irvine, R. (December 1999). *PR Lessons from the Battle in Seattle.* Retrieved from www.epublicrelations.org.

Jaques, T. (2011). Greenpeace campaign on the issue of GM foods. In J. R. Macnamara, *Public relations: Theories, practices, critiques* (pp. 467–471). Sydney: Pearson.

Jaques, T. (2006). Activist 'rules' and the convergence with issue management. *Journal of Communication Management, 10*(4), 407–420.

Jaques, T. (2004). Issue definition: The neglected foundation of effective issue management. *Journal of Public Affairs, 4*(2), 191–200.

Lipsky, M. (1968). Protest as a political resource. *American Political Science Review, 62*(4), 1144–1158.

Lucy Lawless fined $547 for trespassing on Arctic oil drilling ship. (2013, 7 February). *Christian Science Monitor.* Retrieved from www.csmonitor.com/ Environment/Latest-News-Wires/2013/0207/Lucy-Lawless-fined-547-for-trespassing-on-Arctic-oil-drilling-ship.

Moore, P. (2005, 28 January) Environmental movement has lost its way. *Miami Herald.* Retrieved from www.seas.columbia.edu/earth/wtert/sofos/Moore_ Environmental_Movement_Has_Lost_Its_Way.pdf.

Raymond, D. (2003). Activism: Behind the banners. In S. John & S. Thomson (Eds.), *New activism and the corporate response* (pp. 207–225). Basingtoke: Palgrave Macmillan.

Shaw, R. (2001). *The activist's handbook* (2nd ed.). University of California Press.

Smith, M. F. & Ferguson, D. P. (2010). Activism 2.0. In R. L. Heath & M. J. Palenchar (Eds.), *The Sage handbook of public relations* (2nd ed., pp. 395–408). Thousand Oaks, CA: Sage.

Stine, R. (2011, 5 August). Social media and environmental campaigning: Brand lessons from Barbie. *Ethical Corporation.* www.ethicalcorp.com.

Storr, W. (2103, 10 March). Mark Lynas: Truth, treachery and GM food. *The Observer.* Retrieved from www.guardian.co.uk/environment/2013/mar/09/ mark-lynas-truth-treachery-gm.

Thomas, C. (2003). Cyberactivism and corporations. In S. John & S. Thomson (Eds.), *New activism and the corporate response* (pp. 115–135). Basingtoke: Palgrave Macmillan.

Whitehaven coal share plunge after media hoax. (2013, 7 January). *ABC News.* Retrieved from www.abc.net.au/news/2013-01-07/whitehaven-coal-shares-plunge-after-media-hoax/4455362.

Winter, M. & Steger, U. (1998). *Managing outside pressure: Strategies for preventing corporate disasters.* London: John Wiley.

FURTHER READING

Beaudoin, J.-P. (2004). Non-governmental organisations, ethics and corporate public relations. *Journal of Communication Management, 8*(4), 366–371.

Beder, S. (1997). *Global spin: The corporate assault on environmentalism.* Melbourne: Scribe.

Beder, S. (2002). Environmentalists help manage corporate reputations. *Ecopolitics Thought and Action, 1*(4), 60–72.

Beder, S. (2006). *Suiting themselves: How corporations drive the global agenda.* London: Earthscan.

Bodensteiner, C. A. (2003). Succeeding when environmental activists oppose you. *Public Relations Quarterly, 48*(2), 14–20.

Bourland-Davis, P. G., Thompson, W. & Brooks, F. E. (2010). Activism in the 20th and 21st centuries. In R. L. Heath (Ed.), *The Sage handbook of public relations* (2nd ed., pp. 409–420). Newbury Park, CA: Sage.

Burton, B. (2007). *Inside spin: The dark underbelly of the PR industry.* Sydney: Allen & Unwin.

Cooper, A. (2009). *Two-way communication: A win-win model for facing activist pressure: A case study on McDonalds and Unilever's responses to Greenpeace.* Institute for Public Relations. 12th Annual International Public Relations Research Conference, Coral Gables, Florida. Retrieved from www.instituteforpr.org/ipr_info/two_way_communication_facing_activist_pressure.

Doh, J. P. & Teegen, H. (2003). *Globalisation and NGOs: Transforming business, governments and society.* Westport, CT: Praeger.

Fassin, Y. (2009). Inconsistencies in activists' behaviours and the ethics of NGOs. *Journal of Business Ethics, 90*(4), 503–521.

Fitzpatrick, K. R. & Palenchar, M. J. (2006). Disclosing special interests: Constitutional restrictions on front groups. *Journal of Public Relations Research, 18*(3), 203–224.

Henderson, A. (2005). Activism in 'Paradise': Identity management in a public relations campaign against genetic engineering. *Journal of Public Relations Research, 17*(2), 117–137.

Hon, L. (2006). Negotiating relationships with activist publics. In K. Fitzpatrick & C. Bronstein (Eds.), *Ethics in public relations: Responsible advocacy* (pp. 53–69). Thousand Oaks, CA: Sage.

Illia, L. (2003). Passage to cyberactivism: How dynamics of activism change. *Journal of Public Affairs, 3*(4), 326–337.

Jaques, T. (2013). Ensnared in a gay health controversy: A comparative study in responding to issue activism. *Journal of Public Affairs, 13*(1), 53–60.

Jopson, D. (2012, 20 December). The end of the sheep's back. *The Global Mail.* Retrieved from www.theglobalmail.org/feature/the-end-of-the-sheeps-back/535.

Joyce, M. (Ed.). (2010). *Digital activism decoded: The new mechanics of change.* New York: International Debate Education Association. Retrieved from www.cl.cam.ac.uk/~sjm217/papers/digiact10all.pdf.

Kahn, R. & Kellner, D. (2004). New media and internet activism: From the 'Battle of Seattle' to blogging. *New Media and Society, 6*(6), 87–95.

Kozinets, R. V. & Handelman, J. M. (2004). Adversaries of consumption: Consumer movements, activism and ideology. *Journal of Consumer Research, 31*(3), 691–704.

Lubbers, E. (Ed.) (2002). *Battling big business: Countering greenwash, infiltration and other forms of corporate bullying.* Melbourne: Scribe.

Manheim, J. B. & Holt, A. D. (2013). Contrabrand: Activism and the leveraging of corporate reputation. In C. E. Carroll (Ed.), *Handbook of communication and corporate reputation* (pp. 421–434). New York: Wiley.

Meikle, G. (2002). *Future active: Media activism and the internet.* New York: Pluto Press.

Miller, D. (2007). Spinning farmed salmon. In W. Dinant & D. Miller (Eds.), *Thinker, faker, spinner, spy: Corporate PR and the assault on democracy* (pp. 67–93). London: Pluto Press.

Nalinakumari, B. & MacLean, R. (2005). NGOs—A primer on the evolution of the organisations that are setting the next generation of 'regulations'. *Environmental Quality Management, 14*(4), 1–21.

Newsom, V. A. & Lengel, L. (2012). Arab women, social media, and the Arab Spring: Applying the framework of digital reflexivity to analyze gender and online activism. *Journal of International Women's Studies, 13*(5), 31–45.

Non-governmental organizations and business: Living with the enemy. (2003, 9 August). *The Economist,* 49–50.

Price, T. (2006). *Activists in the boardroom: How advocacy groups seek to shape corporate behaviour.* Washington DC: Foundation for Public Affairs.

Susskind, L. & Field, P. (1996). *Dealing with an angry public: The mutual gains approach to resolving disputes.* New York: The Free Press.

Tesh, S. N. (2002). The internet and the grass roots. *Organisation and Environment, 15*(3), 336–339.

Walton, S. (2007). Site the mine in our backyard: Discursive strategies of community stakeholders in an environmental conflict in New Zealand. *Organisation & Environment, 20*(2), 177–203.

Watson, T., Osborne-Brown, S. & Longhurst, M. (2002). Issues negotiation: Investing in stakeholders. *Corporate Communications 7*(1), 54–61.

Werder, K. P. (2006). Responding to activism: An experimental analysis of public relations strategy influence on attributes of publics. *Journal of Public Relations Research, 18*(4), 335–356.

Zietsma, C. & Winn, M. I. (2008). Mutual Influence in stakeholder conflicts building chains and directing flows: Strategies and tactics of mutual influence in stakeholder conflicts. *Business & Society, 47*(1), 68–101.

6

CRISIS MANAGEMENT— READINESS AND RESPONSE

CHAPTER OBJECTIVES

This chapter will help you to:

+ learn about the origins of crisis management as a business discipline

+ discover some iconic crisis cases and why they are important

+ assess the development of pre-crisis management

+ position crisis management as part of an integrated process of management activity

+ recognise the critical role of good communication in crisis response

+ introduce four key areas of crisis preparedness and the role of public relations.

Two of the important things to know about crisis management as a comprehensive discipline are: (a) the difference between crisis management and crisis response; and (b) the difference between crisis preparedness and crisis prevention. These crucial distinctions are two of the key themes of this chapter, while the next chapter focuses more on crisis tactics and logistics.

Crisis management is one of the poorly understood and misrepresented activities of public relations. And there is a good reason for this deficiency. Crisis management can legitimately be positioned across an entire spectrum of complexity—ranging from purely tactical reactive mode, which is little more than emergency response, right through to a continuous strategic process stretching from identification and management of potential crises to post-crisis issue impacts.

This range of approaches to crisis management was introduced in Chapter 1 and we now consider it in more detail, adding further elements and exploring the specific roles of public relations. But first we need to briefly review the development of crisis management as a discipline.

DEVELOPMENT OF CRISIS MANAGEMENT

In its early manifestations, the accepted understanding of crisis had little to do with the modern concept of business management. It was concerned primarily with natural disasters—such as floods, earthquakes, famines and epidemics—or with military, political or financial crises—such as the Balkan Crisis of 1914 that precipitated the First World War, the Wall Street Crisis of 1929 that triggered the Great Depression, or the Abdication Crisis of 1936 that rocked the foundations of the British establishment.

Scholars such as Allison (1971) and Lagadec (1993) believe the idea of systematic study and analysis of crisis as a defined concept did not gain prominence until after the much-analysed 1962 Cuban missile crisis.[1] Moreover, it has been widely argued that *organisational* crisis management as a formal management discipline did not gain real impetus in the USA until the Tylenol poisoning scandal of 1982. For example, Mitroff (2001) says the modern field of crisis management 'is generally acknowledged to have started with the Tylenol poisonings' (p. 3), and Heath and Palenchar (2009) offer the same conclusion: 'Before the Tylenol case, crisis was probably a major topic. Afterward it became a cottage industry' (p. 366). Across the Atlantic, Falkheimer and Heide (2006) argue that the Chernobyl disaster in 1986 galvanised the development of crisis management in Europe. (The Tylenol and Chernobyl crises are both discussed in the next section of this chapter.)

At the same time that interest in crisis management was becoming established, the discipline itself was undergoing major changes that created new challenges and opportunities for leadership and communication. For many years, organisational crisis management was seen almost entirely as a responsive, tactical activity—what to do when a crisis strikes—and it was not generally perceived as a top management responsibility.

---

1 The Cuban missile crisis occurred when the USA and the USSR came close to war over a Soviet attempt to install nuclear-armed missiles in Cuba, well within range of the American mainland.

> The best-designed organisation is unlikely to function effectively in a crisis if those guiding it have insufficient management skills and exhibit poor leadership.
>
> Alexander Kouzmin and Alan Jarman (2004, p. 189)

Of course, dealing with the *impact* of a crisis—be it financial, reputational, operational or other—has long been acknowledged as a management role. This led to the development of a range of specialisms, such as investor relations, reputation management and root cause analysis, not to mention a boom in media training for senior executives. But the crisis management process itself remained largely tactical and was commonly delegated to operational staff, akin to emergency response. The inevitable result was that fully understanding the *process* of crisis management remained low on the executive agenda.

However, it eventually became clear to scholars and practitioners alike that crisis management is more than simply responding to what Coombs (2007) called 'a sudden and unexpected event that threatens to disrupt an organisation's operations and poses both a functional and reputational threat' (p. 164). It was also clear there is a great deal organisations can do *before* a crisis to reduce the likelihood of it occurring and to lessen its impact if it does occur.

As described in Chapter 1, this is well captured in the neat distinction: 'Crisis management is not the same as crash management' (Pauchant & Mitroff, 1992). Tactical response is just one part of total crisis management effort. But before exploring the modern approach to crisis management as a comprehensive, formal business discipline, it is worth pausing to consider some iconic crises and their impact on crisis management today.

ICONIC CRISES

Most business and professional activities have their 'iconic cases' that are used to underscore key principles. Crisis management is no exception and most are legendary cases that are familiar to just about everyone in the field (see the box, 'Milestone events that helped frame modern crisis management').

MILESTONE EVENTS THAT HELPED FRAME MODERN CRISIS MANAGEMENT

'Classic' crises are important not only because of their magnitude, but also because in each case they were game-changers in our understanding of crisis management and crisis communication. The list is long and the following are just some of the most famous cases:

Three Mile Island (1979) A near-disaster at a Pennsylvania power plant highlighted the dangers of nuclear power and dominated public debate.

Tylenol (1982) The deliberate poisoning of supermarket painkillers caused deaths and a ground-breaking product recall.

Bhopal (1984) The fatal gas release at a chemical plant in India was reputedly the world's worst industrial accident.

Chernobyl (1986) A meltdown at a Ukrainian nuclear power station released a radioactive cloud across the region and Western Europe.

Exxon Valdez (1989) A bulk tanker ran aground in remote Alaska, spilling oil in a pristine natural environment.

Brent Spar (1995) Activists occupied an offshore oil facility in the North Sea to prevent it being dumped in the North Atlantic.

Hurricane Katrina (2005) Response systems were overwhelmed by a massive storm that partly destroyed New Orleans and other cities.

Black Saturday (2009) Australia's worst natural disaster resulted in 173 people being killed and more than 400 injured during bushfires in Victoria.

Deepwater Horizon (2010) A fatal oil rig fire and subsequent spill threatened parts of the Gulf of Mexico and ruined corporate reputations.

Fukushima (2011) An earthquake and giant tsunami devastated the coast of Japan and destroyed a major nuclear power facility.

Most of the crises mentioned in the 'Milestone events...' box not only caught the public imagination, but it has been argued they were also milestones in our understanding of crisis management. In fact, they have become part of the vocabulary of crisis management and have been exhaustively studied, dissected and analysed more than most others, especially in the Western world.

Some cases have actually become somewhat mythologised; in other words, they have gained a significance that has been embellished over the years and may not really be supported by the facts at the time. This leads to questioning whether these famous cases remain relevant in today's world and whether the lessons still apply (Jaques, 2009). For example, would the Tylenol case be presented as the success it was claimed in 1982 if the internet had been available for critics and the media to challenge the strategy of the manufacturer? (Use of the internet and social media in crisis communication is discussed in Chapter 7.)

Nonetheless, these and similar cases remain classics of the field and they need to be understood by practitioners and students, in the same way that cadets at every military academy in the world study and analyse iconic battles such as Cannae (216 BC), Thermopylae (191 BC), Waterloo (AD 1815), Gettysburg (1863) and Gallipoli (1915).

Most importantly, understanding famous crises helps build an appreciation of how crisis management has emerged as a modern, integrated discipline.

WHAT IS A CRISIS?

Precisely defining a crisis is not easy. Indeed, one leading authority has declared that crisis is among the most commonly misused words in the English language, 'often trivialised to such an extent that its use borders on the bland and it has an inherently negative image' (Smith, 1995, p. 167). Smith has also argued that there is 'no real collective acceptance' about the precise meaning of the word (2005, p. 319).

Notwithstanding this challenge, in Chapter 1 we introduced a commonly used definition (Pearson & Clair, 1998, p. 60):

> An organisational crisis is a low probability, high impact event that threatens the viability of the organisation, and is characterised by ambiguity of cause, effects and means of resolution, as well as by a belief that decisions must be made swiftly.

And we defined crisis management as:

> A coordinated cross-functional effort to identify, prioritise and actively manage towards resolution those developments that most impact the organisation and where there is a capacity to make a difference.

We also identified nine broad categories of crises, and introduced the 'issue and crisis management relational model' (Figure 1.2) and its four key elements: crisis preparation and prevention in the pre-crisis readiness phase, and incident management and post-crisis management in the response phase (Jaques, 2007). To recap, each of the four segments in the model is built around clusters of activities and processes, many of which link directly to the practice of public relations:

+ *crisis preparedness*—including systems planning, manuals, documentation, infrastructure, war rooms, functional checklists, resources and training

+ *crisis prevention*—including audits, risk assessment, social forecasting, environmental scanning, anticipatory management, emergency response and issue management

+ *crisis incident management*—including crisis recognition, system activation, response initiation and management of the crisis incident itself

+ *post-crisis management*—including business recovery and operational resumption; post-crisis issue impacts such as public investigations and commissions of inquiry, coroner's hearings, litigation and prosecution; and evaluation and modification of the process.

In line with this integrated approach, another valuable approach to defining a crisis comes from British risk expert David Davies (2005, p. 69):

> A crisis is an unplanned (but not necessarily unexpected) event that calls for real time, high level strategic decisions in circumstances where making the wrong decisions, or not responding quickly or proactively enough, could seriously harm the organisation.

This definition highlights two very important elements that emphasise key aspects of our understanding of crisis management: first, that crises are unplanned, *but not necessarily unexpected*; and second, that a crisis calls for *high-level strategic decisions*. Together these ideas combine in the developments that support the themes of this chapter—the concept of pre-crisis management (and prevention) and the emergence of the process approach.

PLANNING AND FOCUS PAY-OFF

Disastrous floods inundated parts of Bangkok in late 2011, including the Bang Pa-In industrial estate, home to two hard disc drive (HDD) factories operated by Western Digital, Thailand's largest foreign employer. The flood shut down about one quarter of the world's HDD supply, causing significant disruption to the global computer hardware supply chain. But production resumed in just forty-six days. This remarkable effort has been attributed to four factors: strong executive leadership and advanced training to ensure people knew what to do; financial strength to hire expert contractors; well-established stakeholder relationships that paid off in a crisis, including with the Thai Government; and an effective enterprise risk management system that helped protect the supply chain. While other flood-affected companies were still struggling to recover, Western Digital rapidly resumed its position as number one in the world market.

Source: Lau Chee Wai and Winai Wongsurawat (2013).

PRE-CRISIS MANAGEMENT

The essential first step towards well-integrated crisis management was the development of the concept of pre-crisis management.[2] This is not a new idea, although the first substantial academic volume devoted entirely to pre-crisis management was published as recently as 2012.[3]

Pre-crisis management is built on the realisation that there are nearly always warning signs—or 'red flags'—that come before crises. This recognition appeared quite early and is seen in the influential publication *Crisis management: Planning for the inevitable* (Fink, 1986), which is regarded as one of the first business books to promote crisis management as an organisational discipline.

Author Stephen Fink introduced and popularised the idea of the *prodromal* (or warning) phase of crisis. He said that prodromes—named from the Greek for 'running before'—constitute the warning signs, and that recognising *and acting* in response to such prodromes often makes the difference between survival and failure in a crisis. Fink himself said the prodromal stage was occasionally referred to as the pre-crisis stage, but he added: 'Usually that appellation is used after the acute crisis has hit, when, in retrospect, people look back at a series of events and point to something as a pre-crisis' (1986, p. 21).

Following Fink's four stage crisis model—prodrome, acute crisis, chronic crisis and resolution—other step-wise models have been developed with a variety of alternative terminology for the pre-crisis phase. For example, Reynolds and Seeger (2005) called it the 'pre-event stage'. But unlike Fink, who suggested that recognition of a pre-crisis usually reflects the 'wisdom of hindsight', later writers made clear that the early phases should constitute genuine, planned steps to prevent crisis and to reduce the risk of an issue

---

2   For more discussion on pre-crisis management, see Jaques (2010) in this chapter's Further reading section.
3   See Olaniran, Williams & Coombs (2012) in this chapter's Further reading section.

developing into a crisis. Or, as Smith (2005, p. 312) described it: 'To be effective, crisis management should, almost by definition, include systematic attempts to prevent crises from occurring.'

This idea is so strong that the respected crisis authority Ian Mitroff (2002) went so far as to declare that in every crisis he had ever studied, there were always a few key people on the inside of an organisation, or on its edge, who saw the early warning signs and tried to warn their superiors. He went on to conclude that 'in every case the signals were either ignored or blocked from getting to the top or having any effect' (p. 20).

Mitroff's assertion might be rather bold, but it captures the central point that a critical role of pre-crisis management is to *identify and act* on warnings to help prevent crises occurring, as well as having response systems set up in advance ready to react when they happen.

Starting to focus attention on what happens *before* the crisis is very important, and it represented a major advance from just thinking about what to do *after* the crisis strikes. But crisis management as it developed tended to neglect what happens when the initial impact of the crisis is over.

> The detection of early warning signals remains an enigma for most organisations.
>
> Ian Mitroff, Katherine Harrington and Eric Gai (1996, p. 44)

To summarise, the modern conceptualisation of crisis management is much more than just crisis response. For example, Penrose (2000) called this 'proactive crisis management' and argued that pre-crisis and post-crisis activities cluster together and should be considered in aggregate rather than as separate sets of activities. This way of thinking helped to address the potential limitation of pre-crisis management (and prevention) and led directly to the 'process approach' to crisis management, which integrates the pre-crisis, crisis response and post-crisis phase into a single, continuous flow.

THE PROCESS APPROACH

The process approach is a more recent development than the idea of pre-crisis management, and is one of the most important advances in crisis management over the past decade.

The traditional way of thinking about crises is largely responsive—to react to a triggering event. This so-called 'event approach' has a strong emphasis on getting ready for a crisis before it occurs and responding quickly and effectively when it strikes. It is also closely aligned to incident or emergency response and is a largely tactical or operational activity that could fall naturally within the responsibilities of functions such as security, emergency management, business continuity or operational recovery.

The role of public relations or corporate communications would be primarily to explain what has happened and what the organisation is doing about it. These functions are generally dealing with the problem rather than trying to prevent it occurring in the first place. In other words, their focus is largely on damage control.

Such activities are very important, but business continuity and operational recovery are not the same as crisis management. However, this is a common misunderstanding for some students and practitioners, and it is not made any easier by the weight of material available. Early on, Pauchant and Mitroff (1992) claimed that 90 per cent of the crisis management literature at that time was focused on what to do when everything falls apart. Fifteen years later Roux-Dufort (2007) said most of the literature was *still* about this tactical event approach. But by then things had already begun to change, with the emergence of the process approach.

Whereas the event approach treats the crisis as a tactical event, the process approach developed from the realisation that a crisis has its origins long before the triggering event, and continues well after the apparent end of the crisis itself.

The process approach to crisis management is not just about being proactive. It is also about crisis management being an integral part of a continuum of activity embedded deep within the responsibilities of the top management of an organisation. It emphasises that this is a role for the top executives, not just operational or tactical people in the front line. This difference was stylishly characterised by the US practitioner Mark Schannon (2006) who coined the concept of *operational preparedness*—plans to contain the problem and quickly get back to normal—versus *organisational preparedness*, which he described as primarily about the creation of a 'crisis mindset' among those in charge.

The central idea behind the process approach was well described by the Dutch academics 't Hart, Hesye and Boin (2001): 'Crises are not discrete events, but rather high-intensity nodes in ongoing streams of interaction' (p. 185). Boin (2004) later added: 'The modern crisis is not boxed in by set dates that mark a clear beginning and ending; it is an embedded vulnerability that emerges, fades, mutates and strikes again' (p. 166).

This conception of crisis as an 'embedded vulnerability' rather than a triggering event is key to the process approach. French crisis expert Christophe Roux-Dufort (2007) further developed the same notion when he coined the phrase 'an accumulation of imperfections' to characterise the origin of organisational crises. In his analysis he went on to say:

> The process approach to crises … leads us to see the triggering event as the factor that reveals a pre-existing dynamic of crisis. In other words, what the event approach sees as the crisis (i.e. the triggering event) the process approach only sees as the amplifier of a process that started long before (p. 228).

The process approach also emphasises the need for strong and active management involvement in the period after resolution of the triggering event. The greatest risk from a crisis, especially legal and reputational, can arise from how the organisation responds following the triggering event. For example, one of the early writers on the subject warned that 'when the dust begins to settle, the aftershocks are often more devastating and costly to the organisation over the longer term than the original crisis' (Phelps, 1986, p. 5). Later, 't Hart and Boin (2001) characterised this as 'the crisis after the crisis'.

Longer term post-crisis events, as identified in the issue and crisis management relational model (Figure 1.2), including coronial inquests, prolonged litigation and hostile media scrutiny, can persist for years or even decades. Furthermore, they may affect the whole industry and not just the organisation initially affected. A good illustration of this is the notorious *Exxon Valdez* incident, which:

+ began in 1989 as an environmental crisis (a major oil spill)

+ became a management crisis (due to a perceived slow and inadequate response)

+ then a management/litigation issue (legal action wasn't finally settled until 19 years later, in June 2008)

+ and, finally, an operational safety issue for the whole industry (it led to changes in construction of bulk tankers and new rules for navigation in narrow waters).

Most importantly, emergence of the process approach to crisis management is not just an academic exercise about theory and definition. It also has a direct impact on the way organisations implement crisis management, particularly the role of top management. And that in turn directly impacts the role of public relations and communication professionals.

CHOCOLATE PLAN CAME TO A STICKY END

While crisis planning is essential, the plan must not only protect the organisation but must also meet the legitimate expectations of stakeholders. In early 2006 Cadbury's discovered salmonella in one of their UK chocolate factories, caused by a leaking waste pipe, yet decided the contamination was so small they wouldn't tell authorities or recall product. However, when the national rate of salmonella poisoning spiked, the problem was traced back to Cadbury's, and may have been responsible for 180 people being infected. The company recalled one million chocolate bars in the UK and Ireland, but this was six months after the problem was identified. The company also admitted the same thing had happened four years earlier. Although Cadbury's had a plan, the authorities said their safety system was out of date and their risk assessment decision-making was inappropriate. The health scare cost the company an estimated £37 million, and they later pleaded guilty to nine health and safety charges and were fined a further £1 million.

Source: Conor Carroll (2009).

As outlined in Table 1.2 in Chapter 1, crisis communication is what gets said by the organisation during and after the crisis. It also provides insight into societal concerns to help develop and communicate strategy. In addition, professional communicators can play an important part in four broad areas that link issue and crisis management, and that focus attention on what needs to be done for effective readiness and response (Jaques, 2012):

1. proactively addressing underlying systemic causes of potential crises

2. establishing effective signal detection mechanisms

3. properly identifying stakeholders and their perspectives

4. learning and unlearning on an ongoing basis.

1   PROACTIVELY ADDRESSING UNDERLYING SYSTEMIC CAUSES OF POTENTIAL CRISES

We have already discussed the importance of recognising early warning signs or red flags (and will do so again shortly), but aligned with this as a major cause of crises can be underlying systemic failures that threaten the organisation. Sometimes these are structural and sometimes they are just failures of the system. Such systemic causes include:

• A structure or management style that inhibits or discourages upward reporting of bad news (often called 'shooting the messenger'); for example, following the disastrous explosion and fire at BP Texas City in 2005, a researcher found a culture at BP in which many top people knew of problems, but few would speak up. 'Only good news flowed upward,' he reported, 'No one dared say the wrong thing or challenge the boss' (cited in Hopkins, 2009, p. 108).

> Top management, by definition, is the least informed group in the company when it comes to bad news. Nothing moves more slowly than bad news running up a hill, a very steep hill.
>
> Kurt Stocker (1997, p. 192)

• Senior management deliberately ignoring or suppressing a problem; for example, early warnings of the impending Ford Explorer/Firestone tyre crisis were identified outside the USA and were 'explained away' as not applying in other markets.[4] Similarly, the Mitsubishi Motor quality scandal emerged when it was revealed that evidence of vehicle recall faults had been deliberately hidden.[5]

• Groupthink, where senior managers collectively convince themselves to proceed down an incorrect path in order to maintain harmony, despite concerns to the contrary; for example, the space shuttle *Challenger* disaster where peer pressure and NASA management systems outweighed individual doubts and allowed a doomed launch to proceed.[6]

There are also other systemic failures. One example is silo thinking, which is where different departments don't talk to each other or share potential problems, and where potential crises don't 'belong' to any one function and fall between the cracks. Another systemic failure is an unwillingness to discuss 'sensitive' issues (sometimes called the 'undiscussables'), which might be embarrassing to management, such as a culture of bullying or sexual and racial harassment or discrimination, or an acceptance of executive dishonesty or questionable practices, all of which have created reputational crisis for many organisations.

THE ROLE OF COMMUNICATOR

It is not normally the role of the communicator to initiate fundamental structural change within an organisation. But communicators can be well placed to raise the reputational risk that might arise from systemic problems, because they often have a direct line of reporting through to senior management or the CEO; they have the ability to listen and

---

4   The Bridgestone/Firestone crisis is discussed in Bridges (2004) in this chapter's Further reading section.

5   For discussion of the Mitsubishi case, see Hagiwara (2007) in this chapter's Further reading section.

6   For detail on groupthink and the *Challenger* disaster, see Esser and Lindoerfer (1989) in this chapter's Further reading section. For a broader discussion on groupthink, see the classic study by Janis (1982) in this chapter's Further reading section.

understand across multiple functions and audiences; they have the communication skills to raise concerns in an appropriate way; and typically they don't have functional demands that lead to silo-thinking because they frequently operate and engage across the organisation (sometimes called 'boundary spanning').

Nystrom and Starbuck (1984) once argued that top managers should listen to and learn from 'dissenters, doubters and bearers of warnings' to remind themselves that their own beliefs and perceptions may not be correct. Rightly or wrongly, in many organisations this dissenter (or devil's advocate) role falls to the communication professional.

2   ESTABLISHING EFFECTIVE SIGNAL DETECTION MECHANISMS

Detecting and acting on warning signs might seem obvious and simple. But history shows that organisations consistently fail to act, and suffer the consequences. In fact, the Institute for Crisis Management in the USA,[7] which has been tracking crises in the news media around the world since 1992, reports that more than two-thirds of crises are not sudden, unexpected events, but are what they call *smouldering crises*; that is, events that could and should have prompted early intervention. As James and Wooten (2005, p. 143) concluded: 'Smoldering crises nearly always leave a trail of red flags and warning signs that something is wrong. These signals often go unheeded by management.'

An instructive example is the case of the giant French bank Société Générale, which reported in 2008 that about $7 billion (€4.9 billion) had been lost through unauthorised transactions by a single rogue trader. An independent inquiry found that the bank had failed to act on seventy-five red flags over a period of eighteen months (Clarke, 2008).

The key to effective signal detection is the link between information and action. Crises often happen not because there were no warnings, but rather because no one turned warnings into practical steps to prevent a crisis.

FAILURE TO HEED WARNINGS

A gas explosion in 2010 at the Pike River coal mine, near Greymouth in New Zealand, cost twenty-nine lives and was one of the country's worst mine disasters. The ensuing Royal Commission found that in the previous seven weeks there had been twenty-one reports of gas building up to dangerous levels and a further twenty-seven incidents of lesser gas build-up, including on the very morning of the accident. The Commission concluded that the company had 'failed to heed numerous warnings of a potential catastrophe at the mine'.

Source: Royal Commission on the Pike River Coal Mine Tragedy (2012).[8]

---

7   See www.crisisexperts.com.

8   Another deadly example of a coal mine operator failing to heed warnings was when twenty-nine miners died after a gas explosion at the Massey Energy mine in West Virginia in April 2010. It was shown that the explosion was entirely preventable and from 2005 to 2010 the company had been issued with 1342 safety violations, totalling US$1.89 million in fines. It was reported that rather than address the safety violations, the company chose to contest the violations in court by challenging the regulations (cited in Crandall, Parnell and Spillan, 2014, p. 60, in this chapter's Further reading section).

THE ROLE OF COMMUNICATOR

As a coordinator of information flowing into and out from an organisation, the communicator is in a strong position to identify warnings that could signal potential crises. In addition, the communicator is often responsible for, or involved with, research into external events and trends. This may range from basic media monitoring and community engagement through to sophisticated stakeholder and data analysis.

As described in Chapter 3, early signal detection is a fundamental element of issue management. And as the person who often has responsibility for implementing issue management, the communicator has both the tools and the opportunity to help ensure effective signal detection systems are in place.

> Whether a company survives a crisis with its reputation, operations and financial condition intact is determined less by the severity of the crisis—the underlying event— than by the timeliness and quality of its response to the crisis.
>
> John Doorley and Helio Garcia (2007, p. 327)

3   PROPERLY IDENTIFYING STAKEHOLDERS AND THEIR PERSPECTIVES

Stakeholders aren't just 'target audiences' who need to be addressed. Nor are they just customers or people who will be affected by an organisation's decision. It has even been argued that a stakeholder is anyone who *thinks* they are a stakeholder. An effective and more specific definition now in common use is:

> A stakeholder is any person or group that is affected by an organisation's decisions and actions—*or can affect that organisation's decisions and actions.*

It is important to note this definition reinforces that dealing with stakeholders means *all* major stakeholders, not just those the organisation chooses to deal with. That could include stakeholders who are vehemently opposed to you, or stakeholders who drive concerns onto the public agenda that you don't think are legitimate issues. (See Chapter 5 for discussion of the role of activist stakeholders in selecting what *they* believe are the issues of concern.)

Looked at in this way, it is very obvious how stakeholders have the potential to cause or promote a major issue or potential crisis—especially with today's use of the internet and social media. Ignoring that potential can represent a very substantial threat to reputation and organisational success.

THE COST OF FAILING TO READ THE COMMUNITY

When the Walt Disney Company announced plans to build a high-profile historical theme park close to a bloody Civil War battlefield west of Washington DC, they thought the issues would be mainly bureaucratic matters such as air and water quality, noise, traffic and property values, and they emphasised that the project would generate 12,000 new jobs and $1.86 billion of tax revenues. However, the company ignored many influential community opinion leaders and instead focused on courting local political and business bosses. After an angry public decided the real issue was 'desecration of American history' the company claimed to be surprised and the plan was eventually dropped.[9]

A classic example of misreading stakeholders was in 1995 when Shell UK tried to sink the disused oil storage buoy *Brent Spar* in the North Atlantic. While the oil giant saw it as a logical and economical engineering solution, with legal and political backing, Greenpeace characterised the plan as 'dumping toxic waste in the ocean' and used a dramatic and media-savvy occupation of the rig to successfully block the project (the *Brent Spar* case is covered in more detail in Chapter 8).

In a remarkably frank assessment after the event, Christopher Fay, Chairman and CEO of Shell UK, told the BBC: 'We covered all the scientific angles, we covered all the technical angles and we certainly very much covered all the legalistic angles. That was maybe a bit inward thinking. We hadn't taken into account hearts and emotions, where people are coming from, which is in part today's debate' ('The battle for Brent Spar', 1995).

Pursuing an 'engineering solution' was equally disastrous in the notorious Intel Pentium Chip Case, where the company mishandled online complaints about a faulty computer chip raised by their most important stakeholders—customers. After weeks of denials and mounting criticism, Intel finally agreed the fault was more serious than they had admitted and announced a $475 million recall. Intel CEO Andrew Grove later conceded: 'We got caught between our mindset, which is a fact-based, analysis-based engineer's mindset, and customers' mindset, which is not so much emotional but accustomed to making their own choice' (cited in Carlton & Yoder, 1994, B1).

In his detailed analysis of this famous crisis, Hearit (1999) concluded: 'It appears that in the case of Intel, an apology does not necessarily mean admitting guilt, but it does mean acknowledging that the customer is always right' (p. 300).

Another case of misreading customers—though much less serious—happened when the giant US clothing company Gap announced in late 2010 that it would change its famous 'blue box' logo. The result was a social media firestorm of criticism. So the company announced it would instead 'crowd source' a new logo. But that idea also failed as thousands of angry customers posted spoof designs. Most significantly, some influential bloggers argued that not only had the company failed to consult customers, but that the logo itself actually 'belonged' to the customers, not the company. Within less than a week the entire project was abandoned and Gap kept its old design.

Acknowledging that the proposed switch was a mistake, Gap North America President Marka Hansen (cited in Hampp, 2010), said:

> Given the passionate outpouring from customers that followed, we've decided to engage in the dialogue, take their feedback on board and work together as

---

9   For analysis of the classic Disney zoning case, see Wiebner (1995) in this chapter's Further reading section.

we move ahead and evolve to the next phase of Gap. We've learned a lot in this process. And we are clear that we did not go about this in the right way. We recognise that we missed the opportunity to engage with the online community. There may be a time to evolve our logo, but if and when that time comes, we'll handle it in a different way.

In each of these examples the stakeholder perspective was ignored or misunderstood. However, the central lesson here is not just listening to a wide range of stakeholders to understand their perspective, but also establishing processes to include them, including those who don't agree with you.

THE ROLE OF COMMUNICATOR

This is an area where the communicator or public relations professional should have a direct involvement. A key responsibility of communicators is to legitimise and recognise stakeholder viewpoints; to bring those perspectives inside the organisation; and, if necessary, to make sure those perspectives are understood and acknowledged. This may be done through research, such as media monitoring and opinion surveys, or though hands-on participation in stakeholder and community engagement.

The other side of this responsibility is to ensure that communication and messages going out from the organisation not only acknowledge stakeholder perspectives, but also use language and communication channels that are suitable for those audiences. Engineers and other executives in technical fields are prone to using complex language and jargon, which might be accurate and legally approved, but comes across to the stakeholder as arrogant and insensitive. As the organisation's language expert, the public relations person needs to produce communication that is technically correct, but that ensures all stakeholders understand its intended meaning.

4   LEARNING AND UNLEARNING ON AN ONGOING BASIS

In the aftermath of a crisis, organisations basically have two main options: (a) to focus on business recovery and avoid any embarrassing discussion about what went wrong; or (b) to try to learn from what happened and hopefully reduce the chance of it happening again.

Unfortunately it seems that many organisations default to option (a), as there is an extensive literature about the barriers to learning from a crisis, and a litany of 'reasons' that are offered as excuses why organisations resist such learning.[10]

Someday we'll look back on this and laugh nervously—then change the subject.

Anon.

---

10 On failure to learn from crises, see Edmonson and Cannon (2005), Pergel and Psychogios (2013) and Smith and Elliott (2007) in this chapter's Further reading section.

It is commonly said that the lesson of history is that we don't learn the lessons of history. This helps to explain why the same crises keep recurring; why organisations suffer the same type of crisis more than once; and why managers seem to keep repeating the same mistakes. In fact, there are well-documented cases where a major crisis has struck the same organisation twice, such as NASA's response to the 1986 *Challenger* and 2003 *Columbia* disasters, and Firestone's handling of their 1978 and 2000 tyre recalls.

One of the factors that underline a reluctance to learn can be seen in findings from the Institute for Crisis Management. In their analysis of crises over many years around the world, their annual reports consistently show that more than half of all reported crises are caused not by natural disasters or other external forces, or by careless workers, but by the actions (or lack of action) by management.[11] Given this fact, it is not surprising that organisations are sometimes reluctant to look too deeply into the lessons from crises, because this may raise awkward questions about management style and organisational culture, as well as about the capacity of individual senior executives and the decisions they made under pressure.

A less threatening way to learn from crisis, and to 'unlearn' bad practices, is to proactively and systematically review crises that have happened to other organisations, perhaps in the same area or the same industry. Facilitating this type of learning review can be an important job for the organisation's communicator.

THE ROLE OF COMMUNICATOR

While the communicator or public relations professional is not necessarily the organisation's compliance manager or trainer, they often have responsibility to help maintain crisis management preparedness, such as keeping the manual and other materials up to date, organising crisis simulations and liaising with external agencies. In that role they are ideally placed to organise or facilitate formal, structured reviews of crises that have happened elsewhere.

When a crisis strikes another organisation it is a very human response to conclude 'Thank goodness it wasn't us' and move on with business as usual. But the communicator can help facilitate a review to consider much more productive questions: 'Could it have been us?' 'And would we have handed it any better?' The review could also be used to test the organisation's media response capacity—to simulate how it would have handled the same questions in the mainstream and social media.

These are steps the communicator can take to add real value to the organisation's crisis preparedness, and they link closely to the requirements for crisis planning, which is discussed in the next chapter.

Note: Parts of this chapter draw on Jaques (2012) and Jaques (2013).

KEY POINTS ———————————————————————

+ The single greatest threat to reputation is a crisis, and real steps can be taken to reduce the likelihood and the impact of a crisis.

+ Iconic crises have helped shape development of crisis management.

---

11 See www.crisisexperts.com.

+ The majority of crises are preceded by early warnings or red flags.

+ The best method of crisis management is to have processes in place to help prevent crises happening in the first place.

+ Integrated crisis management begins long before the triggering event and continues long past operational recovery.

+ The public relations professional is ideally placed to support the four key areas of crisis preparedness.

≡ ACTIVITIES AND DISCUSSION

1. Research any one of the 'iconic' crises listed. What were the key lessons for crisis management and crisis communication? Are those lessons still relevant today?

2. Look for other definitions of a crisis. What are common themes and what are key differences?

3. Examine a recent crisis that has been covered in the news media. Identify ways in which the post-crisis risks to the organisation may be greater than during the event itself.

4. What is the difference between an apology and an apologia, and why is it important for crisis communication?

5. Mark Schannon coined the concept of *operational* preparedness versus *organisational* preparedness. Is one more important than the other, and which should come first?

6. Review the statement by the Gap President Marka Hansen in the section 'Properly identifying stakeholders and their perspectives'. Discuss the effectiveness of her 'explanation' of the company's failed attempt to introduce a new logo.

FROM DENIAL TO RESPONSE – THE INDONESIAN MUD-FLOW DISASTER

Lyn McDonald

University of Queensland

One of the most important roles of an effective crisis leader is to identify that a crisis exists and then to mobilise the organisation's response. But when the Indonesian mud-flow disaster began in 2006, gas operator Lapindo Brantas failed to take responsibility for the crisis, which is Indonesia's largest environmental disaster.

In May 2006, the Lapindo Brantas exploration company began new gas exploration in the district of Sidoarjo in East Java, Indonesia. The disaster started on 29 May when an 8-metre-high hot mud geyser erupted in a paddy field, causing two deaths and widespread respiratory problems in the local area due to the release of hydrogen sulphide gas.

At first the mud flow affected only the exploration site, but soon the rate of flow reached 40,000 cubic metres a day and inundated four adjacent villages, displacing nearly 7000 people. Within months, 450 hectares were covered in mud. Although Lapindo Brantas built levees in an attempt to contain the mud, in November 2006 a levee broke. Later that day, a gas pipe buried under the mud exploded, resulting in thirteen deaths, mostly police and soldiers who were securing the site.

By May 2008 the mud flow covered 1250 hectares, burying sixteen villages and twenty-four factories, and displacing more than 50,000 people. Soon afterwards it was calculated the mud had inundated 14,000 homes, thirty-three schools, sixty-five mosques, a major toll road and an orphanage. The mud flow is expected to continue for many years.

From the start, Lapindo Brantas asserted that the disaster was triggered by an earthquake 600 kilometres away at Yogyakarta, two days before the mud flow started—that it was a natural disaster. But its own joint venture partner accused the operator of incorrect drilling procedures, and this was affirmed by subsequent independent expert analysis.

Although the courts and the parliament later declared the mud flow a natural disaster, within weeks of the event Indonesian President Susilo Bambang Yudhoyono stated that Lapindo Brantas was responsible and soon ordered them to appropriately compensate residents. The government also agreed to share the multibillion-dollar clean-up costs with the politically powerful Bakrie family, the ultimate owner of the company.

Regardless of whether it was human error or a natural disaster, the key issue is: did the company provide the correct response strategy for either crisis cause?

Lapindo Brantas failed to take responsibility for the crisis, despite evidence that the company's procedures were at fault, and in spite of being held responsible for compensation

via presidential decree. In addition, Lapindo Brantas failed in its crisis response strategy, ignoring its relationship with the main crisis stakeholder group: the 50,000 displaced villagers. Further, although the company agreed to pay compensation, despite consistently claiming it was not at fault, its tardy response to the dispossessed resulted in a major humanitarian crisis. Reports early in 2013 said the compensation was still not paid in full.

An examination of newspaper reports examined over the 20-month period at the time indicated that Lapindo Brantas managers avoided a proactive response, avoiding media conferences and making very few statements. Those few statements were usually limited to commenting that the crisis was a natural disaster. No media conference attended by company representatives was identified except a joint one held with Indonesia's president in June 2007 (more than 12 months after the event). No company statement was identified where concern for victims' plight or environmental damage was expressed, or that covered future preventative action. No located stories covered any company announcements on how displaced residents, farmers, employees and businesses were to handle the situation, although this may have been provided on the ground in the affected villages by company officials.

In 2007, a Lapindo vice-president reported that the company handled the evacuations of employees and villagers, and had organised and paid for basic necessities such as food, medical help and amenities for displaced people. But in May 2008, the company stopped providing food for the 600 families still living in a relief centre, stating that they wanted the villagers to accept the compensation offer. The following month, the company placed newspaper advertisements proclaiming its 'social commitment' to the area, but still insisting the mud volcano was a natural phenomenon.

In view of the extent of the disaster in terms of death, social disruption and environmental damage, the company failed to follow even basic crisis communication strategies, such as expressing concern for those affected by the crisis or for the extent of environmental damage, or promising that action would be taken to ensure that this crisis never again occurred.

From an outside view, it appears Lapindo Brantas may have considered that consistently refusing responsibility may create less negative impact for the company's reputation. But the company's inappropriate and conflicting response strategies appear to have directly contributed to the continuing negative emotion and behaviour displayed by the main impacted stakeholder group: the displaced families. All evidence indicates that Lapindo Brantas' poor handling of the Sidoarjo crisis may, in fact, have made the reputational damage even worse.

For more detailed discussion of this case see:

McDonald, L. M. & Widaningrum, W. (2009).
Muddied waters: Lapindo Brantas' response to the Indonesian mudflow crisis.
Paper presented at ANZCA09, *Communication, creativity and global citizenship*. Brisbane, July 2009.

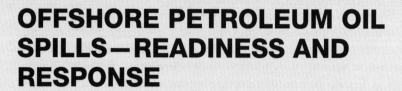

OFFSHORE PETROLEUM OIL SPILLS—READINESS AND RESPONSE

Tina Hunter

University of Queensland

In August 2009 the unthinkable happened. An oil platform in Australia's Exclusive Economic Zone in the Timor Sea (almost 700 kilometres from Darwin, 260 kilometres from the Western Australia coast and 250 kilometres from Indonesia) experienced a loss of control of the exploration well known as H1 in the Montara field. As a consequence of the loss of control of the H1 Well ('Montara'), an initial small oil spill occurred containing approximately 40–60 barrels. This release subsided, but was followed by another oil spill, of higher pressure and volume, which contained a mix of unignited oil and gas.

The platform was abandoned by all personnel soon after, since safety of workers on the platform was compromised due to the presence of unignited oil and gas. The spill and subsequent fire is regarded as one of Australia's worst oil disasters. The identified causes of the spill were a failure to control the well, not installing the necessary pressure containment caps and an incorrectly cemented well.

Oil spills in Australia are regulated under the National Oil Plan (NatPlan), which provides a national framework for responding promptly and efficiently to marine pollution incidents by designating competent national and local authorities to respond to spills. The Commonwealth primarily has the role of coordination, training, technical and logistical support, equipment and materials, and finance. State authorities have jurisdiction from the coast to three nautical miles out to sea, with the Commonwealth having jurisdiction seaward from three nautical miles. On oil platforms, the operator oil company has responsibility for oil spills from the platform, and is required to have a current oil spill plan in place.

In the case of the Montara oil spill, PTTEPAA, the oil company concerned, was responsible for the incidents at its oil exploration rig. Soon after the second oil spill commenced, control was transferred to the Australian Maritime Safety Authority (AMSA). The spill was not finally contained until 3 November 2009, a total of 104 days after the incident began, during which international media attention focused on the spread of a huge oil slick drifting towards the Australian coast and Indonesia.

Australia's response to oil spills is based on three primary aims:

+ to protect human health and safety

+ to minimise environmental impacts

+ to restore the environment, as near as practicable, to pre-spill condition.

In order to meet these aims, it is necessary to maintain readiness to respond to a spill. Preparedness to respond to a marine oil spill such as Montara is contingent upon having the necessary equipment and personnel to respond to an oil spill incident. As such, the training of personnel and the stockpiling of equipment required to respond to oil spills underpin the NatPlan.

Integral to readiness is access to equipment. This equipment is owned by a number of agencies, including AMSA, port authorities and the Australian Marine Oil Spill Centre (AMOSC) in Victoria. The stockpiled equipment includes booms, self-propelled oil recovery vehicles, static oil recovery devices and sorbents, and storage bags and bladders. The equipment stockpiles are located at various Australian ports, with the majority housed at the AMOSC Centre on the east coast in Victoria.

Location of equipment in Victoria is historical, because the majority of Australia's petroleum was originally extracted from the adjacent Bass Strait area. However, the majority of Australia's petroleum activities currently occur in areas offshore of northwest Western Australia. The location of the equipment thousands of kilometres away in Victoria caused major delays in responding to the Montara incident. In reality, in order to maintain best readiness to respond to an oil spill, the majority of oil spill response equipment should be relocated to the mid-north Western Australia coast.

Training comprises regular exercises for personnel likely to be involved in responding to marine oil spills. The training involves federal and state bodies and industry, and the exercises are designed to test the administrative and operational arrangements for responding effectively to a major oil spill, and to test the efficiency and effectiveness of the Oil Spill Response Incident Control System that was implemented in the late 1990s. Each of the four major training exercises since 2000 focused on response to ship-sourced pollution, with the exercises including collisions between an oil tanker and another large vessel, and operational spills from an oil tanker in harbour. As a result, there had been no previous experience in responding to an oil spill from an oil platform.

The difficulty of oil spills from platforms is that, unlike the known quantity of oil on a ship, an oil well poses a limitless source of oil pollution. As such, it is vital to cap the well to contain the spill as soon as possible. Australia's readiness for an oil spill from a petroleum well to date has been poor, and the response to the Montara spill was based on no previous experience. Hopefully lessons have been learnt from the spill, and changes to legislation and regulatory bodies will ensure adequate preparedness and ultimately a better response to future oil spills in Australia.

For more detailed discussion of this incident see:

Hunter, T. (2010). The Montara oil spill and the National Marine Oil Spill
Contingency Plan: Disaster response or just a disaster?
Australia and New Zealand Maritime Law Journal, 24(4), 46–58.

REFERENCES

Allison, G. T. (1971). *Essence of decision: Explaining the Cuban missile crisis.* Boston, MA: Little Brown.

Boin, A. (2004). Lessons from crisis research. *International Studies Review, 6*(1), 165–174.

Carroll, C. (2009). Defying a reputational crisis—Cadbury's salmonella scare: Why are customers willing to forgive and forget? *Corporate Reputation Review, 12*(1), 64–82.

Carlton, J. & Yoder, S. K. (1994, 21 December).Humble pie: Intel to replace its Pentium chips. *Wall Street Journal,* p. B1.

Clark, N. (2008, February 21). Société Générale posts record loss on trading scandal, subprime exposure. *The International Herald Tribune.* Retrieved from www.iht. com/articles/2008/02/210business/socgen.php.

Coombs, W. T. (2007). Protecting organisation reputations during a crisis: The development and application of situational crisis communication theory. *Corporate Reputation Review, 10*(3), 163–176.

Davies, D. (2005). Crisis management: Combating the denial syndrome. *Computer Law and Security Report, 21*(1), 68–73.

Doorley, J. & Garcia, H. F. (2007*). Reputation management: The key to successful public relations and corporate communication.* New York: Routledge.

Falkheimer, J. & Heide, M. (2006). Multicultural crisis communication: Towards a social constructionist perspective. *Journal of Contingencies and Crisis Management, 14*(4), 180–189.

Fink, S. (1986). *Crisis management: Planning for the inevitable.* New York: American Management Association.

Hampp, A. (2010, 11 October). Gap to scrap new logo, return to old design. *Advertising Age.* Retrieved from http://adage.com/article/news/ gap-scrap-logo-return-design/146417.

Hearit, K. M. (1999). Newsgroups, activist publics and corporate apologia: The case of Intel and its Pentium chip. *Public Relations Review, 25* (3), 291–308.

Heath, R. L. & Palenchar, M. J. (2009). *Strategic issues management: Organisations and public policy challenges* (2nd ed.). Thousand Oaks, CA: Sage.

Hopkins, A. (2009). *Failure to learn: The BP Texas City refinery disaster.* Sydney: CCH Australia.

James, E. H. & Wooten, L. P. (2005). Leadership as (un)usual: How to display competence in times of crisis. *Organisational Dynamics, 34*(2), 141–152.

Jaques, T. (2013). Protecting reputation and preventing crisis: The strategic use of issue management. In J. Wrench (Ed.), *Workplace communication for the 21st century: Tools and strategies that impact the bottom line.* (Vol. 2, External workplace communication, pp. 39–61). Santa Barbara, CA: Praeger.

Jaques, T. (2012). Issue management as a strategic aspect of crisis prevention. In B. A. Olaniran, D. E. Williams & W. T. Coombs (Eds.), *Pre-crisis planning, communication, and management: Preparing for the inevitable* (pp. 17–35). New York: Peter Lange.

Jaques, T. (2009). Learning from past crises—Do iconic cases help or hinder? *Public Relations Journal, 3*(1), 1–16. Retrieved from www.prsa.org/prjournal.

Jaques, T. (2007). Issue management and crisis management: An integrated, non-linear, relational construct. *Public Relations Review, 33*(2), 147–157.

Kouzmin, A. & Jarman, A. M. G. (2004). Policy advice as crisis: A political redefinition of crisis management. *International Studies Review, 6*(1), 182–194.

Lagadec, P. (1993). *Preventing chaos in a crisis: Strategies for prevention, control and damage limitation.* (J. M. Phelps, Trans.). London: McGraw-Hill.

Mitroff, I. I (2002). Crisis learning: The lessons of failure. *The Futurist, 36*(5), 19–21.

Mitroff, I. I. (2001). Managing crises before they happen. New York: AMACOM.

Mitroff, I. I., Harrington, K. L. & Gai, E. (1996). Thinking about the unthinkable. *Across the Board, 33*(8), 44–48.

Nystrom, P. C. & Starbuck, W. H. (1984). To avoid organisational crises, unlearn. *Organisational Dynamics, 12*(4), 53–65.

Pauchant, T. C. & Mitroff, I. I. (1992). *Transforming the Crisis-Prone Organisation: Preventing individual, organisational and environmental tragedies.* San Francisco: Jossey-Bass.

Pearson, C. M. & Clair, J. A. (1998). Reframing crisis management. *The Academy of Management Review, 23*(1), 59–76.

Penrose, J. M. (2000). The role of perception in crisis planning. *Public Relations Review, 26*(2), 155–171.

Phelps, N. L. (1986). Setting up a crisis recovery plan. *Journal of Business Strategy, 6*(4), 5–8.

Reynolds, B. & Seeger, M. W. (2005). Crisis and Emergency risk communication as an integrative model. *Journal of Health Communication, 10*(1), 43–55.

Roux-Dufort, C. (2007). A passion for imperfections: Revisiting crisis management. In C. M. Pearson, C. Roux-Dufort & J. A. Clair (Eds.), *International Handbook of Organisational Crisis Management* (pp. 221–252). Thousand Oaks, CA: Sage.

Royal Commission on the Pike River Coal Mine Tragedy. (2012). *Commission report: Volume one.* Retrieved from http://pikeriver.royalcommission.govt.nz/Volume-One—Overview.

Schannon, M. (2006). Risk, issue and crisis management: Ten observations on impediments to effectiveness and what can be done about them. *Journal of Promotion Management 12*(3/4), 7–38.

Smith, D. (2005). Business (not) as usual: Crisis management, service recovery and the vulnerability of organisations. *Journal of Services Marketing, 19*(5), 309–320.

Smith, D. (1995). The dark side of excellence: Managing strategic failures. In J. Thompson (Ed.), *The CIMA handbook of strategic management* (pp. 161–191). Oxford: Butterworth Heinemann.

Stocker, K. P. (1997). A strategic approach to crisis management. In C. L. Caywood (Ed.), *The handbook of strategic public relations and integrated communication* (pp. 189–203). New York: McGraw Hill.

't Hart, P. & Boin, R. A. (2001). Between crisis and normalcy: The long shadow of post-crisis politics. In U. Rosenthal, R. A. Boin & L. K. Comfort. (Eds.), *Managing crises: Threats, dilemmas and opportunities* (pp. 28–46). Springfield, IL: Charles C. Thomas.

't Hart, P., Heyse, L. & Boin, A. (2001). New trends in crisis management and crisis management research: Setting the agenda. *Journal of Contingencies and Crisis Management, 9*(4), 181–188.

The battle for Brent Spar. (1995, 3 September). *BBC Public Eye.* Broadcast on BBC2.

Wai, L. C. & Wongsurawat, W. (2013). Crisis management: Western Digital's 46-day recovery from the 2011 flood disaster in Thailand. *Strategy and Leadership, 41*(1), 34–38.

FURTHER READING

Bridges, J. (2004). Corporate issues campaigns: Six theoretical approaches. *Communication Theory, 14*(1), 51–77.

Coombs, W. T. & Holladay, S. J. (Eds.). (2012). *The handbook of crisis communication.* Malden, MA: Wiley.

Crandall, W., Parnell, J. A. & Spillan, J. E. (2014). *Crisis management: Leading in the new strategic landscape* (2nd ed.). Thousand Oaks, CA: Sage.

Edmonson, A. & Cannon, M. D. (2005, August 22). The hard work of failure analysis. *Harvard Business School Working Knowledge.*

Esser, J. K. & Lindoerfer, J. S. (1989). Groupthink and the space shuttle *Challenger* accident: Toward a quantitative case analysis. *Journal of Behavioral Decision Making, 2*(3), 167–177.

Fearn-Banks, K. (2011). *Crisis communications: A casebook approach* (4th ed.). New York: Routledge.

Gottschalk, J. (1993). *Crisis response: Inside stories on managing image under siege.* Detroit: Visible Ink Press.

Griese, N. (2002). *How to manage organisational communication during crisis.* Tucker, GA: Anvil.

Hagiwara, T. (2007). The eight characteristics of Japanese crisis-prone organisations. In C. M. Pearson, C, Roux-Dufort & J. A. Clair. (Eds.), *International handbook of organisational crisis management* (pp. 253–270). Thousand Oaks, CA: Sage.

Heath, R. (1998). *Crisis management for managers and executives.* London: Financial Times.

Huzey, D., Betts, S. C. & Vicari, V. (2013). *Learning the hard way vs vicarious learning: Post crisis learning for small business.* Paper presented at the Academic and Business Research Institute Conference, Las Vegas, NV.

Janis, I. (1982). *Groupthink: Psychological studies of policy decisions and fiascoes.* Boston: Houghton Mifflin.

Jaques, T. (2010). Embedding issue management as a strategic element of crisis prevention. *Disaster Management and Prevention, 19*(4), 469–482.

Lagadec, P. (1993). *Preventing chaos in a crisis: Strategies for prevention, control and damage limitation.* London: McGraw-Hill.

Mitroff, I. I. (2005). *Why some companies emerge stronger and better from a crisis.* New York: AMACOM.

Olaniran, B. A., Williams, D. E. & Coombs, W. T. (Eds.). (2012). *Pre-crisis planning, communication, and management: Preparing for the inevitable.* New York: Peter Lange.

Pergel, R. & Psychogios, A. G. (2013). Making sense of crisis: Cognitive barriers of learning in critical situations. *Management Dynamics in the knowledge economy, 1*(2), 179–205.

Rosenthal, U., Boin, R. A. & Comfort, L. K. (Eds.). (2001). *Managing crises: Threats, dilemmas, opportunities.* Springfield, IL: Charles C. Thomas.

Sapriel, C. (2010). Why do we keep making the same mistakes? *Communication World, 27,* 28–30.

Seeger, M. W., Sellnow, T. L. & Ulmer, R. R. (2009). *Communication and organisational crisis.* Westport, CT: Praeger.

Seymour, M. & Moore, S. (2000). *Effective crisis management: Worldwide principles and practice.* London: Cassell.

Sheehan, M. & Xavier, R. (2013). *Public relations campaigns* (2nd ed.). Melbourne: Oxford University Press.

Smith, D. & Elliott, D. (2007). Exploring the barriers to learning from crisis: Organisational learning and crisis. *Management Learning, 38*(5), 519–531.

Ulmer, R. R., Sellnow, T. L. & Seeger, M. W. (2006). *Effective crisis communication: Managing from crisis to opportunity.* Thousand Oaks, CA: Sage.

Wiebner, M. (1995). The Battle of Bull Run: How insurgent grassroots lobbying defeated Disney's proposed Virginia Theme Park. *Campaigns and Elections, 16*(1), 44–48.

7

CRISIS MANAGEMENT— PLANNING

CHAPTER OBJECTIVES

This chapter will help you to:

+ understand the difference between issue planning and crisis planning

+ introduce the core elements of a formal crisis management plan

+ assess the role of social media and dark websites in a crisis

+ learn how to establish, equip and train a crisis management team

+ discover why choosing the right crisis spokesperson is so important

+ recognise the special requirements of communication during a crisis

+ evaluate how case study analysis adds to our understanding of the need for planning.

A crisis, by definition, is a situation out of control, when routine responses and processes may not apply. As a result, some organisations take the position that, because a crisis is out of the ordinary and unpredictable, it's a waste of time to plan. In reality, the right answer is the precise opposite. It is exactly *because* crises are beyond routine experience that planning is even more essential—to help provide form and structure for operating in volatile situations.

Before discussing this topic in detail, it is essential to recognise that crisis planning is very different from issue planning. As described in Chapter 4, issue management planning is about the need to develop and implement a specific plan to respond to a defined issue. By contrast, crisis planning is about putting processes in place to identify and deal with future undefined crises if and when they occur.

Of course, every organisation has its most likely crises to prepare for. These can be called 'natural' crises; in other words, the industry-specific or organisation-specific crises that are relatively predictable and should be clear priorities. For example, a chemical company would be expected to plan for a major fire or explosion; for a food manufacturer it might be a fatal product contamination; for an airline a plane crash; for a car-maker a major vehicle recall; for a mining company an underground cave-in; for a hotel a highly publicised outbreak of food-poisoning; and for a bank, men in ski-masks making very large unauthorised cash withdrawals.

> When you look at the majority of crises ... what happened should have been on or near the top of the list of possible events. Why wasn't anyone prepared?'
>
> Kurt Stocker (1997, p. 192)

Planning for such specific potential crises is very important, but for the purposes of this chapter, crisis planning is taken to mean preparing an organisation to respond to any sort of crisis from across the range of operational, procedural, reputational and ethical crisis categories listed in Chapter 1.

However, no crisis plan can cover every possible situation and eventuality. This challenge was well expressed by Andy Grove, co-founder and former CEO of Intel, in the wake of his company's famous Pentium chip crisis (summarised in Chapter 6): 'You need to plan the way a fire department plans. It cannot anticipate where the next fire will be, so it has to shape an energetic and efficient team which is capable of responding to the unanticipated' (Grove, 1995, p. 5). This chapter is about the planning needed to build such a team and to prepare organisations to 'respond to the unanticipated'.

OVERCOMING DENIAL

The first step in crisis planning is accepting the need to plan. This might seem obvious, but research around the world consistently shows that organisations fail to put proper crisis planning in place.

The terrorist attacks on New York and Washington on 11 September 2001 predictably triggered a close interest in crisis preparedness. However, a survey of members and customers by the American Management Association immediately afterwards found that only 49 per cent had a crisis management plan, and only 39 per cent had ever carried out a drill or simulation. A follow-up survey a year later (Ebersole, 2005) showed the number of companies with a crisis plan had increased to 64 per cent, but that soon started to fall back again.

Similarly, a survey of companies in Europe (Burson-Marstellar, 2009) showed that although 60 per cent of the business decision-makers polled had experienced a crisis—more than half within the past year—only 53 per cent currently had a crisis plan in place. There is no reason to think that the level of crisis planning would be any better elsewhere in the world.

So why don't organisations put proper planning in place? One of the most detailed studies to address the question was reported by Mitroff and Pauchant (1990) based on over 350 interviews with top executives in more than 120 companies, which analysed the explanations for why organisations fail to be properly crisis prepared. They identified more than thirty different rationalisations managers have given for *not* putting crisis planning in place. The following is just a sample:

+ Well-managed companies just don't have crises.
+ It is good enough to react once a crisis has already happened.
+ Most crises resolve themselves. Therefore time is our best ally.
+ In a crisis, just refer to the procedures laid out in the manual.
+ We are a team that will function well in a crisis.
+ Every crisis is so different it is not possible to prepare for them.
+ We know how to manipulate the news media.
+ The most important thing in a crisis is to protect our image through clever public relations and advertising (Mitroff & Pauchant, 1990, p. 98).

> The time to repair the roof is when the sun is shining.
>
> Former US President John F. Kennedy

More recently, a survey of CEOs in Australia (Jaques, 2011) suggested this lack of commitment to crisis planning is not so much linked to wilful blindness as to a lack of willingness or experience to prioritise resources. As one CEO commented (Jaques, 2011):

> People prioritise based on day-to-day issues and pressures. And, hopefully, on more than 99% of days, crisis management is not an issue or priority. Consequently, I think there is a tendency for people to put it off. When it's time to do the crisis management stuff, there is always something else which is more important in the short term. It's a matter of planning and priority setting and leadership.

Relating this attitude directly to leadership, Boin and 't Hart (2003, p. 547) summarised the challenge:

> Top business managers are generally averse to take crisis contingency planning seriously. They always seem to have something better to do at the time. The drive for efficiency usually wins out over long-term efforts to improve reliability.

As mentioned in the previous chapter, it is not normally the role of the communicator to initiate fundamental structural change within an organisation. But the communicator is often well placed to work with other functions to highlight the importance of crisis planning, as well as highlighting the very real consequences of failing to do so.

ELEMENTS OF THE CRISIS PLAN

While a crisis management plan must be a written document, it does not need to be a complex production, and the basics can be put in place relatively simply and cost effectively.

Modern practice has certainly moved beyond the four-inch thick binder that hardly anyone ever refers to, and which may be littered with the names of long-departed managers and functional leaders. Best practice today is a practical, relevant and up-to-date 'living document' that reflects the needs of the organisation and focuses on practical guidelines and information rather than flowcharts and needless data. Furthermore, the plan is not only quite brief, but ideally also should be developed as both a printed document and as an electronic version, which can be held in mobile devices and accessed remotely. This is critical for managers working away from head office or the crisis site, or when the crisis itself forces evacuation of offices.

> If only one or two people in your organisation remember the contents of the plan, that's as good as having no plan at all. To make the plan viable, you'll need an ongoing crisis team that actively and regularly trains for a variety of emergency situations.
>
> Richard Levick (2010, p. 57)

There is no one-size-fits-all crisis plan, but there are many common elements in a good plan, which should be seen as a standard management tool and not as a shelf ornament. In reality a good plan comprises three separate components:

1. a readiness and response plan

2. a crisis communication plan

3. a business continuity or operational recovery plan.

Business continuity is typically a largely technical pursuit that focuses on tactical operational matters such as restoring lost power and other utilities; re-establishing online capability and recovering electronic data; maintaining service to customers and suppliers; protecting the logistics supply chain; and restoring business-as-usual as quickly as possible.

As such, this third component is largely outside the present discussion and we will focus on readiness and response and crisis communication.[1]

While each organisation's crisis plan will be constructed differently, these are some of the common elements, which will each be explored separately:

1. designated crisis management team

2. activation process

3. crisis management location

4. clear roles and responsibilities

5. contact lists

6. pre-approved information

7. checklists

8. training

9. crisis communication

10. designated spokespersons.

1 DESIGNATED CRISIS MANAGEMENT TEAM

The crisis management team (CMT) should be named and clearly communicated to people in the organisation. Most importantly, it should not be just the executive team under another label. It should comprise the people who will be the most help in a crisis, some of whom might not be regular members of the executive team.

The main criteria for inclusion should not be rank and status, although whoever is included should have sufficient seniority and influence to make decisions and get things done without unnecessary delays waiting for approval. In other words, the team should be chosen for what they bring to the task, not just because of their job titles.

A common practice is to designate a core team (sometimes called the central or inner team), which assembles regardless of the nature of the crisis. Specialists are then added who would be called on as their particular skills and knowledge are needed. While every organisation has its own specific needs, a typical core CMT might include representatives from:

+ corporate leadership

+ communications (including social media)

+ legal

+ finance

+ human resources

---

1 For discussion on integrating contingency planning and crisis management, see Sapriel (2003) in this chapter's Further reading section.

+ operations
+ business
+ administration (to provide documentation and facilities support).

Other CMT functional or specialist members added, depending on the nature of the crisis (sometimes called the supplementary or outer team), might include:

+ logistics
+ transport
+ health/medical
+ environmental management
+ specific business units
+ emergency response
+ security.

Given the modern demands of travel and other business commitments, many organisations also have a roster of designated alternates or deputies, who are available to step in if one of the main team members is absent. To be effective these alternates *must* be equally well equipped and trained.

2 ACTIVATION PROCESS

Although it seems obvious, some crisis management plans lack a clearly defined process for activating and calling out the team. There should be a clear statement and policy about who is responsible to summon the team and how it is to be activated, though this needs to be flexible enough to cope with extraordinary situations.

Typically this authority lies with the CEO or the CMT chairperson, but the process has to be robust enough to work even when key people are absent or out of contact. Moreover, the activation process needs to work not only during normal business hours but also at night or at 3.00 pm on a Sunday afternoon, or during public holidays.

A common mistake is to delay activating the team 'to wait for more information' or to 'avoid looking as if we are over-reacting'. These responses are understandable, but are potentially very dangerous. An important consideration here is that activating the CMT does not necessarily mean that a crisis has been declared. The team might meet and decide it is *not* a crisis and assess that existing response systems are working well. Or it might decide that it is not a crisis *yet*, and reschedule to meet again later in the day to review developments, while ensuring that key people remain on standby and available at short notice.

Activation can be done in different ways—most commonly by direct phone calls or e-alerts—but whatever method is used, the team members summoned must know what to do and where to go.

3 CRISIS MANAGEMENT LOCATION

This does not have to be a sophisticated 'war room' or 'crisis control centre', but there should be a very clearly identified location where the team assembles. It should be equipped with at least the basic requirements, such as multiple telephones and internet connections, television, radio, photocopier, maps, contact lists and copies of key data (see below). It might be a well-equipped meeting facility or conference room, but should not be the office of the CEO or CMT chairperson, as these will almost certainly be required for other purposes during a crisis.

Beyond basic equipment, other considerations could include:

+ 24-hour access
+ catering and restroom facilities
+ accessible and secure parking
+ back-up power
+ available secretarial and staff support
+ proximity to key managers.

The location should also include a suitable place to meet and brief the news media, preferably well separated from the crisis management room itself and located so that reporters don't need to pass through controlled or sensitive areas.

In addition to the designated crisis management room, it is highly recommended to have a pre-planned back-up location, usually offsite, in the event that the regular location is unavailable or inaccessible; for instance, if it is damaged or evacuated because of the crisis itself. The back-up site may be as simple as a conference room in another building or at a nearby hotel, but the team members need to know where it is and how to gain access.

4 CLEAR ROLES AND RESPONSIBILITIES

Identifying the chairperson of the CMT is a key decision, especially as the best person may not be the CEO, who could be better used dealing with strategic stakeholders or the news media rather than personally leading the team. A common practice is to have alternative chairpersons; for instance, one person if it is a business crisis and another if it is an operational or technical crisis. This approach also helps ensure a back-up if either person is not available. As well as leading the team, the chairperson is often also the person who takes or delegates responsibility to call the team and activate the process.

Apart from this key role, the crisis management plan should spell out the roles and responsibilities of all CMT members, making it clear that these may be different from their day-to-day duties. Similarly, the usual reporting lines for individual CMT members may be different when there is a crisis. They may temporarily be reporting exclusively to the chairperson or another team member, not their usual boss.

Ideally the plan should focus on decision-making and on absolute clarity about who is responsible for each task. Moreover, the CMT members are there to contribute to the team in all respects, not just for their own line or functional role. For example, the organisation may not have a full-time in-house public relations professional, so the business unit representative may be designated to act as contact point and liaison with an external communications expert. Similarly, the organisation may not have an in-house lawyer, so the human resources representative could be designated to oversee any legal aspects and liaise with external counsel.

These supplementary roles are not necessarily complex, but they need to be clearly stated in the plan and understood in advance. In addition, if the crisis is a physical event at an external or remote location, a team member would typically be designated by the CMT to coordinate with the on-site response team to avoid duplication and possible confusion.

LEADERSHIP AND PLANNING

Australian CEOs were surveyed to understand what top leaders involved in hands-on management believe are their roles in crisis preparedness and crisis prevention. The leadership roles identified can be categorised under eight headings and, not surprisingly, many have a strong focus on the importance of planning:

+ Encourage a proactive crisis culture.

+ Establish and enforce standards and processes.

+ Prioritise and set an example.

+ Properly assess the full range of risks.

+ Promote open upward communication.

+ Build relationships before the crisis.

+ Be ready to deal with the news media.

+ Encourage a learning environment and share experience.

Source: Tony Jaques (2012a).

5 CONTACT LISTS

Up-to-date and comprehensive contact lists are an essential tool for effective crisis management, and are often neglected or incomplete. The crisis management plan should include—and regularly review and update—the names and contact details for anyone who might be required in a crisis, not just during office hours but at home if needed. This would typically include:

+ 24/7 contact for all CMT members and alternates

+ senior staff at all locations

+ emergency services

+ news organisations (local and national)

+ government agencies and regulators

+ elected political representatives

+ community leaders

+ major customers

+ key suppliers

+ trade or business associations

+ local hospitals

+ police
+ insurers
+ major shareholders and joint venture partners
+ union leaders
+ external legal and public relations counsel
+ third-party independent experts.

This list is not intended to be comprehensive, and every organisation will have its own requirements. But the time to develop the contact list is *before* it is needed, not during the crisis when it is too late. While the full crisis management plan is often made available online or in electronic format, the contact list (or relevant parts of it) absolutely should be programmed into the phones of all key managers.

6 PRE-APPROVED INFORMATION

When a crisis occurs there is frequently confusion and lack of accurate information about the event itself. Therefore, reliable information that is prepared in advance can become a solid foundation for communication and decision-making. This might include the following.

+ Organisational background:
    - size of operation
    - how many employees
    - key products or services
    - biographies and photos of key executives
    - history of the organisation
    - copies of key policies such as values or mission statement.
+ Facility fact sheets:
    - location maps of operations
    - description of local activities
    - site layout diagrams
    - names of local managers
    - detail of local emergency and back-up capability.
+ Technical data:
    - technical detail about products and services
    - product specifications
    - material safety and data sheets (including hazardous materials)
    - volumes stored.
+ Media templates:
    - pre-written and approved media statements (with blanks to be filled in)
    - extracts from key policies
    - approved summaries of organisational background (as above)

- approved history of past incidents or crises
- frequently asked questions and pre-approved answers
- list of who the media should contact.

The rise of social media has seen the emergence of another important element of pre-approved information: the 'dark website'. This is a micro-website that is formatted and prepared in advance, waiting to be activated very rapidly in the event of a crisis.[2] The dark site is not cluttered with all the usual organisational messages and material, but is focused purely on the present crisis. When activated it would typically include:

+ relevant but brief organisational background (as described above)
+ basic information about the crisis
+ what the organisation is doing to deal with it
+ copies of any media statements that have been made
+ contact information for the news media
+ contact information for the public who may be affected (for example, family of people missing in a major accident)
+ recommendations for what to do (for example, a community near a chemical spill)
+ indication of when fresh information is expected to be available.

7 CHECKLISTS

Checklists are not instructions for what the CMT should do, but provide a formal reminder to ensure important actions or stakeholders are not overlooked in the heat of the crisis.

When there is a temporary lull in the pace of the crisis, team members can use the pre-prepared checklists to continuously review one critical question: is there something or someone we have overlooked? Analysis of crisis case studies shows that communication during a crisis is one of the most frequently criticised failures, often by stakeholders who believe they should have been better informed.

The checklist may collate many of the items already mentioned above, such as roles and contacts. It may also outline key mandatory requirements that are easily overlooked. An organisation may be required to report the potential financial impact of a crisis to its insurer, or to the stock exchange if it is a listed company. Similarly, in many environmental crises, the organisation may be required by law to report the incident to a regulatory authority within a very specific time frame.

Crisis checklists may be generic (across the whole organisation) or may be divided up along functional or departmental lines. Either way, they deliver proven value in ensuring important actions and decision points don't get lost when the pressure comes on.

8 TRAINING

The crisis management plan is of only limited value if it sits on a shelf gathering dust, or if the people concerned are not familiar with its contents and don't know what is expected of them.

---

2   For discussion on the creation of dark websites, see Snellen (2003) in this chapter's Further reading section.

A survey of financial analysts and investor relations officers at companies across Canada and the USA found that while many companies are mindful of the potential damage crises can cause to their sales, reputation and share value, few have an effective crisis management plan in place to deal with negative scenarios—and if they do, it is likely out of date. Of responding analysts, 85 per cent said a corporate crisis had the greatest negative impact on a company's value, yet over 50 per cent said their company plan prepared them only for an operational crisis, and 50 per cent didn't even know if their company conducted crisis simulations (Canadian Investor Relations Institute, 2011).

The most familiar form of training is to hold planned exercises or simulations that present the CMT with a hypothetical situation they must respond to. Good training simulations test the team's capacity to:

+ make decisions against the clock
+ work with incomplete or uncertain information
+ maintain a high-level strategic perspective
+ keep calm under pressure
+ ensure key actions or communications don't get overlooked
+ make effective use of the checklists
+ balance competing priorities
+ work as a team.

Crisis simulations can be complex events involving a large number of people, including emergency services and actors playing roles such as reporters or angry stakeholders, and a full multimedia format. They can equally be table-top exercises focused solely on the CMT itself (plus the designated alternates). The table-top exercise may involve an unexpected operational or management crisis, or may even involve re-running a crisis that has happened to another organisation.

Each approach can be effective, but the key point is that exercises should be held on a regular basis. Most experts believe some formal crisis training should take place at least once a year, and preferably more often.

9 CRISIS COMMUNICATION

Crisis communication is in some ways unlike any other area of public relations. It frequently requires developing and communicating messages under pressure of time, when the information available is confusing or incomplete, when emotions may be running high, and when the organisation is under intense public and media scrutiny.

These challenges when communicating in a crisis were underlined by a US study that showed 57 per cent of the public surveyed believed companies lie or withhold damaging information in the event of a crisis, and a remarkable 95 per cent said they were more offended by a company lying about a crisis than they were about the crisis itself ('U.S. corporations lack credibility', 1993). In fact, long before the invention of the internet, Joseph Scanlon (1975) highlighted the importance of communication in a crisis: 'Every crisis is also a crisis of information. Failure to control the crisis of information can ultimately result in failure to control the crisis' (p. 431).

The detailed demands and techniques of communicating in a crisis are addressed in an extensive body of literature (see examples of manuals and handbooks in the Further reading section of this chapter). While there is a lot more to crisis management than communication, public and media scrutiny is a fact of life in a crisis, and effective communication is vital. Some basic dos and don'ts set the framework for success, and these are listed in Table 7.1.

Table 7.1 Dos and don'ts of crisis communication

Do	Don't
Respond quickly	Speculate about cause or effect
Speak with a single voice	Lie or stonewall
Be informed and accurate	Be 'unavailable'
Admit what you don't know	Treat the media as the enemy
Demonstrate empathy and caring	Say 'no comment'
Stop rumours and correct misinformation	Apportion blame or point fingers
Focus on what you are going to say	Let legal considerations dominate
Say when more information will be available	Use jargon and acronyms

In addition to the use of dark websites to prepare for future crisis (as discussed above), communication using social media is an important development for crisis management, both as a communication tool, and also as the trigger of crises.

At a general level, use of the internet and social media is central to crisis communication. The traditional news media were always important in increasing the exposure of any crisis. Given the focus on speed when crises develop, social media has added to this process of exposure and have created further channels for this to occur.[3] For example, during the shooting rampage at Virginia Tech in 2007, the university's website became a key communication channel with the public, and received up to 150,000 visits per hour (Carlson, 2007).

MULTIPLE ROLES FOR SOCIAL MEDIA

Social and digital media can play three separate roles during a crisis.

1 *Instigator*—where an ill-considered comment or thoughtless response on a social platform can trigger a crisis, and without it the crisis wouldn't have occurred.

2 *Accelerant*—where a similar crisis in the past would not have spread so widely or so quickly without social media.

---

3 For discussion on the role of social media during crises, see Gonzalez-Herrero and Smith (2008, 2010), Kovoor-Misra and Misra (2007), Landau (2011), Perry, Taylor and Doerfel (2003), Phillips (2004), Segars and Jones (2005), Stephens and Malone (2009) and Sweetser and Metzgar (2007) in this chapter's Further reading section.

3   _Extinguisher_—where social media are used effectively before, during and after a crisis to mitigate the damage, and in some cases actually eliminate the crisis.

Source: Dallas Lawrence (2013).[4]

But while digital communication has provided both organisations and stakeholders with new mechanisms for sharing time-sensitive information during a crisis, it can also hinder effective crisis communication by spreading misinformation very rapidly.

In fact, the extraordinary speed and spread of communication via social media can create crises, or potential crises, even when the organisation concerned has done nothing wrong.[5] For example, a newspaper in Florida was archiving old stories and removing their datelines, when one of those stories—a six-year-old article about United Airlines bankruptcy—inadvertently hit a financial wire service's Google alerts. The airline's shares fell more than 90 per cent before recovering later in the day (Myers, 2008).

Similarly, when hackers took control of the Associated Press Twitter account in 2013 and sent hoax reports that the US President had been injured in two explosions at the White House, the US stock market briefly plunged, wiping US$136.5 billion off the S&P share index before quickly recovering (Selyukh, 2013).

HOW A VIRAL VIDEO SHREDDED AN AIRLINE'S REPUTATION

One of the most famous social media reputation crises occurred after United Airlines baggage-handlers in Chicago damaged the expensive guitar of Canadian singer-songwriter Dave Carroll. Following nine months of emails and failed discussion, United refused to pay the $1200 repair bill and in July 2009 Carroll wrote and posted online the humorous music video 'United Breaks Guitars'.

The catchy tune was viewed on YouTube over a million times within a month, and while United tried to fix the problem, they were too late and their reputation suffered badly. According to the _Times_ of London, 'within four days of the song going online, the gathering thunderclouds of bad public relations caused United Airlines' stock price to suffer a mid-flight stall, and it plunged by 10%, costing shareholders $180 million'.

As the website Fast Company commented: 'Can United's 180 million dollar loss be chalked up entirely to a song on YouTube? Probably not. Did the song have a very real and very negative effect on United's brand equity? Absolutely.'

Within four years the video had been viewed an astonishing 13 million times, and Carroll published a book (Carroll, 2013) detailing his experiences and his analysis of the power of social media.

---

4   Dallas Lawrence, Vice President for Corporate Affairs at Mattel, speaking at a PR Conference in Washington DC, December 2013. Retrieved from www.burrellesluce.com/freshideas/2013/12/14-tips-for-building-your-social-media-crisis-communications-plan.

5   For a business magazine view of how crises mushroom with social media, see Conlin (2007) in this chapter's Further reading section.

Even when real events occur, false internet rumours can create chaos. After an engine exploded on a Qantas airliner leaving Singapore in November 2010, sections of the engine fell on an Indonesian island, and a local blogger's false report that the aircraft had crashed was picked up on Reuters. Before the damaged plane could burn off fuel and land back in Singapore, the company's shares had already started to fall. The case has been widely discussed as a reminder of the importance of organisations closely monitoring what is being said about them in social media ('Qantas A380 incident', 2010). In the aftermath of the near-disaster, Qantas CEO Alan Joyce told the *Wall Street Journal*: 'We were ready for traditional media and we had a press conference by 4 o'clock that afternoon, which I fronted. And we had our press statement out within half an hour of us knowing the issue. But we'd missed this whole [social media] end of communication' (Kelly & Critchlow, 2010).

At the same time, when a real crisis occurs, social media is a vital tool for organisations to get information out quickly and remain ahead of rumours. It also enables an organisation to respond via the same channel. Two bored Domino's Pizza employees in North Carolina famously filmed themselves doing disgusting things to a pizza and posted the video on YouTube. The result was a brand reputational crisis when their antics had about a million views in two days before being taken down. The company responded with a message on its corporate website within a day, but it got little traction and Domino's was criticised for not speaking out. Then the CEO uploaded a recorded apology onto YouTube and gained widespread praise for his response.[6] In a social media world, the company had demonstrated 'the critical importance of reaching out to a target audience on its own terms and in its own preferred space' (Levick, 2009).

As part of crisis communication planning, every organisation should have experienced staff responsible for managing social media monitoring and communication. And every organisation should have its own established social media presence; at the very least its own Twitter account and Facebook page. However, the rate of practical adoption in many areas is disappointingly slow. For example, a survey of business continuity practitioners in US companies in 2013 found that more than half (57 per cent) did not officially use social media as a crisis management resource, and only 8 per cent believed that social media had become an enabler for their organisation to proactively identify and respond to crisis events (PwC, 2013).

Apart from social media, crisis communication planning demands proficient implementation of some very basic tactical and logistical aspects, many of which have already been mentioned. In addition, there is the issue of selecting the best spokesperson, which is addressed below. While specific circumstances vary for every crisis, effective crisis communications typically should be built around the following five key steps, regardless of the channels used:

1. *Briefly state the facts as currently known.* Don't speculate and don't guess, but recognise that you need to address perceptions as well as what actually happened.

2. *Apologise.* To be effective, any apology must be swift and sincere. Apologies that are only grudging or reluctant, or are really non-apologies, can be worse than no apology at all.

---

6   Business Insider included the Domino's case in their 'Biggest PR disasters of the decade' (see www.businessinsider.com.au/the-biggest-corporate-pr-disasters-of-the-decade-2009-12?op=1). For strategic analysis of the case, see Young and Flowers (2012) in this chapter's Further reading section.

3. *Express sympathy.* Those affected by a crisis not only need to hear that you are sorry for the crisis, but that you are also sorry for how it has affected them personally.

4. *Express empathy.* You need to show those affected that you know how they feel. Crises are about feelings as well as facts. Demonstrating empathy shows you are human, not just a brand or organisational figurehead.

5. *Focus on actions.* Describe what actions you have already taken and what actions you plan to take to deal with the problem and prevent it happening again.

> One of the most difficult problems executives face during crises is confronting the fact that a crisis actually exists.
>
> Former US Securities and Exchange Commission Chairman
> Harvey Pitt (cited in Levick, 2010, p. 24)

Cover these five basic requirements and you will go a long way towards avoiding disaster and protecting your reputation. Note that these five initial steps do not include blaming, justification, explanation or recovery. There will be plenty of time for that later, when the initial crisis is over. (See Chapter 11 for discussion of the concepts of image restoration theory and post-crisis discourse.)[7]

Yet effective crisis communication is much more than tactical requirements; it also requires special understanding and genuine management commitment. These formidable management hurdles were well summarised by Seymour and Moore (2000, pp. 85–6):

+ You will need to recognise that you are facing a crisis.
+ You will need to make communications a priority.
+ You will need to establish yourself as a credible source of information.
+ You will need to be honest and open.
+ You will need to be sensitive to the human side of the story.
+ You will need to take cultural differences seriously.
+ You will need to explain yourself in uncomplicated, non-technical language.
+ You will need to see the situation as your audiences see it.
+ You will need to understand the motivations of all your audiences, including critics, and not ignore them.
+ You will need to reorganise your operations to deal with the crisis.
+ You must use and recognise the importance of feelings and emotions.
+ You will need to identify good opportunities to deliver your messages.
+ You must rebuild your reputation for the future.

And, of course, if that wasn't hard enough, it is also important to remember that crisis communication, no matter how good, will never satisfy all your critics.

---

7 For discussion on the concepts of image restoration theory and post-crisis discourse, see Benoit (1995), Jaques (2009a) and Ulmer, Sellnow and Seeger (2009) in this chapter's Further reading section.

10   DESIGNATED SPOKESPERSONS

Choosing the right spokesperson is a frequently underestimated part of crisis management planning. Yet the spokesperson has one of the most important roles in dealing with a crisis. *What* the spokesperson says, *how* it is said and *where* it is said are all critical elements in helping to determine the perception of how well the organisation is responding to a crisis.

Despite the critical importance of this role, many organisations simply revert to the default position that 'the CEO is our only spokesperson' without properly considering whether that is the best option. This decision revolves around two distinct questions: first, who should be the spokesperson? And second, what qualities should that person display?

There are many cases of a leader being a positive and inspiring spokesperson in response to a crisis. One of the most frequently mentioned examples is the role of Mayor Rudy Giuliani of New York in the wake of the 9/11 terror attacks on the city's twin towers. Another less publicised instance was when there was a major oil spill off Huntingdon Beach in Orange County, California. Even though the spill came from a contract carrier, *American Trader*, after it ran over its own anchor, the CEO of BP America flew to the scene and told a press conference: 'Our lawyers tell us it's not our fault. But we feel like it's our fault and we are going to act like it's our fault' (cited in Sandman, 2002). The BP legal department may not have been very happy, but because the communication and clean-up were relatively well handled, the spill was soon out of the headlines (though BP and tanker owner Attransco were eventually fined). Contrast this with the *Exxon Valdez* oil spill, which happened only a year earlier and remains to this day a persistent blot on Exxon's reputation.

Sadly, there are also many examples of a CEO who performs badly and further damages the organisation's reputation. In the case of the *Exxon Valdez* crisis, the CEO/chairman made no statement for six days, and when he did eventually emerge he gave a disastrously mismanaged television interview in which he tried to blame others for the crisis.

There are even cases where a statement by the CEO has actually triggered a crisis, most famously when Gerald Ratner, CEO of a British high street jewellery chain, gave a speech in which he described his own products as 'total crap' and said his company's earrings were 'cheaper than a prawn sandwich and probably wouldn't last as long'. [8] The result was virtual destruction of the business, which lost £500 million in shareholder value and led to the closure of 330 stores and the loss of 2500 jobs, including his own. Ratner certainly isn't the only CEO who has made an appalling verbal gaffe, but he is one of that rare group whose statements have crossed the line from personal and corporate embarrassment to an actual corporate crisis.

So should the CEO be the crisis spokesperson? The problem here is that the question itself is easily misunderstood. Absolutely the CEO should be visible and speak when there is a crisis, especially to address issues of policy and to show the organisation cares. However, that does not mean the CEO should be the *only* spokesperson; nor does it mean they should speak on each and every aspect of the crisis on a 24/7 basis. The CEO should speak to demonstrate compassion and commitment to fixing the problem. Yet it is entirely

---

8   For detail on the Gerald Ratner case and a catalogue of other high-profile CEO gaffes, see www.mirror.co.uk/news/uk-news/gerald-ratner-and-the-top-10-business-1305316.

appropriate—indeed, even desirable—to have a number of different spokespersons to talk about technical or operational details, or to provide routine media updates.

Having qualified and well-trained alternative spokespersons helps reduce the risk of over-exposing the CEO and also allows the CEO to focus on providing leadership to manage the crisis. Furthermore, it allows the CEO to be held 'in reserve' to step in if things start to go wrong.[9]

The argument against this approach is the idea that, in the event of a crisis, the organisation must 'speak with one voice'. That is true, but speaking with one voice does not mean having only one spokesperson—it means consistency of message. It means that while new facts may emerge about the crisis, the overall message doesn't keep changing from hour to hour. And it means that the message remains unchanged across all the designated spokespersons—a calm, consistent and qualified voice.

WHEN THE SPOKESPERSON GETS IT DISASTROUSLY WRONG

Crises put everyone involved under intense pressure, and the organisation spokesperson more so than almost anyone else. An explosion at the Sago coal mine in West Virginia on 2 January 2006 trapped thirteen men underground. After almost 40 hours of desperate effort, the CEO announced at 9 p.m. that twelve of the miners still missing had been found and a rescue was underway. Then, just before midnight, unverified reports emerged that all twelve men had been rescued alive. Within minutes the company realised it wasn't true, yet the spokesman said nothing while the local community celebrated and newspapers around the country headlined the 'miracle'. After waiting three hours, the company finally announced the awful truth—that all twelve were dead. By way of explanation, the distraught CEO said: 'In the process of being cautious, we allowed the jubilation to go on longer than it should have.' He was certainly right but it wasn't much comfort for the families ... or for scores of embarrassed newspaper editors.[10]

THE QUALITIES OF AN EFFECTIVE CRISIS SPOKESPERSON

A common problem is that the designated spokesperson for routine non-crisis situations may be unsuited to speak for the organisation during a crisis. For example, the CEO may be highly professional and respected when announcing business results or a new corporate takeover to an audience of shareholders and financial analysts. But the same person may appear pompous and uncaring when speaking to the families of people killed in a terrible accident.

The way a spokesperson speaks and how they engage with key—sometimes hostile—audiences is never more important than in a crisis. A range of skills can be taught, but some

---

9   For discussion of the role of CEO as spokesperson, see Jaques (2012b).

10   For detail on this widely analysed communication failure, see Center et al. (2008) and Schimmoeller (2008) in this chapter's Further reading section. The Sago disaster is also a case study of failing to heed warning signs before a crisis. Over the previous year, the mine had been cited 208 times for safety violations, ninety-six of them 'significant and substantial'.

requirements rely more on personal qualities. This checklist provides a good starting point for selecting the right crisis spokesperson. They should have:

+ the capacity to communicate empathy as well as authority
+ the ability to make commitments on behalf of the organisation
+ a good understanding of the crisis and organisational response
+ enough technical knowledge to avoid embarrassing mistakes
+ the ability to stay calm under pressure
+ previous experience with news media and other stakeholders
+ the capacity to operate in a highly fluid and unstructured situation
+ the ability to avoid jargon and corporate speak
+ a willingness to listen as well as talk.

Then, and only then, should you ask: has the person been media trained?

SHOULD THE CEO GO TO THE SCENE TO TAKE CHARGE?

A further tactical question for crisis planning—and one of the more contentious—is where the CEO should be during the crisis. In fact, the US crisis expert William Small (1991) says no other issue has been debated so much as the role of the CEO in the first few hours of a crisis, and whether he or she should race to the scene.

In some ways this question is almost unanswerable, and it links closely to the previous discussion about the CEO as spokesperson. At one level the solution seems quite simple: the CEO should be where he or she can do the most good for the organisation—perhaps out in the field comforting victims, perhaps in the board room directing recovery or perhaps at external meetings to reassure investors, regulators and other stakeholders.

But as the essayist and satirist H. L. Mencken is reported to have said: 'For every complicated problem there is a solution which is clear, simple and wrong.' That is certainly the case here. In the fast-moving world of social media, the answer is not only about doing the right thing but about being seen to do the right thing—about perception and reputation.

US President George Bush was famously attacked for failing to go to New Orleans soon enough after it was ravaged by Hurricane Katrina, even though it was claimed he was in Washington with his experts closely monitoring and managing the situation. Similarly, BP Chief Tony Hayward was bitterly criticised after being photographed at a yachting regatta in Britain during his company's Gulf of Mexico oil spill disaster, despite the fact that he had been constantly on call for the media for weeks. By contrast, the Chairman of Union Carbide was praised for flying to India immediately after the chemical leak at Bhopal in 1984 to take charge on the scene. However, he was promptly arrested on arrival and spent almost a week cut off from proper communication in an Indian prison, leaving the company leaderless at a critical time.

The window of opportunity for the CEO to do the right thing in a crisis is very narrow, and it is sometimes extremely hard to know what is the right thing to do. Broadly, however, there are good grounds to argue that the CEO *should* go to the scene of a crisis, even if for no reason other than to be visible and to show the organisation cares.

LEARNING FROM PAST CRISES

The final contribution to learning about crisis planning—as with many other areas of public relations—is to review past cases and look for lessons that can be applied to planning for the future.

The case study approach is popular because it tests public relations theories and models against real-life events and lends colour to the discipline. It also leads to three key questions in every case: What did the organisation concerned do well? What could they have done better? And, most importantly, what can be learned from the case? That is one of the reasons why relevant case studies appear throughout this book. When case studies are examined in detail through formal analysis, it provides time and a structured framework to:

+ apply communications theory in real-world situations
+ reflect in depth on the actions of direct participants
+ explore and develop alternative courses of action
+ reinforce key concept learning through practical application
+ research cases from original sources
+ critique the conclusions and hypotheses of other scholars
+ develop worst-case scenarios
+ assess the impact on a wider range of stakeholders
+ apply current attitudes, expectations and technology to past cases
+ consider the case in different cultural, political and geographic contexts.[11]

There are some broad limitations to organisational learning from case studies, especially in the area of issue and crisis management.[12] One limitation is that emphasis on high-profile cases can wrongly suggest that issues and crises only happen—or mainly happen—to big organisations. Another is that, because many published cases rely heavily on publicly available material such as news media reports, there can be an unwarranted impression that media coverage should be the main management focus and main tool for evaluation. A further limitation that relates directly to crisis planning is the need to draw the *correct* lessons from the case, and to ensure that those lessons are still applicable or relevant to the circumstances today.

> You'll never have a crisis someone else hasn't experienced.
>
> US crisis expert Larry Smith (cited in Smith & Miller, 2002, p. 1)

---

11 For further discussion on the case study approach, see Jaques (2008, 2009b) in this chapter's Further reading section.

12 For an exploration of the issue of barriers to post-crisis learning see Smith and Elliott (2007) and Veil (2011) in this chapter's Further reading section.

As discussed in the previous chapter, some crises have become so well known they have effectively entered into the vocabulary of crisis management. It's worth examining one of these 'iconic' cases to consider whether or not it really does add value to modern crisis planning.

In late September 1982 an unknown person spiked Tylenol headache capsules with cyanide, killing seven people in the Chicago area. Johnson & Johnson eventually recalled 31 million bottles of capsules, and the adoption of tamper-resistant packaging was accelerated before the capsules were reintroduced. While the killer was never found, the company was widely acclaimed for its prompt voluntary recall and its commitment to openness with the public and the news media.

Many aspects of Johnson & Johnson's response were rightly praised, and the case is sometimes cited as the 'gold standard' for crisis response. But in a contrarian analysis, Gorney (2002) highlighted that changing variables since 1982 render many of the crisis management and crisis communication aspects meaningless. She concluded that the principal point at issue is whether the Tylenol model should be assumed as the most appropriate for all crises *today*, in particular for product recalls; and, arising from this, the expectation that applying the model would have the same result as it did there decades ago, when the communication, legal and public opinion environment was entirely different.

> A case study is a fiction, written after the fact, to make the practice of public relations more real.
>
> John Pauly and Liese Hutchison (2001, p. 382)

For example, one of the actions for which Johnson & Johnson received most praise was its nationwide recall of Tylenol capsules, despite the fact that the cyanide deaths were confined to the Chicago area, and that it had no legal requirement to do so. However, the initial company recall after the fatalities was, in fact, limited to Chicago and extended only to certain batches of Tylenol Extra-Strength, the variety in which the poison was found. Johnson & Johnson then extended their own recall to seven midwestern states. Yet the full nationwide Tylenol recall was not implemented until five days after the first death, a decision reportedly taken only after a copycat case occurred in Northern California.

Amid today's news media, public and regulatory expectations, and social media scrutiny, it is difficult to conceive that seven deaths would *not* lead to an immediate national recall. Any company today that took five days to initiate a national recall after multiple deaths would probably not be praised for promptness but would most likely be unmercifully attacked for delay.

Many other aspects of this case also warrant critical review,[13] but for the present discussion one other detail is important. Despite being held up as a 'standard-setting'

---

13 See Jaques (2009c) in this chapter's Further reading section.

case, during the Tylenol crisis Johnson & Johnson had no formal crisis management plan (these were not common at that time) and claimed they relied instead on the corporate credo, which sets out the company's values. In fact, Mitroff and Anagnos (2000) said Johnson & Johnson top management later stated that no prior special training would have helped them manage the poisonings better. Furthermore, despite the passage of time, they asserted that, 15 years later and contrary to most contemporary opinion, the company apparently *still* believed that no special crisis training was necessary for executives to prepare for a crisis.

It is possible that this thinking—and their much-vaunted reputation—contributed to severe criticism of Johnson & Johnson in 2010 when they had to recall forty-three medicines because of recurring manufacturing faults ('Johnson & Johnson's recalls infant', 2010), and in 2012 when they had to recall half a million of bottles of infant Tylenol because of a faulty bottle design. Following these and other serious problems, one respected online source described Johnson & Johnson as 'recall-plagued' (Johnson, 2012)—not exactly the preferred description if crisis planning has been effective.

CONCLUSION

It is widely held that an organisation's reputation is impacted as much by the way it responds to the crisis as by the impact of the crisis itself. Although the crisis event may be wholly or partly outside the organisation's control, the management response is typically very much within the organisation's control.

In other words, while the organisation doesn't control the crisis, it does control the crisis plan. However, it is essential to recognise that the plan is not a blueprint. It is a framework for making logical and informed decisions when the risks are greatest and when the organisation is most in need of effective leadership. That leadership and effectiveness is often a reflection of prior commitment to proper crisis planning.

Note: parts of this chapter draw on Jaques (2013).

KEY POINTS ————————————————————————

+ A crisis plan needs to be a 'living document', not an outdated folder on a shelf gathering dust.

+ Individual roles and responsibilities during a crisis may different substantially from what is required during 'business as usual'.

+ Business continuity planning is not the same as crisis preparedness.

+ The CEO is not always the best choice for crisis spokesperson.

+ Some companies and industries face 'natural' crises that are specific to their field of activity.

+ While analysing past crises helps understand the need for planning, some iconic crisis cases may have limited relevance today.

≡ ACTIVITIES AND DISCUSSION

1. List some reasons why organisations fail to properly prepare for crises. What can be done to overcome these failures?

2. Select an organisation and draft a pre-written media template for use in a crisis (with blanks left to be filled in). Would a single template cover all eventualities or are several needed?

3. Research cases where the spokesperson had a major role in the perception of a crisis. What qualities distinguished successful leaders? If the spokesperson made the situation worse, what did they do wrong?

4. Write a brief hypothetical crisis simulation scenario for an organisation you are familiar with that would test the capability of the management team. The scenario should have at least six phases of 'escalation'.

5. Identify William Benoit's five image repair strategies. Are they still relevant today? (See, for example, www.prsa.org/intelligence/prjournal/documents/2012fergusonwallacechandler.pdf.)

PLANNING FOR A CRISIS—EVEN WHEN IT'S A HOAX

Timothy Sellnow

University of Kentucky

On 10 May 2005, New Zealand's Prime Minister received a threat letter claiming a release of a vial of the foot and mouth disease (FMD) virus on Waiheke Island, near Auckland.

New Zealand's Ministry of Agriculture and Forestry (MAF) was charged with managing the case as the disease could devastate the country's vital farming industry. So even though MAF suspected the letter may have been a hoax, the threat was considered viable and they triggered their full crisis-response plan. It was very swift, particularly on the first day, and a great deal of information was developed in a short period of time and disseminated to media outlets to alert farmers who could have been affected by the attack.

MAF held daily press conferences and involved many industry organisations in the emergency response to deal with concerns expressed by farmers and the general public. The press conferences were led by the Assistant Director-General of Biosecurity for New Zealand, with police and Food Safety Authority officials also present. They also held a public meeting on Waiheke Island and contacted farmers. The agency tested cattle in the alleged area of infection, but found no cases of foot and mouth disease.

Although they suspected from the start the letter was a hoax, MAF recognised and acknowledged the catastrophic consequences an FMD outbreak would create for New Zealand. (A subsequent government report estimated that such an outbreak would cost more than 10 per cent of the country's Gross Domestic Product and devastate the economy.) In an effort to maintain or regain the confidence of worried farmers and the general public, MAF officials showed patience in challenging the evidence used by the hoaxer, revealing an overwhelming suspicion that the claims were unlikely or impossible.

The lead communication officer at MAF illustrated this criticism of the evidence: 'Some information contained in the letter regarding the alleged method of contaminating livestock with FMD also raised concerns with our animal health experts as to the veracity of the letter.' The Biosecurity Director summarised his review of the evidence from the letter: 'Simply, we didn't think it was a terrorist action. We thought it was a hoax and the nature of the letter took us that way.'

As the responders challenged the evidence proclaimed by the hoaxer, the threat became suspect. The Post-clearance Director of Biosecurity for MAF explained:

> I guess one of the things that helped we had an early assessment from the police, saying they have a threat assessment unit, who looked at the letter and said it was credible enough to be taken seriously that there were enough inconsistencies or questions ... things around it that made them think that the release probably

hadn't happened and they deduced from their own [findings] things like we don't have foot and mouth disease anywhere in the country ... so it would have had to be brought over. We thought it was a little odd that if someone was going to do it they'd chosen [Waiheke]. So there was enough in there to make us doubt that it was real but you know we had to take it seriously.

Through a process of questioning the scientific evidence, and using the content, form, and sequence of the actual hoax document, responders were able to demonstrate a level of confidence that, while responding with caution and compassion for worried farmers, the MAF was able establish its credibility in managing the case.

On 14 May 2005, a newspaper in Wellington received a second letter, which was verified to be from the original hoaxer. Further tests continued to show no cases of foot and mouth disease on Waiheke Island and two days later MAF issued a press release officially declaring the foot and mouth disease threat a hoax. Two weeks after the first letter was received, and after the maximum incubation period for clinical symptoms of FMD, the task force was stood down.

The success of the crisis response plan was based on three key guiding principles that shaped the strategy and messaging:

1   making a direct attack on the incident and credibility of the hoaxer in order to publicly weaken the legitimacy of the claim

2   demonstrating confidence, preparedness and the capability to deal with the hoax as if it were routine

3   gaining public attention and support through a clear acknowledgment of the potential cost to the country should the threat turn out to be real, but not being willing to take that chance and responding accordingly.

This case has important lessons for other countries facing potential terrorism or biological threats. Terrorism thrives on uncertainty, and no matter how much time and financial resources are devoted to mitigating the risk it poses to citizens and economies, governments can never be certain they have done enough. In the Waiheke hoax case, the MAF's crisis response plan of displaying a balance of scepticism and caution proved effective.

For more detailed discussion of this case see:

Sellnow, T. L., Littlefield, R. S., Vidoloff, K.G. & Webb, E. M. (2009). Interacting arguments of risk communication in response to terrorist hoaxes. *Argumentation and Advocacy, 45,*135–150.

CRISIS PLANNING—CONSISTENCY OF MESSAGE AND RESEARCH ARE THE KEYS

Gwyneth Howell

University of Western Sydney

When MasterFoods received the first of seven anonymous letters, the author claimed that if certain demands were not met, Mars and Snickers bars in New South Wales would be poisoned. Included in the package was a Snickers bar claimed to be laced with household pesticide. Little did the company know that this would lead to a state-wide product recall that would cost the company more than $10 million in terms of sales and product removal.

The cost could have been far greater, but the proactive crisis response by MasterFoods to the extortion threat reinforced that the company placed public interest and safety above the financial costs, and illustrated the impact of research on communication strategies and planning.

MasterFoods is the Australian and New Zealand manufacturer of Mars and Snickers; both listed in the 'top ten' of chocolate bars consumed in Australia. On average one million Mars bars are eaten in Australia every week. The US-based Mars organisation, owner of MasterFoods, champions the five principles of quality, responsibility, mutuality, efficiency and freedom in their business strategy and operations. These principles were key to the effective management of the recall crisis.

The crisis began on receipt of the first letter in 2006 when MasterFoods and the authorities undertook a low-key investigation to prevent public panic and any copycat extortion bid, be it real or a hoax. However, MasterFoods announced and enacted the product recall on receipt of the third letter that contained a specific threat made to the community.

At this acute stage, MasterFoods recognised the need for external crisis communication support and appointed an external consultancy to that role for the duration of the crisis. A core crisis management team (CMT) was established and a crisis management plan (CMP) developed, with MasterFoods Chief Executive Officer Andy Weston-Webb appointed spokesman. To track public opinion and shape their key messages to have the greatest influence during the crisis, MasterFoods retained a market research firm to conduct field research throughout the period. This enabled the company to measure and track the key messages developed for the response strategy. The five key communication messages were:

1 tampering crisis

2 product safety

3 police investigation

4 corporate reputation and

5 product reputation.

The research measured key message effectiveness during the seven-week crisis period on two key target publics: women aged 25–45 years with children and young male adults aged 18–25 years. This research established consumers' understanding of the extortion, how MasterFoods was responding to the situation, when consumers felt it would be safe to purchase products again, and who should inform the public that it was again safe to consume the products. The hotline/call centre also provided additional anecdotal research to supplement the formal focus groups and survey data. This data confirmed individual concerns and opinions during the telephone conversations. These data were combined to provide MasterFoods with a clear and expansive view of the current options of the key target market segments.

A media conference was used to announce that the company would begin its recall of Mars and Snickers bars. Weston-Webb explained that the recall of products would require the assistance of 40,000 outlets throughout New South Wales. During the crisis, the use of video news releases was persuasive and effective. The first depicted the CEO physically removing the recalled products off supermarket shelves.

The company used traditional advertising to detail the reasons for the recall. Further, the company established a crisis hotline number that allowed a two-way dialogue between consumers and MasterFoods. (Today, this would occur through various social media channels and the company website.) Through this hotline, consumers could enquire, report any illnesses arising from eating one of the bars, and access information on where they could get refunds for already purchased products.

During the initial twenty-four hours of recall, MasterFoods was questioned and criticised in the media over its delay in recalling the products after the company said it had received two earlier letters, one of which contained a contaminated Snickers bar. However, Weston-Webb defended the company's procedures and asserted that New South Wales police were contacted after the first chocolate bar and note were received.

More letters would be received, with one letter from the extortionist identifying Sydney's Star City Casino as the target of the extortion, not MasterFoods. The threat to the public was deemed negligible, and snack bars returned to shelves heralded by a state-wide advertising 'We're Back' campaign, with Weston-Webb as its spokesperson. With the product returned to shelves, sales rose 250 per cent.

The lesson is that throughout the crisis MasterFoods was consistent and coherent in its planned communication. It employed an open, honest and direct communication with the key publics, informed through sound research. Finally, throughout the crisis it maintained the same, consistent message that public safety was the number one priority, and at the conclusion of the crisis the company's image and reputation was enhanced.

For more detailed discussion of this case see:

Howell, G. V. J. (2006). MasterFoods and the
Mars Snickers recall—Practitioners using
research to develop, craft and measure the message.
Asia Pacific Public Relations Journal, 7(2), 193–208.

REFERENCES

Boin, A. & 't Hart, P. (2003). Public leadership in times of crisis: Mission impossible? *Public Administration Review, 63*(5), 544–553.

Burson-Marsteller. (2009). *New survey shows that only half of European firms have a crisis plan in place in spite of the significant financial and reputational benefits of crisis preparedness.* Retrieved from www.oursocialmedia.com/category/brussels/bursonmarsteller-brussels.

Canadian Investor Relations Institute (2011, 12 April). Few companies are prepared to manage a crisis. *Business Wire.* Retrieved from www.businesswire.com/news/home/20110412005462/en/Survey-Companies-Prepared-Manage-Crisis.

Carlson, S. (2007). Emergency at Virginia Tech shows the power of the web, says campus official. *Chronicle of Higher Education, 53*(48), 28.

Carroll, D. (2012). *United break guitars: The power of one voice in the age of social media.* Carlsbad, CA: Hay House.

Ebersole, J. G. (2005). *Crisis management planning—What's happening where we work?* Retrieved from www.evancarmichael.com/Business-Coach/223/Crisis-Management-Planning--Whats-Happening-Where-We-Work.html.

Gorney, C. (2002). The mystification of the Tylenol crisis. *Public Relations Strategist, 8*(4), 21–25.

Grove, A. S. (1995). *Only the paranoid survive: How to survive the crisis points that challenge every company and career.* New York: Currency-Doubleday.

Jaques, T. (2013). The leadership role in crisis prevention. In A. DuBrin (Ed.), *The handbook of research on crisis leadership in organisations* (pp. 270–289). New York: Edward Elgar.

Jaques, T. (2012a). Crisis leadership: A view from the executive suite. *Journal of Public Affairs, 12*(4), 366–372.

Jaques, T. (2012b). Is the CEO really the best crisis spokesperson? Four myths exposed. *CEO Magazine*, April, 10–12.

Jaques, T. (2011). Barriers to effective crisis preparedness: CEOs assess the challenges. *Asia Pacific Public Relations Journal, 12*(1).

Johnson, L. (2012, 17 February). Infant Tylenol recall: Johnson & Johnson recalls medicine over bottle design problems. Retrieved from www.huffingtonpost.com/2012/02/17/infant-tylenol-recall-joh_n_1284545.html.

Johnson & Johnson's recalls infant, children's Tylenol, Motrin, (2010, 2 May). *Reuters.* Retrieved from www.reuters.com/article/2010/05/02/us-fda-recall-children-idUSTRE6401AK20100502.

Kelly, R. & Critchlow, A. (2010, 28 December). Qantas copes with aftermath of A380 crisis. *Wall Street Journal*. Retrieved from http://online.wsj.com/news/articles/SB10001424052748703734204576019190757330026.

Levick, R. S. (2010). *The communicators: Leadership in the age of crisis*. Washington DC: Watershed Press.

Levick, R. S. (2009, April 21). Domino's discovers social media. *Bloomberg Businessweek*.

Mitroff, I. I. & Anagnos, G. (2000). *Managing crises before they happen: What every executive and manager needs to know about crisis management*. New York: AMACOM.

Mitroff, I. I. & Pauchant, T. C. (1990). *We're so big and powerful nothing bad can happen to us: An Investigation of America's crisis-prone corporations*. New York: Birch Lane.

Myers, S. (2008, 9 September). Tribune Co., Google explain revival of outdated United bankruptcy story. *Poynter*. Retrieved from http://www.poynter.org/latest-news/top-stories/91401/tribune-co-google-explain-revival-of-outdated-united-bankruptcy-story.

Pauly, J. J. & Hutchison, L. L. (2001). Case studies and their use in public relations. In R. L. Heath (Ed.), *Handbook of public relations* (pp. 381–388).Thousand Oaks, CA: Sage.

PwC. (2013). *Many companies still not leveraging social media as a crisis management resource*. PwC Business Continuity Survey. Retrieved from www.pwc.com/us/en/press-releases/2013/many-companies-still-not-leveraging-social-media.jhtml.

Qantas A380 incident: A lesson in social media and web PR. (2010). *Tnooz*. Retrieved from www.tnooz.com/2010/11/04/news/qantas-a380-incident-a-lesson-in-social-media-and-web-pr.

Sandman, P. M. (2002). *Lawyers and outrage management*. Retrieved from www.psandman.com/col/lawyers.

Scanlon, J. (1975). *Communication in Canadian society*. Toronto: B. D. Singes.

Selyukh, A. (2013, 24 April). 'White House explosions' Twitter hoax shakes US markets. *Sydney Morning Herald*. Retrieved from www.smh.com.au/it-pro/security-it/white-house-explosions-twitter-hoax-shakes-us-markets-20130424-2idbc.html.

Seymour, M. & Moore, S. (2000). *Effective crisis management: Worldwide principles and practice*. London: Cassell.

Small, W. J. (1991). Exxon Valdez: How to spend billions and still get a black eye. *Public Relations Review, 17*(1), 9–25.

Smith, L. R. & Millar, D. P. (2002). *Before the crisis hits: Building a strategic crisis plan*. Washington DC: Community College Press.

Stocker, K. P. (1997). A strategic approach to crisis management. In C. L. Caywood (Ed.), *The handbook of strategic public relations and integrated communication* (pp. 189–203). New York: McGraw Hill.

U.S. corporations lack credibility: Poll finds 57% think they lie. (1993, 14 August). *Toronto Star,* p. E3.

FURTHER READING

Benoit, W. L. (1995). *Accounts, excuses and apologies: A theory of image restoration strategies.* Albany, NY: State University Press of New York.

Berg, D. M. & Robb, S. (1992). Crisis management and the 'Paradigm Case'. In E. L. Toth & R. L. Heath (Eds.), *Rhetorical and critical approaches to public relations* (pp. 93–19). Hillsdale, NJ: Lawrence Erlbaum.

Bland, M. (1998). *Communicating out of a crisis.* London: Palgrave Macmillan.

Burns, J. P. & Bruner, M. S. (2000). Revisiting the theory of image restoration strategies. *Communication Quarterly, 48*(1), 27–39.

Center, A., Jackson, P., Smith, S. & Stansberry, F. (2008). The West Virginia mine disaster: An emotional roller coaster and public relations train wreck. In *Public Relations practices: Managerial case studies and problems* (pp. 301–304). Upper Saddle River, NJ: Pearson Hall.

Conlin, M. (2007, 15 April). Web attack. *Businessweek online.* Retrieved from www. businessweek.com/stories/2007-04-15/web-attack.

Coombs, W. T. (1999). *Ongoing crisis management: Planning, managing, responding.* Thousand Oaks, CA: Sage.

Devlin, E. S. (2007). *Crisis management planning and execution.* Boca Raton, FL: Auerbach Publications.

Elliott, D. (2006). *Key readings in crisis management: Systems and structures for prevention and recovery.* London: Routledge.

Freeo, S. K. C. (2008). *Crisis communication plan: A PR blueprint.* Retrieved from www3. niu.edu/newsplace/crisis.html.

Gonzalez-Herrero, A. & Smith, S. (2010). Crisis communications management 2.0: Organisational principles to manage in an online world. *Organisational Development Journal, 28*(1), 97–105.

Gonzalez-Herrero, A. & Smith, S. (2008). Crisis communications management on the web: How internet-based technologies are changing the way public relations professionals handle business crises. *Journal of Contingencies and Crisis Management, 16*(3), 143–153.

Heath, R. L. & O'Hair, D. (Eds.). (2010). *Handbook of risk and crisis communication.* New York: Routledge.

Hoffman, J. C. (2006). *Keeping cool on the hot seat: Dealing effectively with the media in times of crisis.* New York: Four C's Publishing.

Henry, R. A. (2008). *Communicating in a crisis: A guide for management.* Seattle, WA: Collywobbler Productions.

Hyer, R. N. & Covello, V. T. (2005). *Effective media communication during public health emergencies: A WHO handbook.* Geneva: World Health Organization. Retrieved from www.who.int/csr/resources/publications/WHO_CDS_2005_31/en.

Jaques, T. (2009a). Issue management as a post-crisis discipline: Identifying and responding to issue impacts beyond the crisis. *Journal of Public Affairs, 9*(1), 35–44.

Jaques, T. (2009b). The case for case studies: Optimising the use of communication cases. *PRism, 6*(1). Retrieved from http://praxis.massey.ac.nz/prism_on-line_journ.html.

Jaques, T. (2009c). Learning from past crises: Do iconic cases help or hinder? *Public Relations Journal, 3*(1). Retrieved from www.prsa.org/prjournal.

Jaques, T. (2008). A case study approach to issue and crisis management: Schadenfreude or an opportunity to improve? *Journal of Communication Management, 12*(3), 192–203.

Kovoor-Misra, S. & Misra, M. (2007). Understanding and managing crises in an online world. In C. M. Pearson, C. Roux-Dufort & J. A. Clair. (Eds.), *International handbook of organisational crisis management* (pp. 85–103). Thousand Oaks, CA: Sage.

Landau, D. A. (2011). *How social media is changing crisis management.* Masters Dissertation. Madison, NJ: Fairleigh University.

McKendree, A. G. (2011). Synthesising and integrating the crisis literature: A reflective practice. *Review of Communication, 11*(3), 177–192.

Millar, D. & Smith, L. (2010). *Crisis management and communication* (3rd ed.). San Francisco: IABC.

Mitroff, I. I., Pearson, C. M. & Harrington, L. K. (1996). *Essential guide to managing corporate crises: A step by step handbook for surviving major catastrophes.* New York: Oxford University Press.

Pang, A., Cropp, F. & Cameron, G. T. (2006). Corporate crisis planning: Tensions, issues and contradictions. *Journal of Communication Management, 10*(4), 371–389.

Perry, D. C., Taylor, M. & Doerfel, M. L. (2003). Internet-based communication in crisis management. *Management Communication Quarterly, 17*(2), 206–232.

Phillips, D. (2004). Crisis management in the internet mediated era. In S. M. Oliver (Ed.), *Handbook of corporate communications and public relations: Pure and applied* (pp. 305–328). London: Routledge.

Reynolds, B. S. & Seeger, M. W. (2012). *Crisis and emergency risk communication, 2012 Edition.* Atlanta, GA: Centres for Disease Control. Retrieved from http://emergency.cdc.gov/cerc/pdf/CERC_2012edition.pdf.

Roemer, B. (2007). *When the balloon goes up: The communicator's guide to crisis response.* Victoria, BC: Trafford.

Sapriel, C. (2003). Effective crisis management: Tools and best practice for the new millennium. *Journal of Communication Management, 7*(4), 348–355.

Schimmoeller, M. (2008). The Sago Mine disaster: Can lightning strike twice? *Public Relations Quarterly, 52*(2), 38–42.

Segars, A. & Jones, L. (2005). Crisis management through strategic communication: Using effective internet messaging. *Innovations in Sustainable Enterprise, 1*(4), 1–3.

Skinner, C. & Mersham, G. (2002). *Disaster management: A guide to issues management and crisis communication.* Cape Town: Oxford University Press.

Smith, D. & Elliott, D. (2007). Exploring the barriers to learning from crisis: Organisational learning and crisis. *Management Learning, 38*(5), 519–531.

Snellen, M. (2003). How to build a 'dark site' for crisis management: Using internet technology to limit damage to reputation. *Strategic Communication Management, 7*(3), 8–21.

Stephens, K. K. & Malone, P. C. (2009). If the organisation won't give us information: The use of multiple new media for crisis technical translation and dialogue. *Journal of Public Relations Research, 21*(2), 229–239.

Sweetser, K. D. & Metzgar, E. (2007). Communication during a crisis: Use of blogs as a relationship management tool. *Public Relations Review, 33*(3), 340–342.

Ulmer, R. R., Sellnow, T. L. & Seeger, M. W. (2009). Post-crisis communication and renewal: Understanding the potential for positive outcomes in crisis communication. In R. L. Heath & H. D. O'Hair (Eds.), *Handbook of risk and crisis communication.* New York: Routledge.

Veil, S. (2011), Mindful learning in crisis management. *Journal of Business Communication, 48*(2), 116–147.

Vidoloff, K. G. (2009). New Zealand beef industry: Risk communication in response to a terrorist hoax. In T. L. Sellnow, R. R. Ulmer, M. W. Seeger & R. S. Littlefield (Eds.), *Effective risk communication: A message-centered approach* (pp. 91–103). New York: Springer.

Young, C. L. & Flowers, A. (2012). Fight viral with viral: A case study of Domino's Pizza's crisis communication strategies. *Case Studies in Strategic Communication, 1,* 93–106. Retrieved from http://cssc.web.unc.edu/files/2013/01/art6.pdf.

8

CRISIS MANAGEMENT — INTERNATIONAL

CHAPTER OBJECTIVES

This chapter will help you to:

+ position international crisis management within the context of global public relations

+ distinguish the different applications of the term 'international crisis management'

+ appreciate aspects of multinational organisations that complicate management of cross-border crises

+ learn about barriers to assessing crisis potential in other countries

+ understand how crises can have far-reaching consequences beyond borders

+ recognise the importance of different culture when managing a cross-border crisis.

Practising public relations in a global environment is one of the more complex areas of the discipline, where a hotly discussed question is whether uniform standards are applicable in places other than their country of origin: 'A sample of public relations practitioners, clients or publics in Akron, Ohio, however carefully selected and tested, does not necessarily reveal truths about public relations principles applicable in Ankara, Turkey' (Freitag, 2001, p. 239).

In their review of this controversial subject, Curtin and Gaither (2007) said the cultural dimension of globality introduces variables that resist categorisation and structure. Furthermore, they found there is scant evidence that standardised public relations approaches work across varied socio-economic, political and cultural systems.

Experts working in this field have identified three main approaches to international public relations:[1]

+   *The ethnocentric theory* is a 'one-size-fits-all' approach based on the idea that public relations is built around core principles that apply in most circumstances, despite external factors such as cultural diversity.

+   *The culturally relative or polycentric approach* takes exactly the opposite view—that public relations should be practised differently in every culture.

+   *The hybrid approach* is a bridging theory that suggests there are some generic public relations principles appropriate to all cultures and societies, while there are also some generic variables that apply differently in unique cultures.

While scholars may disagree about these competing approaches,[2] there is very little argument that one of the most challenging areas of international public relations is found in the heat and intensity of crisis management across borders.

Although the broad concept of international crisis management may appear to be self-evident, the term can legitimately be applied to at least three distinct meanings:

1.   crises spanning multiple nation states

2.   multinational organisational crises

3.   organisational crises across borders.

It is important to define and characterise all three, though the focus here will be primarily on the third category.

CRISES SPANNING MULTIPLE NATION STATES

Much of the international crisis management literature addresses major events that threaten across multiple territorial jurisdictions—most often managed at a government or quasi-government level. These are sometimes called transboundary crises. A term to describe these was coined by 't Hart, Heyse and Boin (2001), who defined such crises as being

---

1   This summary of the alternative approaches draws on Curtin and Gaither (2007, pp. 113–114). The authors also discuss in detail a model called 'the circuit of culture' that identifies the factors that work together to provide a shared cultural space in which meaning is created, shaped, modified and re-created.

2   For different approaches to cross-cultural communication, see Bardhan and Weaver (2010) and Freitag and Stokes (2008) in this chapter's Further reading section.

increasingly *deterritorialised*—that is, they have 'cross-border impacts and trigger cross-national contagion effects at the mass-psychological level' (p. 183).

Typical crises across multiple nation states might include the international response to a disease outbreak (for example, AIDS, SARS or mad cow disease); natural disasters that affect more than one country (for example, the Southeast Asian tsunami of 2004 or the deadly heatwave across Europe in 2003); or international terrorist threats (for example, piracy or kidnapping in international waters). For the present discussion, this level of crisis response spanning between countries is better defined as 'disaster management' or 'disaster response'. (See definition of disaster in Table 1.1 in Chapter 1.)

However, even this distinction can sometimes be blurred. Take, for instance, the Baia Mare disaster in Romania in 2000. A gold processing plant in Romania—which was a joint venture between the Romanian government and an Australian company (Esmeralda Exploration)—had a massive spill of waste water contaminated with cyanide and heavy metals into the Tisza River. It then flowed into the Danube, carrying pollution through Romania, Hungary, Yugoslavia and Bulgaria, killing fish and other wildlife and poisoning drinking water supplies. It was undoubtedly an international crisis for the Australian company and its Romanian facility, but at the same time it was also clearly a disaster for the various governments concerned.[3] Government-level disasters are a distinct subset of crises, and the topic of disaster management is discussed in detail in the next chapter.

MULTINATIONAL ORGANISATIONAL CRISES

These are events or developments that threaten corporate or organisational interests in many or all of the different countries where a multinational or transnational organisation operates, and are usually perceived as a specific corporate risk. They directly impact the organisation as a whole—for example, financially or in terms of corporate or brand reputation—and are typically managed from head office using standard organisational crisis response techniques, as described in Chapter 7.

The focus in these crises is often a centralised 'command and control' model designed to ensure consistency of messaging and response across the entire corporate structure and in all countries impacted. Examples of multinational corporate crises that would have the same or similar effect across the organisation's entire international domain might include an accounting or ethical scandal among top executives; a global product recall triggered by health or safety concerns; financial losses and large-scale restructuring and layoffs; or a hostile corporate takeover.

Most importantly, in this category the crisis response is typically mobilised, directed and coordinated from head office using established tools and processes that are familiar to the executives in charge. More often than not, the same or very similar crisis response is mandated in all countries and the crisis communication strategy is driven by public relations practitioners at corporate level.

---

3   Cunningham (2005) analysed the Baia Mare case and suggested that the spill could be categorised as an incident, an accident or a catastrophe, based on different perspectives of culpability.

ORGANISATIONAL CRISES ACROSS BORDERS

By contrast, organisational crises across borders are where a multinational corporation or organisation faces a crisis initiated in a foreign location outside the parent country, often removed from the culture and experience of head office executives; and, more specifically, where the 'standard corporate crisis response' may not be appropriate elsewhere. Such crises are the main subject of this chapter.

This category may involve organisational operations in only one or a small number of locations, sometimes not initially seen by head office as warranting corporate intervention. However, experience shows that 'local' crises have the potential to develop and adversely impact the broader organisation. In fact, growing globalisation of business, and the accelerating pace and spread of communication via the internet and social media, has markedly increased both the likelihood and risk of organisations becoming embroiled in cross-border crises in foreign countries.

> The real challenge is not just to recognise crises, but to recognise them in a timely fashion and with a will to address the issues they represent.
>
> John Darling, Hannu Seristö and Mika Gabrielsson (2005, p. 347)

While many of the basic tools and processes of crisis management are common between multinational crises and crises across borders, the latter present some particular problems, and we focus mainly on how to deal with those challenges.

THE NATURE OF MULTINATIONALS

Before addressing how to deal with crises across borders, it is important to consider some generic aspects of multinational organisations that influence their vulnerability to crises and their capacity to respond. These factors potentially affecting multinational organisations in a crisis situation can be grouped under seven headings (adapted from Nigh & Cochran, 1991).

1. *Long distances and multiple time zones.* Despite the advances bestowed by modern communication technology, working across different time zones is a constant limitation, especially in the time-critical context of a crisis. Moreover, when a crisis occurs, getting experts and specialist equipment to distant locations quickly enough, and getting sufficient information out, can be hurdles. For example, during the notorious Bhopal crisis in 1984, with Union Carbide Headquarters in Connecticut desperate for information, it is reported there were only two open telephone lines between Bhopal and Mumbai, where Union Carbide India had its office.

2. *Being a 'foreigner' outside the home country.* It is easy to underestimate the extent of anti-foreign feeling about multinational corporations, even though the domestic

subsidiary may be locally incorporated and employ local staff. As Nigh and Cochran (1991, p. 221) warned:

> This status as a foreigner has important implications for how local stakeholders such as the media, governments and the society in general treat the multinational corporation. The effects of this status are most pronounced during the crisis and post-crisis phases. In the immediate aftermath of the crisis, the status as foreigner in the host country makes it more difficult to secure successful outcomes in public opinion, public policy and judicial areas.

The reality of such sentiment is regularly on display around the world during riots or other civil unrest when high-profile foreign banks and airlines and multinational fast-food chains frequently become the symbolic targets of choice for protesters determined to smash windows and wreak havoc.

3. *Geographic diversity.* Operating in different countries offers some protection in a crisis when the multinational organisation can attempt to 'isolate' a problem while still maintaining full operations elsewhere. Some multinationals also operate under less identifiable names overseas to shield the parent brand. Social media and instant access to information today makes such 'separateness' harder to sustain, especially in a crisis situation. However, geographic diversity does make it easier to sell off or shut down a crisis-prone subsidiary in order to limit damage to the broader enterprise.

4. *Portability of operations.* Linked to geographic diversity is the capability of a multinational organisation to relocate plants or other facilities to avoid crisis risks because of operating in a particular country. An example was the high-profile social media campaign to force some US multinationals to cease operations in Burma as a protest against the government,[4] or moving operations out of countries that threaten nationalisation of foreign assets. However, moving operations can in itself create a potential crisis, as was shown when Finnish mobile-phone maker Nokia announced it would close its plant at Bochum in Germany and transfer operations to Romania, resulting in mass demonstrations and a threatened boycott ('Decision to close factory', 2008); or when Australian company Pacific Brands triggered national protests after announcing it would relocate production of some of the country's most iconic clothing labels to China ('Bonds latest brand to head offshore', 2009).

5. *Technology–society mismatch.* With companies becoming increasingly dependent on technology for competitive advantage, the transfer of technology by multinationals to operations in foreign countries can be both a strength and a potential crisis risk. These potential risks include the possibility of technology loss in societies where the legal system favours domestic operators over foreigners; or a mismatch with skills or standards in the local work force. Given different levels of political, legal and social development and different standards of regulations and work practices (such as maximum work hours, workplace safety standards, environmental emissions and discrimination), some multinationals attempt to address any mismatch by enforcing

---

4   For details of the Burma (Myanmar) boycott campaign, see Spar and LaMure (2003) in this chapter's Further reading section.

a policy of implementing 'our standard or the local standard, whichever is the higher'. Such a policy certainly makes communication easier to manage.

6. *Different national environments.* Linked to a technology–society mismatch is the more general issue of a different national environment, which can create potential crisis risks for a multinational organisation, and can also pose additional problems when a crisis occurs. Differences in language and culture, education systems, political and legal systems and economic systems all create challenges for multinational organisations responding to a crisis in another country. At the most basic level, communicating with external stakeholders such as government officials and the news media is more difficult in a different language and is more prone to misunderstanding, especially in a crisis situation when time pressure and uncertainty are high. Moreover, the way in which government officials and the media (and other stakeholders) perceive their role in society can differ greatly in different cultures.[5] This directly impacts how they will react in a crisis and the way they expect to interact with the foreign company. Arpan and Sun (2006) have written about what they call the 'liability of foreignness' often experienced by multinational organisations, which can lead to host country groups (such as citizens and government officials) scrutinising the foreign company more closely or judging a little-known foreign company based on unhelpful stereotypes about its home country.[6]

7. *National employee differences.* Building on these broader national differences is the fact that the organisation must work through local employees who may have very different cultural and language backgrounds. Within any multinational organisation there is a constant tension between the central push for global integration and uniformity of policies and practices versus the need for national differentiation and appropriate local adaption. This tension is never greater than in a crisis, with the country leader trying to manage the crisis on the ground within the framework of local culture while keeping head office in another country informed. Meanwhile, the top management team has responsibility to ensure global consistency and transparency in the crisis response, and also to manage the broader strategy and potential impact on the organisation as a whole. The result can be misinterpretation, miscommunication and potential damage to reputation.

RECOGNISING POTENTIAL CROSS-BORDER CRISES

As with all issues and potential crises discussed throughout this book, early recognition of the problem and prompt implementation of a response is essential. But, because of the nature of multinational organisation as outlined, recognition of potential cross-border crises faces additional problems.

---

5 For an example of a differing media perception of a crisis between Colombia and the USA, see Bravo et al. (2013) in this chapter's Further reading section.
6 For detailed discussion of intercultural communication, see Neuliep (2012) in this chapter's Further reading section.

The first of these problems is the risk that an organisation's executives in a location far away from the parent country may try to manage the potential crisis themselves without involving head office, at least in the early stages, in order to avoid 'looking as if they can't manage their own problems'. This is an understandable response, particularly in some national cultures where requesting help may be perceived as a sign of weakness or failure. Such unwillingness to communicate early enough can be very dangerous for the organisation, especially when local managers may lack the experience or global perspective to properly comprehend the potential adverse impact on the organisation as a whole. Moreover, the explosion of social media has meant it is now much harder to 'hide' a potential crisis from head office, certainly once it has appeared in the local news media or online.

The other side of the same coin is when head office recognises the potential cross-border crisis, but attempts to quarantine the impact to just one country or region in an effort to protect the wider organisation. A legendary example occurred when the toxic chemical benzene was detected in bottles of Perrier water in the USA. The French parent company initially tried to argue that the problem was confined to North America and ordered a local recall. Even before the source of the contamination was confirmed, Perrier's North American arm was confidently announcing that the problem was limited to their region. But within days the same contamination was found in Europe, leading to a recall in 120 countries, a temporary shutdown of the entire production process and an international product crisis that cost Perrier almost US$263 million. The proud French company never fully recovered and was eventually sold to Nestlé of Switzerland.[7]

Another example of failing to recognise the full impact of a problem overseas—and the role of the news media—was in early 2006 when the US eye-care giant Bausch and Lomb lost 3 per cent of its share value after the Singapore government announced a link between potentially blinding fungal infections and one of the company's contact lens solutions. Baush and Lomb withdrew ReNu solution, but only in Singapore and Hong Kong where the story had received widespread media coverage. Two months later, the Centers for Disease Control in the USA issued a similar report and the company's share value fell by about 17 per cent in a single day. After further sustained destruction of shareholder value, the company was sold to a private equity firm. Diermeier (2011, p. 207) concluded:

> Companies rarely have the luxury of receiving such a clear warning. This lack of anticipation may have been the consequence of underestimating the crisis or not realising its full reputational impact. But given the particular characteristics of the issue (a quality issue, possible blindness and a clear connection to the company's core competency) this is hard to believe. What more could have gone wrong?

Perhaps Bausch and Lomb's sluggish response was influenced by the fact that the recall in Singapore and Hong Kong received little media attention in the USA.

Similarly, in the case of the Firestone tyre recall (see the box, 'Failing to identify an international crisis') it has been claimed that one reason for the seemingly adequate response

---

7   For an overview of the Perrier case, see Barton (1991) and Kurzbard and Siomkos (1992) in this chapter's Further reading section.

by the Japanese manufacturer (Bridgestone)was a lack of perceived media impact at home. Japan-based *Wall Street Journal* reporters (cited in Gibson, 2001, p. 21) concluded:

> Another reason for silence at Bridgestone headquarters is that the company is feeling no public pressure in Japan over the recall. The Japanese press have shown scant interest in the story as there have been no reports of Japanese dying in accidents and the scope of the recall here was tiny.

In any potential cross-border crisis, local management and head office need to work together so that warning signs are recognised early, and so there is a mutual understanding of how events in one place can affect other locations or the parent organisation. As can be seen from these examples, effective monitoring and strategic analysis of news media coverage can be a critical factor in this issue.

> In an age of global media, when any threat—whether true or unfounded—is aimed at your brand's reputation, you must react immediately from the highest levels within the organisation, no matter where in the world the threat is being launched.
>
> Editor of *Reputation Management Magazine*, Paul Holmes (cited in Wakefield, 2000, p. 60)

FAILING TO IDENTIFY AN INTERNATIONAL CRISIS

A well-known failure to recognise an impending international crisis was the Ford–Firestone crisis of 2000, when 6.5 million tyres were recalled after more than 200 deaths attributed to tyre failures, more than half of them involving Ford SUVs.

Both Ford and Firestone had plenty of warnings from their overseas operations. Ford acknowledged it had replaced tyres on almost 47,000 SUVs in Saudi Arabia, Venezuela, Thailand and Malaysia, but claimed it was a 'customer satisfaction issue' in hot climates where tyres were more vulnerable to problems. Despite explicit warnings from regional managers, the company insisted that tyre failures in overseas markets reflected driving conditions unique to those countries and they 'didn't immediately suspect similar issues in the US'. Firestone agreed that driving conditions in the Middle East were 'extreme and unusual'.

In the wake of well over 100 deaths in the USA and the ensuing recall, Ford CEO Jacques Nasser told a Congressional committee that, despite replacing tyres overseas, Ford held off taking action in the USA 'because review of its various databases assured the company there was not a problem here'. The whole fiasco is a much-studied case book example of how not to manage a crisis, and also highlights the importance of cross-border coordination. It was one of the largest tyre recalls in history, second only to *another* Firestone recall crisis in 1978.[8]

---

8 For a detailed analysis of the Ford–Firestone case, see Pinedo, Seshadri and Zemel (2000) in this chapter's Further reading section.

RECOGNISING CROSS-BORDER CRISIS IMPACT

While recognising a potential crisis in another location can present challenges, recognising the possible impact of a crisis across borders can be even more difficult, and can have far-reaching consequences. For instance, the Montara oil spill case study presented in Chapter 6 highlights how an operational crisis off the northwest coast of Australia threatened environmental and economic damage in Indonesia. And the Alang shipyard case study, presented with this chapter, reinforces how a political–military decision in France had repercussions far beyond French national waters in India. Similarly, the Ribena case study presented in Chapter 3, while about an issue rather than a crisis, highlights how mismanagement in one country can create a very real reputational challenge for the company and the brand in other countries.

In reality, simply gaining a full appreciation of an emerging crisis across borders is not always easy. As Ansell, Boin and Keller (2010, p. 201) observed:

> A transboundary crisis makes it hard to arrive at a *common operating picture* (sometimes called *shared cognition* or *situational awareness*). Such a picture must somehow be pulled from incomplete, often contradictory or continuously changing information that is distributed over a large and shifting number of actors.

Therefore, it is not surprising that the crisis management literature features some well-known and high-profile examples of how organisations misread and misjudged the impact of a crisis elsewhere. Indeed, some cases of crisis management across borders have become so widely analysed that they have generated a substantial literature of their own.

HOW A LOCAL ACTION THREATENED A GLOBAL REPUTATION

When three Hyatt hotels in the Boston area fired almost 100 housekeeping employees, the seemingly local action triggered an online reputational crisis that reverberated around the world. As part of a cost-cutting drive, management directed ninety-eight housekeeping staff to train a new team under the guise of 'vacation replacements'. But they were, in fact, outsourced replacement workers paid almost half the old hourly rate, and the so-called 'Hyatt 100' were then fired without notice (Whitford, 2009).

The result was an unprecedented backlash from politicians, unions and the public, and within less than a day the online site www.hyattboycott.com was fuelling the outrage. Although Hyatt's Chicago HQ said the move was a local decision based on local economic conditions, and was not part of a corporate-wide initiative, the story was picked up by traditional and social media around the world, with Hyatt's corporate name in the glare of global condemnation. As often happens, the story eventually died down, but the *Economist* ('Hyatt vs Massachusetts', 2009) in the UK concluded: 'Sensible business cases do not always provide good public relations, and Hyatt's brand has been damaged'.

One such much-studied case (introduced in Chapter 6) concerns the *Brent Spar*, a disused floating oil-storage buoy in the North Sea that Shell UK decided to tow into the North Atlantic to sink in deep water. When Greenpeace occupied the massive 14,500 tonne facility in 1995 to protest against the principle of deep sea disposal, the story gained enormous international attention, particularly in continental Europe where Shell faced massive protests, a boycott of its products and even firebombing of petrol stations.

This famous case has been analysed from many angles, including the role of activism, and the struggle between science and technology on one hand and emotion and politics on the other.[9] The case also illustrates how activists can selectively frame a campaign. Although *Brent Spar* was jointly owned by Shell and Esso, the public attack was aimed exclusively at Shell, the facility operator, and Esso's involvement was seldom, if ever, mentioned. Greenpeace have asserted this was a deliberate strategic decision to ensure a single focus for the campaign.

However, for the present discussion, the case presents a vivid example of what happens when cross-border impacts shape the outcome of a crisis. Shell UK found itself under pressure not just from politicians and activists in the UK and across Western Europe, but also from its own management outside Britain, particularly Shell in Germany. In addition, the nature of the demands varied substantially. For example, one of the main German Greenpeace leaders subsequently commented that in Britain the debate was largely technical and scientific, while in Germany it was more about Shell's societal responsibility (Jochen Vorfelder, cited in Neale, 1997, p. 98).

In the face of irresistible demands, the plan to sink the buoy was abandoned and *Brent Spar* was eventually scrapped on land in Norway. The impact of the crisis outside the UK was well captured in a speech by Cor Herkstroter (1996, p. 101), Corporate Chairman of the Royal Dutch Shell group of companies:

> We found that what was the best option on the UK was not acceptable elsewhere. We were caught between two different approaches to the environment. The public reacted in a way that we did not expect and the pressure groups used the *Spar* as a symbol in a way we did not anticipate. So, expectations are very rarely consistent. We are sometimes expected to behave one way in one part of the world and rather differently in another part. We are caught in the tensions between these differing expectations.

A few years later, Eric Faulds (Faulds & Morrison, 1998, p. 17), the Shell manager in charge of decommissioning the *Brent Spar*, was even franker about the company's failure to recognise the cross-border impact:

> There was a lack of appreciation that other countries would be interested in our plans and that they would see the issue quite differently. Shell companies across Europe hadn't foreseen how a plan that was the preserve of a sovereign UK government and of Shell UK could rouse public protest across national borders.

Another company caught up in an unexpected cross-border crisis was the Danish dairy giant Arla, which became the innocent victim of an international event. As businesses globalise, so too does the vulnerability of their functions, including crisis management. For Arla this vulnerability was exposed in late 2005 when the Danish newspaper *Jyllands-Posten*

---

9   For a discussion of the *Brent Spar*, see Entine (2002) and Bakir (2006) in this chapter's Further reading section.

published offensive cartoons portraying the prophet Muhammad, causing predictable outrage throughout the Islamic world.

Incensed by the Danish government's refusal to sanction the newspaper—citing the cause of free speech—Moslem leaders launched a boycott of Danish products early in 2006. As a result, Arla's products disappeared off the shelves of 50,000 supermarkets across the Middle East; regional sales dropped from $1.8 million daily to basically nothing in just five days; and the company was forced to shut down its cheese processing plant in Saudi Arabia and lay off staff in Denmark (Gaither & Curtin, 2008). Despite coming under severe criticism at home for 'cowing to fundamentalism', Arla (a Danish–Swedish farmer-owned cooperative) began a strategy to distance itself from the cartoons in order to protect its important Middle Eastern market, and the boycott began to slowly turn around.[10]

Commenting later on the cross-border impact of the crisis, Corporate Communication Director Astrid Gade Nielsen (2008, p. 63) said that before the boycott Arla would have said it was an international company that thought globally:

> After having experienced this, I would rather say we are a Scandinavian company, because we had not fully understood until the cartoon crisis what it really means to be a truly global company, that you have to comprise so many cultures and so many different ways of looking at life. It has changed our communication policy in the sense that we are very much more aware of how we communicate in a global community.

Two years after the boycott crisis (January 2008) Arla announced that it had recovered 95 per cent of its previous sales in the Middle East ('Arla's Middle East sales', 2008).

RECOGNISING CULTURAL DIFFERENCES

While it is important to recognise the threat of an international crisis and also to recognise its potential to spread and have unexpected impacts across borders, the more difficult challenge is to actively manage a crisis in another country, with its different norms and expectations.

As previously discussed, there is a tension between assuming, on the one hand, that 'one size fits all' (ethnocentricity), and on the other hand that everything must be done differently (polycentricity). Indeed, lack of appreciation of these distinctions may be behind some of the better-known failures of crisis-border crisis management.

The value of taking the best from each approach was neatly captured by Robert Wakefield, who has written extensively on international public relations: 'World class public relations is done through application of *strategic consistencies* with *cultural sensitivities*' (Wakefield, cited in 'Notes from PRSA/IPRA', 2000). However, communications professionals often fail to heed this advice. Consequently, as in many fields of public relations, lessons are

---

10 For detail on the Arla case, see Frandsen and Johansen (2010) and Holstrom et al. (2010) in this chapter's Further reading section.

often more readily drawn from crises that are badly handled rather than by situations well managed.

While there are many high-profile examples of misjudging situations and attitudes across national borders, two famous cases stand out and have been intensively studied. Interestingly, both relate to US multinationals assuming that policies and processes that apply at home would be equally applicable in Europe. The first case involves the response by Coca-Cola to a claimed product contamination in Europe, and the other concerns the efforts of Monsanto to establish genetically modified crops in the region.

In the summer of 1999, when around 200 schoolchildren in Belgium and France became ill and blamed 'tainted' Coca-Cola, the initial response of the company was to deny responsibility and to suggest it was a case of mass hysteria. But after it was claimed that the cause was defective carbon dioxide in some drinks, and that other products had been contaminated by chemicals from wooden shipping pallets, government officials in Belgium, France, the Netherlands, Germany, Luxembourg, Switzerland and Spain imposed bans or partial bans on Coca-Cola products (Wakefield, 2000). The drink-maker ordered a recall amounting to an estimated 15 million cases, but delayed a week before issuing a public apology. And it was ten days before CEO Douglas Ivester arrived in Europe to address the emerging crisis, which was later acknowledged as the worst health scare in the company's history.

In newspaper advertisements in Belgium, Ivester apologised for not speaking to consumers earlier, but the recall reportedly cost over $200 million, and Coke's quarterly earnings dropped by 21 per cent. Although independent tests eventually showed the symptoms were largely psychological and the product did not contribute to illness, Taylor (2000) says the incident resulted not so much from the tainting and company's delayed communication and perceived 'arrogance', but from its 'inability to accurately understand and react to the complex cultural dynamics of the European marketplace' (p. 289).

The company misjudged the reality that European regulators were acutely sensitive to food contamination issues, having very recently been severely embarrassed by a widely condemned poor response to a scare involving dioxin in the food chain. The company also underestimated the impact of European sentiment against foreign multinationals and 'Americanisation' of European culture. Based in Atlanta, Georgia, where Coke invests heavily in civic and community causes and enjoys a stellar reputation, the company failed to properly gauge long-term issues relating to the differences between conducting business globally versus the domestic US market. And they were certainly unprepared for the idea that government officials would react so swiftly against a global brand in response to a perceived threat to public health.

As Wakefield (2000) concluded: 'The crisis suffered by Coca-Cola in Europe in 1999 can be a lesson to multinationals, small and large, who are not fully prepared to handle cross-border issues' (p. 59).[11]

---

11 For additional analysis of the Coke case, see Schmidt (1999) and Johnson and Peppas (2003) in this chapter's Further reading section.

CROSS-CULTURAL CONFLICT IN THE RHETORIC OF ATONEMENT

The effect of different cultural approaches to crisis management was seldom more starkly evident than in the 2010 Toyota recall. Announcing the recall of nine million vehicles, Toyota and its CEO initially said very little. This was in accordance with accepted Japanese emphasis on implicit rather than explicit messaging and on non-verbal cues. However, in the USA, with its strong emphasis on explicit and verbal response, Toyota came under sustained attack because of its apparent lack of communication, and CEO Akio Toyoda was widely criticised for going 'missing in action'. Some US commentators even predicted the demise of the Toyota brand. Recognising that the recall demanded a response that functioned to address the US audience's expectation for explicit explanation and action, Toyota launched an extraordinary campaign of atonement that included the unprecedented decision to shut down its US operations while quality issues were addressed. And instead of focusing on justification and blame-shifting, the company apologised for failing the confidence of its customers and committed to return to the 'Toyota way'—built on quality and trust.[12] Toyota rapidly recovered lost sales and within twelve months regained its ranking as the world's most valuable automotive brand ('Toyota wins back global auto sales crown', 2013).

The other widely examined case was less dramatic than the Coke crisis, but lasted longer and ultimately had a much greater adverse impact on the company's reputation and on its business model.

The US corporation Monsanto had been highly successful in applying biotechnology to food production in the USA, and in the late 1990s attempted to introduce what they called 'genetically improved' crops to the United Kingdom and the rest of Europe. Monsanto expected their product would be equally welcome across the Atlantic, but they had gravely misread the social and political environment in Western Europe. Their arrival triggered a storm of objection and protest, with consumer groups accusing the multinational of 'biocolonialism'. In a blunt assessment of the crisis, British public relations expert Judy Larkin (2003, p. 26) said:

> Monsanto had the arrogance to assume that UK consumers would fall over themselves to buy the apparent innovations associated with genetically modified food. Not a single thought was given to an embedded anxiety and sense of confusion over who to trust about safety of food production in the aftermath of a string of public health scares associated with food consumption.

With European retailers rushing to remove GM products from their shelves and Monsanto's reputation in tatters, the company's share price started to plummet. This led to a forced merger with Phamarcia Upjohn in 1999, who subsequently sold off Monsanto's biotechnology division. As Larkin (2003, p. viii) memorably quipped: 'By the end of 2000 Monsanto had wrecked an entire industry as well as its own brand'.[13]

---

12 While the Toyota recall generated an extensive literature, Jones (2012) specifically explores the Shinto background to the Toyota response and the challenges of managing an issue across cultures. See also Heller and Darling (2012), Hiles (2011) and Meisenbach and Feldner (2013) in this chapter's Further reading section.

13 For a detailed analysis of differences between US and European attitudes to GM foods, see Gaskell et al. (1999) and Doh and Guay (2006) in this chapter's Further reading section.

The essential need to properly identify stakeholders and their perspective was perfectly captured in a remarkably frank subsequent statement by Monsanto's former CEO Bob Shapiro (cited in Vidal, 1999):

> We started with the conviction that biotechnology was useful and valuable, but we have tended to see it as our task to convince people that we were right and that people with different points of view were wrong. We have irritated and antagonised more people than we have persuaded. Our confidence in biotechnology has been widely seen as arrogance and condescension because we thought it was our job to persuade. But too often we forgot to listen.

More than a decade later the company finally admitted defeat in the struggle to persuade the Europeans to see it their way. In July 2013, Monsanto announced it was withdrawing all of its EU applications for approval for new crops. The company pointed to the fact that the EU had not approved a new GM crop for cultivation in Europe since 1998 and concluded: 'As the EU today is effectively a conventional seed market we have been progressively de-emphasising cultivation of biotech crops in Europe' (Hope, 2013).

A more recent example of failure to appreciate cultural differences in a cross-border crisis was seen during criticism in China of SK-II cosmetics. In late 2006 Chinese authorities detected toxic heavy metals in SK-II products made in Japan for the US multinational Proctor & Gamble (P&G). The company had recently provoked concern and an online protest in China by insisting on using as brand spokesperson a Taiwanese model who was an outspoken advocate for independence for her home island, a highly sensitive political issue in mainland China. Now the company further offended China by rejecting the findings of the country's quality authority and refusing to apologise.[14]

When P&G finally agreed on a recall of SK-II products, the company closed its ninety-seven sales counters across the country and instituted a refund process that was so limited and complex that near-riots broke out as angry consumers stormed P&G's specified locations in China. About one month after the product recall, Chinese authorities and those in Korea, Singapore and Taiwan confirmed the traces of any metals in the SK-II product were harmless and the cosmetics returned to sale in China. However, P&G undoubtedly suffered significant financial and reputational damage.[15]

Some Western analysts have suggested the SK-II case illustrates how Chinese institutions allow state agencies to actively resist foreign products by presenting test results in negative ways (for example, Whiteman & Krug, 2008). But it is clear that P&G tried to react to the crisis as a global issue of product testing standards rather than addressing China's perceived concerns. They also failed to recognise the way in which Chinese media influence the legal system, and the fact that Chinese consumers tend to trust their government far more than companies, especially foreign multinationals.

Before leaving ways in which multinational organisations assess cultural differences when dealing with a crisis, it is important to emphasise that they don't always get it wrong. When Nike produced a new range of footwear, it featured a logo on the heel and sole that incorporated the word 'Air' in a design intended to represent flickering flames or heat rising from the pavement. However, some Moslem critics claimed the logo could be interpreted as

---

14   For a discussion on when the leader should or should not apologise, see Kellerman (2006) in this chapter's Further reading section.
15   For an extensive analysis of the SK-II case, see Tai (2008) in this chapter's Further reading section.

the word 'Allah' in Arabic script. Despite Nike reportedly receiving independent advice from respected Islamic scholars that this was a misinterpretation of the logo, the company decided this was a cross-cultural debate it could not 'win'. As a result, they recalled more than 30,000 pairs of the offending shoes and ceased distribution of the remainder (Jury, 1997). They also agreed to build several playgrounds in Moslem communities as part of their apology.

Like Arla (discussed earlier), Nike was attacked by some critics for giving in to a 'noisy minority'. But the company took a business decision in recognising the cultural concern, and averted the threat of a global boycott. Crisis management is never easy. Managing international crises is even harder.

KEY POINTS

+ International public relations sees tension between a 'one-size-fits-all' approach and those who believe public relations should be practised differently in every culture.

+ International crisis management can be interpreted as crises that span multiple nation states (disasters); corporate crises that affect most parts of a multinational organisation; and crises that start in one part of a multinational organisation and may threaten the whole enterprise.

+ There are common characteristics of multinational organisations that influence their vulnerability to crises and their capacity to respond.

+ International crisis management creates three key challenges for multinationals:

   – recognising cross-border crises
   – recognising cross-border crisis impact
   – recognising cultural differences when a crisis strikes.

≣ ACTIVITIES AND DISCUSSION

1. Research one of the high-profile international crises introduced in this chapter. What key themes emerge for future practice and do different authors present alternative perspectives?

2. Robert Wakefield is quoted in this chapter as saying: 'World class public relations is done through application of *strategic consistencies* with *cultural sensitivities*'. Discuss what this means and how it could influence the practice of managing crises across borders.

3. List some of the special problems for multinational organisations attempting to manage crises in a region remote from head office. What steps can be taken to address those challenges?

4. Review the McDonald's case study presented in Chapter 3 about reaction to a highly critical documentary film. What factors may have influenced the fundamentally dissimilar approaches to the same reputational threat that existed in different countries?

5. Define the role of culture in managing cross-border crises. How does the ethnocentric view of culture distort an organisation's capacity to respond effectively?

THE GLOBALISATION OF ACTIVISM—CASE OF AN ENVIRONMENTAL DISPUTE

Manoj Thomas

Xavier School of Management, Jamshedpur

Though the decommissioned French aircraft carrier *Clemenceau* never reached Indian shores for scrapping as planned, it created a controversy in Indian and international media about the problem of toxicity in waste generated from ship-breaking. The major instigator of the campaign to halt the project was Greenpeace, an independent global organisation that followed the passage of the ship and used a strategy of protest and activism across the globe to push its agenda against dumping waste in Asia.

After being decommissioned from the French navy, the ship was initially headed for the port of Alang on the western coast of India in 2005. At this time, Alang was the major centre for ship-breaking in India as it offered natural advantages of a gentle slope and high difference in tide levels, plus cheap migrant labour from the poorer regions of Orissa, Bihar and Andhra Pradesh. The ship-breaking process was labour-intensive, involving removal of ship material, including asbestos, with bare hands. Most of the pollutants and hazardous materials were collected and reused commercially in the process—making the industry even more profitable. Even asbestos—one of the main scrap materials of concern—was recovered and sold for reuse in India.

The breaking activity also benefited the economy of the region by creating a large number of jobs directly and also indirectly through ancillary businesses, transport and supporting industries. But critics pointed out that the process that kept the cost of breaking low (and thereby the breaking yard competitive) did not take into account the human costs associated with handling such hazardous material.

Environmental laws in India at this time were lax compared with developed countries in Europe, and due to resulting cost differences, ships were sent to Alang for breaking not only by the private owners but also by different governments that had military and non-military vessels to dispose of.

Although well over 4000 ships had been broken up at Alang, international agencies such as Greenpeace and the international media focused on the *Clemenceau*, which had already been refused entry to two other countries because of asbestos contamination. Greenpeace identified the French ship as 'a symbol of moral injustice of rich countries dumping their waste on poorer countries'. Their actions to halt the ship created such international concern about the problems at Alang that the local Indian media took up the issue, soon followed by Indian politicians. Facing a blaze of publicity, the Supreme Court of

India blocked *Clemenceau* entering national waters, and legal concern in France forced the French President to recall the ship.

For the government of India the options were: to let the status quo continue as the activity was adding to economic activity in the country; to introduce stronger laws and to enforce them (which might drive the activity to other countries where laws continued to be lax); or to facilitate the introduction of technology and support provide for creation of infrastructure, improving the living conditions and health facilities for the workers.

A clear decision among the possible options was difficult because the different stakeholders involved in the decision had different interests. Ship-breakers saw the industry as an act of entrepreneurship by using the difference in laws and labour rates to create a centre of activity. Local workers saw it as an opportunity for employment and livelihood in an economy where jobs for unskilled and semi-skilled workers were scarce. However, environmental activists saw it as a ploy for the developed world to shirk their responsibility and save a little money by endangering the workers of the less developed countries. The role of activists and the international media had been in raising the issues using the lens of an international value system.

An international organisation like Greenpeace, with no affiliation to any single country or private organisation, could raise issues that became important only if viewed in an international context, and helped focus the attention of the international and local media. Greenpeace had access to information across the globe; had developed technical expertise on this subject; and had built up capabilities in lobbying across the globe. This in turn exerted a pressure on the government institutions such as the legislature and judiciary to bring about change.

Footnote: After two years waiting off the French coast, *Clemenceau* was taken to England and broken up in 2010. Alang remains one of the world's largest ship-breaking operations.

For more detailed discussion of this case see:

Thomas, M. T. (2007). The Alang Ship-breaking Yard. *Asian Case Research Journal, 11*(2), 327–346.

POLITICAL AND MEDIA SYSTEMS IMPACT CRISIS RESPONSE—THE MELAMINE-TAINTED MILK CRISIS

Joanne Chen Lyu

Chinese University of Hong Kong

In 2008 a large-scale melamine-tainted milk powder crisis broke out in mainland China. On 11 September, the *Oriental Morning Post* reported that infants were diagnosed with kidney stones and other kidney damage after being fed Sanlu infant formula milk, bringing the crisis to the public. More victims were reported by media outlets, and several days later the General Administration of Quality Supervision (AQSIQ) released its investigation report concluding that Sanlu milk powder was adulterated with melamine, a toxic industrial chemical used to increase the apparent protein level of milk. Facing the crisis, Sanlu responded passively, arousing media criticism and public outcry. After the crisis, the once-prestigious dairy giant began to wither away and was declared bankrupt half a year later.

The melamine crisis was not confined to mainland China. Across the strait, several Taiwan dairy companies suffered a similar crisis because imported creamer (a main ingredient of milk products) from the mainland may have been contaminated by melamine. The largest Taiwanese company affected was the KingCar Group, a leading dairy producer, which responded in a quick and active manner until their mainland supplier finally acknowledged their creamer contained melamine. Though it was confirmed that KingCar's product contained melamine, its corporate reputation was not damaged; on the contrary, it was acclaimed by the media for its responsible attitude and action. KingCar successfully safeguarded its thirty-year corporate reputation in the crisis.

A detailed analysis of media coverage of the two cases reveals very different approaches to crisis communication by the two companies. Besides the variant crisis communication strategies (CCSs) adopted, there was a considerable difference between Sanlu and KingCar in terms of the CCS sequence. Specifically, Sanlu's first response was denial—a very defensive CCS—but as time went by its strategies became more and more accommodative under pressure. By contrast, KingCar's CCSs started with mortification, but the following CCSs were more and more defensive as facts unfolded. A further analysis of how government and the media create different post-crisis social contexts for two corporations confronted with crisis sheds light upon the above findings.

Sanlu was a majority state-owned corporation (its minority owner was the New Zealand dairy giant Fonterra). Involvement of the Chinese government itself partly hampered the functioning of corporate autonomy in crisis and to a large extent determined Sanlu's response style that was characterised by official inertia and featured denial, cover-up and

waiting for direction from superiors in the official hierarchy. In the Sanlu case, it was found that except for the denial immediately after the occurrence of the crisis, when the government began to intervene, there were almost no proactive responses from the company. Sanlu did not even provide the consumers with instructive information, which is commonly offered by the organisation at fault after a food safety crisis. According to Sanlu's claim, they identified melamine in their product through self-inspection on 1 August and instantly reported to related official departments, but they did not give explicit instruction to the consumers. However, when the public were fully aware of the crisis, few media outlets in mainland China questioned the bureaucratic negligence. As a mouthpiece of the Party and government, media stood on the side of government, putting the blame on the corporation.

In Taiwan, the relationship between government and corporations is quite different. In most circumstances, government does not interfere in corporate behaviour. In the case of KingCar there was no corporate crisis communication strategy in response to government orders, as happened in the Sanlu case. While the Chinese government tends to directly interfere where it thinks necessary, the Taiwan government is inclined to guide the corporation rather than give it orders, and grant corporations autonomy to handle the crisis in their manner, rather than taking coercive measures. At the same time, Taiwan's liberal media system allowed its media to behave differently from media on the mainland, being the watchdog not only for corporations but also for the government. In the melamine-tainted milk crisis, KingCar received positive comments from the Taiwan media for its positive actions to investigate and keep the public informed. Meanwhile, the media also compared KingCar's active response with what was claimed to be government inefficiency and incompetence, which almost turned the case into a government reputation crisis. Compared to the mainland media's approval of the government's involvement, Taiwan media played the role of the 'fourth power'.

Mainland China and Taiwan are two typical Chinese societies with traditional Chinese culture. Yet, comparison of melamine-tainted milk crises in the two countries indicates that government and media are important factors in creating the post-crisis social environment and influencing different corporate crisis communication and management in a public food safety crisis. In this case Sanlu, at an early stage, relied on the local government and responded passively, then almost turned silent after the central government's involvement. By contrast, KingCar was more active, autonomous and flexible. In the end, Sanlu went bankrupt, while KingCar survived and continued to thrive.

For more detailed discussion of this case see:

Lyu, J. C. (2012) A comparative study of crisis communication strategies between mainland China and Taiwan: The melamine-tainted milk powder crisis in the Chinese context. *Public Relations Review* 38(5), 779–791.

REFERENCES

Ansell, C., Boin, A. & Keller, A. (2010). Managing transboundary crises: Identifying the building blocks of an effective response system. *Journal of Contingencies and Crisis Management, 18*(4), 195–207.

Arla's Middle East sales bounce back after cartoon crisis. (2008, 30 January). *Flexnews.* Retrieved from www.flex-news-food.com/console/PageViewer.aspx?page=13908.

Arpan, L. M. & Sun, H. (2006). The effect of country of origin in judgments of multinational organisations involved in a crisis. *Journal of Promotion Management, 12*(3/4), 189–214.

Bonds latest brand to head offshore. (2009), 25 February). *The Age.* Retrieved from www. theage.com.au/business/bonds-latest-brand-to-head-offshore-20090225-8hmt. html.

Cunningham, S. A. (2005). Incident, accident, catastrophe: Cyanide in the Danube. *Disasters, 29*(2), 99–128.

Curtin, P. A. & Gaither, T. K. (2007). Practising public relations in a global environment. In *International public relations: Negotiating culture, identify and power* (pp. 109–136). Thousand Oaks, CA: Sage.

Darling, J., Seristö, H. & Gabrielsson, M. (2005). Anatomy of crisis management: A case focusing on a major cross-cultural clash within DaimlerChrysler. *Finnish Journal of Business Economics (LTA), 3*, 343–369. Retrieved from http://lta.hse. fi/2005/3/lta_2005_03_a1.pdf.

Decision to close factory results in anti-Nokia backlash in Germany. (2008). *m-GovWorld.* Retrieved from www.mgovworld.org/News/anti-nokia-backlash-grows-in-germany.

Diermeier, D. (2011). *Reputation rules: Strategies for building your company's most valuable asset.* New York: McGraw Hill.

Faulds, E. & Morrison, F. (1998). A new way of doing business. Interview in Shell UK in-house magazine *Focus,* included in the company's online *Brent Spar Dossier* (pp. 17–20). Retrieved from www.shell.co.uk/gbr/aboutshell/shell-businesses/e-and-p/ decommissioning/brent-spar.html.

Freitag, A. (2001). International media coverage of the Firestone tyre recall. *Journal of Communication Management, 6*(3), 239–256.

Gade Nielsen, A. (2008). We had to set things straight. *Communication Director, 1,* 60–63.

Gaither, T. K. & Curtin, P. A. (2008). Examining the heuristic value of models of international public relations practice: A case study of the Arla Foods crisis. *Journal of Public Relations Research, 20*(1), 115–137.

Gibson, D. C. (2001). Two sides to every story: In defence of Bridgestone/Firestone. *Public Relations Quarterly, 46*(1), 18–22.

Herkstroter, C. (1996). Dealing with contradictory expectations: Dilemmas facing multinationals. *Vital Speeches of the Day, 63*(4), 100–104.

Hope, C. (2013, 18 July). Major GM food company Monsanto 'pulls out of Europe'. *The Telegraph.* Retrieved from www.telegraph.co.uk/earth/environment/10186932/ Major-GM-food-company-Monsanto-pulls-out-of-Europe.html

Hyatt vs Massachusetts. (2009, 25 September). *The Economist.* Retrieved from www. economist.com/blogs/gulliver/2009/09/hyatt_vs_massachusetts.

Jones, V. (2012). *Travelling the road to redemption: Toyota Motor Corporation's rhetoric of atonement as response to the 2010 recall crisis.* Doctoral dissertation. University of Kansas, Lawrence, Kansas. Retrieved from http://kuscholarworks.ku.edu/dspace/ bitstream/1808/10251/1/Jones_ku_0099D_12304_DATA_1.pdf.

Jury, L. (1997, 25 June). Nike to trash trainers that offended Islam. *The Independent.* Retrieved from www.independent.co.uk/news/nike-to-trash-trainers-that- offended-islam-1257776.html.

Larkin, J. (2003). *Strategic reputation risk management.* Basingstoke: Palgrave Macmillan.

Neale, A. (1997). Organisational learning in contested environments: Lessons from Brent Spar. *Business Strategy and the Environment, 6*(2), 93–103.

Nigh, D. & Cochran, P. L. (1991). Crisis management in the multinational firm. *Proceedings of the International Association for Business and Society, Sundance, Utah* (pp. 214–227).

Notes from PRSA/IPRA Conference on International PR. (2000, 30 October). *PR Reporter,* p. 1.

Taylor, M. (2000). Cultural variance as a challenge to global public relations: A case study of the Coca-Cola scare in Europe. *Public Relations Review, 26*(3), 277–293.

't Hart, P., Heyse, L. & Boin, A. (2001). New Trends in crisis management and crisis management research: Setting the agenda. *Journal of Contingencies and Crisis Management, 9*(4), 181–188.

Toyota wins back global auto sales crown from GM. (2013, 28 January). *Automotive News Europe.* Retrieved from http://europe.autonews.com/article/20130128/ ANE/301289857/0/SEARCH.

Vidal, J. (1999, October 7). We forgot to listen, says Monsanto. *The Guardian.* Retrieved from www.guardian.co.uk/science/1999/oct/07/gm.food.

Wakefield, R. I. (2000). World-class public relations: A model for effective public relations in the multinational. *Journal of Communication Management, 5*(1), 59–71.

Whiteman, G. & Krug, B. (2008). Beauty and the beast: Consumer stakeholders demand action in China. *Journal of International Business Ethics, 1*(1), 36–51.

Whitford, D. (2009, 30 September). A mess: Hyatt's housekeeping scandal. *CNNMoney*. Retrieved from http://money.cnn.com/2009/09/30/news/companies/hyatt_hotels_boston.fortune

FURTHER READING

Bakir, V. (2006). Policy agenda setting and risk communication: Greenpeace, Shell and issues of trust. *Harvard International Journal of Press/Politics, 11*(3), 67–88.

Bardhan, N. & Weaver, C. K. (2010). *Public relations in global cultural contexts : Multi-paradigmatic perspectives*. London: Taylor and Francis.

Barton, L. (1991). A case study in crisis management: The Perrier recall. *Industrial Management & Data Systems, 91*(7), 6–8.

Boddewyn, J. J. (2007). The internationalisation of the public affairs function in US multinational enterprises. *Business and Society, 46*(2), 136–172.

Bravo, V., Molledab, J-C., Dávilac, A. F. G. & Boteroc, L. H. (2013). Testing cross-national conflict shifting theory: An analysis of Chiquita Brands' transnational crisis in Colombia. *Public Relations Review, 39*(1), 57–59.

Doh, J. P. & Guay, T. R. (2006). Corporate social responsibility, public policy and NGO activism in Europe and the United States: An institutional-stakeholder perspective. *Journal of Management Studies, 43*(1), 47–73.

Entine, J. (2002). Shell, Greenpeace and Brent Spar: the politics of dialogue. In C. Megane & S. J. Robinson (Eds.), *Case histories in business ethics* (pp. 59–95). London: Routledge.

Frandsen, F. & Johansen, W. (2010). Crisis Communication, complexity and the cartoon affair: A case study. In W. T. Coombs & S. J. Holladay (Eds.), *The handbook of crisis communication* (pp. 425–448). Malden, MA: Wiley Blackwell.

Freitag, A. R. & Stokes, A. Q. (2008). *Global public relations: Spanning borders, spanning cultures*. London: Taylor & Francis.

Fronz, C. (2012). *Strategic management in crisis communication: A multinational approach*. Hamburg: Diplomica Verlag.

Gaskell, G., Bauer, M. W., Durant. J. & Allum, N. C. (1999, 16 July). Worlds apart? The reception of genetically modified foods in Europe and the US. *Science, 285*(5426), 384–387.

George, A. M. & Pratt, C. B. (Eds.). (2012). *Case studies in crisis communication: International perspectives on hits and misses*. New York: Routledge.

Gibson, D. C. (2000). Firestone's failed recalls, 1978 and 2000: A public relations explanation. *Public Relations Quarterly, 45*(4), 10–13.

Global Alliance for PR and Communication Management. (n.d.). *PR country landscapes*. Retrieved from www.globalalliancepr.org/website/securepage/country-landscapes.

Heller, V. L. & Darling, J. R. (2012). Anatomy of crisis management: Lessons from the infamous Toyota case. *European Business Review, 24*(2), 151–168.

Hiles, A. (2011). Toyota recalls 2009–2010: Case study. In A. Hiles (Ed.), *The Definitive Handbook of Business Continuity Management* (3rd ed., pp. 597–610). Chichester: Wiley.

Holmström, S., Falkheimer, J. & Nielsen, A. G. (2010). Legitimacy and strategic communication in globalisation: The cartoon crisis and other legitimacy conflicts. *International Journal of Strategic Communication, 4*(1), 1–18.

Johnson, V. & Peppas, S. C. (2003). Crisis management in Belgium: The case of Coca-Cola. *Corporate Communications, 8*(1), 18–22.

Kellerman, B. (2006, April). When should the leader apologise, and when not?. *Harvard Business Review,* 78–79.

Kurzbard, G. & Siomkos, G. J. (1992). Crafting a damage control plan: Lessons from Perrier. *Journal of Business Strategy, 13*(2), 39–43.

Meisenbach, R. J. & Feldner, S. B. (2013). Toyota: Oh what a feeling, or Oh what a mess. In S. May (Ed.), *Case studies in organisational communication: Ethical perspectives and practices* (2nd ed., pp. 99–109). Thousand Oaks, CA: Sage.

Neuliep, J. W. (2012). *Intercultural communication: A contextual approach* (5th ed.). Thousand Oaks, CA: Sage.

Pinedo, M., Seshadri, S. & Zemel, E. (2000). The Ford-Firestone case. *New York University case study.* Retrieved from www.yoest.com/wp-content/uploads/2013/02/ford_firestone_case-study.pdf.

Schmidt, K. V. (1999, 27 September). Coke's crisis: What marketers can learn from continental crack-up. *Marketing News, 1,* 11, 12.

Spar, D. L. & La Mure, L. T. (2003). The power of activism: Assessing the impact of NGOs on global business. *California Management Review, 45*(3), 78–101.

Tai, S. H. C. (2008). Beauty and the beast: the brand crisis of SK-II cosmetics in China. *Asian Case Research Journal, 12*(1), 57–71.

Van Doesum, W. (2008). *Crisis communication in a globalised world: Arla and the cartoon crisis.* Masters dissertation. Copenhagen Business School.

9

CRISIS MANAGEMENT— DISASTERS

CHAPTER OBJECTIVES

This chapter will help you to:

+ understand the main differences between crisis and disaster

+ introduce the concept of catastrophe

+ recognise the main types of disasters—both natural and man-made

+ learn the four key phases of disaster management: mitigation, preparedness, response and recovery

+ distinguish the roles of government, intra-government and multinational agencies

+ assess the importance of communication and social media in a disaster.

Disasters are devastating events that strike whole communities or countries, often at enormous cost in lives, physical damage and financial impact. The Centre for Research on the Epidemiology of Disasters (CRED) reports that there have been more than 18,000 mass disasters from 1900 to the present (CRED, 2014) and, although experts argue about definition, most agree there are now on average over 200 disaster events a year. It was calculated (Singh & Singh, 2010) that natural disasters alone may have killed nearly three million people worldwide over the past 20 years.

The financial cost is also enormous. The United Nations Office for Disaster Risk Reduction estimates that the total global annual loss from earthquakes alone is about US$100 billion, with a further $80 billion a year just from the cost of tropical cyclones (Global Assessment Report on Disaster Risk Reduction, 2013). In fact, CRED reported that 2011 was the costliest year ever for disasters, with economic cost in excess of US$366 billion (Schlein, 2012). And the same report said the Japanese earthquake and tsunami in March 2011 caused economic losses of US$210 billion, making it the costliest natural disaster of all time. In Australia, the insured cost alone of natural disasters has been estimated at over A$1 billion a year (Crompton & McAneney, 2008) and direct economic costs are generally calculated at about twice the insured loss.

Moreover, disaster researchers believe the incidence and number of disasters is increasing as a result of a number of factors, including rapid urbanisation, people increasingly living in disaster-prone areas, technological interdependence, and changing weather events because of climate change.

But despite these frightening facts, in the same way that the word 'crisis' has been 'devalued' through overuse (see Chapter 6), the same can be said for the word 'disaster'. Contrary to typical news media headlines, losing a crucial football match is not a disaster, nor is a fall in a company's share price. In fact, in recent times, the word 'disaster' has progressed from being devalued to actually being entirely trivialised. For example, a celebrity posting an unwise twitter message might be labelled as a 'PR disaster' or a 'social media disaster', while a film star choosing the wrong dress for a red-carpet event becomes a 'fashion disaster'.

Such language is unhelpful and distracts attention from genuine matters of concern. While it is clear that there is a big difference between a popular culture 'disaster' and a true societal disaster, there is a real lack of agreement about the difference between a crisis and a disaster, and this is certainly true at the academic level. Three of the world's leading academics in the field concluded: 'There have been a number of attempts to distinguish between, among and within different kinds of disasters and crises. However no one overall view has won anywhere near general acceptance among self-designated disaster and crisis researchers' (Quarantelli, Lagadec & Boin, 2007, p. 22).

In fact, Ronald Perry (2007) argues that 'in reality anyone has the right to propose a definition of disaster' (p. 2) and the definition proposed depends on the purposes or interests of the definer.[1] Hiltz, Diaz and Mark (2011) have commented that; 'Disaster, crisis, catastrophe and emergency management are sometimes used synonymously and sometimes with slight differences by scholars and practitioners' (p. 1). Despite this lack of consensus, there is no doubt that genuine crises and disasters have a great deal in common,

---

1   For a detailed analysis of the evolving definition of disaster, see Perry (2007).

such as impact, urgency, uncertainty, limited control and risk. Yet there are some very important differences.

Using the working definition presented in Table 1.1 in Chapter 1, a disaster is a major adverse event that affects the broader society, even though it may also trigger a specific crisis for individual organisations. Unlike the highly focused management response to an organisational crisis, disaster management is most often led by statutory or territorial authorities or governments, and requires interagency coordination to mobilise diverse forces.

Some of the key differences then are impact and scale. There is an old saying that 'a disaster is a crisis that ends badly', or as the Dutch crisis experts Boin and 't Hart (2007) put it: 'A disaster is viewed as a crisis with a devastating ending' (p. 42).

Impact is certainly a critical element. A passenger aircraft that crashes in a remote forest and kills everyone aboard would be a crisis for the airline, but would most likely not be classed as a disaster (other than in newspaper headlines). But what if the same aircraft came down in an urban area, not only killing everyone on board but also dozens of children at a local school as well as destroying a major power substation and plunging the entire region into blackout? That would be a legitimate societal disaster, and would almost immediately be taken out of the hands of the airline itself and civil authorities would take over.

> We are the authors of our own disasters.
>
> Latin proverb

The same aspect of impact applies to natural disasters. A major earthquake that strikes in a largely uninhabited area may cause widespread surface damage and landslips, but without human casualties it would not be regarded as a disaster. Yet an earthquake of only half the magnitude that struck a major city and caused severe structural damage or casualties would certainly be a disaster. Perception is also a significant contributor, with people's frames of reference, experience and memory, values and interests determining their perception of a crisis. As Boin and 't Hart (2007) somewhat brutally noted: 'A flood that kills 200 people is a more or less routine experience in Bangladesh, but it would be experienced as a major crisis in, say, Miami or Paris' (p. 53).

In addition to impact and perception, scale is also an important distinction, when the event is so big that it overwhelms local resources and requires a multi-jurisdiction or multi-government response. This is an important aspect in the definitions developed for the United Nations as one of the key global disaster-response agencies. UN Business defines a disaster as: 'A serious disruption of the functioning of a society, causing widespread human, material or environmental losses and exceeding the coping capacities of the affected communities and government' (UN Business, n.d.).

More broadly the UN, through its Disaster Management Training Programme (2003), says:

> A disaster is the occurrence of a sudden or major misfortune, which disrupts the basic fabric and normal functioning of a society (or community). An event or series of events, which give rise to casualties and/or damage or loss of property,

infrastructure, essential services or means of livelihood on a scale which is beyond the normal capacity of the affected communities to cope with unaided.

In other words, disasters are extreme events that result in widespread social disruption, trauma, damage and loss of life, not just organisational impacts. Or, put more simply for the purpose of clarity, organisations have crises while societies or communities have disasters.[2] However, this important distinction can be blurred when one directly causes the other. For example, the notorious *Deepwater Horizon* oil spill in the Gulf of Mexico in 2010 was an organisational crisis for the oil giant BP, while the same event was a societal disaster for the environment, and for communities and businesses along the affected coast of Louisiana.

Likewise, while the collapse of the investment bank Lehman Brothers in 2008 was undoubtedly an organisational crisis for the company and for some other financial institutions, it helped trigger a global financial collapse that was an undoubted societal disaster which affected governments, economies and investors around the world. In this way, an event or series of events can be a crisis for the organisation, and simultaneously can be a disaster for broader society.

> Sometimes it takes a natural disaster to reveal a social disaster.
>
> US minister Jim Wallis (cited in Fletcher, 2005)

The same blurring, or convergence, can also exist in the reverse direction. In other words, a societal disaster can precipitate an organisational crisis. For example, a major flood would represent a societal disaster for the affected community, but for a company located in the flooded area that loses its factory, its stock and all its electronic records, it would be a corporate crisis (see the box, 'Bushfire threatens oyster industry'). Similarly, the earthquake and tsunami that struck Japan in March 2011 was a national disaster for Japan and interrupted supply chains around the world, especially in the automotive industry. It also triggered an unprecedented crisis for the company whose Fukushima nuclear power station lost power and suffered a meltdown (which in turn created a fresh disaster for the country).

BUSHFIRE THREATENS OYSTER INDUSTRY

A stark example of when a community disaster triggers an organisational crisis was seen in January 2013 when a record-breaking heatwave sparked terrible bushfires that isolated part of Tasmania. As well as destroying much of the small town of Dunalley, fires cut the power supply to the local oyster hatchery, which produces about 40 per cent of the immature baby stock supplied to oyster farms across Australia. The fire melted the freshwater tanks at Cameron's Oysters and burned the only back-up generator, leaving the company facing a major crisis with 110 million delicate tiny oysters in the hatchery likely to die without power to drive the pumps.

The owners launched an appeal on Facebook and, despite the whole community struggling in the face of destruction, seven volunteer electricians arrived to help, and

---

2   This distinction was originally developed by Seeger, Sellnow and Ulmer (1998).

two new generators on the backs of trucks appeared on the scene, having made it through the police blockade that cut off the whole area. With just a few hours to spare, fresh saltwater was pumping over the stricken young oyster spat, saving two-thirds and protecting a key employer in the town. Dunalley and the local area were devastated by a community disaster but the organisational crisis was averted.[3]

TYPES OF DISASTERS

This brings us to natural disasters, which represent a substantial share of all disasters that occur. In fact, Singh and Singh (2010) assert that, on a global basis, natural events account for 80 per cent of all people affected by disasters (p. 1). These are typically the events referred to as 'Acts of God'. However, despite the popular focus on natural disasters, they are not the sole area of attention. It is worth listing some of the more common types of disasters, to make sure the discussion on definitions leaves no room for doubt. For example, storms and floods typically represent about 70 per cent of all natural disasters, yet there are many other categories (Ferris, Petz & Stark, 2013). The following list is not intended to be exhaustive, but it captures some of the leading types of disasters, both natural and man-made (even though the distinction can occasionally be blurred).

Natural disasters include:

+ earthquakes
+ landslides and mudslides
+ volcanic eruptions
+ floods
+ hurricanes, cyclones and typhoons
+ ice storms and blizzards
+ heatwaves
+ hail storms
+ sand storms and dust storms
+ plagues of locusts
+ tsunamis
+ tornadoes
+ avalanches
+ wildfires, bush fires and forest fires
+ epidemics and pandemics.

Man-made disasters include:

+ global warming
+ terrorism
+ deforestation and desertification

---

3 For detail on the fires and the local oyster industry, see http://www.abc.net.au/am/content/2013/s3671092.htm.

+ genocide
+ water and land pollution
+ technological failures; for example:
    - Aberfan (1966)—an unstable coal waste heap overwhelmed a small Welsh town
    - Bhopal (1984)—a chemical leak devastated a nearby Indian city
    - Basel (1986)—a chemical fire and spill polluted the Rhine in Switzerland, Germany, France and Holland
    - Chernobyl (1986)—a nuclear accident spread radioactivity over Western Europe
    - Auckland (1998)—a power blackout shut down New Zealand's largest city
    - Baia Mare (2000)—a gold-processing plant failure polluted the Danube in Romania, Hungary, Yugoslavia and Bulgaria.

WHAT ABOUT CATASTROPHES?

Before leaving the question of how disaster events are defined, it is important to consider one other term and how it has come to be used—'catastrophe'. In recent years, catastrophe has emerged as a term to describe events beyond disasters (sometimes referred to as mega-disasters or hyper-complex events). Indeed, Clifford Oliver (2011) argues that what are now referred to as catastrophes may appear in older publication as crises, disasters or mega disasters, terminology that he says has become outdated.[4] In support of his position, Oliver proposed what he calls a 'continuum of magnitude' (see Figure 9.1).

In summary Oliver offers these descriptions:

+ *Emergency*—an event, usually sudden, that threatens life or property, where local emergency response resources are adequate to immediate needs of the people affected, usually managed within a single jurisdiction.

+ *Disaster*—an event that involves multiple people or locations, where local response resources are not adequate to meet the immediate needs of people affected, and where responders may be required from multiple jurisdictions.

+ *Catastrophe*—an event similar to disaster but where multiple jurisdictions, governments or countries may be involved and the populations affected are so large that many needs may go unmet, at least in the short term.

+ *Extinction level event*—an event so serious that humans may not survive, such as a new ice age or the Earth being struck by a giant asteroid (Oliver, 2011, pp. 7–8).[5]

---

4 Oliver (2011) has detailed chapters on the definition and history of catastrophes, and how catastrophes differ from disasters.

5 This level of impact has also been called 'planetary scale disasters' (Vallero and Letcher, 2013, p. 20).

Following this argument, a disaster event may be classified as a catastrophe if its magnitude is sufficiently devastating; for example, the tsunami caused by the volcanic explosion of Krakatoa in the East Indies in August 1883, which reportedly killed over 36,000 people. Catastrophes in modern times include the Southeast Asian tsunami on Boxing Day 2004, one of the deadliest natural disasters in recorded history, which killed around 230,000 people in fourteen countries; the 2003 Great Sichuan Earthquake in China with a reported 70,000 killed, 374,000 injured and more than four million made homeless;[6] Cyclone Nargis, which struck Myanmar in 2008 causing devastating damage and taking as many as 90,000 lives; and the Haiti earthquake of 2010 that killed perhaps 100,000 people and displaced well over a million.

The concept of catastrophe has another very important distinction. It does not necessarily arise just as the result of a sudden disaster event. It may emerge more slowly, to potentially affect the lives of millions of people, and even cause millions of casualties. Historically, such gradually emerging catastrophes might include the bubonic plague (black death) that devastated Europe in the 1300s;[7] the potato famine that overwhelmed and depopulated parts of Ireland in the 1840s;[8] and the 1918–1919 influenza pandemic in the wake of the First World War, which claimed an estimated 40–50 million lives internationally, with some experts claiming the figure might be as high as 100 million.[9] More recently, perhaps 30 million have died from AIDS since the disease was first recognised in 1981.

Looking forward, potential gradual catastrophes might include the impact of global warming and rising sea levels; devastating droughts and famines; or new pandemics such as SARS or avian flu. Damon Coppola (2007, p. 25) describes these as 'creeping disasters':

> Sudden onset disasters often happen with little or no warning and most of their damaging effects are sustained within hours or days ... Creeping disasters occur when the ability of response agencies to support the people's needs degrades over weeks or months, and they can persist for months or years once they are discovered.

However, for the present discussion we will focus on disasters that are triggered by specific events, rather than such slowly emerging disasters or catastrophes.[10]

DISASTER MANAGEMENT

As outlined in Chapter 1, disaster management is a coordinated response, often led by statutory or territorial authorities, which mobilises diverse forces to respond to disaster threats. Here, again, the UN Disaster Management Programme (2003) provides a useful definition of disaster management:

> The range of activities designed to maintain control over disaster and emergency situations and to provide a framework for helping at risk persons avoid or recover

---

6   For a case study of the Wenchuan Earthquake in 2008, see Chen and Booth (2011) in this chapter's Further reading section.

7   For more on the black death, see Kelly (2005) in this chapter's Further reading section.

8   For more on the Irish potato famine, see Woodham-Smith (1962) in this chapter's Further reading section.

9   For more on the great influenza epidemic, see Barry (2004) in this chapter's Further reading section.

10 For another perspective on catastrophe versus disaster, see Quarantelli (2006).

> from the impact of a disaster. The attempt to minimize the disruption caused by these adverse events and prevent as much additional damage as possible.

Just as disasters and crises have many common characteristics, disaster management has many parallels and overlaps with crisis management. But it also has some important factors that set it apart.

There is a large and well-established disaster management literature.[11] While much of this literature has a strong focus on international disasters and intergovernmental agencies, there is a consistent view[12] that the fundamentals of disaster management can be properly addressed and summarised in four overall phases:

1. mitigation

2. preparedness

3. response

4. recovery.

PHASE ONE: MITIGATION

The first phase is mitigation, which basically means taking steps to reduce the likelihood of a hazard manifesting as a disaster, and to reduce the negative effects if it were to occur. Taking the perspective of an international disaster relief agency, the UN Disaster Management Programme (2003) offers this definition of mitigation:

> The process of planning and implementing measures to reduce the risks associated with known natural and manmade hazards and to deal with disasters when occurring. Strategies and specific measures are designed on the basis of risk assessments and political decisions concerning the levels of risk which are considered to be acceptable and the resources to be allocated (by national and sub-national authorities and external donors).

Placing mitigation in the broader context of the sequence of phases, Coppola (2007, p. 175) said: 'While preparedness, response and recovery are performed either in reaction to hazards or in anticipation of their consequences, mitigation measures seek to reduce the likelihood or consequences of hazard risk before a disaster ever occurs.'

There is also another important distinction between the phases. While actions involved in the preparedness, response and recovery phases are related to specific events, mitigation activities have the potential to produce repeated benefits over time and should concern events that may occur in the future (Organisation of American States, 1997). The OAS plan added that in this way, whether applied in post-disaster reconstruction or during pre-disaster planning efforts, hazard mitigation provides planners with guidelines for

---

11 For recent examples of disaster literature, see Coppola (2007) and Oliver (2011). In this chapter's Further reading section, see also Fraustino, Lui and Jin (2012), Haddow and Haddow (2009), Helsloot et al. (2009), Jennex (2012), McEntire (2006), Pinkowski (2009), Rodriguez, Quarantelli and Dynes (2007), Valedro and Letcher (2013) and Wisner Gaillard and Kelman (2012).

12 See Edwards (2009) in this chapter's Further reading section.

reducing vulnerability to future disaster-related damages. By developing mitigation programs that affect the impact of future disasters, planners can 'break the cycle of damage, reconstruction and repeated damage'.

However, mitigation doesn't come cheap. Coppola (2007) went so far as to emphasise that mitigation has traditionally been the luxury of rich nations, with many poorer societies regarding it as something they cannot justify or afford in light of other, more immediate societal demands, particularly in relation to natural disasters. This disparity was highlighted by Singh and Singh (2010), who claim that 95 per cent of all natural disasters, and 95 per cent of total disaster-related deaths worldwide, occur in third world or developing nations (p. 6).

Obviously, for most natural disasters, there are not many feasible ways to make them less likely. For example, there is very little humans can do to prevent a blizzard or volcanic eruption. Therefore the focus of mitigation is on reducing the consequences. Most disaster managers divide mitigation strategies into two categories: structural and non-structural.

STRUCTURAL MITIGATION

Structural mitigation basically means physical or engineering measures designed to protect humanity against the forces of nature. At the simplest level this might mean building houses on stilts (or with non-residential ground-level space) in flood-prone communities or installing storm cellars in areas where tornadoes are common; right through to complex and costly engineering and design to make houses and other buildings more resistant to earthquakes. Mitigation might also include regulations to require the use of ignition-resistant building materials in bushfire-prone areas, or requiring strengthened or steep roofs to protect against heavy hail or snow.

Beyond protection measures for individual homes and other buildings, further structural mitigation is designed to hold back or deflect the hazard, such as seawalls to resist storm surges and tsunamis. However, the failure of such barriers can be disastrous, as was shown when the Great North Sea Storm of 1953 overwhelmed dykes built to protect the Netherlands; or when Hurricane Katrina breached flood protection barriers and inundated New Orleans in 2005. Other physical protective measures include levees, flood barriers or flood banks along rivers to contain rising water levels; or engineered diversion channels in mountainous regions to divert landslides, mud flows or snow avalanches.

The final element of structural mitigation is development of warning systems so that there is time for people to take precautions and hopefully save lives. Examples of such systems include satellite imaging to warn of approaching hurricanes; ground movement seismic monitoring to give advance indication of earthquakes or volcanic eruptions; and ocean movement detection systems to identify tsunamis out at sea before they strike land.

The reality is that complex structural mitigation measures can be extremely costly, such as the massive Thames Barrier, one of the world's largest movable flood barriers, built near Woolwich to protect central London from flooding causes by tidal surges; or the multibillion-dollar walls and floodgates built as part of the MOSE project, to prevent high tides from inundating the historic city of Venice.[13] Moreover, some of these huge projects can be highly controversial, not only because of their cost but also because of social disruption they can create, and because of concern they may not be a complete guarantee against the power of nature.

PREDICTING DISASTERS

In 2001 the US Federal Emergency Management Agency (FEMA) analysed the potential disasters facing the USA and formally identified the three most probable disaster events: a terrorist attack in New York City, a catastrophic earthquake in San Francisco and a hurricane and levee break in New Orleans. The first of these happened just four months later, when terrorists struck the World Trade Centre in New York on 11 September 2001, and Hurricane Katrina destroyed much of New Orleans in August 2005. The people of San Francisco are still waiting for that catastrophic earthquake.

Source: FEMA study, cited in Phelps (2005).

NON-STRUCTURAL MITIGATION

Non-structural mitigation is fundamentally about non-engineering techniques to reduce the likelihood or consequences of disaster risk, which is sometimes called humanity *adapting to* nature rather than *fighting against* nature.

Unlike structural mitigation, non-structural measures are generally less costly and require fewer resources, which means they are more easily within the reach of developing countries. But they do require strong public and political commitment to do the work and be prepared. A key area of non-structural mitigation is regulatory measures designed to use legal processes and compliance to enforce limitations and restrictions that will mitigate risk. One of the most important of these is zoning, or land use management, to restrict how land can be used—such as limiting development in flood-prone or bushfire-prone areas, on unstable hillsides or exposed coastal areas, or in avalanche or volcanic eruption risk zones.

However, increasing population stress and urbanisation can put pressure on rational planning. A study of home construction in the United Kingdom showed that 7–11 per cent of all new housing since 1989 has been built in areas with 'high flood risk' (Global Assessment Report on Disaster Risk Reduction, 2013).

Zoning regulations can also be used to ensure that developments are not permitted where they would affect storm run-off or where they would disrupt wetlands or forest cover that stabilise or protect the land. Similarly, zoning and safety regulations can be used to ensure residential developments are kept appropriately separated from potentially hazardous industries.

Such legal, regulatory mitigation measures must be reinforced by political and public support, which in turns needs public education programs. The public not only have to

---

13 For discussion about European public perception of coastal flood risk, see Kellens et al. (2011) in this chapter's Further reading section.

comply with legal mitigation requirements, and accept that such measures are in place for the greater good, but they also need to be educated to understand their own role in disaster mitigation. While this communication and education has a strong focus on individual and community preparedness (which we will come to shortly), the mitigation element is to be aware of disaster hazards—to be aware of warning systems and community alarms, and to know what to do when things go wrong.

Another area of non-structural mitigation relates to physical and environmental controls, such as improved coastal vegetation to protect against erosion and storm surges; forest planting and protection to stabilise landslides and erosion; river and harbour dredging to avoid silting and flooding; controlled explosions to reduce the threat of avalanches; and controlled burns to reduce the risk from bushfires.

The final area of non-structural mitigation, which touches on preparedness, is development and maintenance of national emergency response capacity. This means, of course, not just efficient police, fire-fighting services and hospitals, but also specialist disaster capability, such as expert search and rescue teams, helicopter rescue, mass casualty identification, fire-bombing aircraft, rescue dogs, emergency communication and mass temporary accommodation.

PHASE TWO: PREPAREDNESS

While mitigation is intended to reduce disaster risk, preparedness—as with crisis management—comprises the steps taken well in advance to deliver the best possible response when a disaster occurs. One of the keys to disaster preparedness is that the steps taken may require years to develop and fully implement and are designed to avoid having to identify gaps and throw plans together at the last minute or when the disaster has already struck.

Disaster preparedness falls into two main areas—government and public.

GOVERNMENT PREPAREDNESS

Government preparedness includes a huge range of activities that may happen at different levels of government, across multiple jurisdictions and even across different governments. As with crisis management, the critical focus is a comprehensive plan, sometimes called an emergency operation plan, an emergency response plan or a disaster plan.[14] However, unlike an organisational crisis plan, where established chains of command and authority usually exist, a community or national plan may involve dozens of different organisations, many with their own crisis or emergency plan, all with their own chains of command, and often with different or even contradictory processes.

For this reason many governments establish a statutory authority with strong funding and legal power to take control in order to coordinate the personnel and resources of individual agencies. This might include the power to override normal rights and freedoms, such as forcing evacuation even when individuals are unwilling to leave, bulldozing through private property to create a fire-break, or enforcing curfews or exclusion zones to control public access.

---

14 See Smith (2006) in this chapter's Further reading section.

THE NEED FOR INTERAGENCY COORDINATION

A study of a major plant fire in Canada found that 348 organisations appeared on site. They included seven departments of local government, ten regional government agencies, twenty-five entities from the provincial government and twenty-seven organisations from the federal level, as well as thirty-one fire departments, forty-one churches, hospitals and schools, four utilities, eight voluntary agencies, four emergent groups and at least fifty-two different private sector organisations.

Source: Joseph Scanlon (cited in Quarantelli, 2006).

Many elements of a disaster plan would mirror those included in a standard crisis plan, such as designated teams, central control location, clear roles and responsibilities, pre-approved information, communication guidelines and designated spokespersons (see Chapter 7). However, a community or national plan would also include a range of other functions, which would be activated depending on the nature of the disaster. A typical list (adapted from Coppola, 2007, pp. 215–216) would include:

+ direction and control
+ notification and warning
+ evacuation
+ communications
+ public works
+ public information
+ fire suppression
+ search and rescue
+ emergency medical services and mass care
+ mortuary services
+ security and perimeter control
+ involvement of military resources
+ transport
+ relief
+ short- and long-term recovery
+ financial management
+ international coordination
+ volunteer management
+ donations management
+ vulnerable populations.

In addition, the plan might also include special sections to deal with specific disaster hazards, such as infectious diseases, hazardous chemicals, toxic gases or radioactive materials from a nuclear accident.

Like an organisational crisis plan, the disaster or emergency plan is of only limited value without effective training and exercises. Because of their scale, comprehensive community or national exercises can be very costly. But experience shows that the complexity of interagency and cross-jurisdictional disaster response highlights that regular training is vital for optimal preparedness. However, no government plan can be effective without complementary public preparedness. As Ramirez, Antrobus and Williamson (2013, p. 6) concluded:

> The importance of encouraging community and individual engagement, cooperation and proactive involvement in preparedness initiatives relieves the demand on state resources. This is part of a transition from disaster preparedness and preventive strategies being the sole responsibility of governments to involving and collaborating with members of the community to ensure that, in the event that the government cannot immediately assist citizens, these citizens are capable of effectively responding to disasters.

PUBLIC PREPAREDNESS

Public preparedness is less structured, but no less important. A disaster, by definition, is a situation where official response mechanisms are under extreme stress and therefore the public need to be prepared to help themselves, their families and other people. For example, the Australian Federal Government expects that, in the event of a community disaster, citizens should be able to look after themselves without outside assistance for up to three days (COAG, 2009). This approach is sometimes referred to as 'community resilience'.

The common element of any public preparedness process is education, and that should be focused on two goals: to make the public aware of disasters risks, and to make sure they know what to do before and during a disaster. Although awareness and knowledge about potential disasters would appear to be self-evident, front-line response services find themselves constantly required to repeat messages about the most basic awareness and behaviour:

+ Don't try to drive your car through flood water.
+ Stay away from fallen power lines.
+ Secure your home and anything outside when high winds are forecast.
+ Listen to your radio or television for information and instructions.
+ Move to high ground if a tsunami or flooding is possible.
+ Don't risk your life to save pets or livestock.
+ Leave early if fire threatens your home.
+ Listen for community alarms and know what they mean.
+ Don't run outside during an earthquake.

All are basic awareness, but in almost every disaster lives are lost through foolish actions and failure to comply.

Similarly, public education can play an important role in individual and family preparedness before any disaster, with messages such as:

+ Have an evacuation and emergency meeting plan.
+ Know how to turn off gas and electricity at the mains supply.
+ Learn first aid and have a first aid kit at home.
+ Have emergency contact numbers near the phone (or entered on mobile devices).
+ Teach children how to telephone emergency services.
+ Have a battery-powered radio and flashlight (and spare batteries).
+ Stockpile an emergency supply of water and non-perishable food.
+ Join a community volunteer organisation.

Public education messages can be promulgated via all the usual channels of mass communication—including television, radio, newspapers, magazines, the internet and social media—as well as through community activities such as training courses, special events and awareness days, and through membership organisations, churches, libraries and schools.

In some areas, limited literacy and education are major hurdles to public education, and in developing countries—where disaster risks may be higher—there is sometimes less access to communication technology such as radio, television and the internet. But disaster preparedness at both government and individual level is vital, and the two must work together to protect lives and property.

PHASE THREE: RESPONSE

As with crisis response, disaster response is the group of activities that take place immediately before the disaster is recognised, during the disaster itself, and in its direct aftermath (although usually on a vastly different scale). This phase is when all the steps taken during mitigation and preparedness pay off, and when the focus is on limiting injury and loss of life, and controlling damage to property and the environment.

It is also the most difficult and highest profile stage, often taking place under the scrutiny of the international news media and in the glare of television cameras. Think of the graphic photographs and news film of ruined buildings, dead bodies, weeping relatives, damaged infrastructure, starving children, wounded and sick patients in field hospitals, and hopeless people evacuated to huge tent camps.[15] These are the enduring images of disasters, and they are all from the response phase.

Coppola (2007. p. 252) recognised the special demands of this critical phase:

> Response is by far the most complex of the four functions of [disaster] management, since it is conducted during periods of very high stress, in a highly time-constrained environment and with limited information. During response, wavering confidence and unnecessary delay directly translate to tragedy and destruction.

In the period immediately before a disaster there are some pre-disaster response actions that are still possible, including issuing warnings to take shelter or evacuate, and last-minute

---

15 For discussion of using social media to share photographs during disasters, see Liu et al. (2008) in this chapter's Further reading section.

mitigation and preparedness, such as sandbags to hold out flood water, boarding up windows before a storm, or activating an external building sprinkler system to reduce the risk from bushfires. The reality is that it is usually too late for more complex actions, and the focus of response is those steps which begin *after* the disaster has struck.

In terms of disaster response, the first priority is obviously saving people in distress and protecting lives. These first-order activities include locating and recovering victims (search and rescue); then emergency first aid and medical treatment; followed by evacuation of vulnerable populations to a place of safety, usually well away from the consequences of the disaster.

As these steps are carried out, officials would commence the next response action, which is situation assessment—essentially determining key information including what area has been affected by the disaster; how many people have been affected (killed, injured and relocated); whether there are any emerging or ongoing disaster hazards; and what critical infrastructure or facilities have been damaged, and how long it would take to restore them.

After this comes reporting and planning, and provision for people affected, such as safe water, food, shelter, sanitation and health services. Experience shows that the risk of illness and disease escalates rapidly in the wake of many disasters, and the recovery, identification and safe disposal of bodies is a distasteful but critical part of this planning.

Restoration of critical infrastructure is another vital element of disaster response. Loss of infrastructure can prolong and delay the effectiveness of response, and can create major hurdles to making society safe and secure. Nearly every disaster disrupts critical infrastructure components, which include:

+ electricity and gas supply
+ water and sewerage systems
+ communications
+ transport, such as roads, railways, bridges, ports and airports
+ hospitals and emergency services
+ civil order, such as police and security to protect people and property.

> Hurricane Katrina proved that even the President of the United States cannot personally 'manage' a disaster. In the early days of the Katrina response, when the Governor of Louisiana and the President failed to reach agreement for unified command, an effective response became impossible.
>
> Clifford Oliver (2011, p. 272)

The final element of disaster response is the complicated and sometimes political problem of receiving and distributing donations that typically arrive after any major disaster. Donated goods need to be sorted, stored and distributed, and this can be a major challenge when infrastructure is damaged.

A sadly common scenario is when desperately needed food and medical supplies pile up unused on the dock because there is no transport or no safe roads to get it to starving evacuees;

or when donated goods are completely unsuited for proper use. Even cash donations need reliable systems to make sure money can be recorded properly and accounted for, and then distributed in a fair and transparent way that will stand up to legitimate scrutiny.

The response phase of disaster management highlights more than any other that disasters are very different from organisational crises, and that they demand the involvement of governments and transnational agencies for coordination and resources, far beyond the capability of any single organisation.

PHASE FOUR: RECOVERY

The fourth and final element of disaster management is the recovery stage, which highlights one of the major differences with the post-event stage of crisis management.

In organisational crisis management the post-crisis phase is strongly focused on operational continuity, restructuring and getting back to 'business as usual' as quickly as possible (see Chapter 6). As previously discussed, the post-crisis management phase also includes a range of specific threats to the organisation in the form of legal action, such as prosecution and litigation, as well as official inquiries with a strong emphasis on allocating blame, plus a range of image restoration strategies.

By contrast, while the recovery phase after societal disasters may also include some form of investigation or commission of inquiry, the primary focus is typically to determine exactly what happened and how to prevent it happening again, rather than legal action against individuals. However, individual recriminations do sometimes happen, such as in 2012 when six Italian earthquake experts and a government official were each sentenced to six years in prison after falsely giving public reassurances just days before the 2009 earthquake that levelled the city of L'Aquila and killed more than 300 people (Kington, 2012).

Unlike the post-crisis phase for organisations, post-disaster recovery is largely about how to repair, rebuild or regain what has been lost as result of the disaster. As a result, some experts refer to this recovery phase as reconstruction or rehabilitation. According to Coppola (2007, p. 300), typical actions and actions performed in the recovery period of a disaster include:

+ ongoing communication with the public
+ provision of temporary housing or long-term shelter
+ assessment of damages and needs
+ demolition of damaged structures
+ clearance, removal and disposal of debris
+ rehabilitation of damaged infrastructure
+ inspection and repair of damaged structures
+ new construction
+ social rehabilitation programs
+ creation of employment opportunities
+ reimbursement of property losses

+ rehabilitation of the injured

+ reassessment of hazard risk.

However, this list may understate the longer-term scale of recovery. Major recovery work can take years or even decades. For example, within two years of the 2004 Southeast Asian tsunami, half of the permanent homes needed in Indonesia had been completed, and almost 700 schools had been rebuilt or repaired. By contrast, two years after the March 2011 tsunami flattened parts of northeast Japan, few homes had been rebuilt ('Two years later', 2013).

THE SCALE OF RECOVERY

The scale of the recovery task after a major disaster can be illustrated by the earthquakes that struck Christchurch in September 2010 and February 2011, New Zealand's costliest natural disaster, which killed 189 people.

BUILDING DAMAGE

Over 100,000 houses were damaged and required repair or rebuilding. A significant number of properties were unable to be redeveloped in the short to medium term due to serious land damage. More than 50 per cent of the buildings in Christchurch's CBD were severely damaged. The earthquakes closed many swimming pools, historical buildings, museums, churches and sports clubs, with many facing demolition or extensive restoration work. Many heritage buildings were damaged and destroyed, and the New Zealand Historic Places Trust estimated that about 40 per cent of these listed heritage places had been demolished or severely damaged.

ECONOMIC DISRUPTION

More than 60 per cent of the 5000 businesses in the CBD and their 50,000 employees were displaced. The closure of the CBD meant closure or relocation of many businesses, sometimes to an area outside of Canterbury. More than one-third of central city businesses were unable to operate, with another third operating from makeshift premises.

PORT DAMAGE

The city's port at Lyttelton suffered significant damage in each of the major earthquakes. While working services were quickly restored, six of the port's ten working berths (used to transfer cargo) required significant restoration work or rebuilding in the short-term.

WATER-RELATED INFRASTRUCTURE

Freshwater, sewerage and stormwater systems were severely affected. For example, 124 kilometres of water mains and 300 kilometres of sewer pipes were damaged, with structural damage also to some reservoirs and wells. All but sixty-four of the city's 175 freshwater wells required some repair and twenty-one wells were damaged so badly that they could not be used. Christchurch's largest reservoir in Huntsbury was seriously damaged. The quakes damaged eight of the ninety-seven sewer pumping stations within the city so badly that they needed to be completely replaced.

ROADS

These suffered substantial damage and it is estimated that 895 kilometres of road need rebuilding—46 per cent of Christchurch's urban sealed roads. Major renewal projects will rebuild these roads and in some cases the road will need full reconstruction. More than 50,000 individual road surface defects were recorded across the city—this covers anything from a hump or hole to major damage.

Source: Christchurch Earthquake Recovery Authority (www.cera.govt.nz).

After some disasters the damage is so severe that entire communities are abandoned, never to be reoccupied. For example, the Ukraine city of Chernobyl, with a population of 14,000, was abandoned after the nearby nuclear accident in 1986; the Illinois town of Valmeyer was totally demolished and relocated after being overwhelmed by the flooding Mississippi River in 1993; and the 21,000-strong population of Namie abandoned the Japanese city in 2011 after the nuclear accident at the nearby Fukushima nuclear facility, which was destroyed by a tsunami.

Even after massive recovery investment the impact can be long-lasting. According to the Global Assessment Report on Disaster Risk Reduction (2013), prior to the massive earthquake that struck the Japanese city of Kobe in 1995, its port was the world's sixth busiest. Despite a massive investment in reconstruction and efforts to improve competitiveness, by 2010 it had fallen to forty-seventh place.

While community impact can be devastating, the long-term impact of natural disasters on individual organisations also can be dramatic. For example, the US Chamber of Commerce estimates that in the wake of a natural disaster such as Hurricane Katrina or Hurricane Sandy, 52 per cent of the small businesses affected never reopen (cited in Greenfield, 2012).

Although the disaster recovery phase can be very prolonged and extremely costly, most experts believe that recovery can be greatly aided if the mitigation, preparedness and response phases are effectively established and fully implemented.

SOCIAL MEDIA IN DISASTER COMMUNICATION

Social media and digital communication have an important role in all aspects of issue and crisis management (see Chapter 11). But that role is nowhere more evident than in disaster communication.[16] In a disaster there is always a very high level of uncertainty. At the same time there is a critical thirst for accurate information, which drives massive spikes in social media demand.

---

16 For a thorough overview of social media in a disaster, see Fraustino, Lui and Jin (2012), Lang and Benbunan-Fich (2010) and White (2012) in this chapter's Further reading section.

Social media communication in a disaster essentially falls into two categories: (a) information disseminated by first responders and official agencies; and (b) citizen-generated information and communication with family and friends. The combined impact is that the scale of social media traffic in the wake of a disaster can be extraordinary. Following the Japanese tsunami and nuclear fallout in March 2011, tweets on the topic were running at 5500 per second,[17] and on a single day Facebook recorded 4.5 million tsunami-related status updates from 3.8 million users around the world. Similarly, following flash floods in Queensland in January 2011, the Queensland Police Service Facebook page 'likes' jumped from 17,000 to 100,000 in a day, and the page generated 39 million post impressions, equating to 450 post views per second over the same twenty-four hours (Queensland Police Service, 2011). There has also been a detailed study of the role of social media following Cyclone Yasi, which was one of the major events that struck Queensland at this time (Taylor et al., 2012).

The reasons for such reliance on social media are not hard to find, and are consistently supported by researchers around the world.[18] The first is that social media provide real-time information about the disaster at a speed that cannot be matched by traditional media. As a result, social media becomes both the fastest and first source of information. In fact, Utz, Schultz and Glocka (2013) found that communication via social media in a disaster was more effective than other types of media. The reach of social media was demonstrated during the Icelandic volcanic ash crisis in Europe in 2010, which affected the travel plans of nearly nine million people around the world. Social media were used by citizens to organize themselves, as well as by official organisations such as Eurocontrol to get in touch with a huge and massively scattered population (cited in Hiltz, Diaz & Mark, 2011).

The second reason is the belief that social media provide information that has not been filtered by traditional media or by official agencies (or, in some countries, by government censors). Indeed, disasters create unprecedented opportunities for citizens to become news creators rather than just being news consumers.[19] A key difference is that official communication after a crisis is generally 'top down'—focusing on instructions—while citizen communication is perceived as being 'bottom up'—based on personal experience, often from within the disaster area.

A powerful example of the impact of citizen-generated information was in January 2009 when a US Airlines flight from New York to North Carolina was forced to make a crash landing in the Hudson River. Bystander Janis Krums uploaded a picture of the plane from his iPhone to TwitPic, and within three hours the iconic photo was viewed 40,000 times online (causing the site to crash) and appeared on news networks and newspaper around the world (Sillito, 2009). The flipside of this benefit is, of course, the uncontrolled sharing of information that is false or, in some cases, deliberately misleading (discussed later in this chapter).

The third and final reason for the explosion in social media after a disaster is the need to check in with family members, which traditional media cannot be expected to address.

---

17 http://crisiscommunicationsmanagement.blogspot.com/2012/04/impact-of-social-media-in-emergencies.html
18 See Velev and Zlateva (2012) in this chapter's Further reading section.
19 See Freeman (2011) and Stelter and Cohen (2008) in this chapter's Further reading section.

This trend is reinforced by analysis reported by the University of San Francisco in 2013, which found that 76 per cent of the Americans who have experienced a disaster used social media to contact friends and make sure they are safe, while 24 per cent let loved ones know they were safe. In addition, the analysis found 37 per cent used information on social media to buy supplies and find shelter, and 18 per cent retrieved emergency information through Facebook, while 25 per cent had downloaded disaster-related apps.

Another important role for social media following disasters is locating 'missing' people. For example, following the disastrous Typhoon Haiyan that struck the Philippines in late 2013, Google launched a service to help individuals share information about people they were looking for, or to identify families for victims who had been found (Schroeder, 2013).

> Social media takes time and careful, strategic thought. It doesn't happen by accident.
>
> US author on social media Brian E. Boyd (2013)

In Australia, a study at the University of Western Sydney into the use of social media during natural disasters (Howell & Taylor, 2012) found it performs a valuable role coordinating official information, assisting isolated people to receive help, and providing psychological first aid by supporting the needs of individuals and connecting communities. The study surveyed data from social media during floods and a cyclone in Queensland, the tsunami disaster in Japan and earthquakes in Christchurch, New Zealand, all in early 2011. The study found that:

+ Around a quarter of respondents used social media to request help from neighbours or the authorities.

+ More than a third of the sample spent most of their time on social media providing general information, responding directly to questions or directing people.

+ About half of the respondents offered help or practical assistance, and over three-quarters posted messages of support and sympathy.

However, reliance on social media as a communication vehicle in disaster situations may be developing at a rate beyond what is reasonable and practicable. A 2010 survey by the American Red Cross found that 69 per cent of respondents said emergency responders should be monitoring social media sites in order to quickly send help, and that a worrying 78 per cent expected help to arrive in less than an hour after their tweet or Facebook post. Expressing concern about such unrealistic public expectations, Red Cross told a US Congressional Committee (Defrancis, 2013) their follow-up surveys in 2011 and 2012 reinforced that Americans are becoming increasingly reliant on social media in disasters.

The power of social media in a disaster is undoubted, whether it is people trapped under rubble sending tweets about their location, or citizens reporting disasters before officials have been able to react. Social media have also been a powerful tool in exposing the impact of disasters against the wishes of repressive governments, as occurred after Cyclone Nargis hit Myanmar in 2008.[20]

---

20 For a detailed analysis of how citizen journalists used social media to report from inside Myanmar, see Downman (2013) in this chapter's Further reading section.

However, the speed of social media has a distinct downside, which is the rapid proliferation of malicious or misleading information. It is inevitable that 'citizen journalists' and even mainstream media will sometimes get it wrong in the race to be first. It is sadly also inevitable that social media in a disaster bring out the worst in society, from fake online 'charities' stealing aid from victims to the deliberate online distribution of false information.

While 'joke' photographs often surface after a disaster, Hurricane Sandy, which struck the northeast coast of the USA in 2012, was notorious for the volume of faked or misidentified photographs that circulated via digital media. But, as was shown in the Queensland Police Service case study, a well-managed and responsive official social media strategy can be extremely effective in reducing rumours and falsehoods and providing the community with timely and reliable communication when a disaster strikes.

KEY POINTS

+ While crises affect organisations, disasters affect societies or communities.

+ Disasters can create crises for individual organisations.

+ A single event can be an organisational crisis and a societal disaster at the same time.

+ Most disasters arise from nature, but some are man-made.

+ Most disasters arise from sudden events, but creeping disasters may develop over weeks or months.

+ Disaster preparedness requires both government and public participation.

+ While response is short term, recovery can take years or even decades.

+ Social media in a disaster have great benefits, but also have some worrying challenges.

≡ ACTIVITIES AND DISCUSSION

1. List some of the key differences between a crisis and a disaster. How do these differences affect the management of communication during a disaster?

2. Timely distribution of essential materials can present serious challenges following a disaster. Identify some of those challenges and discuss how they can be addressed.

3. Assume a major earthquake has occurred in your community. Develop a response plan and how to communicate the balance between societal and individual interests.

4. List and debate the traits of a successful leader in a disaster.

5. While social media facilitate citizen engagement in disaster response, discuss whether it is possible or desirable to take steps to reduce distribution of false information.

THE IMPACT OF SOCIAL MEDIA ON PUBLIC INFORMATION MANAGEMENT

Gary Mersham

Open Polytechnic, Wellington.

Social media plays an increasing role in the awareness of emergencies and impact on reporting processes and media coverage, causing a blurring of the line between 'official' and 'non official' messaging in the minds of the public, and creating a widening asynchrony between them.

When a magnitude 8.0 earthquake off Samoa created a tsunami in September 2009, it caused significant damage and loss of life in Samoa, American Samoa and Tonga. With social media and traditional media depicting a worsening situation and emphasising a potential threat to New Zealand, the New Zealand Ministry of Civil Defence and Emergency Management (MCDEM) appeared to be uninformed about the avalanche of social media discussions and traditional news coverage taking place.

Although the MCDEM ultimately issued a national alert and managed some media enquiries, timely public statements were not issued. This was highlighted when the ministry participated in a news interview, during which its representative clearly was not well informed about social media reporting. This triggered widespread criticism in the print, broadcast and social media.

In 2006 MCDEM had signed agreements with public and commercial radio and television media organisations to provide reliable and guaranteed channels of communication for official warnings and emergency information messages before and during civil defence emergencies. However, the activation of the agreement required a separate process from the one undertaken for media releases and was not activated for this event. This created a vacuum where the public turned to the social media for updates and where the demand for information by broadcast media was amplified, but often frustrated.

Social media is replacing broadcast communication as the predominant points of access to news and information. Public attention paid to the traditional mass media and their largely uni-directional channels of delivery is being replaced by a mix of instant and ubiquitous two-way communication, dialogue and public discourse through the social media.

The challenge for emergency management organisations is how to recognise and integrate this phenomenon into their messaging. Social media now feed into and trigger the newsgathering agendas and timeframes of traditional broadcast and print media, and major news agencies, providing sources for leads to be verified.

Another consequence of social media is that the flow of information cannot be 'locked down' or controlled. Highly structured emergency management organisations are accustomed to tightly controlling information flow to their stakeholders during an emergency or disaster. Social media directly challenge the controlled dissemination of messages, and query and test the legitimacy of 'official' messages.

THE SEQUENCE OF EVENTS

At 6.48 a.m. (New Zealand time) the earthquake occurred, generating the deadly tsunami. At 7.04 a.m. the Pacific Tsunami Warning Centre (PTWC) issued a publicly accessible warning of a tsunami threat to New Zealand. A blog post on Newswire.co.za by a journalism student illustrated the speed, reach and impact of text and twitter messages in comparison to official messages thereafter:

> I was probably one of the first people in New Zealand to know about today's tsunami—and I heard about it from a friend in Germany. It was shortly before 7am when a text on my cellphone woke me, saying: 'Saw on TV there's tsunami warning for NZ. Are you ok?'

Around the same time, Reuters tweeted about the earthquake and resulting tsunami. This was followed almost immediately by reports on CNN.

Trade Me is one of the most popular social media sites in New Zealand. Primarily an internet-auction website, it also hosts popular message boards where people participate in discussions on current events and topics, ask questions and seek advice. The PTWC warning was posted on the Trade Me site shortly after release, triggering a train of exchanges from 7.28 am onwards, resulting in 430 postings on the tsunami threat, discussing the implications and (lack of) guidance from the authorities. These discussions referred to eyewitness accounts from Samoans and New Zealand tourists who were in communication with their New Zealand-based relatives.

Postings referred to a breakfast television interview with an emergency management representative who had said in an interview at 8.39 am that they could not yet formally confirm the event, referring to (social media) reports of damage in Samoa as 'unconfirmed rumour'.

At this point synchronisation between the MCDEM frontline (official warnings/advisories) and its formal public information (media releases) unravelled, and coherence of the system's public voice was put at risk. The interview highlighted the disjunction between what broadcast and social media were showing, saying and asking, and the response of officials. As a result, it did not convey the public information messages necessary to reassure the public.

Social networking sites are challenging the age-old concept of 'official sources', including during emergencies and disasters. Traditional sources, like official spokespersons, are being

relied upon less by the public, who are instead turning to social media outlets. This is in part due to the cultural mind set of public officials to rely only on official sources.

Fortunately, public officials, who were previously barred from accessing social media sites because of perceptions of them as poor sources of information or because of IT security policies, are now engaging and integrating these social communication channels and their commentaries into their communication strategies.

For more detailed discussion of this case see:

Mersham, G.M. (2010). Social media and public information management: The September 2009 tsunami threat to New Zealand. *Media International Australia*, 137.

BUSHFIRE DISASTER TESTS COMMUNICATION CAPACITY

Chris Galloway

Massey University, Auckland

Devastating bushfires that roared across parts of tinder-dry Victoria in 2009 did more than take the lives of many people and lay waste to communities. Subsequent examination of the fires' causes and consequences illustrated how disasters may not only be caused by inattention to issues (including, in this case, alleged failure to maintain rural power lines) but also leave many issues in their destructive wake.

Authorities' plans and preparations for bushfires were shown to have been inadequate to deal with what became Australia's worst natural disaster. Deficiencies were revealed through the direct experience of more than seventy-eight fire-affected communities, through media reportage and analysis and through a Victorian Bushfires Royal Commission. In the media, weather experts struggled to find words to describe a risk that transcended existing categories and made a mockery of existing emergency planning. As a result, confidence in organisations charged with public safety, such as the state government and its agencies, including the Country Fire Authority, was placed in question. Leadership and other organisational changes followed.

Poor communication was central to the debate about the effectiveness (or otherwise) of emergency systems. Amid a sequence of destructive fires—culminating in the 7 February 'Black Saturday' disaster—emergency authorities' communication with one another and the public fell well short of meeting the demands of the evolving threats to lives and property. There were specific failures to communicate the risk that Black Saturday's scorching weather posed to residents in vulnerable regions: in some cases the communication was late or defective; in others, it simply did not happen. The Bushfires Royal Commission noted that while many people tried their best in extraordinarily difficult circumstances, 'some poor decisions were made by people in positions of responsibility and by individuals seeking to protect their own safety'.

The Victorian state government did try to prepare people for the worst by setting expectations in advance. The day before Black Saturday, Premier John Brumby advised Victorians to cancel any plans for the following day, telling them: 'If you don't need to go out, don't go out. It's a seriously bad day ... it's going to be a terrible day for anyone who is ill or who is old.' However, the warning was overwhelmed by a reality far worse than predicted, with 173 lives lost and massive damage to wildlife and property. It became clear that failures in responding were due not only to individual deficiencies but also to systemic issues. As Mr Brumby noted: 'There were system failures on that day [Black Saturday] and for that all of us who were involved ... we're obviously sorry those systems failed.'

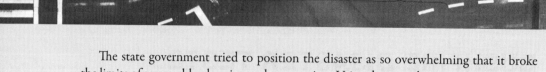

The state government tried to position the disaster as so overwhelming that it broke the limits of reasonable planning and preparation. Using dramatic language in an apparent effort to minimise perceptions of organisational failure, Mr Brumby commented: 'What broke over the state was like a tsunami. It didn't matter how good people's fire plans were.' Mr Brumby's remark came as commentators such as blogger Guy Rundle were claiming that 'some or many [deaths] were caused by a fatal paralysis of action and initiative, a sheer lack of audacity and leadership, an inability to take control in a situation which has totally engulfed and undermined any notion of normality'.

Yet the overwhelming nature of the situation was not enough to save Mr Brumby, whose government lost power in a close election in November 2010. One of the factors in the Brumby government's demise may have been the fact that although the fires swept Victoria in February 2009, it was not until August 2010 that he personally apologised to Victorians. Mr Brumby noted that he felt a 'weight of responsibility to get the arrangements and system right for the future so that we never again see a repeat of those circumstances on February 7'. However, although he established the Victorian Bushfires Royal Commission and a Reconstruction and Recovery Authority, this shouldering of responsibility may well have been too little, too late. Apologies have much more meaning close to the event to which they relate, rather than many months afterwards.

Nor was it only the immediate failures in the cauldron of catastrophe that came to light: it emerged that authorities had not responded adequately to the ramifications of previous fire disasters. One environmentalist noted: 'Apart from the terrible human and animal suffering from the continuing bushfire crisis in Victoria, the tragedy of this event is the continuing failure of public land managers to heed lessons already learned from past holocausts.'

The Bushfires Royal Commission eventually made sixty-seven recommendations, mainly calling for state government action. The disaster, therefore, produced issues not only for those directly affected but especially for those the public perceived as responsible for community safety. The state government and its agencies obviously could not be held responsible for natural events such as the heatwave when temperatures in Victoria topped 43°C. But the public held them accountable for their performance in managing the impacts of these events.

For more detailed discussion of this case see:

Galloway, C. & Kwansah-Aidoo, K. (2012). Victoria burning: Confronting the 2009 catastrophic bushfires in Australia. In A. M. George & C. B. Pratt (Eds.), *Case studies in crisis communication: International perspectives on hits and misses* (pp. 279–289). New York: Routledge.

REFERENCES

Boin, A. & 't Hart, P. (2007). The crisis approach. In H. Rodriguez, E. L. Quarantelli & R. R. Dynes (Eds.), *Handbook of disaster research* (pp. 42–54). New York: Springer.

Boyd, B. E. (2013). *Social media for the executive: Maximise your brand and monetise your business.* Tulsa, OK: One Seed Press.

Centre for Research on the Epidemiology of Disasters (2014). Disaster profiles. Retrieved from http://www.emdat.be/disaster-profiles.

COAG (2009). *National strategy for disaster resilience: Building our nation's resilience to disaster.* Council of Australian Governments. Retrieved from www.ag.gov.au/ EmergencyManagement/Pages/NationalStrategyForDisasterResilience.aspx.

Coppola, D. P. (2007). *Introduction to international disaster management.* Burlington, MA: Butterworth-Heinemann.

Crompton, R. & McAneney, J. (2008). The cost of natural disasters in Australia: The case for disaster risk reduction. *The Australian Journal of Emergency Management, 23*(4), 43–46.

Defrancis, S. (2013, 9 July). Testimony of Suzy C. Defrancis, Chief Public Affairs Officer, before the U.S. Subcommittee on Emergency Preparedness, Response, and Communications. Retrieved from www.redcross.org/images/MEDIA_ CustomProductCatalog/m18989859_2013-Social-Media-Hearing-DeFrancis.pdf.

Ferris, E., Petz, D. & Stark, C. (2013). *The year of recurring disasters: A review of natural disasters in 2013.* Washington DC: Brookings Institution. Retrieved from www. brookings.edu/research/reports/2013/03/natural-disaster-chapter-1-ferris.

Fletcher, M. (2005, 12 September). Katrina pushes issues of race and poverty at Bush. *Washington Post.* Retrieved from www.washingtonpost.com/wp-dyn/content/ article/2005/09/11/AR2005091101131.html .

Global Assessment Report on Disaster Risk Reduction. (2013). *From shared risk to shared value: The business case for disaster risk reduction.* Retrieved from www.preventionweb.net/english/hyogo/gar/2013/en/gar-pdf/ GAR13_PressKit_EN.pdf.

Greenfield, K. T. (2012, 29 November). A pet store fights to survive Sandy. *Business Week.* Retrieved from www.businessweek.com/articles/2012-11-29/a-pet-food-store- fights-to-survive-sandy#p2.

Hiltz, S. R., Diaz, P. & Mark, G. (2011). Social media and collaborative systems for crisis management. *ACM Transactions on Computer-Human Transaction, 18*(4), 1–6.

Howell, G. V. J. & Taylor, M. (2012). When a crisis happens, who turns to Facebook and why? *Asia Pacific Public Relations Journal, 12*(1).

Kington, T. (2012, 24 October). Italian scientist convicted over L'Aquila earthquake condemns 'medieval' court. *The Guardian*. Retrieved from www.theguardian.com/world/2012/oct/23/italian-scientist-earthquake-condemns-court.

News.com.au (2013). Two years later, Christchurch earthquake recovery remains slow. Retrieved from www.news.com.au/world-news/two-years-later-christchurch-quake-recovery-slow/story-fndir2ev-1226582311033.

Oliver, C. E. (2011). *Catastrophic disaster planning and response.* Boca Raton, FL: CRC Press.

Organisation of American States (1997). *USAID/OAS Caribbean Disaster Mitigation Project.* Washington, DC: Unit of Sustainable Development and Environment.

Perry, R. W. (2007). What is a disaster? In H. Rodriguez, E. L. Quarantelli & R. R. Dynes (Eds.), *Handbook of disaster research* (pp. 1–15). New York: Springer.

Phelps, R. (2005, 21 September). *All hazards vs homeland security planning. Disaster resource guide.* Retrieved from www.ems-solutionsinc.com/pdfs/Meetthe Experts.pdf.

Quarantelli, E. L (2006, 11 June). Catastrophes are different from disasters: Some implications for crisis planning and managing drawn from Katrina. *Social Science Research Council.* Retrieved from http://forums.ssrc.org/understandingkatrina/catastrophes-are-different-from-disasters-some-implications-for-crisis-planning-and-managing-drawn-from-katrina.

Quarantelli, E. L., Lagadec, P. & Boin, A. (2007). A heuristic approach to future disasters and crises: New, old and in-between types. In H. Rodriguez, E. L. Quarantelli & R. R. Dynes (Eds.), *Handbook of disaster research* (pp. 16–41). New York: Springer.

Queensland Police Service. (2011). *Disaster management and social media: A case study.* QPS Media and Public Affairs Branch, Brisbane. Retrieved from www.police.qld.gov.au/Resources/Internet/services/reportsPublications/documents/QPSSocialMediaCaseStudy.pdf.

Ramirez, S., Antrobus, E. & Williamson, H. (2013). Preparing for and communicating in disasters and emergencies. *Australian Journal of Communication, 40*(1), pp. 1–21.

Schlein, L. (2012, 17 January). 2011 costliest year in history for catastrophes. *Voice of America.* Retrieved from www.voanews.com/content/article-2011-costliest-year-in-history-for-catastrophes-137585693/159469.html.

Schroeder, S. (2013), 12 November). Google sets up person finder and relief map for Typhoon Haiyan. *Mashable.* Retrieved from http://mashable.com/2013/11/11/google-tools-typhoon-yolanda.

Seeger, M. W., Sellnow, T. L. & Ulmer, R. R. (1998). Communication, organisation and crisis. *Communication Yearbook, 21,* 231–275.

Sillito, D. (2009, 16 January). Twitter's iconic image of US Airways plane. *BBC News.* Retrieved from http://news.bbc.co.uk/2/hi/7834755.stm.

Singh, K. K. & Singh, A. K. (Eds.). (2010). *Natural and manmade disasters: Vulnerability, preparedness and mitigation.* Delhi: MD Publications.

Taylor, M., Wells, G., Howell, G. & Raphael, B. (2012). The role of social media as psychological first aid as a support to community resilience building: A Facebook study from 'Cyclone Yasi Update'. *Australian Journal of Emergency Management, 27*(1), 20–26.

Two years later, Christchurch earthquake recovery remains slow. (2013). *News.com.au.* Retrieved from www.news.com.au/world-news/two-years-later-christchurch-quake-recovery-slow/story-fndir2ev-1226582311033.

UN Business. (n.d.). What is a disaster or emergency? Retrieved from http://business.un.org/en/documents/6712.

UN Disaster Management Programme. (2003). *Words are important.* Retrieved from www.who.int/hac/techguidance/tools/Definitions%20for%20HAC%20Oct%20 2003.pdf.

University of San Francisco. (2013). Infographic: Social media, the new face of disaster response. Retrieved from www.usfca.edu/management/news/Social_Media_and_Disaster_Response_Infographic.

Utz, S., Schultz, F. & Glocka, S. (2013). Crisis communication online: How medium, crisis type and emotions affected public reactions in the Fukushima Daiichi nuclear disaster, *Public Relations Review, 39*(1), 40–46.

Vallero, D. A. & Letcher, J. M. (2013). *Unravelling environmental disasters.* Waltham, MA: Elsevier.

FURTHER READING

ADPC. (2002). *Community based disaster management: Trainers guide.* Asian Disaster Preparedness Centre, Bangkok. www.adpc.net.

ADRC. (2005). *Total disaster risk management: Good practices.* Asian Disaster Reduction Centre, Japan. www.adrc.or.jp.

Argenti, P. (2002). Crisis communication: Lessons from 9/11. *Harvard Business Review, 80*(12), 103–109. Retrieved from http://hbr.org/web/special-collections/insight/communication/crisis-communication-lessons-from-9-11.

Barry, J. M. (2004). *The great influenza: The story of the deadliest pandemic in history.* New York: Viking Penguin.

Burns, R., Robinson, P. & Smith, P. (2010). From hypothetical scenario to tragic reality: A salutary lesson in risk communication and the Victorian 2009 bushfires. *Australian and New Zealand Journal of Public Health, 34*(1), 24–31.

Carter, N. (1991). *Disaster management: A disaster manager's handbook.* Manila: Asian Development Bank.

Chen, Y. & Booth, D. C. (2011). *The Wenchuan earthquake of 2008: Anatomy of a disaster.* Berlin: Springer.

Dougall, E. K., Horsley, J. S. & McLisky, C. (2008). Disaster communication: Lessons from Indonesia. *International Journal of Strategic Communication, 2*(2), 75–99.

Downman, S. (2013). Reporting disasters from inside a repressive regime: A citizen journalism case study of the 2008 Cyclone Nargis disaster. *Australian Journal of Communication, 40*(1), 153–172.

Drabek, T. E. (2003). *Strategies for coordinating disaster responses.* Monograph 61, Boulder, CO: National Hazards Center, University of Colorado.

Edwards, F. L. (2009). Effective disaster response in cross border events. *Journal of Contingencies and Crisis Management, 17*(4), 255–265.

Fraustino, J. D., Lui, B. & Jin, Y. (2012). *Social media use during disasters: A review of the knowledge base and gaps.* US Department of Homeland Security, Maryland University. Retrieved from www.start.umd.edu/start/publications/START_SocialMediaUseduringDisasters_LitReview.pdf.

Freeman, M. (2011). Fire, wind and water: Social networks in natural disasters, *Journal of Cases on Information Technology, 13*(2), 69–79.

Haddow, G. D. & Haddow, K. S. (2009). *Disaster communications in a changing media world.* Burlington, MA: Butterworth-Heinemann.

Helsloot, I., Boin, A., Jacobs, B. & Comfort, L. K. (Eds.). (2012). *Megacrises: Understanding the prospects, nature, characteristics and the events of cataclysmic events.* Springfield, IL: Charles C. Thomas.

Jennex, M. E. (Ed.). (2012). *Managing crisis and disaster with emerging technologies: advancements.* Hershey, PA: IGI Global.

Kellens, W., Zaalberg, R., Neutens, T. & de Maeyer, P. (2011). An analysis of the public perception of flood risk on the Belgian coast. *Risk Analysis, 31*(7), 1055–1068.

Kelly, J. (2005). *The great mortality: An intimate history of the Black Death.* New York: Harper-Collins.

Kirschenbaum, A. (2003). *Chaos organisation and disaster management.* Boca Raton, FL: CRC Press.

Lang, G. & Benbunan-Fich, R. (2010). The use of social media in disaster situations: Framework and cases. *International Journal of Information Systems for Crisis Response and Management, 2*(1), 11–23.

Liu, S. B., Palen, L., Sutton, J., Hughes, A. L. & Vieweg, S. (2008). In search of the bigger picture: The emergent role of on-line photo sharing in times of disaster. *Proceedings of the 5th Information Systems for Crisis Response and Management (ISCRAM) Conference*, Washington, DC. Retrieved from https://www.cs.colorado.edu/~palen/Papers/iscram08/OnlinePhotoSharingISCRAM08.pdf.

Mazmanian A. (2012, 3 June). Of hurricanes and hashtags: Disaster relief in the social-media age. *National Journal.* Retrieved from www.nationaljournal.com/tech/of-hurricanes-and-hashtags-disaster-relief-in-the-social-media-age-20120603.

McEntire, D. A. (2006). *Disaster response and recovery.* Hoboken, NJ: Wiley.

North Atlantic Treaty Organisation. (2001). *NATO's role in disaster assistance.* Brussels, Belgium: NATO Civil Emergency Planning. Retrieved from www.nato.int/eadrcc/mcda-e.pdf.

Pinkowski, J. (2009). *Disaster management handbook* (2nd ed.) Boca Raton, FL: CRC Press.

Rodriguez, H., Quarantelli, E. L. & Dynes, R. R. (Eds.). (2007). *Handbook of disaster research.* New York: Springer.

Sellnow, T. L., Seeger, M. W. & Ulmer, R. R. (2002). Chaos theory, informational needs, and natural disasters. *Journal of Applied Communication Research, 30*(4), 269–292.

Smith, E. (2006). National disaster preparedness in Australia: Before and after 9/11. *Journal of Emergency Primary Health Care, (4)*2, Art 7.

Stelter, B. & Cohen, N. (2008, 29 November). Citizen journalists provided glimpse of Mumbai Attacks. *New York Times.*

Sutton, J., Palen, L. & Shklovski, I. (2008). *Backchannels on the front lines: Emergent uses of social media in the 2007 Southern California wildfires.* Proceedings of the 5th Information Systems for Crisis Response and Management (ISCRAM) Conference, Washington, DC. Retrieved from https://www.cs.colorado.edu/~palen/Papers/iscram08/BackchannelsISCRAM08.pdf.

Troy, D. A., Carson, A., Vanderbeek, J. & Hutton, A. (2008). Enhancing community-based disaster preparedness with information technology. *Disasters, 32*(1), 149–65.

Vanderford, M. L., Nastoff, T., Telfer, J. L. & Bonzo, S. E. (2007). Emergency communication challenges in response to Hurricane Katrina: Lessons from the Centers for Disease Control and Prevention. *Journal of Applied Communication Research, 35*(1), 9–25.

Velev, D. & Zlateva, P. (2012). Use of social media in natural disaster management. *International Proceedings of Economics, Development and Research, 39,* 41–45.

White, C. M. (2012). *Social media, crisis communication and emergency management: Leveraging Web 2.0 technologies.* Boca Raton, FL: CRC Press.

Wisner, B., Gaillard, J. C. & Kelman, I. (Eds.). (2012). *The Routledge handbook of hazards and disaster risk reduction.* Abingdon, Oxford: Routledge.

Woodham-Smith, C. (1962). *The great hunger: Ireland 1845–1849.* London: Hamish Hamilton.

10

RISK MANAGEMENT— PERCEPTION, HAZARD AND OUTRAGE

CHAPTER OBJECTIVES

This chapter will help you to:

+ understand the basics of risk, risk management and risk communication

+ assess the concept of risk society and the risk paradox

+ recognise the factors that influence risk perception

+ discover why expert opinion about risk is often so different from the public viewpoint

+ introduce the notions of hazard and outrage

+ learn about the social amplification of risk framework

+ gain an overview of the key theories that influence risk communication

+ explore guidelines for risk communication and the use of message mapping.

Just about every issue or crisis revolves around risk—usually risk presented by an event, or potential risk if a particular event or development is not properly managed. As a result, communicating about risk—the discipline known as risk communication—is a vital element of issue and crisis management.

As shown in the previous chapters, risks arising from issues and crises can appear in many forms. For organisations there are risks *to the organisation* (for example, adverse regulations or natural disasters) and also risks to others that are generated *by* the organisation (for example, toxic emissions or faulty products). Broadly, organisational risks can be categorised as:

+ *strategic*—threatening the organisation's ability to achieve its objectives
+ *compliance*—arising from breaches or potential breaches of relevant law or regulations
+ *financial*—the possibility of unacceptable financial loss or loss of shareholder value
+ *health and environmental*—health, safety and environmental risk to workers, the local community or society
+ *operational*—breakdown of plant or processes, fires, leaks, flood or explosions
+ *reputational*—damage to reputation and its impact on ability to operate
+ *human or personal*—when people do or say something wrong
+ *supply chain*—problems arising from the actions of others in the supply chain
+ *technology*—IT or e-business failures or breaches of data security.[1]

By contrast, individuals or communities are more frequently targets of risk rather than being risk-generators, and are most likely to be concerned with personal health and safety; damage to the environment; potential financial or property loss; and also loss of reputation.

> A firm's ability to weather storms depends on how seriously executives take risk management when the sun is shining and no clouds are on the horizon.
>
> Robert Kaplan and Anette Mikes (2012, p. 60)

Reputation risk is a major subject on its own, especially for organisations, and Chapter 11 is devoted specifically to reputation management and addressing threats to reputation. In addition to the broad categories of risk, defined above, there are also other specific types of risk. These include:

+ *investment risk*—the business risk considered when making a new investment or possible adverse changes to an existing investment
+ *actuarial/insurance risk*—mathematically calculated predictions based on measurable data, often used in finance or insurance to identify and assess risk
+ *societal risk*—potential threats to broader society, including structural or social change or natural disasters

---

1   These broad categories of risk are not unlike the types of crisis listed in Chapter 1. Kaplan and Mikes (2012) suggest three umbrella corporate risk categories: preventable risks (which arise within the company and generate no strategic benefits), strategic risks (taken for superior strategic returns) and external risks (uncontrollable risks from outside the organisation).

+ *exchange risk*—business exposure to adverse movement in exchange rates between different currencies
+ *product/recall risk*—when products endanger consumer health or safety and may have to be recalled
+ *infrastructure risk*—the vulnerability to loss of infrastructure such as water, power, fuel or transport.

However, while these may be significant, some are beyond the scope of this book. The present chapter addresses the broader question of risk and in particular the role of risk management and risk communication in response to issues and crises.

DEFINING TERMS

In order to understand this topic is it essential to briefly define three key terms: risk, risk management and risk communication. We explore them in more detail later in this chapter.

RISK

The word risk has a wide range of meanings and interpretations across different groups and people, including business, governments, NGOs, activists, community groups, families and individuals. A conventional understanding is that risk is the chance of something happening, with its impact calculated by multiplying probability and magnitude; that is, how likely it is to happen, and how serious the impact is likely to be if it does.

RISK MANAGEMENT

Risk management is the systematic ongoing process by which an organisation or society identifies and catalogues risks; assesses and prioritises those risks; develops and implements programs to avoid risk, reduce the negative impact or accelerate recovery; and continuously evaluates the effectiveness of those actions and monitors for new or emerging risks.

As with issue and crisis management versus issue and crisis communication, there is much more to risk management than just risk communication.

RISK COMMUNICATION

The US National Research Council and National Academy of Sciences (NRC/NAS, 1989) developed a definition of risk communication that remains in common use today. They defined risk communication as

> ... an interactive process of exchange of information and opinion among individuals, groups and institutions involving multiple messages about the nature of risk, and other messages, not strictly about risk, that express concerns, opinions or reactions to risk messages and to legal and institutional arrangements for risk management.

The NRC/NAS report *Improving risk communication* (1989) also emphasised that risk communication is a *component* of risk management; that successful risk communication does not guarantee risk management decisions will maximise general welfare, but only that it ensures decision makers will understand what is known about the implications for welfare and available options. From an organisational perspective, its primary objectives are 'to build, strengthen or repair trust; educate and inform people about risks; and encourage people to take appropriate actions' (Covello, 2011, p. 511).

A commonly used, more modern approach is that risk communication is any 'purposeful exchange' of information about risk or about perception of risk. As with the original NRC/NAS definition, the emphasis on multidirectional consultation implied in the word 'exchange' is crucial and appears throughout this chapter. It is also important to highlight at this stage that risk communication is *not* about 'educating the public' and is *not* about the information you give out after you have made all your plans. Furthermore, while risk often involves controversial issues, successful risk communication does not necessarily result in consensus on those issues.

HOW THE ELEMENTS FIT TOGETHER

+ A community may face a *risk* of loss of life and property through bushfire.

+ *Issues* it faces might include the bushfire-prone forest surrounding the community; lack of willingness and/or resources to reduce the risk; inadequacy of local fire-fighting capability; and a local attitude of 'it can't happen to us'.

+ The *crisis* is when the bushfire strikes and threatens terrible destruction.

+ *Risk management* would include strategies before, during and after the fire to identify and reduce risk and communicate to stakeholders.

+ *Post-crisis risk issues* might include whether and where to rebuild; who was to blame; what can be done to reduce risk in future; and who will pay.

+ *Risk communication* would apply at every stage—to raise concern and promote action before the fire; to ensure people are prepared and know what to do in the event of a fire; to direct people to safety when the fire strikes; and to calmly assess future actions after the fire.

+ *Risk controversy* might arise between authorities who want prescribed burns in spring to reduce the risk of worse fires in summer, and some residents and environmentalists who oppose prescribed burns because of the risk of needless damage to nature and lifestyle.

Source: adapted with permission from work by Dr Chris Galloway.

THE RISK PARADOX

Before entering into the detail of risk communication, it is worth pausing to consider why it has become so important. Risk is nothing new, and decisions over 'fight or flight' when facing a threat are said to have ensured the survival of our cave-dwelling ancestors.

Modern society's attitude to risk, and opinion about what is or is not acceptable, is obviously a much more recent phenomenon. This modern new attitude has given rise to what is sometimes called the 'risk paradox'—that the technological age has made us safer, healthier and living longer than ever before, yet we worry more than ever before about our health and safety. As Kasperson et al. (1988, p. 177) concluded (in a ground-breaking paper we will discuss shortly):

> Despite the expenditure of billions of dollars and steady improvements in health, safety and longevity of life, people view themselves as more rather than less vulnerable to the dangers posed by technology. Particularly perplexing is that even risk events with minor physical consequences often elicit strong public concern and produce extraordinarily severe social impacts, at levels unanticipated by conventional risk analysis.

This paradox is partly explained by the rise of what has been called the 'risk society'. This term is used to describe how modern society responds to risk, and how its expectations of protection against risk have changed the way society operates.[2]

Developed mainly by the British sociologist Anthony Giddens (1990) and his German counterpart Ulrich Beck (1992, 2006), the concept of the risk society draws attention to what Beck called 'manufactured risks' generated as a result of technology and modernisation. Whereas earlier generations accepted risk as a natural state, generally beyond the control of humanity, modernisation of industry created new and unfamiliar risks. They are generated by the decisions and actions of people and organisations; they may involve materials that are invisible or hard to measure (such as nuclear radiation and atmospheric gases); and they can spread across borders and affect communities far away.[3] They can also affect society in unequal ways—as Beck put it 'wealth accumulates at the top, risk at the bottom'. In other words, manufactured risks can produce wealth for the select few, but create risks for the poorer many.[4]

Most importantly, within modern risk society ordinary people are less willing to accept these risks as 'natural' or as an inevitable price of progress, and they demand measures for control and mitigation. While it is entirely reasonable to focus on smaller hazards once the bigger hazards have been attended to, another impact of the risk society is a focus on a regulatory response to risks that may be regarded as personal choice, such as proposing laws to reduce consumption of high-fat or high-sugar 'junk food'. Critics of this approach sometimes refer to it as the 'nanny state', and others would argue that this is a debate about personal freedom rather than risk.

The junk food debate is a good example of how discussion concerning such risk issues is not simply academic but remains a high-profile topic in the community today. However, risk is the underlying driver, and the concept of the risk society has a fundamental importance for issue and crisis management. Societal perception of risk, regardless of whether or not it

---

2   For more on the risk society, see Boudia and Jas (2007) in this chapter's Further reading section.
3   The work of Giddens, Beck and others was first published in the wake of the unprecedented Chernobyl nuclear disaster in the Ukraine in 1986, which spread dangerous radiation across parts of Western Europe.
4   For discussion on measuring risk, see Soprano et al. (2009) in this chapter's Further reading section.

is justified, can directly influence major decisions, such as whether a country should allow the marketing of genetically modified foods, or the development of nuclear power.[5]

> (Risk is something that is never a problem, until it is.
>
> Australian business writer David James (2004)

RISK PERCEPTION

Closely linked to the concept of a risk society—with its heightened awareness and reduced tolerance of some kinds of risk—is a substantial body of work on the idea of risk perception, which is now an essential building block for effective risk communication. It arose from recognition of a massive gulf between the expert assessment of risk and the view of the public (non-experts), and it attempts to explain and address this major difference. Work on risk perception emerged with academics including Paul Slovic, Baruch Fischhoff, Roger Kasperson and Ortwin Renn, and continues to the present day, through specialists including Vincent Covello, Peter Sandman and William Leiss, as one of the most active areas of risk research.

The challenge risk perception explores is that there is very little correlation between the risks that experts know will harm people and the environment, and the risks that cause people to be concerned and upset. Early studies typically showed that the priority assigned to risks by experts had little or no alignment with how non-experts, or lay people, prioritised the same risks.[6] In other words, there are many risks that worry people but cause little harm, while there are many other risks that do pose a real threat but don't make people concerned and upset. Research suggests that this is explained, at least in part, by factors that influence how risks are perceived.

In reality, risk is understood and acted upon in two fundamental ways. The first is *risk as analysis*, which brings logic, reason and scientific deliberation to bear on risk assessment and decision-making. The other approach is *risk as feelings*, which refers to our instinctive and intuitive reactions to danger (Slovic & Peters, 2006).

When it comes to personal perception, Sandman (2012) says there are at least thirty-five factors. The most commonly recognised of these risk perception factors include:

+ *trust*—risks generated by a trusted source are more accepted than risks perceived to be generated by an untrusted source
+ *voluntariness*—risks that are voluntary are more accepted than risks that are imposed.
+ *controllability*—risks under an individual's control are more accepted than risks mainly controlled by others

---

5   See Chapter 2 for discussion of the notorious Three Mile Island nuclear incident, which caused little or no health or environmental damage, yet effectively put a halt to any new nuclear power projects in the USA. See also Song, Kim & Han (2013) in this chapter's Further reading section for risk assessment and public response to continuing commitment to nuclear power plants in South Korea.

6   See the pioneering study by Slovic (1987) in this chapter's Further reading section.

+ *familiarity*—risks that are familiar are more accepted than risks regarded as exotic

+ *fairness*—risks seen to be fairly distributed are more accepted than risks perceived to be unfairly distributed

+ *dread*—risks that are linked to diseases that are not dreaded (for example, asthma) are more accepted than those linked to dreaded illness (for example, cancer)

+ *benefit*—risks that have clear benefits are more accepted than risks perceived to have little or no benefit

+ *performance history*—risks more likely to be accepted when the organisation does not have an adverse history of past incidents or transgressions

+ *natural*—risks regarded as natural are more accepted than risks perceived to be man-made

+ *effect on children*—risks that are believed to affect mainly adults are more accepted than risks to children or other vulnerable populations.

As one of the most prolific authorities on these perception factors, Peter Sandman has written and spoken very widely on this topic over more than 30 years.[7] While others have contributed strongly to the perception concept at a mainly academic level, Sandman developed a unique approach in which he calls the perception factors 'components of outrage'. His approach to practical risk perception is built on a simple but elegant formula:

RISK = HAZARD + OUTRAGE

Given the many and varied definitions of risk, Sandman's innovative formula combines the two principal elements. He defines *hazard* as what experts regard as risk; namely probability multiplied by impact (as previously mentioned). Hazard is typically based on science and statistics, such as toxicity data and mortality; that is, how dangerous it is and how many people it kills. He defines *outrage* as what the public regard as risk; namely all the things that people are worried about and which experts often ignore.

Sandman argues that it is a serious mistake to treat hazard as 'real risk' and outrage and 'just perception'. Most importantly, he championed the idea that when it comes to risk communication, hazard (risk as analysis) and outrage (risk as feelings) are equally real, equally measurable and equally manageable; and that *both* must be properly addressed. It will always be ineffective, he argues, to address hazard while ignoring outrage, or to address outrage and not pay proper attention to hazard. As Sandman (2012, p. 8) concluded:

> Experts, when they talk about risk, focus on hazard and ignore outrage. Therefore they tend to overestimate the risk when the hazard is high and the outrage is low, and underestimate the risk when the hazard is low and the outrage is high— because all they are looking at is the hazard. The public, in precise parallel, focuses on outrage and ignores hazard. The public, therefore, overestimates the risk when the outrage is high and the hazard is low, and underestimates the risk when the outrage is low and the hazard is high.

---

7   His website www.psandman.com contains a valuable archive of his writings and speeches, including journal articles, columns, presentations and videos, which are freely available to students and practitioners.

Given the complex and sometimes contradictory nature of risk perception, there are essentially three categories of risk communication: preventive, precautionary and crisis.

1. *Preventive risk communication* attempts to calm people down and to provide assurance about risk to which they might be exposed—for example, that the health and environmental risk from the chemical plant near their community is not as great as they believe.

2. *Precautionary risk communication* is designed to inform people about risk and make them concerned—for example, to encourage people to wear car seatbelts, or to get vaccinated against disease (see vaccination case study at the end of this chapter).

3. *Crisis risk communication* is about guiding justifiably upset people through serious hazard situations—for example, advising people what to do during a disease epidemic or a major food poisoning outbreak or an earthquake (see discussion of crisis communication in Chapter 7).

> The difference between a risk and an opportunity is how soon you discover it.
>
> Anon.

Some organisations that are seen as 'risk creators' lament about how hard it is to calm people down (preventive risk communication) and how seemingly easy it is for activists to provoke what they regard as needless concerns. This is highlighted when such citizen concern generates high-profile public activities and media attention. However, Sandman (2012) believes it is, in fact, easier to calm people down than it is to create concern about legitimate threats (precautionary risk communication). While this may seem counter-intuitive, he points out that many activist and community organisations struggle to generate concern in an apathetic public: 'The natural state of humankind vis-à-vis risk is apathy. Most people, most of the time, are apathetic about most risks, and it is very hard to get them upset' (p. 2).

SOCIAL AMPLIFICATION OF RISK FRAMEWORK

A key factor in how risk is perceived, and whether people will get upset, is the social amplification of risk framework (SARF). The SARF is the mechanism by which forces within society amplify risk, increasing (or sometimes decreasing) the amount of attention they receive, and often also directly influencing the perception of the degree of risk and the degree of concern generated.

In the mid-1980s a group of renowned risk analysts applied themselves to what they called the perplexing problem of why some relatively minor risks or risk events, as assessed by technical experts, often generate strong public concerns and lead to substantial impacts on society and the economy. They believed the answer lay beyond just the recognised risk perception factors (Sandman's components of outrage), and the result of their research was a ground-breaking article (Kasperson et al., 1988) that introduced the concept of the social amplification of risk. By this they meant the phenomenon by which information processes, institutional structures, social-group behaviour and individual responses shape the social experience of risk and thereby contribute to the risk consequences.

This seminal paper said that while direct personal experience is the most obvious mechanism by which we amplify (or diminish) risk, many risks are not experienced directly and therefore information flow becomes a key ingredient in the public response to risk. Although there are many social agents involved, it was recognised that the news media were the primary amplifiers. As a result, the process is sometimes referred to as 'media amplification of risk' (and social media has further augmented this phenomenon).

Repeated news stories direct public attention towards particular risks; provide information that is regarded as credible by interested members of the public; and often dramatise events. If the risks are already feared by the public, then increased concern is the likely result.

RISK MANIPULATION OR LEGITIMATE ISSUE MANAGEMENT?

A classic case of how risk can be communicated and interpreted to suit a cause is the notorious Alar controversy, which involved a chemical used on apples to enhance colour and shelf-life. Although US government regulators agreed that Alar did not pose a health risk to the public, an anti-pesticide activist report in 1989 branded it as 'the most potent cancer-causing agent in the American food supply'. A high-profile public relations and media campaign, including the intervention of actress Meryl Streep, created a health panic that saw apples taken off supermarket shelves and banned in some school cafeterias. With huge quantities of apples and apple juice destroyed, and the US apple industry temporarily on its knees, the manufacturer 'voluntarily withdrew' the product, even though European and international regulators saw no need for action. As the *Wall Street Journal* concluded: 'Alar was not banned because of a cool and informed appraisal of the best scientific evidence, but because of the coinciding interests of an advocacy group, a celebrity, a public relations company and the media.'

Source: Tony Jaques (2011).

Since it was first developed, the SARF has continued to attract further research as scholars try to more fully understand the mechanism by which risk becomes amplified or diminished in society.[8] At the same time, the framework has been applied to analyse high-profile cases where perceived risk has been a major factor, such as genetically modified food in the UK (Frewer, Miles & Marsh, 2002); the *Brent Spar* oil platform disposal crisis in the North Sea (Bakir, 2005); artificial sweetener in the USA (Lofstedt, 2008); a Greek food contamination incident (Yannopoulou, Koronis & Elliott, 2011); and how bird flu and mad cow disease were perceived in South Korea (Chung & Yun, 2013).

It is important to note that when social amplification of risk increases when hazard is high, the process is regarded as a positive benefit. But if SARF increases concern when

---

8   For further discussion on the process of social amplification of risk, see Pidgeon, Kasperson and Slovic (2003) and Pidgeon and Henwood (2010) in this chapter's Further reading section.

hazard is low, it may be regarded as distortion (although opinions will differ about which is the case).

The original research that developed the SARF recognised that, in addition to traditional news media, informal communication channels also have a major role to play in how risks are amplified within society, as information flows between friends, co-workers and social groups. The widespread adoption of the internet and social media has accelerated and expanded the speed and reach of that information flow, creating the possibility that a risk controversy may 'go viral'. In addition, the sheer volume of information about risk has increased dramatically. But the underlying concept of the framework remains unchanged: that forces within society act in an important way to increase or decrease perception of risk.

RISK COMMUNICATION

Recognising the vital importance of perception, risk communication must include not only announcements, warnings and instructions from expert sources to non-expert audiences, but also other kinds of messages—about risk information; about personal beliefs and feelings concerning risks and hazards; and about reactions to risk management actions and institutions. Importantly, it is not just about messages from experts and risk managers to stakeholders and publics, but equally about messages from publics to risk managers.

Effectively, risk communication is that part of risk management that focuses on *purposeful exchange* of information about risk and ensuring that all stakeholders are involved in the process. It usually begins as a result of a perceived, potential or actual threat to the environment or to personal safety and health, and involves development of *risk messages*, which are written, verbal or visual statements about risk. Risk messages may or may not include advice about risk reduction behaviour, but are developed with the express purpose of presenting information about risk.

> Learning to listen better is much more central to risk communication than learning to explain better.
>
> Peter Sandman (2012, p. vii)

It is essential to remember that risk communication is not simply dissemination of information. Ideally it has four primary goals:

+ Increase knowledge and understanding.
+ Enhance trust and credibility.
+ Effect behaviour change.
+ Resolve or avoid conflict.

(Sadly, however, sometimes is it used to misinform, to shut down dialogue, and to arouse rather than resolve conflict.)

Since risk communication emerged as a specific discipline in 1984 (cited in Leiss, 1996), it has developed an extensive literature[9] and has become a very important subset of the modern practice of public relations and organisational communication.

Apart from the important risk perception theory (introduced above), there are five other main theories (sometimes called models) that influence risk communication, which may come to bear at the same time:

+ trust determination theory

+ mental noise theory

+ negative dominance theory

+ prospect theory

+ cultural theory.

TRUST DETERMINATION THEORY

In the complex and sensitive field of risk communication, trust is one of the most important factors in determining how people perceive risk. Essentially, people are less concerned and upset about a risk when they trust the organisation responsible for the risk, or when they trust the organisation or individual talking to them about that risk.[10]

Only when trust exists can an organisation show progress on other goals of risk communication, such as open dialogue and building consensus. Research shows that the most important factors determining trust are:

1. listening, caring, empathy and compassion

2. competence, expertise and knowledge

3. honesty, openness and transparency.

Other factors in trust determination include accountability, perseverance, dedication, commitment, responsiveness, objectivity, fairness and consistency (Covello, 2011).

For organisations seeking to establish trust, turning to third-party experts is a proven effective method. However, those third-parties must be genuinely independent, not secretly funded front organisations, and not internet 'sock puppets' (people using a false identify online to make controversial comments).

For individuals, trust is often promoted by showing how much you care rather than showing how much you know. As discussed in Chapter 7, a misstatement by the organisational spokesperson, or non-verbal communication that undermines the message, can be very damaging to trust and credibility.

---

9   For more recent publications on risk communication, see Bennett et al. (2010), Covello (2010, 2012), Fischhoff (2009), Heath and O'Hair (2010), Lundgren and McMakin (2013), Palenchar (2010), Palenchar and Heath (2007), Ulmer, Seeger and Littlefield (2009) and Walaski (2011) in this chapter's Further reading section.

10 For more discussion on the role of trust in communication, see Trettin and Musham (2000) in this chapter's Further reading section.

THE EVOLUTION OF RISK COMMUNICATION

Modern experts accept that risk communication should be a two-way process involving genuine consultation. But it wasn't always like that. US academic Baruch Fischhoff used colloquial language to illustrate the progressive steps in the 20-year development of the discipline:

+ All we have to do is get the numbers right.

+ All we have to do is tell them the numbers.

+ All we have to do is explain what we mean by the numbers.

+ All we have to do is show them they've accepted similar risks in the past.

+ All we have to do is show them it's a good deal for them.

+ All we have to do is treat them nice.

+ All of the above.

Source: Baruch Fischhoff (1995).

MENTAL NOISE THEORY

The mental noise theory (sometimes called the attention span theory) is built on the simple recognition that when people are stressed and upset it is much more difficult for them to understand and process information. This reality can easily be seen in day-to-day life and in relationships between friends and families.

But this obvious reality has a particular significance in risk communication.[11] When people are exposed to a risk, or believe they are exposed to a risk, they are often stressed and upset. Moreover, the various risk perception factors listed in the earlier section—such as fairness, benefit and dread—add further to the 'mental noise' or 'cognitive static' that interferes with the ability to receive messages.

Psychologists have shown that in low-stress situations the brain can process on average seven separate messages or facts, while in high-stress situations this goes down to an average of three messages (Miller, 1994). They also believe that stress cuts the capacity to process information below a person's usual education level.

For risk communicators, the mental noise theory suggests that the most effective strategy is to:

+ limit the number of messages to three to five

+ repeat messages at least twice

+ use simple language to keep the communication clear and easily understood.

This does not mean 'speaking down' to stakeholders and treating them like children. But it does mean remaining calm; keeping messages short (and repeating them); avoiding technical jargon; and using authentic language and realistic examples the audience will identify with. It also means including enough information to explain the risk, yet

---

11 For more discussion on mental models, see Morgan et al. (2001) in this chapter's Further reading section.

maintaining a balance between overwhelming with detail and over-simplification that leaves out important facts.

Regardless of the language used and the volume of information, the complexities and uncertainties of risk must be explained in a manner that the audience will accept and understand.

NEGATIVE DOMINANCE THEORY

An important aspect of the way people under stress process information is that they tend to think negatively, and that negative information carries significantly more weight that positive information.

Here, again, psychologists have shown that when people are under stress they will focus much more on what they could potentially lose (negative impact) than on what they could possibly gain (positive impact). For example, people upset over learning their homes will be demolished for a new freeway would initially find it hard to focus on the offer of a much more modern home in a better area (see prospect theory in the next section). This negative dominance is so strong that psychologists have also shown that, in stress situations, it can take three or more positive messages to counter just one negative message. For risk communicators this does not mean ignoring the negatives—which would reduce trust and credibility—but means focusing as much as possible on the positives instead.

Proponents of the negative dominance theory believe it also means avoiding negative words—such as no, not, never, can't, won't, nothing and none. They believe such words tend to get remembered longer than positive words. Risk communications are typically more effective when they focus on constructive action—what is being done—rather than on what is not being done (Covello, 2011). However, it should be pointed out that some other risk communication experts believe a strongly stated negative can actually increase rather than decrease effectiveness; for example, 'We promise we will *never* do that again'.

PROSPECT THEORY

Aligned to the negative dominance theory is the prospect theory, which addresses how people trade off gains and losses when faced with a risk decision. Built on the work of Adam Tversky and Nobel prize-winner Daniel Kahneman, prospect theory (sometimes known as risk heuristics) includes the idea that people are *risk averse* when it comes to possible gains, and are *risk seeking* when considering possible losses.

This seemingly contradictory position was demonstrated in experiments which showed that people typically preferred a guaranteed gain of $100 to a 10 per cent chance of getting $1000 (risk averse), but rather than certainly lose $100, people would gamble instead on a 10 per cent chance of having to pay $1000 (risk seeking). Detail of this famous experiment is explained in Kahneman and Tversky (1979).

For issue and crisis managers, the importance of this theory is that potential loss and potential gain are not weighted equally, and that people often make judgments on the short-term potential of loss and gain rather than the final outcome.

CULTURAL THEORY

The cultural theory of risk was developed by Mary Douglas and Aaron Wildavksy (1982)[12] and argues that in addition to individual perceptions of risk, the structure and nature of social organisation influences how perceptions evolve. This includes the way individuals see dangers to society, along with the cultural norms of society. These can be characterised on a grid along two dimensions: collective control versus self-sufficiency, and egalitarianism versus individuality. Examples would include the way security of the society as a whole is regarded vis à vis the security of members of that society, or how people within that culture have a particular perspective on balancing individual risk against risk to the group.

The theory leads to the conclusion that societies and groups within society can be categorised as having a particular way of life. Each cultural norm is in turn associated with their view of risk and their view of commercial and government organisations that are involved in the management of risk. In other words, understanding where groups and individuals stand within these cultural categories is very important to how risk communication proceeds.

SEVEN CARDINAL RULES OF RISK COMMUNICATION

Recognising the importance of risk theories, academics and practitioners have developed a number of important principles to maximise the effectiveness of risk communication. One of the pioneering efforts to capture such principles was the 'seven cardinal rules' (Covello & Allen, 1988), originally developed for the US Environmental Protection Agency by risk expert Vincent Covello (Director of the Center for Risk Communication in New York) and Frederick Allen (then Associate Director Public Policy at the USEPA). The 'rules' have subsequently been adapted and widely republished (for example, Covello, 2011) and remain a widely used practical summary to guide communicators.

1. Accept and involve the public as a legitimate partner.

2. Plan carefully and evaluate your efforts.

3. Listen to the public's specific concerns.

4. Be honest, frank and open.

5. Coordinate and collaborate with other credible sources.

6. Meet the needs of the media (including social media).

7. Speak clearly and with compassion.

THE MESSAGE MAP

In line with these 'rules', a major challenge of risk communication is to develop messages that are accurate and focused, yet easily conveyed and understood. One technique developed to achieve this important balance is the 'message map', championed by Vincent Covello (see, for example, Covello, 2006).

---

12 The cultural theory of risk is expanded in Douglas (1992) in this chapter's Further reading section.

At its simplest level, the message map follows a hierarchically organised template to respond to anticipated questions or concerns, as illustrated in Table 10.1.

Table 10.1 Message map template

Stakeholder:		
Question or concern:		
Key message 1	Key message 2	Key message 3
Supporting fact 1-1	Supporting fact 2-1	Supporting fact 3-1
Supporting fact 1-2	Supporting fact 2-2	Supporting fact 3-2
Supporting fact 1-3	Supporting fact 2-3	Supporting fact 3-3

The conventional question and answer sheet (Q&A) or list of frequently asked questions (FAQ) may appear to be about two-way communication, but tends to be based largely on what the organisation wants to convey. By contrast, the message map is a visual aid that provides, at a glance, key messages in relation to a particular concern or question, each with supporting facts, which is more likely to promote open dialogue and exchange of information about risk.

Each key message is limited to ten to twelve words, which means they are readily available as a 'sound bite' to respond to a reporter or stakeholder, but they can also be used as a firm foundation for written communication. The supporting facts for each key message provide accessible material for further information and discussion. Their brevity also makes them well suited to Twitter and other social media amplifiers.

The following example is taken from an extensive series of message maps developed with the US Department of Health and Human Services for a hypothetical outbreak of avian influenza or pandemic influenza.

Table 10.2 Pre-event risk communication message map for pandemic influenza

Stakeholder: Public and media		
Question or concern: How is pandemic influenza different from seasonal flu?		
Key message 1	Key message 2	Key message 3
Pandemic influenza is caused by an influenza virus that is new to people.	The timing of an influenza pandemic is difficult to predict.	An influenza pandemic is likely to be more severe than seasonal flu.
Supporting fact 1-1	Supporting fact 2-1	Supporting fact 3-1
Seasonal flu is caused by viruses that are already among people.	Seasonal flu occurs every year, usually during winter.	Pandemic influenza is likely to affect more people than seasonal influenza.

Supporting fact 1-2	Supporting fact 2-2	Supporting fact 3-2
Pandemic influenza may begin with an existing influenza virus that has changed.	Pandemic influenza has happened about thirty times in recorded history.	Pandemic influenza could severely affect a broader set of the population, including young adults.
Supporting fact 1-3	Supporting fact 2-3	Supporting fact 3-3
Fewer people would be immune to a new influenza virus.	An influenza pandemic could last longer than the typical flu season.	A severe pandemic could change daily life for a time, including limitations on travel and public gatherings.

Source: Covello (2008).

While such maps are a very useful communication tool, the actual process of developing the message maps is another invaluable benefit for the organisation. Fundamental to all good communication is not just to decide what you want to tell stakeholders, but to understand what they *already* know and what they *want* to know. There is no area where this is more important than in risk communication, and the first step in message mapping is to identify the stakeholders and compile a list of their questions and concerns. After that, the list is typically categorised into common areas, and teams of subject matter experts and communicators work together, sometimes with a facilitator, to develop the key messages and supporting facts.

As with the issue management strategy development (described in Chapters 3 and 4), experience shows that the message mapping process for risk communication often exposes different points of view within the organisation about the same stakeholder question or concern, or reveals gaps in knowledge. As a result, the experts need to arrive at agreed positions that are consistent with the facts and that support the organisation's risk strategy—and do it *before* any possible crisis.

The process also forces the message mapping team to capture facts, which are sometimes very complex, in a strictly limited number of words that are clearly understandable by the intended audience. This is crucial for risk communication.

As previously discussed, the mental noise theory proposes that when people are upset or angry they often have difficulty hearing, understanding and remembering facts. The message map approach is specifically designed to overcome this hurdle by presenting accurate information in a way that is logical, brief and readily understood.

KEY POINTS

+ Just about every issue or crisis involves some type of risk.

+ Risk communication is one of the most important components of risk management.

+ In the 'risk society' we are healthier and live longer, but worry more about risk.

+ There are clearly identified factors that determine how people perceive risk.

+ How people feel about risk (outrage) is just as important as technical danger (hazard).

+ Risk communication is not simply dissemination of information.

+ Preventive risk communication seeks to calm people down, while precautionary risk communication tries to make them concerned.

+ There are powerful forces in society—including the media—that amplify how we perceive risk.

+ Five important theories influence risk communication: trust determination, mental noise, negative dominance, prospect and culture.

+ There are proven effective guidelines for how to communicate risk to people who are upset and concerned.

☰ ACTIVITIES AND DISCUSSION

1. While risk communication is a very important component of risk management, what are some of the other ways in which risk is managed?

2. Why do experts and non-experts have such different views of risk? Is it really true that they are equally important?

3. Since the social amplification of risk framework (SARF) emerged in the late 1980s, social media has changed the ways in which society is able to amplify and communicate risk. Identify some of the main ways social media has impacted how risk is perceived.

4. Research the famous *Brent Spar* crisis in the North Sea in 1995 (introduced in Chapter 8). What can this ground-breaking case tell us today about how risk is communicated and how it can affect policy?

5. Activists and the media are sometimes accused of deliberately exaggerating risk to achieve a particular purpose. Is this ever justified?

6. The chapter refers to the 'nanny state' argument used when governments try to legislate against, for example, 'fast food'. Is the fast food–obesity debate really about risk or about personal choices?

RISK MANAGEMENT AND UNDERSTANDING THE REAL ISSUE

Chris Galloway

Massey University, Auckland

Natural resource development of all kinds often generates issues, and one of the latest battlegrounds is the lucrative coal seam gas (CSG) industry, based on 'mining' gas trapped in underground coal deposits.

The gas can be turned into LNG (liquefied natural gas) as well as being used directly to power domestic and industrial energy needs. However, extraction companies are being confronted by activists who seek not just to hinder but ideally—from their point of view—to halt the growth of an industry that already generates company profits, jobs and substantial government revenue, with the potential to produce much more. In Australia, a coalition of opponents called the Lock the Gate Alliance (LTGA) is at the forefront of calls to shut down coal seam gas mining.

Companies facing activist strategies such as rallies, lobbying and promotional stunts might consider engaging with them as a sensible option. Surely if the activists understood the facts of coal seam gas extraction better, they might feel inclined to tolerate, if not support, it? However, in this case and others like it, real engagement is not possible when activists choose a strategy that rules out compromise. As their name suggests, the Lock the Gate Alliance sees landowners (often, farmers) on their side of the gate and all others outside. There is no middle way; no meeting point. But this uncompromising all-or-nothing approach may have dealt the group out of a role in developing policy around the future of the CSG industry.

The LTGA case illustrates how an issue that seems to be at the centre of an activist campaign (here, the perceived environmental and health risks associated with CSG extraction) may be only one aspect of what motivates them. The environmental risks most commonly associated with CSG are understood to be chemicals used in 'fracking' technology to release gas from coal seams, which may affect underground water resources, as well as the inadvertent release of gas into the air. While these risk issues were the trigger for the formation of the alliance, it now taps into a wider agenda centred on what it calls 'inappropriate mining'.

Describing itself as a national grass-roots organisation, LTGA articulates a sweeping mission focused on protecting Australia's natural, environmental, cultural and agricultural resources. LTGA is concerned not just about risks to farmland (some of the best CSG deposits lie under top-quality agricultural land) but also to the physical surrounds of that land, the local wildlife and the Indigenous people who may seek a voice in how the land and its resources are used.

Moreover, LTGA wants to 'empower all Australians to demand sustainable solutions to food and energy production'. The organisation's statement of aims is also broad: to protect Australia's water systems, agricultural land for food and fibre production; bushlands, wetlands and wildlife; the health of all Australians; and Australia's Aboriginal and cultural heritage.

Therefore, an issue management strategy that sought to deal with LTGA simply on the basis of its most visible issue—the direct risks of CSG mining—would fall short. The strategy would need to take into account the diverse strands of the various issues on which the alliance says it wants to take a stand.

Yet confronting a group such as LTGA, with its non-cooperation stance, may be more a matter of seeking to contain its influence through counter-publicity and lobbying. Such coalitions often regard cooperation with big business and big government as 'selling out', and this may be particularly so in the LTGA case, where an anti-capitalist value appears to be at work. The LTGA's website notes that members are 'concerned that the short-term greed associated with these [mining] industries (including that of governments through royalties and other returns) is compromising the welfare of future generations of Australians'. It adds that what it sees as the out-of-balance power relationship between governments and communities indicates 'a system that is no longer working for all Australians and ... has lost a moral and ethical compass'.

While LTGA's wide-ranging agenda is evidently appealing to a broad cross-section of predominantly rural groups, its inclusive orientation to a long list of environmental, cultural, social, heritage and moral factors has weakened its focus at the same time as it has enlarged the group's constituency. This means it expends effort on areas that are not on the immediate agenda of the principal actors in the CSG issue. These include the federal and state governments, who mainly want the industry—within proper safeguards—to thrive and produce ever-increasing revenue streams.

Against this background, there are lessons both for activists and for companies dealing with their demands. Successful activist organisations need a relentless focus on a key issue or clearly identified cluster of issues. For companies, looking beyond the issue the activists are most vocal about in order to recognise the broader base of their concerns may pay dividends.

For more detailed discussion of this case see:

Galloway, C. & Jaques, T. (2012). Coal seam gas in Australia: Can activists be effective from the margins? *Asia Pacific Public Relations Journal, 13*(2), 35–44.

THE HPV SCHOOL VACCINATION FACTSHEET—COMMUNICATING RISKS AND BENEFITS

Deborah Wise

University of Newcastle

Gardasil is the brand name for a vaccine that prevents the development of human papilloma virus (HPV) types 16 and 18—the two types of HPV held to be responsible for causing approximately 70 per cent of all cervical cancers. Globally, Gardasil has been promoted as being the world's first anti-cancer vaccine, and its endorsement by the World Health Organization has ensured that to date more than thirty countries have approved Gardasil for use in female populations. Both Australia and New Zealand have publicly funded HPV vaccination programs, and in Australia all girls are offered the vaccine at high school when they are in Year 7 (aged approximately 12–13). Nevertheless, numerous media reports of girls said to be suffering adverse side effects after vaccination have led some parents, and their daughters, to be concerned about the risks associated with HPV vaccination.

In New South Wales all parents/caregivers are given, through their daughter's school, an HPV vaccination pack prior to vaccination. This pack contains a consent form as well as a double-sided fact sheet titled 'Questions & Answers (Q&A) about HPV Vaccination Program: A prevention strategy for cervical cancer'. The fact sheet is an example of a controlled message whereby public relations practitioners not only have control over the creation of the text, but they also select the colours, typefaces, fonts, paper and visuals as well as the final distribution of the document. The HPV vaccination fact sheet is also an example of risk and benefit communication.

The risks and benefits of vaccination are initially communicated in the fact sheet's title—the use of 'prevention' inferring that cancer can be stopped from occurring (a benefit), while the counter inference is that cervical cancer will happen without the vaccine (a risk). This risk of cervical cancer is then reinforced in the first two questions and answers that mention 'cancer' a further five times.

Risk is further foregrounded in statements such as 'HPV infections of the cervix usually do not cause any symptoms', implying that because HPV is usually without symptoms, women will not know if they have, or have had, an HPV infection. As such, all women are at risk. Similarly, the statement 'women can be infected with HPV through sexual contact and it is estimated that up to 79 per cent of women in Australia will be infected with HPV at some point in their lives' implies that 79 per cent of women will get sexually transmitted HPV, and this will be a form of HPV likely to cause cancer. However, what the brochure omits to mention is that there are more than a hundred different types of HPV, and only a few are linked to cervical cancer.

The use of 'up to' (*'up to* 79% of women in Australia will be infected with HPV at some point in their lives' and 'two particular types of HPV are responsible for causing *up to* 80% of cancers') is also telling. Most readers will probably overlook the qualifier 'up to' and instead recall only the certain risk that statistics convey. Statistics are also juxtaposed throughout the brochure against phrases such as 'a group of viruses' and 'most women who have HPV clear the virus naturally'. The use of these vague terms, as opposed to scientifically arrived at statistical 'facts', suggests certitude about the risk of getting cervical cancer while providing much less certain information in terms of the varieties of HPV; whether or not a woman will have any symptoms; and whether or not women will clear the virus naturally. For some readers the uncertainty suggested through the use of 'usually' and 'most', together with the certainty of statistical evidence, may induce them to think they (and their daughters) are at greater risk of getting cervical cancer than not.

These framing techniques of presenting readers with a risk (HPV infection and cervical cancer), offering a solution to averting that risk (HPV vaccination) and providing a benefit (not getting cervical cancer) mean the HPV vaccination fact sheet effectively fulfils one of the first aims of persuasive health messages; namely that a message should convince people they are susceptible to a severe risk, and that adopting a recommended response will avert that risk (a benefit).

In NSW, 70 per cent of Year 7 schoolgirls were vaccinated in the first year of the program. And, although some areas of the brochure could be seen as manipulative, it could also be argued that there is no need to change the content, the layout or the method of delivery when it succeeds in convincing parents to vaccinate their daughters. However, it could also be asked: Whose interests is the vaccine serving? Vaccine producers? Researchers? The population? And, although commissioned by a government agency, in whose interests are public relations practitioners working?

For more detailed discussion of this case see:

Wise, D. & James, M. (2012). The HPV school vaccination program: A discourse analysis of information provided to parents. *Public Communication Review, 2*(1), 3–15.

REFERENCES

Bakir, V. (2005). Greenpeace v. Shell: Media exploitation and the social amplification of risk framework. *Journal of Risk Research, 8*(7–8), 679–691.

Beck, U. (2006). Living in the world risk society. *Economy and Society, 38*(3), 329–345. Hobhouse Memorial public lecture given on 15 February, 2006 at London School of Economics.

Beck, U. (1992). *Risk society: Towards a new modernity.* London: Sage.

Chung, J. B. & Yun, G. W. (2013). Media and social amplification of risk: BSE and H1N1 cases in South Korea. *Disaster Prevention and Management, 22*(2), 148–159.

Covello, V. T. (2011). Risk communication, radiation and radiological emergencies: Strategies, tools and techniques. *Health Physics, 101*(5), 511–530.

Covello, V. T. (2008). *Risk communication: Principles, tools and techniques.* In series 'Global health technical briefs' developed by Johns Hopkins Bloomberg School of Public Health for US Agency for International Development (USAID). Retrieved from www.epa.gov/superfund/community/ciconference/download/ presentations/2013/thursday/thurs_grand_e_915_covello_adv_risk_comm_ risk_comm_fs.pdf.

Covello, V. T. (2006). Risk communication and message mapping: A new tool for communicating effectively in public health emergencies and disasters. *Journal of Emergency Management, 4*(3), 25–40.

Covello, V. T. & Allen, F. (1988). *Seven cardinal rules of risk communication.* Washington DC: Environmental Protection Agency. Retrieved from www.epa.gov/care/ library/7_cardinal_rules.pdf.

Douglas, M. & Wildavsky, A. (1982). *Risk and culture: An essay on the selection of technical and environmental dangers.* Berkeley, CA: University of California Press.

Fischhoff, B. (1995). Risk perception and communication unplugged: Twenty years of process. *Risk Analysis, 15*(2), 137–145.

Frewer, L. J., Miles, S. & Marsh R. (2002). The media and genetically modified foods: Evidence in support of social amplification of risk. *Risk Analysis, 22*(4), 701–711.

Giddens, A. (1990). *The consequences of modernity.* Cambridge: Polity Press.

Jaques, T. (2011). Managing issues in the face of risk uncertainty: Lessons 20 years after the Alar controversy. *Journal of Communication Management, 15*(1), 41–54.

James, D. (2004). *The business devil's dictionary.* Milton, Queensland: Wiley Australia.

Kahneman, D. & Tversky, A. (1979). Prospect theory: An analysis of decisions under risk. *Econometrica, 47*(2), 263–291.

Kaplan, R. S. & Mikes, A. (2012, June). Managing risks: A new framework. *Harvard Business Review,* 47–60.

Kasperson, R. E., Renn, O., Slovic, P., Brown, H. S., Emel, J., Goble, R., Kasperson, J. X. & Ratick, S. (1988). The social amplification of risk: A conceptual framework. *Risk Analysis, 8*(2), 177–187.

Leiss, W. (1996). Three phases in the evolution of risk communication practice. *The Annals of the US Academy of Political and Social Science. 545*, 85–94.

Lofstedt, R. E. (2008), Risk communication, media amplification and the Aspartame scare. *Risk Management, 10*(4), 257–284.

Miller, G. A. (1994). The magical number seven, plus or minus two: Some limits on our capacity for processing information. *Psychological Review, 101*(2), 343–352. Partly reprinted from the 1956 paper in *Psychological Review, 63*(2), 81–97.

National Research Council/National Academy of Sciences. (1989). *Improving risk communication.* Washington DC: National Academy of Sciences/National Academy Press.

Sandman, P. M. (2012). *Responding to community outrage: Strategies for effective risk communication.* Fairfax, VA: US Industrial Health Association. First published 1993. Retrieved from http://psandman.com/media/RespondingtoCommunity Outrage.pdf.

Slovic, P. (1987, 17 April). Perception of risk. *Science, 236*, 280–285.

Slovic, P. & Peters, E. (2006). Risk perception and affect. *Current Directions in Psychological Science, 15*(6), 322–325.

Yannopoulou, N,. Koronis, E. & Elliott, R. (2011). Media amplification of a brand crisis and its affect on brand trust. *Journal of Marketing Management, 27*(5–6), 530–546.

FURTHER READING

Anderson, L. N. & Walsch, D. L. (2013). Every organisation faces risk, but effectively communicating risk is a skill. In J. S. Wrench (Ed.), *Workplace communication for the 21st Century* (Vol. 2, External workplace communication, pp. 215–234). Santa Barbara, CA: Praeger.

Bennett, P., Calman, K., Curtis, S. & Fischbacher-Smith, D. (2010). *Risk communication and public health* (2nd ed.). Oxford, UK: Oxford University Press.

Bergmans, A. (2008). Meaningful communication among experts and affected citizens on risk: Challenge or impossibility? *Journal of Risk Research, 11*(1–2), 175–193.

Boudia, S. & Jas, N. (2007). Risk and 'risk society' in historical perspective. *History and Technology, 24*(3), 317–331.

Charlebrois, S. & Watson, L. (2009). Risk communication and food recalls. In A. Lindgreen, M. K. Hingley & J. VanHamme (Eds.), *The crisis of food brands: Sustaining safe, innovative and competitive food supply* (pp. 29–43). Farnham: Gowe.

Covello, V. T. (2012). Risk communication and environmental health: Principles, strategies, tools and techniques. In R. H. Friis (Ed.), *The Praeger Handbook of environmental health* (pp. 367–390). Santa Barbara, CA: Praeger.

Covello, V. T. (2010). Risk communication. In H. Frumkin (Ed.), *Environmental health from global to local.* (2nd ed., pp. 1099–1140). San Francisco: Jossey-Bass.

Douglas, M. (1992). *Essays in cultural theory.* London: Routledge.

Fischhoff, B. (2009). Risk perception and communication. In R. Detels, R. Beaglehole, M. A. Lansing & M. Gulliford (Eds.), *Oxford textbook on public health* (pp. 940–953). Oxford, UK: Oxford University Press.

Frewer, L. (2004). The public and effective risk communication. *Toxicology Letters, 149*(1), 391–357.

Galloway, C. (2012). Developing risk-literate public relations: Threats and opportunities. *Asia Pacific Public Relations Journal, 13*(1).

Gurabardhi, Z., Gutteling, J. M. & Kuttschreuter, M. (2004). The development of risk communication: An empirical analysis of the literature in the field. *Science Communication, 25*(4), 323–349.

Gutteling, J. M. & Wiegman, D. (1996). *Exploring risk communication.* Dordrecht: Kluwer.

Heath, R. L. & O'Hair, D. (Eds.). (2010). *Handbook of risk and crisis communication.* New York: Routledge.

Hiles, A. (2011). Lessons in risk management from the Auckland power crisis. In A. Hiles (Ed.), *The definitive handbook of business continuity management* (3rd ed. pp. 554–564). Chichester: Wiley.

Hopkin, P. (2012). *Fundamentals of risk management: Understanding, evaluating and implementing effective risk management* (2nd ed.). London: Kogan-Page.

Kallenberg, K. (2007). The role of risk in corporate value: A case study of ABB asbestos litigation. *Journal of Risk Research, 10*(8), 1007–1025.

Kaplan, S. (1997). The words of risk analysis. *Risk Analysis, 17*, 404–417.

Lundgren, R. E. & McMakin, A. H, (2013). *Risk communication: A handbook for communicating environmental, safety and health risks* (5th ed.). Hoboken, NJ: Wiley.

Leiss, W. (2001). *In the chamber of risks: Understanding risk controversies.* Montreal: McGill-Queens University Press.

Morgan, M. G., Fischhoff, B., Bostrom A. & Altman, C. J. (2001). *Risk communication: A mental models approach.* Cambridge UK: Cambridge University Press.

Palenchar, M. J. (2010). *Risk* communication. In R. L. Heath (Ed.), *The Sage handbook of public relations* (2nd ed., pp. 447–460). Newbury Park, CA: Sage.

Palenchar, M. J. & Heath, R. L. (2007). Strategic risk communication: Adding value to society. *Public Relations Review, 33*(2), 120–129.

Pidgeon, N., Kasperson, R. & Slovic. P. (Eds.). (2003). *The social amplification of risk.* Cambridge, UK: Cambridge University Press.

Pidgeon, N. & Henwood, K. (2010). The social amplification of risk framework: Theory, critiques and policy implications. In P. Bennett, K. Calman, S. Curtis & D. Fischbacher-Smith (Eds.), *Risk communication and public health* (2nd ed., pp. 53–68). Oxford: Oxford University Press.

Powell, D. & Leiss, W. (1997). *Mad cows and mother's milk: The perils of poor risk communication.* Montreal: McGill-Queen's University Press.

Reiss, C. (2001). *Risk identification and analysis: A guide.* Fairfax, VA: Public Entity Risk Institute.

Reynolds, B. S. & Seeger, M. W. (2012). *Crisis and emergency risk communication, 2012 edition.* Atlanta, GA: Centers for Disease Control. Retrieved from http://emergency.cdc.gov/cerc/pdf/CERC_2012edition.pdf.

Ropeik, D. & Slovic, P. (2003). Risk communication: A neglected tool in protecting public health. *Risk in Perspective, 11*(2), 1–4.

Song, Y., Kim, D. & Han, D. (2013). Risk communication in South Korea: Social acceptance of nuclear power plants. *Public Relations Review, 39*(1), 55–56.

Soprano, A., Crielaard, B., Piacenza, F. & Ruspantini, D. (2009). *Measuring operational and reputational risk: A practitioner's approach.* Chichester, UK: Wiley.

Trettin, L. & Musham, C. (2000). Is trust a realistic goal of environmental risk communication? *Environment and Behaviour, 32*(3), 410–426.

Ulmer, R. R., Seeger, M. W. & Littlefield, R. S. (Eds.). (2009). *Effective risk communication: A message-centered approach.* New York: Springer.

Walaski, P. (2011). *Risk and crisis communications: Methods and messages.* Hoboken, NJ: Wiley.

Waring, A. & Glenson, A. L. (1998). *Managing risk: Critical issues for survival and success into the 21st century.* London: Thomas Business Press.

Young, E. (1998). Dealing with hazards and disasters: Risk perception and community participation in management. *Australian Journal of Emergency Management, 13*(2), 14–16.

11

RISK MANAGEMENT— REPUTATION

CHAPTER OBJECTIVES

This chapter will help you to:

+ evaluate how reputation is defined

+ appreciate the importance and value of reputation

+ understand why reputation is emerging as a major organisational issue

+ learn how issues and crises are the greatest threats to reputation

+ discover the danger of the gap between reputation and reality

+ introduce some key theories of post-crisis reputation risk management

+ assess how social media has changed the threat to reputation.

Reputation has been called the 'risk of risks' (Economist Intelligence Unit, 2005). Not all experts agree with this characterisation, but in the context of issue and crisis management, potential impact on reputation is a critical factor. In fact, the link between issue management and reputation has increased substantially in recent years. Heath (2013) says that although issue management originally centred on the public policy battle, with reputational undertones, there is now a serious consideration that issue management has become 'the disciplinary keeper of matters relevant to corporate reputation' (p. 388). Moreover, nothing damages reputation faster or deeper than a crisis or an issue mismanaged (Jaques, 2012). That risk to reputation is the focus of this chapter.[1]

While our attention here is on managing risk to reputation, it is not useful to proceed without some understanding of the basic concepts. In fact, reputation is one of those qualities that are reasonably easy to comprehend, but much less easy to explain. Organisational reputation has been defined in many different ways, and Table 11.1 includes just a sampling of definitions, although there are many more.[2]

Table 11.1 Pinning down the intangible: how to define organisational reputation

Frombun (1996)	Corporate reputation is a perceptual representation of a company's past actions and future prospects that describes the firm's overall appeal to all of its key constituents when compared with other leading rivals.
Preston (2004)	Reputation is an integral, but distinct, asset (or where negative, liability) and like most assets it can be enhanced by investment and innovation and it is subject to risk, depreciation and obsolescence.
Eccles, Newquist and Schatz (2007)	A company's overall reputation is a function of its reputation among its various stakeholders (investors, customers, suppliers, employees, regulators, politicians, NGOs and the communities in which it operates) in specific categories (product quality, corporate governance, employee relations, customer service, intellectual capital, financial performance, handling of environmental and social issues).
Barnett, Jermier and Lafferty (2006)	Corporate reputation is observers' collective judgments of a corporation based on assessments of the financial, social and environmental impacts attributed to the corporation over time.
Wartick (2002)	Corporate reputation is the aggregation of a single stakeholder's perceptions of how well organisational responses are meeting the demands and expectations of many organisational stakeholders.
Watson (2007)	Reputation is the sum of predictable behaviours, relationships and two-way communication as judged affectively and cognitively by its stakeholders over a period of time.
Argenti and Druckenmiller (2004)	Corporate reputation is the collective representation of multiple constituencies' images of a company built up over time and based on a company's identity programs, its performance and how constituencies have perceived its behaviour.

---

1   The link between risk and reputation is discussed in Kewell (2007) in this chapter's Further reading section.
2   For an executive view on reputation, based on interviews with more than a dozen key business leaders in Australia, see Mulvey (2008) in this chapter's Further reading section.

Dowling (1994)	Corporate reputation is the evaluation (respect, esteem, estimation) in which an organisation's image is held by people.
Hannington (2004)	Reputation is the product of infectious history. It reflects the reactions of people to how you have behaved, their experience of your products and services, and the referred experience of others. It measures the ability to satisfy your stakeholders' requirements and is a predictor of future behaviour.
Fombrun and Rindova (2005)	Corporate reputation is a collective representation of an organisation's past behaviour and outcomes that depict its ability to render results to stakeholders in the future.
Llewellyn (2002)	Reputation occurs as stakeholders evaluate their knowledge of, or encounters with, an organisation vis-à-vis their expectations, which are couched within their individual values or collective norms.

Argenti, P. A. & Druckenmiller, B. (2004). Reputation and the corporate brand. *Corporate Reputation Review, 7*(4), 368–74.

Barnett, M. L., Jermier, J. M. & Lafferty, B. A. (2006). Corporate reputation: The definitional landscape. *Corporate Reputation Review, 9*(1), 26–38.

Dowling, G. (1994). *Corporate reputations*. Melbourne: Longman Professional.

Eccles, R. G., Newquist, S. C. & Schatz, R. (2007, February). Reputation and its risks. *Harvard Business Review*, 104–114.

Fombrun, C. (1996). *Reputation: Realising value from the corporate image*. Boston: Harvard Business School Press.

Fombrun, C. J. & Rindova, V. (2005). Fanning the flame: Corporate reputations as a social construction of performance. In J. Porac & M. Ventresca (Eds.), *Constructing Markets and Industries*. New York: Oxford University Press.

Hannington, T. (2004). *How to measure and manage your corporate reputation*. Aldershot, UK: Gower.

Llewellyn, P. G. (2002). Corporate reputation: Focusing on the zeitgeist. *Business and Society, 41*(4), 446–55.

Preston, L. E. (2004). Reputation as a source of corporate social capital. *Journal of General Management, 30*, 43–49.

Wartick, S. L. (2002). Measuring corporate reputation: Definition and data. *Business and Society, 41*(4), 371–391.

Watson, T. (2007). Reputation and ethical behaviour in a crisis: Predicting survival. *Journal of Communication Management, 11*(4), 371–384.

From the sampling in Table 11.1, some consistent themes are evident:

+ Reputation depends on the perceptions and judgments by stakeholders of past behaviour and experience.

+ It is built over time.

+ It can be a predictor of future behaviour.

Added to those themes is the fact that the emergence of social media has changed the way in which reputations are built and the ease with which reputations can be destroyed.

A valuable, broad perspective on the nature and importance of reputation comes from US public relations veteran Bill Pendergast, former Washington DC Manager of public relations consultancy Fleishman-Hillard (cited in Hannington, 2004, p. 5):

> Reputation is a corporation's most important asset. Strong and durable reputations are built over time by doing the 'right things right' across the organisation, and taking appropriate credit for achievements. Reputation influences all the goals a corporation can set—getting a higher stock multiple, generating higher profit margins, attracting and retaining the best employees, finding strong business partners and capturing both the attention and loyalty of customers. Reputation is a critical factor in how well an organisation weathers a crisis.

A confounding factor when considering organisational reputation is the fact that it overlaps or touches on so many other concepts. As Wartick (2002, p. 373) commented: 'In the last decade the following list of constructs and concepts has been used synonymously with, or in very close relationship to, corporate reputation: Identity, Image, Prestige, Goodwill, Esteem and Standing.'

One attempt to distinguish some of these concepts comes from Argenti and Aarons (2011, p. 118):

> Reputation is the sum of all an organisation's constituencies' perceptions. It differs from image in that it is built gradually, and is therefore not simply a perception in any moment of time. It differs from identity because it is a product of both internal and external constituencies, whereas identity is constructed by the company itself.

In line with this approach, some experts argue that because reputation is the global result of an organisation's behaviour, it is not generally something that can be directly 'managed'. Hutton et al. (2001, p. 249) suggested that attempting to manage one's reputation can be likened to trying to manage one's own popularity: 'a rather awkward, superficial and potentially self-defeating endeavour'.

However, while there is little disagreement about the importance of reputation, debate continues about exactly how to define organisational reputation and its relationship to other constructs.[3] For the present discussion, we will briefly consider one of those other related constructs not mentioned by Wartick, which is brand.

Brand is not generally seen as synonymous with reputation. In fact, they are quite distinct, yet the two are intimately linked. At the simplest level it can be said that:

BRAND IS WHAT YOU SAY ABOUT YOURSELF.

REPUTATION IS WHAT OTHER PEOPLE SAY ABOUT YOU.

---

3   For a detailed definitional analysis on reputation, see Barnett, Jermier and Lafferty (2006) and Gotsi and Wilson (2001) in this chapter's Further reading section.

Clearly, though, they have a strong influence on each other. Reputation can influence brand and brand can affect reputation.[4] One of the problems is that there can be a disconnect between brand and reputation. For example, high brand awareness does not necessarily equate to good reputation. Indeed, it may equate to bad reputation. For example, some fast-food chains have very high brand awareness and high brand loyalty, yet they are also at the top of the awareness list when it comes to the products that critics target as unhealthy. Similarly, some cigarettes have very high brand awareness, but that doesn't translate into positive reputation for the manufacturers.

The reason this distinction is important here is that companies can get blinded by 'brand awareness' and may forget that the real goal is not just reputation, but *good* reputation. In fact, there are well-known cases where an organisation has changed its brand specifically to distance itself from poor reputation. Examples include the telecommunication company WorldCom, which changed its name to MCI in the wake of an accounting fraud scandal and record bankruptcy; the budget airline ValuJet which adopted the name AirTran after a high-profile airline crash exposed its poor safety record; and tobacco giant Philip Morris— makers of brands such as Marlboro and Chesterfield—whose parent organisation became the neutral-sounding Altria Group.[5]

SO WHY IS GOOD REPUTATION IMPORTANT?

As Pendergast commented above, reputation is a very important asset not only for corporations and individuals, but also for governments, NGOs, not-for-profits and other organisations. Moreover, it is quantifiable and it is an acknowledged wealth generator.

But what is it actually worth? In theory, the value of reputation is calculated by taking the market value of the company and subtracting the tangible assets. That leaves a net figure for intangibles, of which reputation is an important part. In this respect, the Institute of Practitioners in Advertising (2006) reports that intangible assets such as ideas, knowledge, expertise, talent, identity, customer service and reputation comprise over 70 per cent of the market value of companies listed on the Fortune 500 and FTSE 500. Moreover, they report that this proportion has tripled over the past 30 years. Similarly, a Weber Shandwick international reputation survey (2007) found that global business influencers attributed 63 per cent of a company's value to reputation. Other studies produce slightly different percentage results, but broadly there is a consistent belief that reputation alone can account for at least half of an organisation's value.

At the same time, executive understanding of the importance of reputation has increased dramatically. For example, the MORI Captains of Industry survey found that in 1983 only 8 per cent of business leaders mentioned reputation as a significant component in their company's valuation. In the same survey 20 years later, 48 per cent of CEOs, chairpersons

---

4   For analysis of branding versus reputation, see Karmark (2013) in this chapter's Further reading section.

5   For comment on the media reaction to the name change for the world's largest tobacco company, see Alsop (2004), and for analysis of the strategic thinking behind the change, see Smith and Malone (2003) in this chapter's Further reading section.

IS REPUTATION REALLY LIKE A BANK ACCOUNT?

It's a common idea that reputation is like a bank account, which you build up in good times and draw from when things go wrong. But as risk guru Peter Sandman (2010) has concluded, it is simplistic to accept that events that improve your reputation are deposits, events that damage your reputation are withdrawals, and that the objective is to maintain a healthy balance of 'reputational capital'.

The problem with this idea is that deposits and withdrawals—good actions and bad actions—are not in common currency, and good reputation and bad reputation can exist at the same time. The bank account metaphor also wrongly suggests that badly behaved organisations can 'buy back' reputation with some high-profile good citizenship. When failed Australian tycoon Alan Bond was jailed for dishonesty, some of his supporters tried to mitigate his company's record bankruptcy by emphasising that he helped Australia win the America's Cup yachting trophy. It made a good story of reputational redemption, but it meant nothing to the investors who had lost millions. They knew the real meaning of an empty bank account. And it was no metaphor.

and senior board members of FTSE 500 companies spontaneously mentioned image and reputation as the main criteria they use to judge a company—ahead of more conventional indicators such as financial performance and product/service quality (cited in Woodcock, n.d.). In the Economist Intelligence Unit (2005) global survey of 269 senior risk managers, 90 per cent declared that corporate reputation was one of the primary assets of the firm, and nearly 60 per cent said reputation is a key source of competitive advantage as products and services become less differentiated.

 A risk to its reputation is a threat to the survival of the enterprise.

Peter J. Firestein (2006, p. 25)

While there is no doubt that organisational reputation is of enormous value, it is never static and is constantly at risk, so organisations need to commit resources to protecting it. Understanding the factors that determine reputation risk enables an organisation to take action to address them.

Eccles, Newquist and Schatz (2007) propose that effectively managing reputation risk involves five steps: assessing your organisation's reputation among stakeholders; evaluating your organisation's real character; closing reputation–reality gaps; monitoring changing beliefs and expectations; and putting a senior executive in charge who has sufficient authority to get things done and is able to ensure the CEO doesn't fall into the trap of listening only to good news.

Figure 11.1 A framework for managing reputation risk

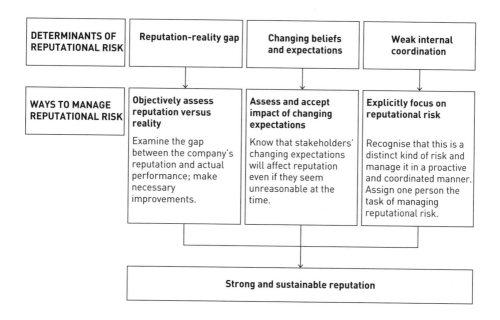

Source: Eccles, Newquist and Schatz (2007). Reprinted by permission from *Harvard Business Review.*

THE REPUTATION–REALITY GAP

While it is true that reputation is largely based on the perception of stakeholders, there must still be a clear link to reality, as identified in Table 11.1.

When an organisation's good reputation far outstrips a possibly weak underlying reality, a major threat arises that the gap will be exposed and reputation will be badly damaged as perception and reality begin to rebalance. This concept is closely aligned with the 'expectation gap' approach to issue management introduced in Chapter 1. The expectation gap approach says an issue arises where a gap opens up between an organisation's *actual behaviour* and the legitimate expectation of stakeholders as to how it *should behave*. In addition, that can also occur when stakeholder beliefs and expectations change and the organisation has failed to recognise and adapt to change.

Obviously, reputation depends on more than just expectations of organisational behaviour. The concept of a perception gap is a good illustration of the strong relationship between issue management and reputation protection.

> A reputation once broken may possibly be repaired, but the world will always keep their eyes on the spot where the crack was.
>
> English bishop Joseph Hall (1574–1656)

One of the best known examples of the devastating impact of a reputation–reality gap is the sustained damage suffered by UK energy giant BP. Moreover, BP's experience provides a vivid example of the complex link between issues, crises, risk and reputation. Beginning in late 2000, the company embarked upon an aggressive and extremely costly rebranding and reputation-building program designed to portray itself as a responsible corporation that cares about the environment. Under CEO John Browne, tens of thousands of petrol stations around the world were rebadged with the new green and yellow 'Helios' sunburst logo intended to allow the company to differentiate itself, to show a commitment to the environment, and to symbolise 'dynamic energy in all its forms, from oil to gas to solar' (Macalister & Cross, 2000).

At the same time, the company launched a massive 'Beyond Petroleum' advertising program to support expansion and promotion of its alternative energy program. The program triggered predictable scorn from environmental activists and other critics, who argued that the company would have been far better advised to spend this investment on improving its performance and its real dependence on oil rather than trying to 'greenwash' its way to respectability. Greenpeace called it a triumph of style over substance, and the NGO Corpwatch (Bruno, 2000) awarded BP its 'Greenwash Award' and described the program as 'beyond preposterous'.

Even inside the company there were doubters who were prepared to speak out. 'Externally, the issue is often one of suspended disbelief,' said Greg Bourne, who was then BP's regional President/Director for Australia and New Zealand. 'Changing your logo won't change society's mind. It is only by exhibiting changed behaviour and attitudes over a long period of time that you will slowly but surely differentiate yourself' (cited in Lamb & McKee, 2008, p. 235).

Unfortunately, BP did not have the luxury of time to reap the reputational benefit. In March 2005 an explosion and fire at its Texas City Refinery near Houston killed fifteen people and injured scores of others in the USA's worst industrial accident for decades. Later investigations blamed mismanagement and cost-cutting.[6] Less than a year later, an oil leak at the Prudhoe Bay oil field in Alaska caused BP to slash production. It was caused after failure of a corroded pipeline and followed warnings about corrosion and maintenance problems.

With the company's reputation taking a battering, CEO Browne was forced to resign after lying in court about his personal life (Swartz, 2007). Then came the *Deepwater Horizon* disaster in April 2010 when a BP-contracted oil rig in the Gulf of Mexico caught fire and sank, with the loss of eleven lives and widespread damage to the marine and coastal environment.

There is no space here to describe the prolonged and painful aftermath of this disaster, which would have caused massive damage to any company.[7] But it is clear that BP's prior efforts to differentiate itself as being environmentally responsible made the reputational

---

6   For detail on the Texas City disaster, see Heffernan (2011) and Hopkins (2009) in this chapter's Further reading section.

7   An extensive literature has been developed about the BP *Deepwater Horizon* disaster for example, Balmer (2010), Harlow, Brantley and Harlow (2011). See also Baron (2010), Brown (2011) and Steffy (2011) in this chapter's Further reading section.

damage even greater. Analysing the case from the perspective of corporate branding and reputation, Balmer (2010, p. 97) concluded: 'BP's brand positioning was, at best, an aspiration and was, in truth, never really attainable. To a large degree, it was divorced from reality.'

As the BP case shows, when there is a major gap between reputation and reality, and where society's expectation of performance has changed, the risk to reputation is very real.

REPUTATION, ISSUES AND CRISES

Although there is an extensive literature about all aspects of reputation, the focus here is specifically on the ways in which organisations respond to crises and major issues, and how that can impact on organisational reputation. This question has seen the development of some key theoretical concepts, each viewing the challenge from a different perspective. One important early study was the work of Myria Allen and Rachel Caillouet (1994), who drew on the framework of impression management to explore how organisations use different strategies to respond to different audiences.[8]

> It takes 20 years to build a reputation and five minutes to ruin it. If you think about that, you'll do things differently.
>
> US entrepreneur Warren Buffet

They collected and analysed almost 800 external organisational statements—including press releases, brochures, media articles and testimony at hearings—to determine how messages were targeted to different stakeholders in the context of a crisis or major issue. The authors identified seven main communication strategies utilised to protect reputation following an adverse event, as listed in Table 11.2.

Table 11.2 Impression management strategies

Strategy	Objective
Excuse	Attempts to avoid responsibility for the event
Justification	Accepts some responsibility for the event but tries to avoid responsibility for the negative effects
Ingratiation	Attempts to gain audience approval for the organisation
Denouncement	Tries to move the blame to someone else
Factual distortion	Claims the allegations/accusations are taken out of context or are untrue
Intimidation	Suggests danger or a threat (rarely found in this study)
Apology	Admits fault and accepts punishment (not found at all in the data)

Source: adapted from Allen and Caillouet (1994, p. 52).

---

8   See also Caillouet and Allen (1996) in this chapter's Further reading section.

Research building on Allen and Caillouet led to development of two key theories relating to how organisations respond to protect their reputation: image restoration theory and situational crisis communication theory. These two theories have subsequently become well-established concepts and are commonly in use as the basis to analyse issue and crisis case studies.

IMAGE RESTORATION THEORY

The first of these seminal ideas came from William Benoit (1995, 1997a, 2013), who used communication and sociology to develop the theory of image restoration discourse. He described it as an approach for understanding corporate crisis situations, and for determining how to design messages during and after a crisis in order to explain a corporation's behaviour, and to protect and restore its reputation with key stakeholders.[9] Importantly, he also described it as a tool for critics, students and academics to formally evaluate messages produced.

Rather than describe the kinds of crisis situations, or the stages in a crisis (which had been a focus of previous study), the theory of image restoration discourse focuses on message options—what an organisation can say when faced with a crisis—which Benoit asserted was more exhaustive than earlier theories (1997a).

As shown in Table 11.3, this theory offers five broad categories of image repair strategies—denial, evasion of responsibility, reducing offensiveness, corrective action and mortification—along with a number of sub-strategies.

Table 11.3 Benoit's image restoration strategies

Strategy	Sub-strategy	Message
Denial	Simple denial	We didn't do it.
	Shift the blame	Someone else did it.
Evasion of responsibility	Provocation	Someone else forced us into this situation.
	Defeasibility	We lacked the information or ability to prevent it.
	Accident	It was just an accident.
	Good intentions	We never intended this outcome.
Reducing offensiveness	Bolstering	We've always behaved well in the past.
	Minimisation	It's not really all that serious.
	Differentiation	It's not as bad as other crises.
	Transcendence	We were trying to achieve something worthwhile.
	Attack accuser	Our accusers are bad people.
	Compensation	We will help/reimburse the victims.
Corrective action	Plan to solve or prevent problem	We'll fix it and do better in the future.
Mortification	Apologise for act	We did it and we are really sorry.

Source: adapted from Benoit (1995, 1997a).

---

9   For broader discussion of post-crisis communication and post-crisis issue impacts, see Sims (2009), Ulmer, Sellnow and Seeger (2009) and Jaques (2009) in this chapter's Further reading section.

While Benoit's strategies might at first seem simple, they provide a reliable and consistent basis on which to assess an organisation's communication to minimise risk to reputation during and after a crisis. This approach also provides common terminology to help make informed comparisons and commentary about high-profile cases, from international corporate crises such as the BP oil spill disaster in the Gulf of Mexico in 2010 (Harlow, Brantley & Harlow, 2011) down to individual reputational damage to British actor Hugh Grant after being arrested in Hollywood for lewd behaviour with a prostitute (Benoit, 1997b).[10]

A CRISIS DOESN'T HAVE TO BE REAL TO DAMAGE REPUTATION

A notorious case of an unreal crisis that caused very real corporate damage was in California in late 2005 when a woman claimed to have found the tip of a human finger in her bowl of chilli at a Wendy's restaurant. Initially, the company tried to play it down, but the story generated massive media coverage and became the subject of late-night talk shows and comedians' routines. Wendy's then launched an ill-timed new sales promotion to divert attention, but sales continued to fall. When a US$100,000 reward was offered for information, a tipster rang the company hotline to identify the man who had lost his finger in an accident. He had sold it for $100 to the husband of the hoaxer, who cooked it before placing it in her chilli. The couple pleaded guilty and went to prison. Meantime Wendy's had been forced to lay off staff and reduce hours in some restaurants, and lost $2.5 million in sales. It was a devastating example of the impact of rumours and hoaxes on real-life reputation.[11]

SITUATIONAL CRISIS COMMUNICATION THEORY

Although previous researchers had focused mainly on categorising crises and developing possible response strategies, American academic Tim Coombs set out to build on this by attempting to match crisis response strategies to the crisis situation that represented a risk to reputation. Using attribution theory, Coombs' early work developed a list of crisis types categorised by responsibility—how much a stakeholder believes the organisation is responsible for the crisis event—and then possible crisis response strategies for each broad category (Coombs, 1995).

The situational crisis communication theory (SCCT) first appeared as a formally named concept in 2002 (Coombs & Holladay, 2002) and is built around protecting the organisation's reputation during a crisis. The foundation of the SCCT approach is a matrix of crisis types to help make initial assessment of responsibility that publics will attribute to

---

10 See this chapter's Further reading section for other examples of the image restoration theory in practice. Brinson and Benoit (1996) used the theory to analyse the Dow Corning breast implant crisis, and later the image strategy used by Queen Elizabeth II (Benoit & Brinson, 1999). See also Meyers (2011), who assessed the 2009 and 2010 Toyota vehicle recalls, and Blaney, Benoit and Brazeal (2002) who used the theory to analyse the 2000 Firestone tyre scandal. For further examples of how this theory has been applied to case analysis, see references in Benoit (2013).

11 As part of Wendy's response, the company's PR executive gave a lengthy profile interview to the *New York Times* (Richtel & Barrionuevo, 2005). For analysis of the company's advertising strategy, see Braun-LaTour, LaTour and Loftus (2006) in this chapter's Further reading section.

a crisis situation. These crisis types are allocated to distinct clusters: the victim cluster, the accidental cluster and the preventable cluster (see Table 11.4). In summary:

+ The victim cluster involves crisis types in which harm is inflicted on the organisation as well as on stakeholders.

+ The accidental cluster involves harm from unintentional actions by the organisation, where the organisation did not intend for the crisis to occur.

+ The preventable cluster involves intentionally placing stakeholders at risk, or not doing enough to prevent the crisis.

Situational Crisis Communication Theory

Table 11.4 SCCT crisis types

Cluster	Crisis type	Attributions of responsibility	Reputational threat
Victim cluster Organisation is also a victim of the crisis	Natural disasters—acts of God	Weak attribution of responsibility	Mild reputational threat
	Rumour—fake or damaging information		
	Workplace violence—current or former employees		
	Product tampering/malevolence—caused by external agent		
Accidental cluster Organisational actions leading to crisis were unintentional	Challenges—to appropriateness of operations	Minimal attribution of responsibility	Moderate reputational threat
	Technical-error accidents—technology or equipment failure causes industrial accident		
	Technical-error product harm—technology or equipment failure causes product recall		
Preventable cluster Organisation knowingly put people at risk, took inappropriate actions or broke law/regulation	Human error accidents—cause industrial accidents	Strong attribution of responsibility	Severe reputational threat
	Human-error product harm—causes product to be recalled		
	Organisational misdeed without injuries—stakeholders deceived with no injury		
	Organisational misdeed, management misconduct—laws or regulations broken		
	Organisational misdeed with injuries—stakeholders put at risk or injured		

Source: adapted from Coombs (2006, 2007).

In addition to the degree of responsibility set out in Table 11.4, SCCT also provides for adjustments to be made to this initial assessment by considering two important variables: severity and performance history. *Severity* is the amount of damage generated by the crisis, including financial, human and environmental damage. *Performance history* refers to the past actions or conduct of an organisation, including whether it has had previous crises, and its prior relationship history—especially how well or how poorly it has treated stakeholders in the past.

SCCT makes it clear that as severity increases or performance history deteriorates, the public will attribute greater crisis responsibility to the organisation and the risk to reputation increases. Moreover, the greater the perceived acceptance of responsibility for the crisis, the more accommodative the chosen response strategy must be; that is, greater concern must be shown for the victims.

Coombs and his colleagues have developed a list of thirteen crisis response strategies for SCCT (for the detailed list, see Coombs, 2007, p. 170). These are not substantially different from the strategies originally developed by Benoit (see Table 11.3) and reflect three broad categories:

+ *Deny strategies*—attempting to remove any connection between the organisation and the crisis.

+ *Diminish strategies*—arguing that the crisis is not as bad as people think, or that it was outside the organisation's control.

+ *Rebuild strategies*—where the organisation attempts to improve its reputation by material and/or symbolic forms of aid to victims.

However, a key advance with SCCT over other approaches is that it not only provides an effective framework for properly assessing crises and their reputational impact, but it also directly links assessment to strategy, as shown in the box, 'SCCT crisis response strategy guidelines'.

SCCT CRISIS RESPONSE STRATEGY GUIDELINES

1   Informing and adjusting information alone can be enough when crises have minimal attributions of crisis responsibility (victim crises), no history of similar crises and a neutral or positive prior relationship reputation.

2   Victimage can be used as part of the response for workplace violence, product tampering, natural disasters and rumours.

3   Diminish crisis response strategies should be used for crises with minimal attributions of crisis responsibility (victim crises) coupled with a history of similar crises and/or negative prior relationship reputation.

4   Diminish crisis response strategies should be used for crises with low attributions of crisis responsibility (accident crises) that have no history of similar crises, and a neutral or positive prior relationship reputation.

5   Rebuild crisis response strategies should be used for crises with low attributions of crisis responsibility (accident crises) coupled with a history of similar crises and/or negative prior relationship reputation.

6   Rebuild crisis response strategies should be used for crises with strong attributions of crisis responsibility (preventable crises) regardless of crisis history or prior relationship reputation.

7   The deny posture crisis response strategies should be used for rumour and challenge crises, when possible.

8   Maintain consistency in crisis response strategies. Mixing deny crisis response strategies with either the diminish or rebuild strategies will erode the effectiveness of the overall response.

Source: Tim Coombs (2007, p. 173), reprinted with permission.

To summarise, SCCT centres on the crisis manager examining the crisis situation in order to assess the reputational threat level presented by the crisis. The threat is the amount of damage a crisis could inflict on the organisation's reputation if no action is taken. SCCT theorises that by understanding the crisis situation, the crisis manager can determine which crisis response strategy or strategies will maximise reputational protection (Coombs, 2007, p. 166). More recently, Kim and Wertz (2013) have researched the factors that predict the strategy organisations are more likely to select, identifying in particular the degree of crisis preparation and perception of crisis as an opportunity.

ONLINE AND SOCIAL MEDIA REPUTATION RISK

As with reputation, the rise of digital communication and social media has generated an enormous literature, from technical and operational aspects, through to software and programming, on to communications protocols and right up to boardroom responsibility.

More specifically, the rise of social media has had a profound impact on all aspects of public affairs and organisational communication,[12] and that impact has most especially been felt in terms of how social media can affect reputation.[13] For example, US digital strategist Peter LaMotte (cited in Working, 2013) says the old days of being able to ignore 'the armies of trolls beyond the walls of your organization' are gone: 'There's a massive hole in the castle wall, and anyone out there can come in hurt your brand and leave and be OK with it.'

There is strong evidence that the internet and social media have changed how issue managers must operate (Coombs, 2002); and how they have, in fact, made permanent change across the whole continuum, from issue to crisis to reputation. More than ever, it is important to remember that understanding the interrelated processes introduced in

---

12 For more on public affairs and organisational communication, see Breakenridge (2008), Christ (2005), Fitch (2012), Macnamara (2009), Wright and Hinson (2011) in this chapter's Further reading section.

13 For a detailed discussion on social media and corporate reputation, see McCorkindale and DiStaso (2013) in this chapter's Further reading section.

this book—issue management, crisis management, risk communication and reputation management—remain the essential foundation. As Andriole et al. (2013, p. 19) warned: 'Process always precedes technology, so technology integration should stand on the shoulders of process integration.'

But while the fundamental nature of the issue and crisis management processes changes only slowly, the development of digital communication has dramatically altered the spread and speed of implementation. And the impact on reputation has seen perhaps the most dramatic change.

> Social media today has the unbridled ability to create and destroy reputations at the speed of an electron.
>
> US business commentator Davia Temin (2012, p. 12)

A great deal has been written about how social media has 'democratised' the relationship between the powerful and the not-so-powerful.[14] However, our focus here is primarily on organisational communication and risk to organisational reputation. (Many of the same ideas apply to individual reputations, although for a CEO the line between organisational and individual reputation can become very blurred.)[15]

As mentioned at the start of this chapter, nothing damages reputation faster or deeper than a crisis or an issue mismanaged, so the central question here is: how has social media changed issue and crisis management?

The first step in the issue management process (as detailed in Chapter 4) is to identify emerging issues early and to communicate about them to key stakeholders. Two pioneering studies (Thomsen, 1995; Heath, 1998) highlighted the importance of the internet in enabling organisations to execute this identification role—to research emerging issues very efficiently and to communicate with stakeholders faster than ever before. Later development of social media reinforced that advantage.

Similarly, these pioneers also identified the closely related theme that has been further developed in almost all subsequent scholarship; namely that the capacity social media provides the organisation to identify and manage issues also energises the power of activists and other stakeholders to escalate problems into issues and to place these issues on the public agenda.

As long ago as 1998, Heath said 'the electronic playing field helps to democratise public policy debate' (p. 276), with the internet and social media enabling any organisation— no matter how financially limited—to sustain its messages over time and to reach people around the world. As a result, an organisation's reputation can be at risk not only in its

---

14 See the Further reading sections for Chapter 2 and Chapter 5.
15 A famous case of blurring between the CEO and the organisation was the impact on Martha Stewart Living Omnimedia (MSO) when founder and CEO Martha Stewart was jailed for unrelated dishonesty. See, for example, Cheng (2011) in this chapter's Further reading section.

home country, but also wherever like-minded people raise awareness about an issue and communicate to one another about it. As Coombs (2002, p. 218) wrote:

> Stakeholders no longer have to rely on generating favourable media coverage because they can post their own information directly to the Internet. Instead of depending on the unreliability of an uncontrolled medium, the stakeholders can utilise a controlled medium—websites and discussion group postings.

Moreover, newer social networks such as Facebook, Twitter and Instagram (most notably since 2006) have even further accelerated what Coombs called 'issue contagion'— the notion that an issue can spread very much like a cold virus, with people being the 'hosts' spreading the contagion through social media. The infamous case of the Intel Pentium chip failure (summarised in Chapter 6) is sometimes regarded as one of the first 'internet-generated crises'. CEO Andy Grove later said Intel's failure to properly follow up the original online complaints was the single biggest business mistake he ever made (cited in Coombs, 2002).

Through issue contagion, social media is changing forever the way in which organisations identify and prioritise issues, and has also changed the capacity of issues to damage reputation. If there is any doubt about how rapidly reputations can suffer since the advent of social media, Andriole et al. (2013), for example, describe 100 recent case studies of what they call 'social media disasters'.[16]

The catalogue of mistakes and misjudgements presented by Andriole and colleagues leads directly to the other major impact of social media; that is, not only the way in which digital communication allows issues to be raised and spread, but also the way in which the ill-advised use of social media can actually generate reputational damage. This may be through misusing social media in a way which invites criticism and threatens reputation, or in failing to respond to legitimate issues raised on social media.

HOW NOT TO RUN A SOCIAL MEDIA COMPETITION

It's not uncommon for a social media competition to get hijacked by critics, but Australian airline Qantas couldn't have chosen worse timing or a worse topic. Soon after industrial action stranded thousands of passengers when the entire fleet was grounded by management, the airline invited Twitter followers to win a pair of first-class pyjamas by tweeting their idea of a 'dream luxury flight experience'.

The invitation urged followers to 'be creative' and within minutes the site was filled with sarcastic and abusive comments such as: 'A plane that doesn't have an exploding engine! #QantasLuxury'. Mainstream media throughout Australia and around the world picked up the story and branded the blunder 'an excellent case study in corporate cultural tone deafness' (Taylor, 2011). It was hardly the biggest public relations failure in Australia, as one commentator claimed, but it was an embarrassing gaffe that damaged reputation and served as a reminder of the risks with social media.

---

16 This book recommends using the term 'disaster' in a more specific way; namely as a major event that adversely affects broader society beyond individual organisations. See Table 1.1 in Chapter 1.

The concept of contagion via social media was also taken up by Alsop (2004, p. 22), who wrote:

> Companies can think of a Web-based threat to their reputation as a particularly dangerous virus that can spread to infect millions of people in a matter of hours or even minutes. The appropriate response has to be determined swiftly and implemented without delay. You certainly don't want to answer every crank. One can protest too much, adding credibility to otherwise groundless gossip. But companies must respond to legitimate threats to their reputations.

Another important aspect of contagion is how social media crises can rapidly migrate across into the traditional news media. Pang, Hassan and Chong (2014) concluded that crises are often triggered online when stakeholders are empowered by social media platforms to air their grievances; and that when crises are covered by mainstream media because of their newsworthiness, the crises gain credibility offline.

A particular social media threat to reputation is in the form of rumours, which can spread extremely rapidly and take on a life of their own. We have seen examples of the damage that can be done, such as the 'finger in the chilli' incident at Wendy's (summarised earlier in this chapter); the fake Whitehaven coal report (mentioned in Chapter 5); the hoax report of an explosion at the White House that damaged the stock market (mentioned in Chapter 7); and the role of social media in falsely reporting a Qantas plane crash (also mentioned in Chapter 7).

Another notorious example of the speed of disruption was in 2008 when Apple shares fell 10 per cent in ten minutes following false rumours on a user-generated content site run by CNN that then CEO Steve Jobs had suffered a major heart attack (Hargreaves, 2008).

While such social media driven events can have a very rapid impact, damaging rumours can also be extraordinarily long-lasting. One of the most famous cases involved allegations that began in the early 1980s that the 'man in the moon' logo used by Proctor & Gamble for over 100 years was a secret Satanist symbol. The logo was eventually dropped in 1995, but a lawsuit against former Amway distributors who spread Satanist rumours about their competitor was not settled until 2007, when Proctor & Gamble was awarded over $19 million ('Procter & Gamble awarded', 2007).

A good example of an online rumour that was promptly and effectively dealt with involved the same company, when some animal lovers claimed the Proctor & Gamble fabric freshener product Febreze could poison pets. Using supporting statements from the US Humane Society and expert veterinary authorities, P&G mounted a counter-offensive, replying almost entirely via online sources.[17] The rumours died down within a few weeks.

In his assessment of how firms should fight rumours in the digital age, Hiles (2011, p. 6) concluded:

> Rumours can come from any direction, at any time. They are frequently a mix of fiction and fact, but they may also be unconfirmed fact that has escaped control. 360 degree environmental scanning is essential to provide an early warning. A predetermined strategy is needed to ignore or combat them. A rebuttal needs to be quick and comprehensive.

---

17 For details on the Febreze case, see Crawford (1999) in this chapter's Further reading section.

Beyond mere rumour, an effective strategy to respond to reputational threats requires strong and focused management. But social media remains a vulnerability for many organisations that have yet to put effective scanning and monitoring in place. In fact, Andriole et al. (2013, p. 50) reported that while study after study revealed that well over 50 per cent of executives believe that reputational risk associated with social media should be a board room issue, only around 15 per cent of companies have a program in place to capture and analyse social data. However, there are also cases when even a board decision can trigger a social media threat to reputation (see the box, 'When the board gets it wrong').

These days, risk to reputation, online or otherwise, should be a top priority for all executives. The US academic Daniel Diermeier (2011, p. 161) has said: 'Reputation management is not a corporate function, but a capability.' If reputation risk is to be minimised, it is a capability that should be developed in every manager, especially communications professionals.

WHEN THE BOARD GETS IT WRONG

One of Australia's best known marketing fiascos was when Kraft ran an online competition to find a name for a new product that combined cheese with its famous yeast-based spread Vegemite. The board of Kraft Australia made the decision, and the chosen name from 48,000 entries was iSnack 2.0. But the public hated the name and the ensuing storm of criticism, mainly through social media, was overwhelming. In fact, a reported 700,000 Australians tweeted about the choice. More importantly, questions were asked about the capacity of the local company to manage an iconic brand. The new name was abandoned and the company handed the choice back to the public. About 50,000 customers voted online in just five days and they chose the new name—Cheesybite.[18]

KEY POINTS

+ Reputation may be an 'intangible' asset but it has critical, measurable value.

+ Nothing damages reputation faster or deeper than a crisis or an issue mismanaged.

+ Reputation is what others say about you. Brand is what you say about yourself.

+ A gap between reputation and reality is a major potential risk.

+ A crisis doesn't have to be real to damage reputation.

+ Two key theories provide a framework for protecting reputation during and after a crisis:

    – Benoit's image restoration theory

    – Coombs' situational crisis communication theory.

+ Social media is both a powerful tool and a major vulnerability in managing reputation risk.

---

18 For discussion of the Cheesybite case, see Howell (2012) and Keinan, Farrelly and Beverland (2012) in this chapter's Further reading section.

☰ ACTIVITIES AND DISCUSSION

1. Examine a current crisis and assess the organisation's communication against Benoit's image restoration strategies (Table 11.3). Which strategy did the organisation use, and would another strategy have been more effective?

2. Can reputation be 'managed' in a traditional business sense? If so, what role can corporate communicators have?

3. Research examples of companies that changed their corporate identity or a brand name to avoid reputational risk. Was it successful?

4. Social media has dramatically increased the speed at which rumours spread. But has experience of social media made people more likely or less likely to believe online rumours? Develop arguments to support or refute this proposition.

5. Online competitions can very easily go wrong and damage reputation. Explore some recent examples and suggest what the organisation could have done differently.

6. Social media relies on authentic peer communication and opinion. Discuss how an organisation can engage in a genuine way.

7. If reputation is to be a guiding philosophy for some large corporations, how should it be measured?

RISK MANAGEMENT—PROACTIVE VERSUS REACTIVE PUBLIC RELATIONS

Gwyneth Howell

University of Western Sydney

In 2009, Australia's then Prime Minister Kevin Rudd suggested that every university student in the country should study the James Hardie asbestos crisis as 'there is no place for asbestos in today's global economy. No material is worth dying for'.

The deadly legacy of asbestos—a lightweight, cheap, fire-retardant material—is most apparent in Australia, where the main producer of this product, James Hardie Industries (JHI), sought to manage the issue of liability through a series of business decisions that required a precise communication strategy to limit the damage to the company brand. The company's actions during the early 2000s adversely affected thousands of Australian victims and their families. Public pressure was brought to bear, a Royal Commission was undertaken, and today there is certainty about compensation. JHI employed both proactive and reactive public relations, with very different outcomes and a dramatic impact on the company's reputation.

JHI's core business is the production of fibre cement and other building materials. Between 1917 and 1987 the organisation manufactured asbestos-related products and dominated the Australian market for asbestos cement products, with market share approximating 90 per cent. However, the inhalation of asbestos fibres can cause a number of painful and lethal conditions. Today, an estimated 7000 Australians have already died from asbestos-related cancers, and this is predicted to rise to 18,000 deaths by 2020. The financial estimates of Australia's total liability for future asbestos claims are $6 billion and rising.

In 1998, JHI began to explore ways of managing risk in the asbestos business, and particularly by separating any legacy issues that may be associated with asbestos by relocating the company to the Netherlands. This project was instigated in 2001 and featured a communication plan that became known as the 'Project Green Board Paper Communication Strategy'. JHI employed proactive issues management to limit media coverage and influence government policy related to its asbestos liabilities. To do so, JHI established the Medical Research and Compensation Foundation (MRCF) to cover future compensation payouts, providing partly paid shares to fund the MRCF. The announcement of this foundation and the move to the Netherlands attracted only positive media converge due to the carefully crafted proactive communication campaign.

However, in 2003 JHI cancelled $1.9 billion partly paid shares in its Australian company, without disclosure to the Australian Stock Exchange, the NSW Supreme Court, the MRCF or any other stakeholders. The cancellation of the partly paid shares resulted in

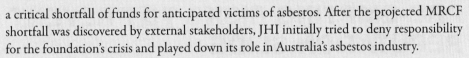

a critical shortfall of funds for anticipated victims of asbestos. After the projected MRCF shortfall was discovered by external stakeholders, JHI initially tried to deny responsibility for the foundation's crisis and played down its role in Australia's asbestos industry.

By 2004, the company's failure to manage the funding shortfall crisis illustrated the poor outcomes of reactive public relations during a crisis. As the company struggled to respond to external publics, including high levels of media interest, their actions and responses created a national focus. JHI's public relations strategy in 2004 was a complete contrast to its 2001 public relations strategy where the organisation had employed openness, transparency and conviction to its key publics. Now various affected publics and stakeholder groups used media coverage and public protests to bring pressure to bear on the New South Wales Government, leading to the establishment of a Special Commission of Inquiry. The inquiry critiqued the highly successful proactive communication strategy of 2001, and illustrated the poor outcomes of the reactive communication strategy in 2004. On 21 December 2004, after the Special Commission of Inquiry's damning findings against JHI were made public, and facing extensive media and public pressure, JHI agreed to a deal negotiated by Greg Combet, then Secretary of the Australian Council of Trade Unions, on behalf of all present and future asbestos disease claims. The company agreed to make up the $1.5 billion shortfall of the MRCF's funding. This marked the largest financial settlement in Australian history.

From 2004 onwards, JHI maintained information on its company website about the fund, while asbestos campaigners maintained their communication strategy, engaging online media to increase awareness in the community about the dangers of asbestos and the actions of JHI. The company subsequently linked the payments to company earnings and for three years the New South Wales government extended loans to the MRCF to ensure certainty for the victims and their families.

Today, thanks to online and social media activism, this issue continues to be prominent in the media. In late 2012, the telemovie *Devil's Dust* premiered on Australian television, telling the story of JHI, asbestos and its legacy. While this issue will continue for JHI, for public relations professionals the case illustrates that their most important challenge in dealing with a risk and reputational crisis is maintaining control of the message through proactive strategic communication.

For more detailed discussion of this case see:

Howell, G. V. J. (2009). Issues and crisis management: James Hardie Industries. In M. Sheehan & R. Xavier (Eds.), *Public relations campaigns* (pp. 189–205). Oxford University Press, Melbourne.[19]

---

19 See also Howell and Miller (2006) and Patel and Xavier (2005) in this chapter's Further reading section.

PRE-EMPTING RISKS TO PREVENT REPUTATION SLIDE

Augustine Pang

Nanyang Technological University, Singapore

With Christmas and year-end festivities approaching, the commuters jostling to get into the trains during the evening peak hours on the Singapore subway seemed hurried, but less harried than usual. But the mood of holiday optimism soon turned sour when train breakdowns began to occur. Like falling dominos, progressive breakdowns eventually paralysed the entire North–South line, one of the major metro lines that connects downtown Singapore to several heavily populated suburban towns, causing the most serious train breakdown in the 24-year history of metro network operator, SMRT. The first crisis, on 15 December 2011, lasted five hours, while the second, on 17 December, lasted seven hours.

With more than 220,000 commuters affected, confusion reigned. Trains were stalled in underground tunnels and some commuters had to be guided onto the tracks and walked in the dark along the tunnels to enter the stations. When the doors of some trains did not open, and ventilation stated to fail, train windows were smashed to let air in. Those who did get out of the station were then faced with further frustration as replacement bus services did not appear for hours.

Commuters were seething. They spared no one in publicly lambasting SMRT, both online and offline. Within days, Singapore Prime Minister Lee Hsien Loong announced a Committee of Inquiry to get to the root of the problem, and try to restore SMRT's reputation. As so often happens with crises, the problems proved to have been in place long before the critical events. The issues and risks had emerged over time but were not adequately managed.

First, increasing ridership as a result of a denser population was not holistically managed. When commuters complained about constantly packed trains, CEO Saw Phaik Hwa's response showed little understanding of the risk to her organisation's reputation. She simply said: 'People can board the train—it is whether they choose to.'

Second, although SMRT increased train services to cater for higher demand, it emerged that SMRT's maintenance program had not kept pace. Saw, who resigned from SMRT shortly after the crises, was accused of focusing on generating profits by converting open spaces into rentable retail space. During her nine years in charge she doubled profits for SMRT's shareholders, but neglected to ensure trains were well maintained for her key stakeholders: the city's commuters.

Third, increased stress on the rail system should have signalled to SMRT that there would be increased risks of trains breaking down—and that SMRT needed to be more crisis-prepared. Weeks after the crises, Transport Minister Lui Tuck Yew declared in Parliament that the crises 'exposed gaps in emergency preparedness and crisis response, and we need to do better'. The lack of crisis preparedness to manage these risks later began to emerge. Train drivers said they had not been trained in emergency situations, so when trains stalled in tunnels they did not know to turn on the ventilation to ensure air circulation. And while SMRT did have a rail incident management plan, an expert witness declared it was 'too complicated'. The witness observed that senior management also lacked formal operational training.

Fourth, effective risk management begins with good communication, yet messaging from SMRT served only to damage reputation even further. When the first indications of train breakdown occurred on 15 December, a message was sent out to SMRT taxi drivers. The message, which was flashed on SMRT taxi drivers' screens, read: 'Income opportunity. Dear partners, there is a breakdown in our MRT train services from Bishan MRT to Marina Bay MRT stretch of stations.' A taxi passenger took a photo of the screen and posted it online. It went viral and drew heavy criticism.

SMRT's use of social media also drew a backlash. SMRT's official twitter @SMRT Singapore used to have this description, 'This is the official Twitter channel of SMRT. We're here, 9am-6pm, Mon-Fri (excl public holidays)'. Only later did SMRT realise that social media does not have 'official hours'.

The Committee of Inquiry met in April 2012, and by July had concluded a six-week investigation and released a 358-page report. Among the key findings were that 'a defective metal fastener in an assembly that held up a power-supplying rail had triggered the first breakdown on 15 December'. The subsequent damage to trains went undetected and that led to the second breakdown on 17 December. More importantly, SMRT's maintenance lapses and incident management were found to be wanting. SMRT promised to shift its focus back to an 'engineering-focused organisation'.

Desmond Kuek, who became CEO in October 2012, admitted there were 'deep-seated issues' within SMRT. 'There are clearly managerial, structural, cultural and systemic issues that need addressing ... And that is one of my top priorities,' he said. He has his work cut out for him. With every subsequent train breakdown, commuters are reminded of the SMRT crisis of 2011. Until commuter confidence is comprehensively restored, SMRT's reputation continues to be on the line—and on the slide whenever a breakdown occurs.

For more detailed discussion of this case see:

Pang, A. (2013). Derailed: The SMRT crisis of 2011.
Media Asia, 40(2), 124–127.

REFERENCES

Allen, M. W. & Caillouet, R. H. (1994). Legitimation endeavors: Impression management strategies used by an organisation in crisis. *Communication Monographs, 61*(1), 44–62.

Alsop, R. J. (2004). Corporate reputation: Anything but superficial—the deep but fragile nature of corporate reputation. *Journal of Business Strategy, 25*(6), 21–29.

Andriole, S. J., Schiavone, V. J., Von Hoyer, E., Langsfeld, M. D. & Harrington, M. R. (2013). *Avoiding #FAIL: Mitigating risk, managing threats and protecting the corporation in the age of social media.* Media, PA: Ascendigm Press. Available from www.listenlogic.com/esrebookdownload5150.

Argenti, P. A. & Aarons, G. (2011). Digital strategies for enhancing reputation. In A. Hiles (Ed.), *Reputation management: Building and protecting your company's profile in a digital world* (pp. 115–125). London: Bloomsbury.

Balmer, J. M. T. (2010). The BP Deepwater Horizon débâcle and corporate brand exuberance. *Journal of Brand Management, 18*(2), 97–104.

Benoit, W. L. (2013). Image repair theory and corporate reputation. In C. E. Carroll (Ed.), *Handbook of communication and corporate reputation* (pp. 213–221). New York: Wiley.

Benoit, W. L. (1997a). Image repair discourse and crisis communication. *Public Relations Review, 23*(2), 177–198.

Benoit, W. L. (1997b). Hugh Grant's image restoration discourse: An actor apologises. *Communication Quarterly, 45*(3), 251–267.

Benoit, W. L. (1995). *Accounts, excuses and apologies: A theory of image restoration strategies.* Albany, NY: State University Press of New York.

Bruno, K. (2000, 14 December). BP: Beyond Petroleum or Beyond Preposterous? *Corpwatch.* Retrieved from www.corpwatch.org/article.php?id=219.

Coombs, W. T. (2007). Protecting organisation reputations during a crisis: The development and application of situational crisis communication theory. *Corporate Reputation Review, 10*(3), 163–176.

Coombs, W. T. (2006). Crisis management: A communicative approach. In C. Botan & V. Hazleton (Eds.), *Public relations theory II* (pp. 171–197). Mahwah, NJ: Lawrence Erlbaum.

Coombs, W. T. (2002). Assessing online issue threats: Issue contagions and their effect on issue prioritisation. *Journal of Public Affairs, 2*(4), 215–229.

Coombs, W. T. (1995). Choosing the right words: The development of guidelines for the selection of 'appropriate' crisis response strategies. *Management Communication Quarterly, 8*(4), 447–476.

Coombs, W. T. & Holladay, S. J. (2002). Helping crisis managers protect reputational assets: Initial tests of the situational crisis communication theory. *Management Communication Quarterly, 16*(2), 165–186.

Diermeier, D. (2011). The cost of reputation: The impact of events on a company's financial performance. In A. Hiles (Ed.), *Reputation management: Building and protecting your company's profile in a digital world* (pp. 153–161). London: Bloomsbury.

Eccles, R. G., Newquist, S. C. & Schatz, R. (2007. February). Reputation and its risks. *Harvard Business Review,* 104–114.

Economist Intelligence Unit (2005). *Reputation: Risk of risks.* White paper by EIU. Retrieved from www.acegroup.com/eu-en/assets/risk-reputation-report.pdf.

Firestein, P. J. (2006). Building and protecting corporate reputation, *Strategy and Leadership, 34*(4), 25–31.

Hannington, T. (2004). *How to measure and manage your corporate reputation.* Aldershot, UK: Gower.

Hargreaves, S. (2008). Apple's stock hit by web rumor. CNNMoney. Retrieved from http://money.cnn.com/2008/10/03/technology/apple/.

Harlow, W. F., Brantley, B. C. & Harlow, R. M. (2011). BP initial image repair strategies after the *Deepwater Horizon* spill. *Public Relations Review, 37*(1), 80–83.

Heath, R. L. (2013). Who's in charge and what's the solution? Reputation as a matter of issue debate and risk management. In C. E. Carroll (Ed.), *Handbook of communication and corporate reputation* (pp. 388–401). New York: Wiley.

Heath, R. L. (1998). New communication technologies: An issues management point of view. *Public Relations Review, 24*(3), 273–288.

Hiles, A. (2011). How firms should fight rumours. In A. Hiles (Ed.), *Reputation management: Building and protecting your company's profile in a digital world* (pp. 1–10). London: Bloomsbury.

Hutton, J. G., Goodman, M. B., Alexander, J. B. & Genest, C. M. (2001). Reputation management: The new face of corporate public relations? *Public Relations Review, 27*(3), 247–261.

Jaques, T. (2012, January). Crisis prevention not a priority, say Australian CEOs. *CEO Magazine,* 13–15.

Institute of Practitioners in Advertising (2006). *The intangible revolution.* Retrieved from www.ipa.co.uk/Document/The-Intangible-Revolution.

Kim, S. & Wertz, E. K. (2013). Predictors of organizations' crisis communication approaches: Full versus limited disclosure. *Public Relations Review, 39*(3), 238–240.

Lamb, L. F. & McKee, K. B. (2005). Helios? A Greek god with a British accent for a global company. In *Applied Public Relations: Cases in Stakeholder Management* (pp. 232–237). Mahwah, NJ: Lawrence Erlbaum.

Macalister, T. & Cross, E. (2000, 25 July). BP rebrands on a global scale. *The Guardian*. Retrieved from www.theguardian.com/business/2000/jul/25/bp.

Pang, A., Hassan, N. B. B. A. & Chong, A. C. Y. (2014). Negotiating crisis in the social media environment: Evolution of crises online, gaining credibility offline. *Corporate Communication, 19*(1), 96–118.

Procter & Gamble awarded $19.25 million in Satanism lawsuit. (2007, 20 March). *FoxNews.com*. Retrieved from www.foxnews.com/story/2007/03/20/procter-gamble-awarded-125-million-in-satanism-lawsuit.

Richtel, M. & Barrioneuvo, A. (2005, 22 April). CSI: Wendy's Restaurants. *New York Times*. Retrieved from www.nytimes.com/2005/04/22/business/22wendys.html?pagewanted=1&_r=0.

Sandman, P. (2010). *Two kinds of reputation management*. Online article posted 3 December, 2010. Retrieved from www.psandman.com/col/reputation.htm.

Swartz, M. (2007, 13 August). Blackmail, sex, and corporate secrets. *Upstart Business Journal*. Retrieved from http://upstart.bizjournals.com/executives/features/2007/08/13/John-Browne-Public-Outing.html?page=all.

Taylor, R. (2011, 22 November). Epic fail for Qantas Twitter competition. *Reuters*. Retrieved from www.reuters.com/article/2011/11/22/us-qantas-idUSTRE7AL0HB20111122.

Temin, D. (2012). What boards must know about social media. *The Corporate Board, 33*(194), 11–15.

Thomsen, S. R. (1995). Using online databases in corporate issues management. *Public Relations Review, 21*(2), 103–122.

Wartick, S. L. (2002). Measuring corporate reputation: Definition and data. *Business and Society, 41*(4), 371–391.

Weber Shandwick. (2007). *Safeguarding reputation*. Issue No.1. Weber Shandwick survey conducted with KRC Research. Retrieved from www.corporatereputation12steps.com/Downloads/PDFs/1_WS_Safeguarding_Reputation_exec_summary.pdf.

Woodcock, C. (n.d.) *Why reputation is a major factor in business continuity management*. Blog retrieved from www.continuitycentral.com/feature0335.htm.

Working, R. (2013, 6 November). Man the barricades: 8 ways to respond to a crisis. *Ragan's PR Daily*.

FURTHER READING

Alsop, R. J. (2004). *The 18 immutable laws of corporate reputation: Creating, protecting and repairing your most valuable asset.* London: Kogan Page.

Balmer, J. M. T. & Greyser, S. A. (2011), Revealing the corporation: Perspectives on identify, image, reputation, corporate branding and corporate-level marketing (2nd ed.) London: Routledge.

Barnett, M. L., Jermier, J. M. & Lafferty, B. A. (2006). Corporate reputation: The definitional landscape. *Corporate Reputation Review, 9*(1), 26–38.

Baron, G. (2010). *Unending flow: Case study on communications in the Gulf oil spill.* Bellingham, WA: PIER Systems, Inc. Retrieved from https://www.piersystem. com/external/content/document/3571/1009367/1/Unending%20Flow_v1.01. pdf.

Benoit, W. L. & Brinson, S. L. (1999). Queen Elizabeth's image repair discourse: Insensitive royal or compassionate Queen? *Public Relations Review, 25*(2), 145–166.

Blaney, J. R., Benoit, W. L. & Brazeal, L. M. (2002). Blowout! Firestone's image restoration campaign. *Public Relations Review, 28*(4), 379–392.

Braun-LaTour, K. A., LaTour, M. S. & Loftus, E. F. (2006). Is that a finger in my chili? Using affective advertising for post-crisis brand repair. *Cornell Hotel and Restaurant Administration Quarterly, 47*(2), 106–17.

Breakenridge, D. (2008). *PR 2.0: New media, new tools, new audiences.* Upper Saddle River, NJ: Pearson Education.

Brinson, S. L. & Benoit, W. L. (1996). Dow Corning's image repair strategies in the breast implant crisis. *Communication Quarterly, 44*(1), 29–41.

Bronn, P. S. (2010). Reputation, communication and the corporate brand. In R. L. Heath (Ed.), *The Sage handbook of public relations* (2nd ed., pp. 307–320). Newbury Park, CA: Sage.

Brown, E. M. (2013). The Deepwater Horizon disaster: Challenges in ethical decision making. In S. May (Ed.), *Case Studies in organisational Communication: Ethical perspectives and practices* (2nd ed., pp. 233–245). Thousand Oaks, CA: Sage.

Caillouet, R. H. & Allen, M. W. (1996). Impression management strategies employees use when discussing their organisation's public image. *Journal of Public Relations Research, 8*(4), 211–227.

Carroll, C. (2009). The Dasani controversy: A case study of how the launch of a new brand jeopardised the entire reputation of Coca-Cola. In A. Lindgreen, M. K. Hingley & J. Vanhamme (Eds.), *The crisis of food brands: Sustaining safe, innovative and competitive food supply* (pp. 3–14). Farnham, Surrey: Gower.

Carroll, C. E. (Ed.). (2013). *The handbook of communication and corporate reputation.* Hoboken, NJ: Wiley.

Casarez, N. B. (2002). Dealing with cybersmear: How to protect your organisation from online defamation. *Public Relations Quarterly, 47*(2), 40–45.

Cheng, S. S. (2011). A corporate hero with scandal: Lessons learned from Martha Stewart's insider trading crisis. *International Journal of Humanities and Social Science, 1*(15), 12–24.

Christ, P. (2005). Internet technologies and trends transforming public relations. *Journal of Website Promotion, 1*(4), 3–14.

Coombs, W. T. (2006). The protective powers of crisis response strategies: Managing reputational assets during a crisis. *Journal of Promotion Management, 12*(3/4), 241–260.

Crawford, A. P. (1999). When those nasty rumours start breeding on the web: You've got to move fast. *Public Relations Quarterly, 44*(4), 43–45.

Diermeier, D. (2011). *Reputation rules: Strategies for building your company's most valuable asset.* New York: McGraw-Hill.

Doorley, J. & Garcia, H. F. (2005). *Reputation management: A key to successful corporate and organisational communication.* London: Routledge.

Ferguson, D. P., Wallace, J. D. & Chandler, R. C. (2012). Rehabilitating your organisation's image: public relations professionals' perceptions of the effectiveness and ethicality of image repair strategies in crisis situations. *Public Relations Journal, 6*(1).

Fitch, K. (2012). Social media. In J. Chia & G. Synnott (Eds.), *An introduction to public relations: From theory to practice.* (2nd ed., pp. 370–391). Melbourne: Oxford University Press.

Fombrun, C. J. & Van Riel, C. (1997). The reputational landscape. *Corporate Reputation Review, 1*(1), 5–13.

Gotsi, M. & Wilson, A. M. (2001). Corporate reputation: Seeking a definition. *Corporate Communications: An International Journal, 6*(1), 24–30.

Gregory, A. (2013). Corporate reputation and the discipline of communication management. In C. E. Carroll (Ed.), *Handbook of communication and corporate reputation* (pp. 81–93). New York: Wiley.

Henderson, T. & Williams J. (2002). Shell: Managing a corporate reputation globally. In D. Moss & B. DeSanto (Eds.), *Public relations cases: International perspectives* (pp. 10–25). London: Routledge.

Heffernan, M. (2011). Out of sight, out of mind: BP Texas City case study. In *Willful Blindness: Why we ignore the obvious at our peril* (pp. 161–166). New York: Walker and Co.

Hiles, A. (Ed.). (2011). *Reputation management: Building and protecting your company's profile in a digital world.* London: Bloomsbury.

Hopkins, A. (2009). *Failure to learn: The BP Texas City refinery disaster.* Sydney: CCH Australia.

Howell, G. V. J. (2012). An issues-crisis perspective. In J. Chia & G. Synott (Eds.), *An introduction to public relations and communication management* (2nd ed., pp. 312–366). Melbourne: Oxford University Press.

Howell, G. V. J. & Miller, R. (2006). Spinning out the asbestos agenda: How big business uses public relations in Australia. *Public Relations Review, 32*(3), 261–266.

Jaques, T. (2009). Issue management as a post-crisis discipline: Identifying and responding to issue impacts beyond the crisis. *Journal of Public Affairs, 9*(1), 35–44.

Karmark, E. (2013). Corporate branding and corporate reputation. In C. E. Carroll (Ed.), *Handbook of communication and corporate* reputation (pp. 446–458). New York: Wiley.

Keinan, A., Farrelly, F. & Beverland, M. (2012). *Introducing iSnack 2.0: The new Vegemite.* Harvard Business School Case study. Published 20 April 2012.

Kewell, B. (2007). Linking risk and reputation: A research agenda and methodological analysis. *Risk Management, 9(4)*, 238–254.

Larkin, J. (2003). *Strategic reputation risk management.* Basingstoke: Palgrave Macmillan.

Macnamara, J. (2010). Public communication practices in the Web 2.0–3.0 mediascape: The case for PRevolution. *PRism, 7*(3).

Macnamara, J. (2009). Public relations in the interactive age: New practices, not just new media. *Asia Pacific Public Relations Journal, 10*, 1–16.

McCorkindale, T. & DiStaso, M. W. (2013). The power of social media and its influence on corporate reputation. In C. E. Carroll (Ed.), *Handbook of communication and corporate reputation* (pp. 497–512). New York: Wiley.

Meyers, A. A. (2011). *Crisis communication and image repair strategies: Audience attitude and perceptions of Toyota in an online environment.* Thesis, Valdosta State University, GA. Retrieved from http://vtext.valdosta.edu:8080/jspui/handle/10428/1102?mode=full.

Mulvey, P. (2008). *Reputation really matters: How to guard your corporate image.* Melbourne: Monterey Press.

Patel, A. & Xavier, R. (2005). Legitimacy challenged: James Hardie Industries and the asbestos case. *Australian Journal of Communication, 32*(1), 53–69.

Rayner, J. (2003). *Managing reputational risk: Curbing threats, leveraging opportunities.* Chichester, UK: Wiley. Retrieved from http://educationists.pbworks.com/f/125481___managing_reputational_risk_curbing_threats__leveraging_opportunities_9780471499510.pdf.

Schwartz, P. & Gibbs, B. (1999). *When good companies do bad things: Reputation and risk in an age of globalisation.* New York: Wiley.

Sims, R. (2009). Towards a better understanding of organisational efforts to rebuild reputation following an ethical scandal. *Journal of Business Ethics, 90*(4), 453–472.

Smith, E. A. & Malone, R. E. (2003). Altria means tobacco: Phillip Morris's identity crisis. *American Journal of Public Health, 93*(4), 553–556.

Steffy, L. C. (2011). *Drowning in Oil: BP and the relentless pursuit of profit.* New York: McGraw Hill.

Ulmer, R. R., Sellnow, T. L. & Seeger, M. W. (2009). Post-crisis communication and renewal: Understanding the potential for positive outcomes in crisis communication. In R. L. Heath & H. D. O'Hair (Eds.), *Handbook of risk and crisis communication.* New York: Routledge.

Walker, K. (2010). A systematic review of the corporate reputation literature: Definition, measurement, and theory. *Corporate Reputation Review, 12*(4), 357–387.

Wright, D. K. & Hinson, M. D. (2010). A three year longitudinal analysis of social and emerging new media use in public relations practice. *Public Relations Journal, 5*(3).

12

LEADERSHIP AND THE FUTURE

CHAPTER OBJECTIVES

This chapter will help you to:

+ understand corporate social responsibility

+ revisit the integrated relational model

+ consider the future of the process approach to crisis management

+ place issue and crisis management within the broader context of executive capability

+ evaluate the importance of leadership in managing risks, issues and crises

+ assess the developing impact of social media

+ recognise developing trends.

Earlier chapters focused on the individual elements of an integrated management process— issue and crisis management, risk communication and reputation—and the mechanisms that link these critical activities and make them part of an integrated management response to potential threats to the organisation and society.

This chapter looks at possible future trends in these activities as they intersect and combine to create a framework for development, and examines one key factor that is common across them all: the role of effective leadership and how it drives success or failure. We also explore additional aspects of the impact and implications of further development in digital communication and social media. Before proceeding, however, it is worth spending a little time looking at one management response that could play a continuing role in the future: corporate social responsibility.

CORPORATE SOCIAL RESPONSIBILITY

Seen in the context of issue management and reputation, corporate social responsibility (CSR) provides a useful model for future development. CSR is not usually regarded as an explicit response to the threat of issues and crises, yet it has a great deal to do with the impact of issues and crises on reputation.[1] Moreover, it has a lot to do with an integrated cross-functional approach to potential threats and other complex challenges.

In risk management there is already a specific practice that addresses this broad approach: enterprise risk management (ERM). The formal definition of ERM (see the box) highlights all of these key elements (and could apply equally to issue management). While the emphasis in this definition is on shareholder value, CSR similarly captures the essential themes: structure, discipline, cross-functional alignment and addressing the needs of the organisation as a whole.

ENTERPRISE RISK MANAGEMENT

Enterprise risk management is a structured and disciplined approach aligning strategy, processes, people, technology and knowledge with the purpose of evaluating and managing the uncertainties the enterprise faces as it creates value. 'Enterprise wide' means the removal of traditional functional, divisional, departmental and cultural barriers. A truly holistic, integrated and future-focused and process-oriented approach helps an organisation manage all key business risks and opportunities with the intent of maximising shareholder value for the enterprise as a whole.[2]

Source: KPMG (2001, p. 3).

---

1 For the idea of CSR as reputation insurance, see Minor and Morgan (2011) in this chapter's Further reading section. See also Bebbington, Larrinaga and Moneva (2008) on the relationship between corporate social reporting and reputation risk management.
2 For a detailed discussion of enterprise risk management, see Chitakornkijsil (2010) and Nocco and Stultz (2006) in this chapter's Further reading section.

CSR has been described as actions that appear to further some social good beyond the interests of the firm, and beyond that which is required by the law (McWilliams & Siegel, 2001). While there have been scores of definitions, one respected formal description is that developed by the International Organization for Standardization for its *Guidance Standard on Social Responsibility* (ISO, 2010), known as ISO 26000:

> Social responsibility is the responsibility of an organization for the impacts of its decisions and activities on society and the environment, through transparent and ethical behaviour that
>
> + contributes to sustainable development, including the health and the welfare of society
>
> + takes into account the expectations of stakeholders
>
> + is in compliance with applicable law and consistent with international norms of behaviour; and
>
> + is integrated throughout the organization and practised in its relationships.

The definition developed by Harvard Business School (n.d.) is also widely cited:

> Corporate social responsibility encompasses not only what companies do with their profits, but also how they make them. It goes beyond philanthropy and compliance and addresses how companies manage their economic, social, and environmental impacts, as well as their relationships in all key spheres of influence: the workplace, the marketplace, the supply chain, the community, and the public policy realm.

The Harvard definition goes on to emphasise that the term 'corporate social responsibility' is often used interchangeably with corporate responsibility, corporate citizenship, social enterprise, sustainability, sustainable development, triple-bottom line, corporate ethics and, in some cases, corporate governance. Although these terms are different, they all point in the same direction: throughout the industrialised world and in many developing countries there has been a sharp escalation in the social roles corporations are expected to play. The Harvard authors conclude that companies are facing new demands to engage in public–private partnerships and are under growing pressure to be accountable not only to shareholders but also to stakeholders such as employees, consumers, suppliers, local communities, policymakers, and society-at-large (Harvard Business School, n.d.).

One activity mentioned in the ISO2600 standard is corporate philanthropy—when organisations perform charitable actions that may be designed to make the corporation feel good, but aren't necessarily linked to the legitimate expectations of society (Tench, 2014). Tench says that philanthropy is often a short-term, one-way relationship that may be unpredictable on behalf of the recipient, and that may not be a reliable guide to the moral or ethical performance of the donor. For example, an organisation may donate generous amounts of cash to a local children's charity, yet at the same time it generates profits by importing goods made by child labour in developing countries.

Companies frequently justify expenditure on CSR programs by referring to the notion of 'enlightened self-interest'—where everyone benefits. However, Somerville and Wood (2012) propose that there are really two distinct approaches. They say public relations practitioners can use CSR as just another element in 'the creation or engineering of consent' in order to foster 'a favourable and positive climate of opinion towards the institution'. Alternatively, it can be used to 'try to realise the idea that public relations can act in the public interest by making genuine attempts to discover the requirements of community stakeholders or help companies be more responsive to social needs' (p. 192).

> Every organisation must assume full responsibility for its impact on its employees, the environment, customers and whomever and whatever it touches. That is its social responsibility.
>
> Peter Drucker (2009, p. 61)

Somerville and Wood say it is clear that many businesses maintain that to act in a socially responsible way implies that business is motivated by more than just self-interest, and is, in fact, an activity that aims to promote the interests of society at large. In this regard, one early definition of CSR came from the respected management academic, Archie Carroll, who described CSR as 'the economic, legal, ethical and discretionary expectations that society has of organisations at a given point in time' (Carroll, 1979, p. 500).

This approach aligns closely with one of the three main issue management models described in Chapter 1—the expectation gap (or legitimacy gap) theme—and also the reputation–reality gap described in Chapter 11. As previously discussed, in recent years the expectation gap theme has attracted renewed attention with the rise of social media creating an increasingly broad circle of stakeholders and other interested parties, and providing them with the tools to express very strongly and widely their opinions about any perceived gap between expectation and performance. This, in turn, has caused managers and boards to once again question the role of the organisation in society, which establishes a very clear alignment between issue management and CSR.

CSR is not without its critics, including some within the profession of communications and public affairs. In fact, it has been called 'a contested concept' (Broomhill, 2007). This contest about CSR comes mainly from two directions:

+ legitimacy—whether it is a proper expenditure for business organisations
+ authenticity—whether it is genuine or just 'spin'.

The question of legitimacy builds on the view of the free-market economist Milton Friedman (1970), who famously argued that the sole social responsibility of a business organisation is to use its resources to engage in activities designed to increase profits for its shareholders. He suggests it is wrong to imply that corporations have other social responsibilities. Similarly, the US academic John Holcomb (2005) has argued that, despite support from some theorists and popular books and journals, many public relations/ public affairs practitioners and senior management are not enamoured with the term and concept of CSR. He says CSR is often seen as 'appendage efforts such as philanthropy, often not centrally related to core functions of the firm' (p. 40). However, this legitimacy argument seems to have waned in recent years and CSR continues as a core enterprise approach.

The more persistent criticism of CSR relates to authenticity—that some organisations use it a publicity shield that focuses on creating a positive image rather than actual positive performance (which is also a criticism of some aspects of issue management). Indeed, Benn, Todd and Pendleton (2010) say that the some of the most trenchant scholarly criticism of CSR has hinged on its role as a public relations or branding exercise. One example is the idea of 'greenwash' (introduced in Chapter 11), which is when an organisation cynically promotes green-based environmental initiatives, images or product claims that are insubstantial or misleading, or when the organisation may actually be operating a way that damages the environment.

As in the field of issue management and reputation, such criticism frequently comes from anti-corporate or environmental activists.[3] An early activist critic who specifically targeted CSR was Amnesty International's Peter Frankental (2001), who argued that CSR had become a 'PR invention'. He said CSR can have real substance only if it embraces all the stakeholders of a company; if it is reinforced by changes in company law relating to governance; if it is rewarded by financial markets; if its definition relates to the goals of social and ecological sustainability; if its implementation is benchmarked and audited; if it is open to public scrutiny; if the compliance mechanisms are in place; and if it is embedded across the organisation horizontally and vertically.

This concern is also expressed by some business commentators worried about authenticity. In fact, de Bussy (2009) notes such concern comes from both ends of the political spectrum. He says, for example, the liberal US corporate critic Joel Bakan and the pro-business conservative Australian journalist Janet Albrechtsen are in agreement that CSR is 'essentially a fraud, designed to mask the true intentions and actions of corporations' (de Bussy, 2006, p. 230).

Although some organisations now incorporate the principles of CSR within a broader approach under the label of sustainability, it is clear that, when properly executed, CSR can contribute to corporate image and reputation; can differentiate organisations; and can provide competitive advantage.[4] Good reputation in turn makes it easier to recruit and motivate employees; to enhance and add value to the organisation's products and services; and to encourage others to be more willing to consider the organisation's point of view (Tench, 2014). This last benefit is especially important when it comes to issue management and risk communication. As explained in Chapter 10 (in discussion of the trust determination theory), stakeholders are more willing and more likely to accept information on controversial issues and complex risks from an organisation they know and trust, and CSR can help build that awareness and trust. Moreover, Jen Boynton (2013), in the *Harvard Business Review* online, says the business case for CSR 'is becoming easier and easier to make':

> You can argue that it boosts a company's brand, manages risk and just plain saves money. But perhaps most importantly the general public is clamouring for companies to enact good, fair business practices—and most of that public pressure comes through social media.

---

3   For an activist view of greenwashing, see Bruno (2012) and Lubbers (2001) in this chapter's Further reading section. For an Australian perspective, see Pearse (2014), also in this chapter's Further reading section.

4   Future developments of CSR are assessed in detail in Golob et al. (2103) in this chapter's Further reading section.

The purpose here is not a detailed analysis of CSR.[5] Rather it is to identify CSR as an example of an enterprise-wide commitment to utilise resources and coordinate actions to achieve certain strategic objectives that may not, in the short term, be just about dollars and cents and the bottom line. Moreover, CSR illustrates that such a holistic approach—especially in sensitive areas such as issue management and reputation—cannot be achieved without effective integration across the organisation.

INTEGRATION OF SYSTEMS

In line with the inclusive nature of CSR—demanding comprehensive involvement across management functions—one of the most important developments over the last decade for the present discussion has been the emergence of a greater integration of issue and crisis management systems and their support programs, and the evolution of the process approach to crisis management.

A relational model was introduced in Chapter 1 (reproduced here in Figure 12.1) and further examination suggests that integration is a trend likely to continue in the future. The model not only highlights the existence of distinct pre-crisis and post-crisis phases, but it also illustrates the way in which many other activities—including issue management, risk communication, emergency response, strategic planning and business continuity—become integrated and contribute to overall reputation.

Figure 12.1 Issue and crisis management relational model

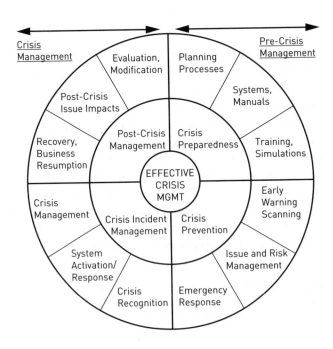

Source: Jaques (2007).

---

5   For analysis of CSR see sources in the chapter's Further reading section.

Previous chapters have provided many instances where there is a lack of agreement over competing definitions of various communication activities and how they relate to each other. As new variations continue to appear, the definitional approach in the future is likely to become more complex rather than simpler. At the same time, the increasingly rapid development of the internet and social media has further blurred the boundaries between activities, between the roles of the participants and between media.

While some professionals continue to argue about which corporate discipline properly 'owns' social media—for example, public relations, marketing, branding, advertising or customer service (to name but a few)—the reality is that traditional media and digital media are themselves increasingly integrating. In fact, it may not be long before these distinctions become irrelevant and we once again simply refer to all communication channels as 'the media'.

As these communication tools increasingly integrate, so too do the management and communication activities they support, none more so than with issue and crisis management and risk communication. Chapter 6 noted that this integration is most distinctly seen in the development of the so-called process approach to crisis management. The traditional event approach presents a crisis as a stand-alone occurrence, with the management focus on getting ready for the event before it happens; responding when it strikes; and restoring business-as-usual as quickly as possible when it is over.

By contrast, the emerging process approach—in line with the relational model above—includes these same basic phases of preparedness, response and recovery, but presents a crisis as one step in a much more complex continuum of activity. It recognises that the contributing elements to any crisis usually appear long before the triggering event; that there are many activities which can help prevent the crisis happening at all (including issue management and risk communication); and that a range of management activities after the crisis itself are critical to how well the organisation recovers in the longer term and the impact on its reputation.

Holladay and Coombs (2013, p. 452) concluded: 'Just as stakeholder perceptions determine whether a crisis or risk exists, stakeholder perceptions of an organisation's response to a threat determines whether the organisation has responded, or has responded appropriately'.

Most importantly for the present discussion, the process approach means the evolution of an increasingly intimate relationship between issue and crisis management, which should only increase in the future to the benefit of both disciplines. However, the desired outcomes of issues better managed and more crises avoided is not inevitable and will not happen without the presence of a crucial ingredient—effective executive leadership.[6]

THE ROLE OF LEADERSHIP

Like many of the terms used in this book, 'leadership' is a difficult concept to define. Waters (2013) says that although academics and industry leaders intuitively know what leadership means, it has different meanings for different people. He cites research that in the past

---

6   For an exploration of leadership styles and motivation in relation to CSR in Australian-based corporations, see Benn, Todd and Pendleton (2010) in this chapter's Further reading section.

50 years more than sixty-five theories have been proposed to describe leadership and quality leadership.

> The first responsibility of a leader is to define reality.
>
> Max DePree (2004, p. 11)

When it comes to public relations, one of the key approaches is the contingency theory. Rather than proposing the two-way symmetrical approach to public relations as the ideal approach for practitioners (see Chapter 5), the contingency theory advocates that as situations and environmental factors change, public relations people should adapt their campaigns and programs based on those factors. Moreover, a study of US practitioners (Waters, 2013) found that they are 'most often oriented to be leaders in situations that focus on organisational relationship issues' (p. 332). This is very important for issue and crisis management, which are concerned largely with organisational relationships.

In the same way that CSR and systems integration (as described above) need effective leaders and commitment from executive management, so too is real leadership needed for issue and crisis management to be successful. Much of the literature on leadership in this area focuses on crisis management rather than issue management.[7] However, a theme throughout this book is that issue and crisis management are different elements on a common management continuum. As a result, the need for leadership and the demands on individual leaders are very consistent between the two.

It's not surprising that a crisis situation turns the spotlight on leaders. As Gaines-Ross (2008) says, CEOs are regarded by many stakeholders as the human face of any organisation: 'Just as CEOs receive most of the credit when things go right, they are also expected to accept the majority of the blame when things go wrong, particularly in times of crisis' (p. 42). She adds that her research found, 'when crisis strikes, nearly 60 per cent of the responsibility for the crisis is attributed to the CEO' (p. 31).

One result of this attention on the CEO is that a lot of the available material concentrates on the role of the leader as spokesperson in a crisis. The subject of the crisis spokesperson is covered in detail in Chapter 7, which also includes results from a survey of Australian CEOs identifying what they believe are the roles of a leader a crisis (Jaques, 2012a). A key conclusion here is that crisis (and issue) leadership is about much more than just speaking on behalf of the organisation—albeit a crucial responsibility. For example:

+ Leaders need to be able to help identify issue and crisis threats early and have the forethought to assign sufficient resources to make a difference.

+ They need to break down functional barriers to drive the integration of issue and crisis management systems.

+ They need to be able to recognise that issues and crisis may represent an opportunity as well as a threat.[8]

---

7 For typical material on crisis leadership, see Berger and Meng (2010), Klann (2003), Levick (2011) and Mitroff (2004) in this chapter's Further reading section.

8 For discussion on how executives can develop an understanding of 'crisis as opportunity', see Brockner & James (2008) in this chapter's Further reading section.

+ They need to provide an example to managers throughout the organisation to take personal responsibility for developing and implementing effective issues plans to help prevent crises happening in the first place.

> Communication is the centrepiece of effective leadership.
>
> American public relations pioneer Edward Bernays

However, it is clear that there are special leadership qualities needed when a crisis actually strikes. Many writers in this field have noted that crisis management is not a discipline to be learned on the job, in the midst of the storm. As shown by the examples given in Chapter 7, some leaders who operate well when the sun is shining are found wanting when everything starts to go wrong. The reality is that crisis management is a test of the quality and character of leaders as much as it is a test of their skills and expertise (Hesselbein, 2002).

Dominic Cockram, CEO of the British crisis consultancy Steelhenge, says that while each crisis situation is unique to the organisation involved, every crisis requires leadership, both internally and externally, in front of the public, the media and a plethora of other stakeholders (see the box, 'Leadership in crisis management'). Cockram (2013) concludes that, as the human face of the organisation, it is not just personal reputation which is at risk but also that of the whole organisation:

> When a leader appears in control, confident and empathetic, they can win the trust of the public and safeguard the reputation both of themselves and their organisation, and move forward towards a resolution.

LEADERSHIP IN CRISIS MANAGEMENT

A good leader provides the crisis management team with:

+ *Focus.* A strong leader provides focus in a complex and fast-moving situation, identifying what really matters and allowing necessary actions to move more quickly.

+ *Direction.* A leader provides direction and guidance to people when they most need it, moving them quickly towards achieving that all-important control of the situation.

+ *Decision.* It is the role of the leader to make difficult decisions, almost always in the face of uncertainty and often with unhappy outcomes as the 'lesser of two evils'.

+ *Support.* An effective leader gives support to those less strong than themselves, helping to manage emotions in very tense environments.

+ *Humanity.* A good leader gives the organisation a human face, which the public needs to see in any crisis.

+ *Drive.* Preventing procrastination and decision avoidance is a leader's role.

+ *Clarity*. This is a great challenge, but if the leader can give clarity to an otherwise chaotic situation, then control will soon follow.

+ *Accountability.* The ultimate accountability for the way the incident is managed lies with the leader; this is often a double edged sword that can—and frequently does—result in resignation.

Source: Dominic Cockram (2013). Reprinted with permission.

FUTURE TRENDS

The great Danish physicist Niels Bohr once quipped: 'Prediction is very difficult, especially about the future.' The purpose here is not to attempt precise predictions, but there are some trends in public affairs and corporate communication that seem likely to influence the future development of issue and crisis management and risk communication:

1. relationships and engagement

2. establishing real systems

3. identifying potential issues and crises

4. the evolving role of issue and crisis management

5. the rise of social media.

1 RELATIONSHIPS AND ENGAGEMENT

One of the fundamental changes in the past 20 years is that organisations are spending less time trying to control public opinion and more time trying to join the conversation. Traditional strategies for improving reputations, serving communities and influencing public policy have been insufficient or ineffective (Pinkham, 2013). As Pinkham summarised it: 'One way communication is out. Stakeholder engagement is in.'

Progress towards greater stakeholder engagement is not new. The notion of 'two-way symmetrical communication' as a model for excellence, as championed by James and Larissa Grunig, was introduced in Chapter 5. It was explained that it now has some critics who suggest it may be an idealisation rather than a practical model.

Working towards engagement and the establishment of real relationships (as, for example, with CSR) is a fundamental shift that continues to gain momentum, especially with social media creating new tools for relationship-building and also creating new expectations among stakeholders that organisations have a duty and obligation to engage.

This is nowhere more evident than in issue management, where the transition from one-way communication to engagement is particularly advanced. This was well illustrated by Fischhoff's evolution of risk communication (see the box in Chapter 10) from 'All we need to do is get the numbers right' to genuine engagement.

Some academics suggest that the study of public relations should actually be about public *relationships*. This is certainly true in issue management, where Robert Boutilier

(2011, p. 3) presented this idea in a vivid analogy: 'Trying to manage issues without developing relationships with the groups and people behind them is like trying to direct a movie by going online and changing the script without ever talking to the actors or crew'.

Of course, authentic engagement is not easy, especially with executives who still persist with the 'We'll tell them what they need to know' approach. Moreover, it takes effort and leadership. As Doug Pinkham (2013), CEO of the Public Affairs Council, concluded:

> It's important to remember that effective stakeholder management is labour-intensive and requires both attention and long-term commitment. Otherwise, in an inter-connected world, even a well-meaning company can look incompetent or hypocritical.

2 ESTABLISHING REAL SYSTEMS

This risk of looking incompetent or hypocritical leads directly to the second trend: the need for real commitment and authentic systems. Not only is the world of social media very fast-moving, but it is also extraordinarily unforgiving.

It is true that some 'social media disasters' are in reality trivial affairs, driven by a handful of over-excited bloggers (see Chapter 9). But it is also true that the speed and spread of social media and data exchange means that genuine failures in issue and crisis management and risk communication are more likely to be exposed and more likely to create lasting damage. Moreover, the growing use of social media for citizen response in real disasters will increase concerns about trust and reputation. Which reports should be trusted and which might be due to malicious behaviour (Hiltz, Diaz & Mark, 2011)? These reasons and more demonstrate why organisations must build issue and crisis management processes that are genuine and robust, with real executive support.

An instructive example of the need for organisational authenticity is the much-analysed case of the ill-fated US energy trading company Enron.[9] The company was a media darling in the 1990s and was regarded as a great corporate citizen. It was the most admired global company in the year 2000; for six years it was ranked the USA's most innovative company; and it enjoyed three years rated as one of the best companies to work for. But in early 2001 it collapsed into financial disaster, with its senior executives sent to prison for dishonesty. While the company then became a media whipping boy for mismanagement and executive hubris, it also demonstrates the vital link between process and reality. Robert Heath (2002, p. 211) says that Enron:

> ... developed a mammoth database monitoring and response system that could track threats and opportunities, calculate impact on business plans and operations, and suggest coordinated responses. This was the essence of an excellent issues management program that had at least one fatal flaw, a commitment to corporate responsibility that truly reflected the reality of sound business practices rather than sheer opportunism.

---

9 The Enron collapse has been widely examined as a case study in areas including accounting, ethics, executive crime and corporate culture. For analysis from the perspective of public affairs and issue and crisis management, see Bowen and Heath (2005), Conrad and Poole (2005), Lordan (2002) and Seeger and Ulmer (2003) in this chapter's Further reading section.

The underlying problem here was well captured by Sims and Brinkmann (2003), who described the Enron case as one where 'culture matters more than codes'.

Some experts argue that better controls today make such a financial disaster less likely. But the evidence suggests that executive dishonesty or misbehaviour is still one of the greatest causes of organisational crises. For example, Gehrke (2012) says: 'the largest category of intentional crises occur due to unethical leadership practices or decisions' (p. 151). Whatever the raw statistics show, it seems clear that issue and crisis management will remain in strong demand to try to prevent such crises and to protect reputations.

3 IDENTIFYING POTENTIAL ISSUES AND CRISES

One of the most important characteristics that distinguish both issue and crisis management when operating at peak effectiveness is proactivity; that is, identifying problems and potential threats early and taking planned action to avoid or reduce impact to the organisation and its reputation. This planned, pre-emptive approach is covered in detail in earlier chapters, which emphasised repeatedly the importance of taking action in advance rather than reacting to situations that are already out of control. To paraphrase Thierry Pauchant and Ian Mitroff (cited in Chapter 1):

> There is a crucial difference between *crisis management*—including why crises happen in the first place and what can be done to prevent them—as opposed to *crash management*—what to do when everything falls apart.

While the importance of identifying potential issues and crisis is now well established, it will probably be even more important in the future, with new tools emerging, including social media. The pace at which issues and crises develop is likely to increase, as is the speed at which they progress along the life cycle from concern to problem to issue to crisis. In fact, the 'new economy' approach has already thrown up what some people call the e-life cycle (see Chapter 2) in which issues can escalate much faster and potentially end more quickly; where multiple platforms increase media momentum and impact on the organisation; and where there is an even higher risk of synergy with or contagion to other issues.

> Spectacular crisis management begins with great issue management.
>
> Canadian public relations practitioner John Larsen (2005)

Not only are issues and crises likely to develop much faster, but the changing expectations of a digital, risk-averse society also suggest the nature of threats that need to be identified are also changing. As mentioned earlier in this chapter, the rise of social media has created an increasingly broad circle of stakeholders and other interested parties, and has provided them with the tools to express very strongly and widely their opinions about what they believe are the issues which need to be addressed. For example, Doh and Guay (2006, p. 51) suggest that 'the emergence of NGOs that seek to promote what they perceive to be more ethical and socially responsible business practices is beginning to generate substantial changes in corporate management, strategy and governance'.

To meet this, organisations will need increasingly sophisticated and flexible tools to identify new varieties of potential threats and issues. This will require senior management support and commitment, as well as skilled issue and crisis management professionals able to navigate an increasingly complex field.

4 THE EVOLVING ROLE OF ISSUE AND CRISIS MANAGEMENT

The future challenge for issue and crisis management is twofold: first, to establish and maintain a strategic focus; and second, for the two disciplines to work more closely together while sustaining distinct identities.

As with the evolution of public affairs more generally (see Figure 12.2), issue and crisis management have the opportunity to develop a much more strategic focus. But it won't just happen. The British practitioner Simon Titley (2003) has argued that the public affairs industry needs to master trends if it is not to be their victim. 'The choice for practitioners,' he says, 'is whether they want the industry to mature into a supplier of business-critical strategic consultancy, or decline into a provider of ad hoc tactics' (p. 84).

While practitioners have this choice, it also depends on the degree to which a more strategic approach is embraced by overloaded and risk-averse executives (Jaques, 2012b).

Figure 12.2 The evolving role of public affairs and issue management

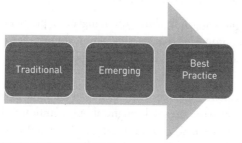

Traditional	Emerging	Best Practice

Problem dump	Resource/consultant to line managers	Integrated part of management team
PR orientation	Communication professional	Strategic partner
Communication outward	Listening and sharing	Two way communication
Reactive	Reactive but moving towards relationship building	Seen as creating commercial advantage
Focus on protecting existing businesses and markets	Focus on changing the policy paradigm	Focus on strategic options
Responding to external threats	Proposing new or alternative policy recommendations	Helping identify new market/business opportunities

Source: adapted with permission from Australasian Centre for Corporate Public Affairs.

It is not simply about communication professionals securing a seat in the boardroom. As illustrated in this book, they need to demonstrate that they can be a strategic partner and add value to the organisation as a whole.

The question of discipline identity is about much more than just professionals protecting their turf. The way issue and crisis management are taught, implemented and positioned within the organisation are crucial to the future of the two disciplines.

The danger of encroachment by more fashionable and more established activities and professions is nothing new and is very real. In some organisations today, issue management is being subsumed into sustainability, government affairs or even marketing, while crisis management may find itself taken over by emergency response engineers or by IT people in business continuity. At the same time, some law firms now have departments offering advice on crisis management; insurance companies provide consulting on risk communication; and accounting firms say they can manage systems for reputation management. And, as previously mentioned, an endless parade of departments and professions claim to be the experts on all aspects of social media.

However, as argued in the chapters of this book, issue and crisis management are distinct, specialist disciplines that embrace a unique range of tools and processes, and offer real value to organisations of all types. The process approach to issue and crisis management, described in detail in Chapter 6, provides a valuable way forward for both disciplines to retain their separate identities and also to become fully integrated as true strategic activities.

5 THE RISE OF SOCIAL MEDIA

In spite of Niels Bohr's warning about the dangers of prediction (see above), there is probably little risk in proposing that the single most important trend to impact the future of issue and crisis management will be the ongoing development of the internet and social media.

The previous chapters included many examples of ways in which the new tools of digital communication have already brought about significant changes to public affairs and communication in general, and specifically to issue and crisis management and risk communication. While this trend will undoubtedly continue, disagreement remains about the extent to which these changes represent simply new tools to achieve old tasks, or changes to the fundamental nature of those tasks.

The former argument is typified by Dallas Lawrence (2013), who wrote: 'From Gutenberg to Zuckerberg, good PR efforts have not changed. We are just so tied up in the new platforms that are out there, we forget the basic media relations practices.' A more moderate position is taken by the US crisis expert, Tim Coombs (2014, p. 325):

> If you believe the hype, the Internet has revolutionised crisis public relations management, rendering all previous knowledge on the subject obsolete. A word of advice, do not believe the hype. Yes, the Internet has changed crisis public relations management, just as it has changed all other aspects of public relations. But we are witnessing evolution, rather than revolution.

Or, as one commentator has noted, social media is an important ingredient in the meal, but it isn't the main course.

However, argument about the relative importance of social media is not very helpful. Marshall McLuhan, the Canadian philosopher of media theory (who reportedly predicted the World Wide Web 30 years before its invention), advised: 'First we shape our tools, and thereafter our tools shape us' (McLuhan, 1994, p. xxi). This is certainly true for issue and crisis management. Both of these disciplines began well before the rise of the internet[10] and, as detailed in previous chapters, have subsequently seen major changes, many of them driven by the new capabilities made possible by social media. In this way, digital communication has become an important tool, and has also created changes that would never have been foreseen by the pioneers of issue and crisis management who have been introduced here.

In precisely the same way, we have no way of foreseeing exactly how issue and crisis management will evolve in years to come. But it seems a sure bet that both will continue to be key influential disciplines for managers and executives everywhere.

KEY POINTS

+ Corporate social responsibility (CSR) is a useful model for aligning organisational functions to achieve strategic objectives.

+ Effective issue and crisis management demands genuine integration of systems and support programs.

+ Leadership is a central common factor in determining success at both strategic and operational level.

+ Some key trends can be identified that are likely to influence the future development of issue and crisis management and risk communication:

    – moving from one-way communication towards authentic relationships and engagement—with critics as well as supporters

    – establishing real systems—changing the organisation's nature, not just its image

    – developing ways to identify new varieties of potential issues and threats

    – responding to the evolution from tactical response to strategic partner

    – recognising and adapting to the demands and opportunities of social media.

≡ ACTIVITIES AND DISCUSSION

1. Why is it important to take a multi-stakeholder approach to identifying standards for CSR?

2. Discuss how CSR can reduce the issue expectation gap.

---

10   The World Wide Web as we know it today began in 1989. Facebook was launched in 2004, Twitter in 2006 and Instagram in 2010.

3. The chapter suggests that growing integration between traditional and social media means the difference in future may become irrelevant. Develop arguments to support or refute this proposition.

4. What are some of the specific leadership qualities required to optimise the linkages between issue and crisis management and to drive alignment with strategic objectives? Can those qualities be taught?

5. Explore different possible models of how issue and crisis management could be positioned within an organisational structure. Which structures and which reporting lines are most likely to produce the best outcome for the organisation?

6. Identify recent examples of crises that originated largely on social media. How did the organisation respond and what could have been improved?

REFERENCES

Benn, S., Todd, L. R. & Pendleton, J. (2010). Public relations leadership in corporate social responsibility. *Journal of Business Ethics, 96*(3), 403–423.

Boutilier, R. (2011). *A stakeholder approach to issues management.* New York: Business Expert Press.

Boynton, J. (2013, 17 July). How the voice of the people is driving corporate social responsibility. *Harvard Business Review Blog.* Retrieved from http://blogs.hbr.org/cs/2013/07/how_the_voice_of_the_people_is.html.

Broomhill, R, (2007). Corporate social responsibility: Key issues and debates. *Dunstan Paper,* 1/2007. Adelaide, Australia: Dunstan Foundation. Retrieved from http://firgoa.usc.es/drupal/files/Ray_Broomhill.pdf.

Carroll, A. B. (1979). A three dimensional conceptual model of corporate social responsibility. *Academy of Management Review, 4*(4), 497–505.

Cockram, D. (2013, February 15). Why is leadership so important in a crisis? *Business2Business* blogsite. Retrieved from www.business2community.com/crisis-management/why-is-leadership-so-important-in-a-crisis-0409549#1Gsy53yIdmWEV1qW.99.

Coombs, W. T. (2014). Crisis public relations management. In R. Tench & L. Yeomans (Eds.), *Exploring public relations* (3rd ed., pp. 313–328). Harlow: Pearson Education.

De Bussy, N. M. (2009). Reputation management: A driving force for action. In G. Synnott & J. Chia (Eds.), *An introduction to public relations: From theory to practice* (pp. 222–247). Melbourne: Oxford University Press.

DePree, M. (2004). *Leadership is an art.* (First published 1987). New York: Doubleday.

Doh, J. P. & Guay, T. R. (2006). Corporate social responsibility, public policy and NGO activism in Europe and the United States: An institutional-stakeholder perspective. *Journal of Management Studies, 43*(1), 47–73.

Drucker, P. (2009). *Managing in a time of great change.* Boston, MA: Harvard Business School Publishing.

Frankental, P. (2001). Corporate social responsibility: A PR invention? *Corporate Communications: An International Journal, 6*(1), 18–23.

Friedman, M. (1970, 30 September). The social responsibility of business is to increase its profits. *New York Times.*

Gaines-Ross, L. (2008). *Corporate reputation: 12 steps to safeguarding and recovering reputation.* Hoboken, NJ: John Wiley.

Gehrke, P. J. (2012). The crisis fallacy: Egoism, epistemology, and ethics in crisis communication and preparation. In J. M. H. Fritz, S. A. Groom, J. M. Harden-Fritz, C. E. Mattson, J. H. Prellwitz & C. G. Seymour (Eds.), *Communication ethics and crisis: Negotiating differences in public and private spheres* (pp. 133–159). Madison, NJ: Fairleigh Dickinson University Press.

Harvard Business School. (n.d). *Defining corporate social responsibility.* The Corporate Social Responsibility Initiative. Retrieved from www.hks.harvard.edu/m-rcbg/CSRI/init_define.html.

Heath, R. L. (2002). Issues management: Its past, present and future. *Journal of Public Affairs, 2*(4), 209–214.

Hesselbein, F. (2002). Crisis management: A leadership imperative. *Leader to Leader, 2,* 4–5.

Hiltz, S. R., Diaz, P. & Mark, G. (2011). Social media and collaborative systems for crisis management. *ACM Transactions on Computer–Human Transaction, 18*(4), 1–6.

Holcomb, J. H. (2005). Public affairs in North America: US origins and development. In P. Harris & C. Fleisher (Eds.), *The handbook of public affairs* (pp. 31–49). New York: Sage.

Holladay, S. J. & Coombs, W. T. (2013). Successful prevention may not be enough: A case study of how managing a threat triggers a threat. *Public Relations Review, 39*(5), 451–458.

International Organization for Standardization. (2010). *Guidance Standard on Social Responsibility.* Retrieved from https://www.iso.org/obp/ui/#iso:std:iso:26000:ed-1:v1:en.

Jaques, T. (2012a). Crisis leadership: A view from the executive suite. *Journal of Public Affairs, 12*(4), 366–372.

Jaques, T. (2012b). Is issue management evolving or progressing towards extinction? *Public Communication Review, 2*(1).

Jaques, T. (2007). Issue Management and crisis management: An integrated, non-linear, relational construct. *Public Relations Review, 33*(2), 147–157.

KPMG. (2001). *Enterprise risk management: An emerging model for building shareholder value*. White paper. Australia: KPMG International. Retrieved from www.kpmg.com.au/aci/docs/ent-risk-mgt.pdf.

Larsen, J. (2005). Issues & Crisis: The Inextricable Link. *Canadian Public Relations Society National Conference*, Calgary, Alberta, 17 June.

Lawrence, D. (2013). Vice President for Corporate Affairs at Mattel, speaking at a PR Conference in Washington DC, December 2013. Retrieved from www.burrellesluce.com/freshideas/2013/12/14-tips-for-building-your-social-media-crisis-communications-plan.

McLuhan, M. (1994). *Understanding media: The extensions of man*. Cambridge, MA: MIT Press.

McWilliams, A. & Siegel, D. (2001). Corporate social responsibility: A theory of the firm perspective. *Academy of Management Review, 26*(1), 117–126.

Pinkham, D. (2013, 18 December). Engaging conversations. *Public Affairs Perspective*. Blog post. Washington, DC: Public Affairs Council. Retrieved from http://pac.org/blog/engaging_conversations.

Sims, R. R. & Brinkmann, J. (2003). Enron ethics (or: culture matters more than codes). *Journal of Business Ethics, 45*(243–256).

Somerville, I. & Wood, E. (2012). Public relations and corporate social responsibility. In A. Theaker (Ed.), *The public relations handbook* (4th ed., pp. 175–194). Abingdon, UK: Routledge.

Tench, R. (2014). Community and society: Corporate social responsibility. In R. Tench & L. Yeomans (Eds.), *Exploring public relations* (3rd ed., pp. 46–69). Harlow: Pearson Education.

Titley, S. (2003). How political and social change will transform the EU public affairs industry. *Journal of Public Affairs 3*(1), 83–89.

Waters, R. D. (2013). The role of stewardship in leadership. *Journal of Communication Management, 17*(4), 324–340.

FURTHER READING

Bebbington, J., Larrinaga, C. & Moneva, J. M. (2008). Corporate social reporting and reputation risk management. *Accounting, Auditing and Accountability Journal, 21*(3), 337–361.

Benn, S., Todd, L. R. & Pendleton, J. (2010). Public relations leadership in corporate social responsibility. *Journal of Business Ethics, 96*(3), 403–423.

Berger, B. K. & Meng, J. (2010). Public relations practitioners and the leadership challenge. In R. L. Heath (Ed.), *The Sage handbook of public relations* (2nd ed., pp. 421–434). Newbury Park, CA: Sage.

Bowen, S. A. & Heath, R. L. (2005). Issues management, systems and rhetoric: Exploring the distinction between ethical and legal guidelines at Enron. *Journal of Public Affairs, 5*(2), 84–98.

Brockner, J. & James, E. H. (2008). Toward an understanding of when executives see crisis as opportunity. *Journal of Applied Behavioural Science, 44*(1), 94–115.

Bruno, K. (2012). *Greenwash+20: How some powerful corporations are standing in the way of sustainable development.* Amsterdam: Greenpeace International. Retrieved from www.greenpeace.org/international/en/publications/Campaign-reports/Climate-Reports/GreenwashPlus20.

Chitakornkijsil, P. (2010). Enterprise risk management. *International Journal of Organizational Innovation, 3*(2), 309–337.

Conrad, C. & Poole, M. S. (2005). Enron as a paradigm case of organizational ethics and rhetoric. *Strategic organizational communication in a global economy* (6th ed., pp. 429–441). Belmont, CA: Thomson Wadsworth.

DuBrin, A. J. (Ed.). (2013). *Handbook of research in crisis leadership in organisations.* Northampton, MA: Edward Elgar.

Golob, U., Podnar, K., Elving, W. J., Nielsen, A. E., Thomsen, C. & Schultz, F. (2013). CSR communication: Quo vadis? *Corporate Communications: An International Journal, 18*(2), 176–192.

Heath, R. L. & Palenchar, M. J. (2009). Corporate social responsibility: Getting the house in order. In *Strategic issues management: Organisations and public policy challenges* (2nd ed., pp. 125–156), Thousand Oaks, CA: Sage.

Heath, R. L.& Ni, L. (2010). Community relations and corporate social responsibility. In R. L. Heath (Ed.), *The Sage handbook of public relations* (2nd ed., pp. 557–568). Thousand Oaks, CA: Sage.

Klann, G. (2003). *Crisis leadership.* Greensboro, NC: CCL Press.

Levick, R. (2010). *The communicators: Leadership in the age of crisis.* Washington DC: Watershed Press.

Lordan, E. J. (2002). The Enron end run—PR lessons from an accounting debacle. *Public Relations Quarterly, 47*(3), 22–24.

Lubbers, E. (Ed.). (2002). *Battling big business: Countering greenwash, infiltration and other forms of corporate bullying.* Melbourne: Scribe.

Macnamara, J. (2012). *Public relations: Theories, practices, critiques.* Sydney: Pearson Australia.

Minor, D. & Morgan, J. (2011). CSR as reputation insurance. *California Management Review, 53*(3), 40–58.

Mitroff, I. I. (2004). *Crisis leadership: Planning for the unthinkable.* Hoboken, NJ: Wiley.

Nocco, B. W & Stulz, R M. (2006). Enterprise risk management: Theory and practice. *Journal of Applied Corporate Finance, 18*(4), 8–20.

Pearse, G. (2014). *The greenwash effect: Corporate deception, celebrity environmentalists, and what big business isn't telling you about their green products and brands.* New York: Skyhorse.

Schwartz, P. & Gibb, B, (1999). *When good companies do bad things: Responsibility and risk in an age of globalization.* New York: Wiley.

Seeger, M. W. & Ulmer, R. R. (2003). Explaining Enron: Communication and responsible leadership. *Management Communication Quarterly, 17*(1), 58–84.

APPENDIX: ISSUE MANAGEMENT PLAN—A FULLY WORKED EXAMPLE

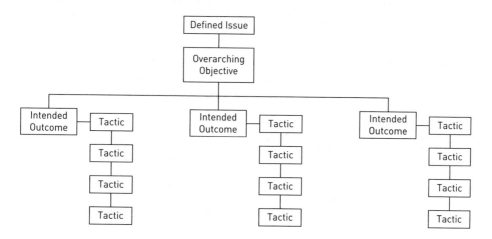

While Chapter 4 includes examples of individual elements of the Do-it Plan©, here is a fully worked hypothetical case study that includes not only suggested approaches but also discussion on the reasoning behind the proposed solutions.[1] Although this scenario has been workshopped, it is crucial to recognise that there is no right answer. Any effective issue management plan depends on appropriate choices and good judgment.

BACKGROUND

Our company is a large and well-respected food producer, with a number of high-profile brand names. One of our products is particularly popular with children and, while there are similar competitors, our product is the best known and is regarded as something of an 'icon'. It is also one of our longest-established and most profitable lines, contributing up to 25 per cent of total company revenue.

SCENARIO

From time to time in the past our product has been criticised for not being a wholesome element of a balanced diet. We have—perhaps unwisely—tended to ignore that criticism on the basis that our product is a snack item eaten for pleasure and is not intended to be a regular food.

---

1 This example is revised and updated from a case study first published in Jaques, T (2000). *Don't Just Stand there— The Do-it Plan © for Effective Issue Management.* Issue Outcomes, Melbourne.

Now, a substantial nutritional study has just been published that examined the health and diet of a large number of children. It concluded that those who consume our product regularly suffer a number of adverse health effects, including overweight, elevated blood pressure and susceptibility to a range of illnesses. Our own extensive research does not support these claims, but our corporate lawyers advise there would be no grounds for us to initiate legal action arising from the report.

While the brief initial news media interest has died down, the organisation that undertook the research is now reviving the issue by a high-profile call for a mandatory health warning on our product and similar snack foods that are marketed to children.

STEP ONE: DEFINITION

Defined Issue	Health allegations threaten the integrity of our brand name and put 25% of revenue at risk

It is essential that the issue is defined concisely and in terms of impact on the organisation itself. It should also be defined as objectively as possible.

DISCUSSION

1. It would have been tempting and even satisfying to define the issue as '*False* health allegations...'. However, that simply permits emotion to enter into the plan, and adds nothing to the issue. Proving the allegations false may be an integral part of the plan, but the issue as defined recognises that our brand product is under attack, regardless of whether or not the allegations are true.

2. It may also have been tempting to broaden the issue to reflect that our product is not the only one under attack; that the issue is an attack on the integrity of a whole class of food rather than just our brand. For example, 'Health allegations threaten the integrity of a range of snack foods ...'. Recognising that we are not alone may provide some comfort, and the involvement of others in our industry may later be an important tactic. But the issue should be defined as it affects us. Our management and shareholders are much more immediately interested in the impact on *our* brand name and *our* revenue than on how it might affect our competitors or the industry overall.

STEP TWO: OBJECTIVE

Experience has shown that agreeing on the *overarching objective* is the single most difficult phase of the Do-it Plan©. But of all the phases, it is also the one that is it most important to get exactly right. This is the core foundation upon which the entire issue management plan is built. Without a clearly defined and agreed *overarching objective*, the plan will be doomed to failure.

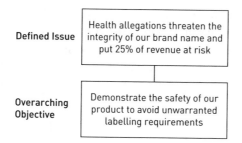

DISCUSSION

1. While the defined issue addresses profitability and market share through the impact of lost revenue, it would not have been sufficient to simply state the *overarching objective* as 'Protect the profitability of the company' or 'Ensure a continuing return on shareholder funds'. These are more appropriate as underlying business assumptions. The *overarching objective* in the issue management plan must be the specific objective for the issue under consideration, not the underlying business objective of the organisation as a whole, though obviously the issue objective must be aligned with the business strategy.

2. An *overarching objective* simply to 'Demonstrate the safety of our product' would also not be sufficient. The rule of thumb for an *overarching objective* is to ensure it is drafted to lead to reasonably self-evident actions and milestones. It would be pointless to demonstrate our product is safe, and yet still be required to provide what we believe are unwarranted health warnings on the label. Demonstrating safety is to a degree a matter of opinion, but whether or not we are required to relabel our icon brand is a demonstrable matter of fact.

3. It might have been tempting to state the *overarching objective* as 'To protect consumer confidence in our product'. That approach, however, highlights the distinction between the *overarching objective* and the *intended outcome*. First, confidence is difficult to objectively measure—other than in sales. Second, and more importantly, consumers in this case will not finally decide the fate of our product. Business history is littered with the corpses of products or services that were extremely popular with consumers, but which were unprofitable to produce or were regulated out of existence. There would be no value in ensuring consumer confidence alone if regulation effectively drove our product off the shelves. Consumer confidence is certainly important in this case, but it is clearly not an objective in itself. It is much better included as an *intended outcome* that supports the *overarching objective*.

STEP THREE: INTENDED OUTCOMES

Not only are the *intended outcomes* the 'bite-sized pieces' that will deliver the *overarching objective*, but they are often interrelated or interdependent. As a result, they sometimes appear to be two sides of the same concept. There is no hard and fast rule, but the general answer usually lies in the detail of potential *tactics* (that is, the actions to deliver each *intended outcome*). If two proposed *intended outcomes* are likely to require different *tactics* they should probably be regarded as separate *outcomes*. But if the likely *tactics* have a high degree of duplication or overlap, the two proposed *intended outcomes* may, in fact, be combined in one.

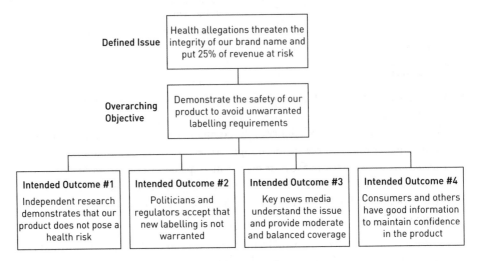

It is important also to remember that *intended outcomes* are written in the form that describes the situation that will apply *after* they are achieved. The construction 'Develop a strategy to persuade the public' focuses on the action—which may or may not succeed— whereas the preferable form 'The public has been persuaded by a well-developed strategy' unambiguously moves the focus from the output to the outcome.

DISCUSSION

INTENDED OUTCOME #1: INDEPENDENT RESEARCH DEMONSTRATES THAT OUR PRODUCT DOES NOT POSE A HEALTH RISK

It is important to recognise that this *intended outcome* is not to refute the most recent, adverse research, but rather to independently demonstrate the safety of our product. By focusing only on the newly reported research, we would be agreeing to debate on the ground set by our critics rather than staking out our own ground. Responding to the new report itself will be captured as a *tactic* to help support intended outcome #2.

INTENDED OUTCOME #2: POLITICIANS AND REGULATORS ACCEPT THAT NEW LABELLING IS NOT WARRANTED

By being outcome focused, the emphasis remains on the need for the key political and regulatory players to be not only well informed but also persuaded that new labelling is not warranted. Simply keeping them well informed is no help if they reject our position.

It is they who are in a position to most directly impact our *overarching objective*. Preparing a response to the adverse new research that provoked this issue is a defensive measure and fits best as a *tactic* under this *intended outcome*.

INTENDED OUTCOME #3: KEY NEWS MEDIA UNDERSTAND THE ISSUE AND PROVIDE MODERATE AND BALANCED COVERAGE

The area of media strategy is the one where outputs are most commonly confused with outcomes. Our real objective in this example is not to maximise column inches or count 'positive mentions' but to help ensure that what is written is informed and balanced. The journalists and social media commentators need to be provided with good, accurate information, but—unlike the politicians and regulators—not necessarily persuaded to accept our position.

Because accurate media coverage may be important in helping persuade the politicians in intended outcome #2, and perhaps also the consumers in intended outcome # 4, it could be argued that the media strategy is really a means to an end rather than an *intended outcome* in itself. However, it appears to offer a distinct set of *tactics* (see below), and is therefore accepted as a stand-alone *intended outcome*.

INTENDED OUTCOME #4: CONSUMERS AND OTHERS HAVE GOOD INFORMATION TO MAINTAIN CONFIDENCE IN THE PRODUCT

It might be argued that loyal consumers would have little direct influence on proving the product safe or whether the product should carry a new health warning label. But it is equally true that angry consumers or potential litigants can exert enormous pressure on the politicians and regulators who are capable of exerting direct influence. Angry consumers can also be a strong negative force on social media. Therefore this *intended outcome* is accepted as helping deliver the *overarching objective*. Others who need accurate information and assurance regarding our product might include retailers or our own employees. It is important to note that in this case the *outcome* is not just that consumers are persuaded, but that their persuasion is based on good information.

STEP FOUR: TACTICS

Tactics are what needs to be done to deliver each outcome. But it is a common mistake to allow discussion about individual *tactics* to get mired in unnecessary detail. The list of *tactics* should be recorded as viewed from a management perspective and should assume that the people designated to implement each *tactic* know how to do their job without the need for it to be spelled out. Thus a listed *tactic* might be as broad as 'Develop and implement a communication plan to ...' or as open-ended as 'Explore options for ...'. However, a *tactic* may also include some examples so that the written plan as finally recorded captures the intent without necessarily pre-empting the answer.

Furthermore, the *tactics* chosen at any one point in time may lead to, or depend on, further decisions, or may prove to be blind alleys. Any issue management plan therefore should be a 'living document' and it is the *tactics* that need to be the most flexible element.

While the *tactics* should be subject to regular progress review and revision, constantly revisiting the *defined issue* or the *overarching objective* can weaken the plan.

The *tactics* included in this case study are not intended to be a fully comprehensive list, but are written to illustrate the style and range required to optimise the Do-it Plan©. It should also be noted that with real-life issues, the *tactics* can seldom be presented in a strictly sequential order. They are often interdependent and frequently would be addressed simultaneously.

Intended outcome #1: Independent research demonstrates that our product does not pose a health risk.		
Tactic	Who	When
Develop detailed scope and consultant brief for new research	Fred and Research Department	End of next week
Identify and commission a respected research organisation	Fred and Research Department	End of this month
Negotiate potential third-party review process for findings	Jim plus team to be identified	Start of next month
Commission international literature search and review for current scientific perspective	Jim and our consultants	End of this week
Develop communication plan for findings (see intended outcomes #2 and #3)	Mary and PR Department	Start of next month
Explore merits and options for involving trade association/ other producers in research project	Katrina	End of next week
Review possible industry alliance to establish independent Industry Scientific Advisory Board	Katrina and Alan	At Trade Association conference next month
Intended outcome #2: Politicians and regulators accept that new labelling is not warranted		
Tactic	Who	When
Identify key politicians/ bureaucrats	Alice and lobby consultants	End of this week
Develop response position on adverse research (see intended outcome #3)	Alice, Fred from Research and Edwin in Media Relations	Agreed draft by end of this week
Develop a pack of up-to-date information and commence dialogue with key players	Alice, lobby consultants and PR Department	End of month

Intended outcome #2: Politicians and regulators accept that new labelling is not warranted		
Tactic	Who	When
Identify respected expert or academic help to prepare and review lobby material	PR Department and Fred from Research	Start of next month
Review overseas political trends on labelling requirements	Celine and Business Development Unit	Commence this week and review progress
Commission external report of legal and regulatory issues raised by new labelling	Celine and Jason in Legal	Start immediately; assess consultants' timeline
Develop full submission when research project completed	Alice and team to be identified	At end of month review progress from intended outcome #1
Review political party policies for threats/opportunities	Donald to work with Alice	By end of month
Intended outcome #3: Key news media understand the issue and provide moderate and balanced coverage		
Tactic	Who	When
Identify journalists/bloggers who have written on this—for and against	Edwin, with consultants and media monitors	By next week
Prepare press statement and Q&A to announce new research (see intended outcome #1)	Edwin and consultants work with Fred in Research	End of this month
Brief specialist writers and bloggers on new research and response to previous study (see intended outcome #2)	Edwin and team to be identified	Start of next month
Agree on shared load with trade association generics versus brand	Edwin and Katrina to explore	Prior to next month's Trade Association conference
Coordinate our media strategy with efforts by trade association and other generic producers	Edwin and Katrina	At next month's Trade Association conference
Commission detailed ongoing news media monitoring/analysis	Edwin, with consultants and media monitors	End of this week
Ensure strong media component to research communication plan (intended outcome #1)	Katrina and consultants work with Mary and PR Department	Start of next month

(Continued)

Intended outcome #4: Consumers and others have good information to maintain confidence in the product		
Tactic	Who	When
Explore options for assessing current consumer opinion; for example, surveys, focus groups and social media	Gary and team to be identified	End of next week
Establish feedback mechanism for consumers; for example, toll-free line, prepaid reply cards and Facebook	Gary's team plus Andrew from Marketing	Mid next month
Develop social media plan to help sales/marketing monitor distributor/consumer attitudes	Andrew, with support from PR Department	Mid next month
Determine what information consumers want and their preferred method for delivery	Gary's team	Mid next month
Develop consumer response tools; for example, information pack, Q&A and FAQs	Gary's team	End of next month
Identify and open dialogue with consumer organisations, nutrition activists, children's health organisations etc; include critics	Donald and consultants	Develop plan end of month; implement mid next month
Develop communication plan to keep our employees and retailers informed and confident	Andrew, PR Department and Mary Beth from HR	Start of next month

USEFUL WEBSITES

Government departments and agencies

Australian Emergency Management—www.em.gov.au

Centers for Disease Control and Prevention (USA)—www.cdc.gov

Chinese Center for Disease Control and Prevention—www.chinacdc.cn/en/

European Centre for Disease Prevention and Control—http://ecdc.europa.eu/en

New Zealand Ministry of Civil Defence and Emergency Management—www.mcdem.govt.nz

US Department of Homeland Security—www.dhs.gov

US Federal Emergency Management Agency (Response & Recovery)—www.fema.gov/response-recovery

Non-government organisations

Amnesty International—www.amnesty.org

Centre for Research on the Epidemiology of Disasters (CRED)—www.cred.be

Friends of the Earth International—www.foei.org

Greenpeace—www.greenpeace.org

United Nations Office for Disaster Risk Reduction—www.unisdr.org

World Wildlife Fund—www.worldwildlife.org

Industry organisations

Arthur W. Page Society—www.awpagesociety.com

Australian Centre for Corporate Social Responsibility—www.accsr.com.au

Bernstein Crisis Management, Inc.—www.bernsteincrisismanagement.com

Business Continuity Institute—www.thebci.org

Business for Social Responsibility—www.bsr.org

Campaign Strategy (Chris Rose)—www.campaignstrategy.org

Centre for Corporate Public Affairs—www.accpa.com.au

Chartered Institute of Public Relations—www.cipr.co.uk

China International Public Relations Association—www.cipra.org.cn

Coalition for Environmentally Responsible Economies (Ceres)—www.ceres.org

Edelman Trust Barometer—http://trust.edelman.com

Hong Kong Public Relations Professionals' Association—www.prpa.com.hk

Institute for Crisis Management—www.crisisexperts.com

Institute for Public Relations—www.instituteforpr.org

Institute of Public Relations Malaysia—www.iprm.org.my

Institute of Public Relations of Singapore—www.iprs.org.sg

International Association of Business Communicators—www.iabc.com

International Institute for Disaster Risk Management (Philippines)—www.rdmhome.org/

International Institute of Communications—www.iicom.org

International Public Relations Association—www.ipra.org

Issue Management Council—www.issuemanagement.org

Issue Outcomes Pty Ltd—www.issueoutcomes.com.au

League of American Communications Professionals—www.lacp.com

National Resources Defense Council—www.nrdc.org

People for the Ethical Treatment of Animals—www.peta.org

Peter M. Sandman Risk Communication—www.psandman.com

Public Relations Association of Indonesia (PERHUMAS)—www.perhumas.or.id

Public Relations Institute of Australia—www.pria.com.au

Public Relations Institute of New Zealand—www.prinz.org.nz

Public Relations Society of America—www.prsa.org

Public Relations Society of India—www.prsi.co.in

Public Relations Society of Japan—www.prsj.or.jp/en/

Public Relations Society of the Philippines—www.facebook.com/PRSPnews

Reputation Institute—www.reputationinstitute.com

Science Media Centre—www.sciencemediacentre.org

Sigwatch: NGO Tracking & Issues Analysis—www.sigwatch.com

World Business Council for Sustainable Development—www.wbcsd.ch

INDEX